Inventory of Estimated Budgetary Support and Tax Expenditures for Fossil Fuels

OECD

This work is published on the responsibility of the Secretary-General of the OECD. The opinions expressed and arguments employed herein do not necessarily reflect the official views of the Organisation or of the governments of its member countries.

This document and any map included herein are without prejudice to the status of or sovereignty over any territory, to the delimitation of international frontiers and boundaries and to the name of any territory, city or area.

Please cite this publication as:
OECD (2011), *Inventory of Estimated Budgetary Support and Tax Expenditures for Fossil Fuels*, OECD Publishing.
http://dx.doi.org/10.1787/9789264128736-en

ISBN 978-92-64-12872-9 (print)
ISBN 978-92-64-12873-6 (PDF)

The statistical data for Israel are supplied by and under the responsibility of the relevant Israeli authorities. The use of such data by the OECD is without prejudice to the status of the Golan Heights, East Jerusalem and Israeli settlements in the West Bank under the terms of international law.

Photo credits: Cover illustration :
© klikk - Fotolia.com
© iamtheking33 - Fotolia.com
© umabatata - Fotolia.com
© Anzelm - Fotolia.com
© Ghost - Fotolia.com

Corrigenda to OECD publications may be found on line at: *www.oecd.org/publishing/corrigenda*.

FOREWORD

The recovery of the world economy from the worst economic crisis of our lifetimes remains fragile. In the meantime, the room for policy manoeuvres is increasingly limited, especially in more advanced economies. In this context, structural reforms are essential to stimulate growth and employment. There are very few quick wins though. One of them is the removal of inefficient subsidies.

Reforming or eliminating support for the consumption or production of fossil fuels can contribute to achieving economic and fiscal objectives, while also helping tackle environmental problems like climate change. In September 2009, G20 Leaders agreed to rationalise and phase out, over the medium term, inefficient fossil-fuel subsidies. A similar commitment was made by leaders of the Asia-Pacific Economic Cooperation (APEC) forum in November 2009. The OECD, together with other inter-governmental organisations, has contributed to several reports on energy subsidies in response to G20 Leaders' mandates and requests.

Any reform of policies to support fossil-fuel production and use necessitates first an examination of what those policies are, and what financial transfers they generate. Previously the only multi-country data series on fossil-fuel support were the estimates of energy-consumption subsidies provided for emerging and developing economies by our sister organisation, the International Energy Agency (IEA). Getting a handle on features of tax codes of countries designed to encourage oil and gas production or relieve particular end-use sectors from excise taxes is a more complex exercise. This *Inventory of estimated budgetary support and tax expenditures for fossil fuels* marks the first attempt to provide such information in a consistent manner for the majority of OECD countries.

This *Inventory* indicates that the value of budgetary support and tax expenditures relating to fossil-fuel production and consumption in the 24 OECD countries examined amounted to between USD 45 billion and USD 75 billion a year during 2005-10. Over 250 individual producer or consumer support mechanisms for fossil-fuels are identified in the *Inventory*. Not all these mechanisms are clearly inefficient, and caution is required in interpreting the support amounts. Nevertheless, there is ample scope for both saving money and improving the environment through fossil-fuel subsidy reform, not only in developing and emerging economies but, as this *Inventory* shows, in advanced economies as well.

I hope that the *Inventory* will inspire more countries to increase transparency in this area, and that it will help spur productive debate about policies that influence the production and use of fossil fuels. Further work to expand the geographical coverage and deepen the *Inventory* to cover more measures applied by sub-national governments is already underway. Both developed and developing countries need to make progress in reforming inefficient support to fossil fuels. The OECD stands ready to help in these efforts.

Angel Gurría
Secretary-General

ACKNOWLEDGEMENTS

This volume is the result of a collective effort by three OECD Directorates: the Trade and Agriculture Directorate (TAD), which provided overall co-ordination; the Centre for Tax Policy and Administration (CTPA); and the Environment Directorate (ENV). The identification, documentation and estimation of budgetary support and tax expenditures was undertaken principally by Jehan Sauvage and Jagoda Sumicka, under the guidance of Ronald Steenblik, Senior Trade Policy Analyst. The following internal OECD staff and external consultants contributed additional information on particular countries:

Belgium	–	Gimin Kang
Canada	–	Anthony Halley
Chile	–	Mattias Salamanca Orrego
Hungary	–	Lukács András, Károly Kiss, Pavics Lázár
Ireland	–	Scott Foster
Israel	–	Tidhar Wald, Philip Hemmings
Italy	–	Laura Giacomassi, Chiara Martini
Japan	–	Tetsuya Uetake, Satoshi Urasawa
Korea	–	Gimin Kang
Mexico	–	Anthony Halley
Netherlands	–	Cees van Beers, El Arkesteijn-van Schaik, Perrine de Vleeschouwer
New Zealand	–	Darryl Jones
Norway	–	Morten Anker, Matias Kristoffersen Egeland
Sweden	–	Jens Lundsgaard, Michelle Harding
United Kingdom	–	Kerryn Lang, Tom Moerenhout
Turkey	–	Heymi Bahar

In several cases, countries themselves provided additional data; these efforts are greatly appreciated. All allocations of transfers to specific fuels (where necessary) were performed by the OECD Secretariat.

Trevor Morgan drafted the overviews of national policies provided at the beginning of each country chapter for Australia, Belgium, Canada, France, Germany, Hungary, Ireland, Italy, Japan, Korea, Mexico, Netherlands, New Zealand, Norway, Poland, Spain, Sweden, Turkey, United Kingdom, and the United States. Chapter 1 (Introduction) was written by Ronald Steenblik, Michael Ash, James Greene, Jens Lundsgaard, and Jehan Sauvage.

Other staff in the OECD provided extensive feedback on the *Inventory* document throughout its development: Nils Axel Braathen, Carmel Cahill, Jonathan Coppel, Anthony Cox, James Greene, Michelle Harding, Chiara Martini, Stephen Matthews, Olga Melyukhina, and Helen Mountford. Thanks is owed to Amos Bromhead and Karen Treanton of the IEA for their inputs. The advice of Masami Kojima, Doug Koplow and Michael Thöne is also gratefully acknowledged.

Special thanks also go to Nadine Rocher and Kristina Jones for their help in preparing contracts for external consultants; Eavan Coyle and Theresa Poincet for formatting early versions of the documents; and Jane Kynaston for the final preparation of the manuscript for publication.

The *Inventory* was discussed in 2011 by two OECD subsidiary bodies: the Joint Meetings of Tax and Environment Experts (JMTEE), and the Joint Working Party on Trade and Environment. The comments and corrections provided by delegates to these bodies have been instrumental to the project.

This book is published on the responsibility of the OECD Secretary-General.

TABLE OF CONTENTS

Tables

Figures

Boxes

ABBREVIATIONS

Abbreviation	Explanation
..	not available
b/d	barrels per day
bcm	billion cubic metres
billion	10^9
boe	barrels of oil equivalent
CCS	carbon capture and storage
CCTs	clean-coal technologies
G-20	The Group of Twenty nations
GJ	gigajoule (1 joule x 10^9)
GSSE	General Services Support Estimate
GW	gigawatt (1 Watt x 10^9)
HS	Harmonized System
IEA	International Energy Agency
kg	kilogramme (1 000 kg = 1 tonne)
kg CO_2-eq	kilogramme of carbon-dioxide equivalent
Kt	kilotonnes (1 tonne x 10^3)
kW	kilowatt (1 Watt x 10^3)
kWh	kilowatt-hour
LNG	liquified natural gas
LPG	liquified propane gas
mb/d	million barrels per day
MBtu	million British thermal units
Mcm	million cubic metres
million	10^6
MJ	megajoule (1 joule x 10^6)
Ml/year	million litres per year
Mt	million tonnes (1 tonne x 10^6)
Mtce	million tonnes of coal equivalent
Mtoe	million tonnes of oil equivalent
MW	megawatt (1 Watt x 10^6)
MWh	megawatt-hour
n.a.	not applicable
n.c.	not calculated
NGL	natural-gas liquids
p	provisional
ppm	parts per million (by volume)
tce	tonne of coal equivalent
toe	tonne of oil equivalent
trillion	10^{12}
VAT	value-added tax
W	Watt (1 joule per second)

CURRENCY ABBREVIATIONS

Abbreviation	Explanation
AUD	Australian dollar
CAD	Canadian dollar
CLP	Chilean peso
EUR	Euro
GBP	British pound
HUF	Hungarian forint
ISK	Icelandic króna
JPY	Japanese yen
KRW	Korean won
ILS	Israeli new shekel
MXN	Mexican peso
NLG	Dutch guilder
NOK	Norwegian krone
NZD	New Zealand dollar
PLN	Polish zloty
SEK	Swedish krona
USD	United States dollar

EXECUTIVE SUMMARY

The need for an inventory

The global economic crisis is not yet over. With increasing understanding of the risks of climate change, countries are struggling at home and internationally to find cost-effective measures to reduce their greenhouse-gas emissions. Policy makers are faced with having to deal with a multitude of challenges at once: nourishing growth while encouraging it to become more "green"; preventing high unemployment rates from becoming entrenched; reducing government deficits; and managing global imbalances. Implementing growth-friendly fiscal structures and public spending patterns is critical to reducing imbalances and stimulating growth.

The importance of reforming policies supporting fossil fuels was explicitly recognised in the OECD's June 2009 Declaration on Green Growth, in which 34 countries vowed to "encourage domestic policy reform, with the aim of avoiding or removing environmentally harmful policies that might thwart green growth, such as subsidies: to fossil fuel consumption or production that increase greenhouse gas emissions …" [www.oecd.org/greengrowth]. Three months later, G-20 leaders committed to "rationalize and phase out over the medium term inefficient fossil fuel subsidies that encourage wasteful consumption", and called upon the rest of the world to do the same. In November 2009, a similar commitment was made by leaders of the Asia-Pacific Economic Cooperation (APEC) forum.

Despite the many benefits of reforming fossil-fuel subsidies, efforts to implement such reforms have long been hampered by a crucial lack of information regarding the amount and type of support measures in place. This lack of information was most profound for fossil-fuel support in industrialised countries, including the membership of the OECD. The International Energy Agency (IEA) has been producing data on fossil-fuel consumer subsidies in emerging and developing countries for several years using an estimation approach known as the "price-gap" method, which measures the extent to which a policy keeps domestic fuel prices below an international reference price. However, the price-gap approach does not capture support to producers and tax concessions to both producers and consumers, which account for much of the support provided by developed countries, since such measures do not push final prices below the level of international reference prices. Such support and tax concessions nonetheless reflect policies that may induce greater production or use of fossil fuels than would otherwise be the case.

To help fill this critical data gap, in 2010 the OECD started collecting data on budgetary support and tax expenditures that relate to fossil fuels. The *Inventory of*

Estimated Budgetary Support and Tax Expenditures for Fossil Fuels contains the first results of that effort, setting out over 250 measures in 24 countries.[1]

How fossil fuels are supported in OECD countries

Governments support energy production in a number of ways, including by: intervening in markets in a way that affects costs or prices; transferring funds to recipients directly; assuming part of their risk; selectively reducing the taxes they would otherwise have to pay; and undercharging for the use of government-supplied goods or assets. Support to energy consumption is also provided through several common channels: price controls intended to regulate the cost of energy to consumers; direct financial transfers; schemes designed to provide consumers with rebates on purchases of energy products; and tax relief.

The OECD inventory takes stock of the broad set of measures identified by governments that effectively "support" fossil-fuel use or production, as defined using the PSE-CSE framework, which has already been used extensively to measure support, most notably in agriculture.[2] The scope of "support" is deliberately broad, and is broader than some conceptions of "subsidy". It covers a wide range of measures that provide a benefit or preference for a particular activity or a particular product, either in absolute terms or relative to other activities or products.

The data in the inventory were sourced from official government documents and web sites, complemented by information provided directly by government agencies themselves. The valuations are generally those estimated by the respective governments, though the OECD has allocated support among the different fuels based on production and consumption volumes where such information is not available from government sources.

Policy features that support fossil fuels have been put in place for various policy reasons. While a number of the measures may be inefficient or wasteful, others may not be. The inventory does not analyse the impact of specific measures or pass judgement on which ones might be usefully kept in place and which ones a country might wish to consider for possible reform or removal. Its purpose is to provide information about policies that provide some level of support, as a starting point for further analysis about the objectives of particular measures, their impacts (economically, environmentally and socially), and possible reforms and alternatives.

---

1. The 24 OECD countries covered by this first inventory collectively account for about 95% of the OECD's total primary energy supply: Australia, Belgium, Canada, Chile, France, Germany, Hungary, Iceland, Ireland, Israel, Italy, Japan, Korea, Luxembourg, Mexico, the Netherlands, New Zealand, Norway, Poland, Spain, Sweden, Turkey, the United Kingdom, and the United States. Inventories for the other ten OECD countries will be developed in the near future.

2. The PSE-CSE framework distinguishes among those measures that benefit producers (PSE: Producer Support Estimate), consumers (CSE: Consumer Support Estimate), and those that benefit producers or consumers collectively, or that do not support current production, such as industry-specific R&D (GSSE: General Services Support Estimate). For more information, see the OECD's PSE Manual, available online at: *www.oecd.org/agriculture/PSE*

The inventory provides important information about incentives created within each national economy. Caution is required, however, in interpreting the support amounts. This is particularly the case as the majority of support mechanisms identified in the inventory are tax expenditures. Tax expenditures are *relative* preferences within a country's tax system that are measured with reference to a benchmark tax treatment set by that country. Since the benchmark or "normal" tax treatment varies considerably from country to country, the value of this type of support is not comparable across countries. Thus, for example, a country that applies high rates of taxation to fossil-fuel end products within the context of an excise-tax system with lower rates for some products than others may have higher measured support to fossil fuels than a country with lower but uniform excise-tax rates, even if the tax system of the former country has higher taxes than the latter country on each type of fuel.

Some countries are more transparent than others when it comes to budgetary support and tax expenditures, which has implications in terms of the coverage of support mechanisms in the inventory, with the largest number of mechanisms listed for those countries that are most transparent. Part of the value of this inventory is that it provides a standardised template for reporting measures. This common platform will encourage countries to become more open in quantifying and reporting on policy measures that affect fossil-fuel production or use.

More generally, the OECD inventory marks the beginning of an ongoing process that will be broadened and deepened over time. The inventory will gradually be expanded to cover all OECD countries. Measures at the sub-national level in federal countries were only canvassed at this stage on a selective basis, due to time and resource constraints. Numerous other forms of support – notably those provided through risk transfers, concessional loans, injections of funds (as equity) into state-owned enterprises, and market price support – were not quantified in this initial inventory. The data requirements for estimating the transfers associated with such measures are greater than for budgetary transfers and tax expenditures, and the calculations to estimate the support elements more complex.

Chapter 1

Introduction

This chapter describes the coverage, method and data sources used in compiling the country information contained in the *Inventory*. It also discusses the way in which this information should be interpreted, with particular attention being devoted to the concept of tax expenditures given the latter's relative importance for the report. A distinction is made among tax expenditures based on whether they relate to the consumption of fossil fuels, to the use of fossil fuels as inputs to production, or to the production of fossil fuels. Measurement issues are also discussed, in particular the role of tax benchmarks and the importance of the broader tax system in understanding the meaning of tax-expenditure estimates.

1. INTRODUCTION

This document provides preliminary quantitative estimates of direct budgetary support and tax expenditures supporting the production or consumption of fossil fuels in selected OECD member countries. This information has been compiled as part of the OECD's programme of work to develop a better understanding of environmentally harmful subsidies (EHS). It is also intended to inform the on-going efforts of the Group of Twenty (G20) nations to reform fossil-fuel subsidies. It may be seen as a complement to the information on fossil-fuel consumption subsidies that has been compiled by the International Energy Agency (IEA), primarily for developing and emerging economies.

The G20 exercise is concerned with "inefficient fossil fuel subsidies that encourage wasteful consumption", which G20 countries have declared their intent to "[r]ationalise and phase out over the medium term" (G20, 2009). A similar commitment was made by leaders of the Asia-Pacific Economic Cooperation (APEC) forum in November 2009. And through the OECD's 2009 Declaration on Green Growth, 34 countries declared that they would "encourage domestic policy reform, with the aim of avoiding or removing environmentally harmful policies that might thwart green growth, such as subsidies: to fossil fuel consumption or production that increase greenhouse gas emissions ..." (OECD, 2009a).

This document proceeds from the fundamental perspective that the identification of "subsidies" to any sector or industry requires first taking an inventory of the full set of measures that may qualify as support to that sector. For one, because of interactive effects among policies, it is difficult to determine *a priori* whether a particular support policy is inefficient, encourages wasteful consumption, or is environmentally harmful. Only with a full picture of the operating policies can various analytical tools be brought to bear on questions about the effects of those policies on human welfare and the environment.

This document marks a first attempt to comprehensively list the various direct budgetary expenditures and tax expenditures that effectively support fossil fuel production or use in OECD countries. The scope of what is considered "support" is here deliberately broad, and is broader than some conceptions of "subsidy". Essentially, it includes both direct budgetary expenditures and tax expenditures that in some way provide a benefit or preference for fossil-fuel production or consumption relative to alternatives.

In interpreting the figures, it is important to underscore that tax expenditures are measures of support only relative to the benchmark tax structure of the country in question. Since the figures measure *relative* support within the context of that country's tax system, they are not comparable across countries. A country that applies high rates of taxation to fossil-fuel end products within the context of a highly differentiated excise-tax system may thus have higher measured support to fossil fuels than a country with lower but uniform excise-tax rates, even if the tax system of the former country has higher taxes than the latter country on each type of fuel.[3]

It is recognised that the policy features that support fossil fuels have been put in place for various policy reasons. A consequence of this broad conception of support is that while a number of these measures may be inefficient or wasteful, others may not be. The report does not provide any analysis of the impacts of specific support measures, and so does not pass any judgement on which measures might be usefully kept in place and which ones a country might wish to consider for possible reform or removal. Its purpose is to provide information about policies that give some level of support, as a starting point for further analysis about the objectives of particular measures, their impacts (economically, environmentally and socially), and possible reforms and alternatives.

Structure of the report

The document is organised by country. The Secretariat has so far been able to identify budgetary support and tax expenditures relating to fossil fuels in 24 OECD member countries. Its intention is eventually to extend the exercise to cover all 34 OECD member countries, as well as selected non-OECD countries.

Each country chapter is structured into three sections. The first section provides an overview of the salient features of the energy economy of the country: the shares of different energy sources in total primary energy supply (TPES); fossil resources; domestic production and international trade; the ownership structure of the industry; pricing and taxation policies in the energy sector; and support policies.

The second section of each country chapter provides documentation of the measures, identified by the OECD Secretariat to date, that support fossil-fuel production or consumption activities involving that country. Measures that do not affect current production or consumption of fossil fuels are also included in the inventory. These are separately itemised in the general services support estimate (GSSE) category and refer mainly to expenditures relating to past production activities (*e.g.* to compensate victims of mine land subsidence following the underground extraction of coal or hydrocarbons), to research and development not directly relating to production, and to activities such as the funding of strategic stockpiles, the benefits of which are not easily attributable to producers or consumers uniquely.

---

[3]   For example, even though gasoline and diesel fuels may both be taxed in Country X (and it could be argued that neither is subsidised in an absolute sense), a lower level of taxation on diesel compared with gasoline would be included in the inventory if the lower rate is treated as a tax expenditure by Country X. This is considered support since the tax structure changes market prices in a non-neutral way that is more favourable to the lower-taxed product. Note that Country Y, which taxes diesel and gasoline at the same rate, would not be considered to provide support even though its common tax rate is lower than the lower of the two rates in Country X. (This would also be the case even if Country Y did not tax these fuels at all). The fact that measured support is higher in Country X than Country Y therefore does not mean that the tax system of Country X is more favourable to fossil fuels than that of Country Y. It merely indicates that there is a preference within Country X's tax system of the measured size relative to the benchmark treatment for that country. While not directly comparable, such preferences or non-neutralities are nonetheless important since they can impact production and consumption decisions.

The entries for individual measures, identified by name and a unique OECD database code, describe the years for which data are available on the cost of the measure. Thereafter follows a succinct description of the measure, highlighting its formal incidence – *i.e.* which aspect of production or consumption is targeted – and how it operates. Each entry concludes with a reference to the data source or sources.

The third section of each country chapter presents the data itself. These are reported according to the organising framework described in Figure 1.1. This framework, which is similar to the one used by the OECD for organising data on support to agriculture, divides incidence into consumption and production, and production into several sub-categories depending on whether the measure relates to output returns (*i.e.* the unit revenues received from sales); enterprise income (the overall income of producers); the costs of intermediate inputs, such as fuel or electricity; and the costs of production factors – labour, land (which includes access to sub-surface natural resources), capital and new knowledge. The other dimension of the figure, transfer mechanism, refers to how the transfer is created.

Coverage, method and data sources

This first attempt at estimating support to fossil-fuel production and consumption provided by a broad range of countries of necessity concentrates on budgetary transfers and tax expenditures relating to fossil fuels. Data on these transfers are relatively straightforward to obtain from official government documents. These measures correspond, respectively, to the first and second rows in Figure 1.1, and also touch on elements in the third row. Numerous other forms of support – notably support provided through risk transfers, concessional credit, injections of funds (as equity) into state-owned enterprises, and market price support – were not quantified, however. The data requirements for estimating the transfers associated with such measures are greater, and the calculations required to estimate the support elements more complex, than for budgetary transfers and tax expenditures. Nonetheless, the OECD Secretariat intends to include these transfers in the future.

Regarding market price support – which refers to the monetary value of gross transfers from consumers and taxpayers to energy producers arising from policy measures creating a gap between domestic producer prices and reference prices of that specific energy commodity, measured at the mine-mouth or well head – an indication of its possible magnitude can be obtained by examining import tariffs on fossil fuels. Tables 1.1 and 2.1 show most-favoured nation (MFN) tariffs applied by OECD countries on the main fossil fuels. These are the highest tariffs applied on imports from other member states of the World Trade Organization (WTO). Weighted-average import tariffs will tend to be lower than those indicated by the MFN tariffs, as most OECD countries are party to one or more bilateral or regional free-trade agreements, which usually set tariffs on industrial products such as fuels to zero. Petroleum products in general attract the highest tariffs, followed by natural gas and coal. Even based on applied MFN tariffs, however, it appears that import tariffs do not protect domestic producers to any important extent. In the few countries that apply a common import tariff on all goods (*e.g.* Chile and Korea), a small degree of protection of domestic producers (where applicable) may exist. The effect on consumers is to raise the domestic price by the level of the tariff, and to slightly dampen demand.

Also not covered by this exercise are measures relating to energy-consuming capital, such as support to the manufacturing of motor vehicles designed to run on petroleum fuels, nor to electricity producers, even where that electricity is derived from fossil fuels. However, support provided through provisions of the income-tax system of many countries that encourages employers to provide employees with fuel credit cards for buying motor fuels used in company-owned automobiles *would be* covered in the inventory, were those data available.

The country coverage is also incomplete. Time and resource constraints meant that the inventory was not able to include Austria, Greece, Portugal, Czech Republic, Denmark, Estonia, Finland, Slovak Republic, Slovenia, and Switzerland. Support provided by sub-national governments (states, provinces, prefectures, *départements, Länder*) is also not comprehensively included.[4] However, in order to gauge the importance of such support, the database does contain estimates of budgetary payments and tax expenditures relating to fossil fuels provided by a few, usually three, sub-national jurisdictions in five countries: Australia, Canada, France, Germany and the United States. The inclusion in the inventory of measures provided by only selected sub-national jurisdictions in federal countries calls for additional caution in interpreting the estimates and further precludes country comparisons. This exercise documents that support provided by sub-national governments is, however, not trivial.

---

[4]   The Secretariat intends to extend the country coverage to the remaining OECD countries not covered in this report. Where applicable, the missing data on sub-national measures will also be added to the relevant country chapters. The data will be regularly updated on a joint IEA-OECD web-based platform, in order to continue to provide transparent and accurate estimates of budgetary support and tax expenditures to fossil-fuel production and consumption.

Figure 1.1. Matrix of support measures, with examples

Transfer Mechanism (how a transfer is created)	Statutory or Formal Incidence (to whom and what a transfer is first given)								
	Production			Costs of Production Factors				Direct consumption	
	Output returns	Enterprise income	Cost of intermediate inputs	Labour	Land	Capital	Knowledge	Unit cost of consumption	Household or enterprise income
Direct transfer of funds	Output bounty or deficiency payment	Operating grant	Input-price subsidy	Wage subsidy	Capital grant linked to acquisition of land	Capital grant linked to capital	Government R&D	Unit subsidy	Government-subsidized life-line electricity rate
Tax revenue foregone	Production tax credit	Reduced rate of income tax	Reduction in excise tax on input	Reduction in social charges (payroll taxes)	Property-tax reduction or exemption	Investment tax credit	Tax credit for private R&D	VAT or excise-tax concession on fuel	Tax deduction related to energy purchases that exceed given share of income
Other government revenue foregone	Reduced resource-rent tax		Under-pricing of a good, government service or access to a natural resource		Under-pricing of access to government land; reduced royalty payment		Government transfer of intellectual property right	Under-pricing of access to a natural resource harvested by final consumer	
Transfer of risk to government	Government buffer stock	Third-party liability limit for producers	Provision of security (e.g., military protection of supply lines)	Assumption of occupational health and accident liabilities	Credit guarantee linked to acquisition of land	Credit guarantee linked to capital		Price-triggered subsidy	Means-tested cold-weather grant
Induced transfers	Import tariff or export subsidy	Monopoly concession	Monopsony concession; export restriction	Wage control	Land-use control	Credit control (sector-specific)	Deviations from standard IPR rules	Regulated price; cross subsidy	Mandated life-line electricity rate

Source: OECD.

Table 1.1. MFN tariffs applied by OECD countries on imported hydrocarbon fuels, as of 1 January 2011

Country	Crude oil	Crude oil and liquid petroleum products						Gaseous hydrocarbons		
		Motor gasoline	Aviation spirit	Kerosene	Jet fuel, kerosene based	Diesel	Heavy fuel oil	LNG	LPG	Gaseous natural gas
HS code:	2709	2710.11 ex	2710.11 ex	2710.19 ex	2710.19 ex	2710.19 ex	2710.19 ex	2711.11	2711.12	2711.21
Australia[1]	0%	0%	0%	0%	0%	0%	0%	0%	0%	0%
Canada	0%	0%	0%	0%	0%	0%	0%	0%	0-12.5%	0%
Chile	6%	6%	6%	6%	6%	6%	6%	6%	6%	6%
Iceland	0%	0%	0%	0%	0%	0%	0%	0%	0%	0%
Israel	0%	0%	0%	0%	0%	0%	0%	0%	0%	0%
European Union	0%	4.7%	4.7%	4.7%	4.7%	0-3.5%	3.5%	0%	0-8%	0%
Japan	0%	JPY 0.995/L	JPY 0.995/L	0-3%	JPY 0.375/L	JPY 0.819/L	JPY 0-0.819/L	0%	0%	4.1%
Korea	3%	5%	5%	5%	5%	5%	5%	3%	3%	3%
Mexico	0%	0%	0%	0%	0%	0%	0%	0%	0%	0%
New Zealand	0%	0%	0%	0%	0%	0%	0%	0%	NZD 0.104/L	NZD 3.17/GJ
Norway	0%	0%	0%	0%	0%	0%	0%	0%	0%	0%
Switzerland	0%	0%	0%	0%	0%	0%	0%	0%	0%	0%
Turkey	0%	4.7%	4.7%	4.7%	4.7%	0-3.5%	3.5%	0%	0-8%	0%
United States	USD 0.0525-0.105/bbl	USD 0.525/bbl	USD 0.0525-0.105/bbl	USD 0.105-0.525/bbl	USD 0.525/bbl	USD 0.0525-0.525/bbl	USD 0.0525-0.105/bbl	0%	0%	0%

Notes: 1. Australia applies excise duties at the point of import, and lists these duties in its tariff schedule. Since these (AUS 0.38143 per litre for motor gasoline, kerosene, diesel and heavy fuel oil, and AUD 0.03556 per litre for aviation spirit and jet fuel) are the same as the normal excise duty applied to domestically produced fuels, the tariffs here are listed as zero.

Sources: **European Union:** Business Link (http://www.businesslink.gov.uk/bdotg/action/tariff); **all other countries:** European Commission, Market Access Database (http://madb.europa.eu/mkaccdb2/indexPubli.htm).

Table 1.2. MFN tariffs applied by OECD countries on imported solid fossil fuels, as of 1 January 2011

| Country | Hard Coal | | | | Lignite | | Peat | Coke and semi-coke of coal, lignite or peat |
| | Anthracite | Bituminous coal | Other | Briquettes of hard coal | Non-agglomerated | Agglomerated | | |
HS code:	2701.11	2701.12	2701.19	2701.20	2702.10	2702.20	2703	2704
Australia	0%	0%	0%	0%	0%	0%	0%	0%
Canada	0%	0%	0%	0%	0%	0%	6.5%	0%
Chile	6%	6%	6%	6%	6%	6%	6%	6%
Iceland	0%	0%	0%	0%	0%	0%	0%	0%
Israel	0%	0%	0%	0%	0%	0%	6%	0%
European Union	0%	0%	0%	0%	0%	0%	0%	0%
Japan	0%	0%	0%	3.9%	0%	0%	0%	3.2%
Korea	0%	0%	0%	1%	1%	1%	1%	3%
Mexico	0%	0%	0%	0%	0%	0%	0%	0%
New Zealand	0%	0%	0%	0%	0%	0%	0%	0%
Norway	0%	0%	0%	0%	0%	0%	0%	0%
Switzerland	CHF 0.80/ tonne	CHF 0.80/ tonne	CHF 0.80/ tonne	CHF 0.80/ tonne	CHF 0.80/ tonne	CHF 0.80/ tonne	CHF 0.80/ tonne	CHF 0.80/ tonne
Turkey	0%	0%	0%	0%	0%	0%	0%	0%
United States	0%	0%	0%	0%	0%	0%	0%	0%

Sources: **European Union:** Business Link (http://www.businesslink.gov.uk/bdotg/action/tariff); **all other countries:** European Commission, Market Access Database (http://madb.europa.eu/mkaccdb2/indexPubli.htm). The identification of support measures was conducted mainly through searches of official government documents and web sites. In a few cases, unpublished data were requested from, and furnished by, OECD governments.

INVENTORY OF ESTIMATED BUDGETARY SUPPORT AND TAX EXPENDITURES FOR FOSSIL FUELS © OECD 2011

Generally, the data provided in this document have been obtained from government sources. Support measures were identified mainly through searches of official government documents and web sites. In a few cases, unpublished data were requested from and furnished by OECD governments. The data presented are as complete as possible, but they are by no means comprehensive. There is more information presented in the inventory for those countries which have been relatively more transparent in terms of their support to fossil fuel consumption and production in their budget books. This does not necessarily mean that these counties have higher levels of support than other countries, but may reflect that they have been more transparent about the support that is provided.

A limiting factor in respect of tax expenditures relating to fossil fuels is the extent to which OECD countries produce such estimates already. In a recent survey of OECD countries, 16 of the 24 responding countries (Australia, Austria, Belgium, Canada, France, Germany, Greece, Mexico, the Netherlands, Norway, Portugal, Spain, Switzerland, Turkey, the United Kingdom, and the United States) stated that they publish full tax-expenditure reports on a regular basis (OECD, 2010). Most of these reports cover both corporate and personal income taxes. Fewer cover VAT, and fewer still attempt to estimate tax expenditures in respect of excise taxes (which, although significant, may in part be because of conceptual difficulties in defining an appropriate benchmark system for a tax that is applied to a specific commodity).[5]

However, few countries include detailed figures in their published tax-expenditure estimates related to the production or consumption of fossil fuels, and in some cases the figures that are published may relate to energy consumption or a range of natural resource production rather than specifically to fossil fuels. Where data do exist[6], they reveal that the tax expenditures are varied, with some providing minor relief to selected consumers or industries, and others providing significant relief to broad groups of taxpayers.

The level of disclosure and accuracy of sub-national tax expenditures relating to fossil fuels can vary widely as well. Moreover, in their corporate income-tax systems, a number of sub-national governments provide the same tax expenditures as federal governments, creating additional tax relief, even absent specific statutory tax breaks.

The main transformation of data carried out by the Secretariat was to allocate support to particular fuels where government data do not provide such a breakdown, and to allocate support for descriptive purposes in terms of its formal incidence (*e.g.* support to output returns, labour, land). Following standard practice (see, *e.g.* OECD, 2009b), transfers associated with policies benefitting more than one fuel or sector were allocated

---

[5]   Governments typically take decisions on tax expenditures simultaneously with decisions on broad programme spending in annual budgets. Except from compliance and policy discussions, there has typically been little oversight thereafter. Recently, however, the judicial branches of some countries have begun to look at the equity perspectives of tax expenditures, in light of constitutional provisions requiring equal treatment under the law.

[6]   In some cases, countries have multiple procedures and definitions of what constitute tax expenditures. In the United States, for example, the Joint Committee on Taxation (a legislative body) publishes a list of tax expenditures that is different from that published by the Department of the Treasury (an executive body). For this report, estimates were derived from the Department of the Treasury, as their numbers are generally more detailed than those produced by the Joint Committee.

according to the relative value of production or consumption, or proportional to the energy-equivalent volume of production or consumption. It is recognised that the actual allocation of support across fuel types may in practice vary based on factors other than the volume or value of production or consumption, but this approach is adapted in the absence of more specific information. For these reasons, while the base data come from government sources, the particular breakdowns may not reflect the views of the responsible governments. In a few cases, mainly pertaining to excise-tax exemptions, the Secretariat also estimated the value of these tax expenditures, based on the published rate of exemption and national or IEA data on the volume of fuel that was exempted.

Interpretation of the data

The data on direct budgetary expenditures constitute a relatively small part of the inventory of transfers compiled for this report. They are concentrated for the most part in three areas: *(i)* support for energy purchases by low-income households; *(ii)* government expenditure on research, development and demonstration projects, both through government laboratories and through grants to non-governmental bodies; and *(iii)* transfers to help redeploy resources in declining fossil-fuel industries, namely coal.[7] Data on direct budgetary support are relatively easy to collect and interpret: the data are usually provided in government budget documents, and there is little need to refer to a hypothetical benchmark – unlike the case for tax expenditures.

Types of tax expenditures relating to fossil fuels

Tax expenditures, by contrast, are always estimated with reference to a benchmark tax level or system. The following section, therefore, explains the main types of tax expenditures examined for this report, and some of the caveats that must be born in mind when interpreting the data.

Tax expenditures with respect to fossil fuels can be categorised into three broad groups: *(i)* those relating to final consumption of fossil fuels; *(ii)* those relating to the use of fossil fuels as inputs to production; and *(iii)* those relating to the production of fossil fuels, including extraction, refining and transport.

Tax expenditures relating to final consumption of fossil fuels

This group of tax expenditures is targeted at final consumption, typically by households, and is generally provided through lower rates, exemptions, or rebates with respect to the two main types of consumption taxes:

- value added taxes (VAT) (which are intended to be broad-based taxes on final consumption, representing a percentage of the value of the good or service sold); and

- excise taxes (which are levied on specific goods, and for which the value of the tax normally is unrelated to the value of the underlying good).

---

[7]   In the coal industry, direct payments are still used by a few countries to help keep high-cost producers from going out of business, but the long-run trend in these types of transfers is downwards. Indeed, since the late 1980s, subsidised coal production has halted entirely in Belgium, France, Ireland, Japan, and Portugal.

These are generally the most visible form of tax expenditures relating to fossil fuels, as they have a direct effect on prices and therefore consumption, though they are not always easy to measure.

Some tax expenditures are levied broadly in the economy through general exemptions or rate reduction in countries' VAT rates. Other tax expenditures are more targeted. In this area, three main categories of tax expenditures stand out: *(i)* those related to specific groups of consumers, *(ii)* those related to specific tax bases, and *(iii)* those related to how the fuels are used. In the first group, qualifying individuals or categories of consumers are taxed less heavily on their fossil-fuel use than users subject to the standard rate of tax. Often, government entities are exempt from fuel taxes (Box 1.1). Sometimes reduced VAT rates are intended to achieve social goals, such as with the exemption of low-income earners from taxes. Such tax exemptions encourage higher rates of consumption of the exempted fuels than would occur in the absence of the exemptions. Governments similarly attempt to achieve social goals through differential tax rates (such as lower tax rates or exemptions on smaller quantities).

Box 1.1. Expenditures relating to governmental activities

When tax expenditures relating to fossil fuels are discussed, most people think first of the beneficiaries as fossil-fuel producers or private consumers of such fuel. Rarely do they think of governments. Yet, in many instances, governments (and their affiliated bodies) are significant beneficiaries of fossil-fuel-related tax expenditures.

In France, for example, the government taxes natural gas consumption at a rate of EUR 1.19 per megawatt hour. The tax structure features a number of exemptions that can be categorised in the other types of tax expenditures mentioned above (such as for households and transportation). In addition, until recently, sub-national governments and other public authorities were exempted from the tax. In 2008, this one tax expenditure was estimated at EUR 37 million. There was also a tax expenditure for fuel used by the military, estimated at EUR 30 million (French Budget, 2010). Both these tax exemptions were eliminated starting in 2009 and 2010, respectively. Many OECD countries provide tax exemptions or reductions for other levels of governments or quasi-governmental bodies, including fuel used in hospitals, schools, and public transport. While such measures may not have a net revenue impact if the government that suffers the lost revenue is the same government that benefits from the concession, just as in the private sector a selective exemption for fossil fuels in the public sector can nonetheless bias decisions by government managers responsible for a spending budget (managed independently of the government's tax revenues) toward greater use of fossil fuels than would otherwise be the case.

In the second group, specific fossil fuels sometimes are subject to reduced rates or are exempted from tax altogether, even though they are intended for the same end purpose as other fuels that are taxed. A common example in the transportation fuel area is a lower tax rate (or exemption) on diesel relative to gasoline (petrol). The broader context, however, must be taken into account. In some countries where the excise tax on diesel is substantially lower than on gasoline (petrol), goods vehicles have to pay distance-based road-user charges. Many countries also levy lower excise taxes on fuels deemed to be "cleaner" than gasoline or diesel, such as CNG, LPG and biofuels, in order to encourage consumers to switch to those fuels. Finally, in the third group are tax expenditures occurring as a result of differences in rates based on how the fossil fuels are used (for example, diesel use on highways versus diesel used in primary industries). Aviation fuels are a special case (Box 1.2).

An important point to bear in mind when interpreting any tax expenditures relating to VAT and excise taxes on fuel is that, in most OECD countries, the majority of the fuel – especially fuel used in motorised vehicles – that is consumed is taxed to some degree. That which is not is generally sold at a price that is at least at world-market parity. (The current exception among OECD countries is Mexico.) The overall net effect of this taxation, even after the exemptions, reductions and rebates, is still to provide some degree of disincentive to consume compared with a situation in which no taxes were applied, and hence no tax expenditures would be measured. The deviations from the standard tax rate nonetheless still distort relative prices *within* an economy, and may favour the consumption of certain fuels in preference to others. This type of non-neutrality reported by governments thus constitutes "support" for purposes of this inventory.

The coverage of this inventory thus departs significantly from that of the estimates of fossil-fuel subsidies published by the IEA and from the lists of subsidies reported by some governments. The IEA uses the so-called "price-gap" approach, which compares domestic fuel prices to an international reference price, in order to provide one type of estimate of the extent to which different countries support the consumption of fossil fuels. This results in most OECD countries not being covered since they tend to have domestic prices that are at least at world-market parity. The broader definition of support used here encompasses policies that may induce changes in the relative prices of fossil fuels. The price-gap approach may also not fully capture those measures that support the production of fossil fuels (to the extent that such support is not entirely reflected in domestic prices). While the present inventory covers measures that provide support (either absolute or relative) to fossil fuels, it does not attempt to assess the impact on prices or quantities of the measures considered, nor does it pass any judgment as to whether a given measure is justified or not.

The relative nature of tax expenditures relating to taxes on consumption can best be illustrated with an example. Assume a country decides to raise additional revenues through a new excise tax on heating oil. Assume also that in an effort to avoid making low-income households worse off, the government exempts them from the new tax. The new tax raises USD 950 million net per year and the government reports a tax expenditure (foregone tax revenue) due to the tax exemption of USD 50 million.

While this new policy results in a net increase in taxes on heating oil of USD 950 million, the country's own reported tax expenditure for low-income households is included in the inventory as support of USD 50 million since it represents more favourable tax treatment for this particular group of taxpayers relative to the treatment that applies to others. Clearly the tax exemption has an important policy purpose – protecting low-income families from cost increases. The inclusion of such measures in the inventory is merely a recognition that support is provided for use of fossil fuels by low-income families when considered relative to the tax treatment that applies to others. This facilitates discussion about the impacts and goals of the policy. For example, it might be asked whether the goals of raising new revenue while protecting low-income families could be achieved without providing a weaker disincentive to use fossil fuels for low-income families relative to the general population by other approaches such as direct income support rather than a tax exemption. Whether or not the tax is intended to reduce fossil-fuel use, it would clearly tend to have this impact, so the issue of differential incentives for different groups is relevant from an environmental point of view. It is, however, noted that some readers may not generally interpret "support" for fossil fuels in this manner. For example, they may interpret support to be the net impact that policies have on the sector, or organisations and individuals consuming fossil fuels (*e.g.* in this case, a net increase in taxes of USD 950 million). This net approach to evaluating support is not, however, the approach used for this study.

Box 1.2 The taxation of fuel used in international aviation

Fuels purchased for use in international aviation are sold free of tax due to an international agreement dating from December 1944: the Convention on International Civil Aviation (also known as the "Chicago Convention"). While fuel taxes may be applied to domestic aviation, Article 24(a) of the Chicago Convention states that "(f)uel ..., on board an aircraft of a contracting state ... shall be exempt from customs duty ... inspection fees or similar national duties or charges." This provision was extended by the Council of the International Civil Aviation Organization (ICAO) in a 1999 Resolution, which states: "fuel ... taken on board for consumption" by an aircraft from a contracting state in the territory of another contracting State departing for the territory of any other State shall be exempt from all customs or other duties ... ." Moreover, the Resolution broadly interprets the scope of the Article 24 prohibition to include "import, export, excise, sales, consumption and internal duties and taxes of all kinds levied upon ... fuel." Most, if not all, bilateral air-services agreements include similar clauses to the ICAO Resolution's expanded view of the Chicago Convention prohibition against taxes on international fuel.

This broad tax exemption was brought about to prevent distortions of aviation markets among countries, such as due to the double taxation of fuel, and to avoid inefficient tax-avoidance behavior, such as airlines shifting routes to reduce tax payments.

Other arrangements generally exempt fuel used in international transport by rail and water as well.

Several OECD countries now apply taxes on fuel used for domestic flights. For example, the United States levies a USD 0.043 per litre charge on domestic jet fuel, and in the Canadian province of Alberta aviation fuel is subject to both a provincial CAD 0.02 per litre tax and a federal levy of CAD 0.04 per litre. In Japan, fuels used for domestic aviation are taxed at JPY 26 (EUR 0.22) per litre, and in Norway they are taxed at NOK 0.69 (EUR 0.09) per litre.

Tax expenditures relating to fossil fuels as inputs to production

A significant portion of fossil fuels (*e.g.* heating in manufacturing plants, inputs to other uses) is consumed by manufacturers and service providers. Some tax expenditures are thus targeted at fossil fuel products that form an input to production. With some types of taxation, such as with VAT, governments attempt to tax only final consumption. In so doing, firms are effectively and necessarily exempted from the VAT that they pay on inputs, through an input refunding system. Such measures are specifically designed not to discriminate among different production methods. As such, exempting energy, including fossil fuels, from VAT when it is only an input to production, can be consistent with the broader tax-policy aims of VATs.

Excise taxes, however, intentionally raise the price of the taxed item – *e.g.* because its use is deemed harmful to society, or because governments can raise revenues easily and relatively efficiently on its consumption. Given this intent, there is much less rationale for exempting businesses who use these goods as inputs to production, as the goal is not to tax final consumption but the specific (potentially environmentally or socially harmful) product or activity. In this case, a tax exemption may actually limit the effectiveness of the tax. Tax expenditures in this area can include exemptions from excise taxes on fuels for certain types of businesses or households and reductions in rates of energy taxes that are related to the energy intensity of firms' production (*e.g.* to attenuate the impact that the standard tax rate might have imposed on firms' competitiveness).[8] Industries engaged in the transformation of fossil fuels into more-refined products or electricity are also often exempted from excise taxes on the fuels used as inputs (Box 1.3). Commonly, fuel used by producers in primary sectors (agriculture, fishing, forestry and mining) is exempted when used in vehicles not operated on publicly financed roads, on the basis that at least part of the tax serves as a means for recovering the cost of building and maintaining those roads or to internalise costs associated with road use (*e.g.* accidents and noise). The intent of the tax may affect whether or not the country in question considers a particular exemption to be a tax expenditure or not.

Box 1.3. Manufacturer privilege

In most OECD countries, and across the EU, industries engaged in the upgrading or transformation of energy from one form to another (*e.g.* oil refineries, coal-briquette plants, and fossil-fuel-fired power plants) are exempted from excise taxes on energy. This is due to what is sometimes called the "manufacturer privilege" – a provision of the tax code which deems that fossil fuel used in the production of final energy products (such as gasoline or coal briquettes or electricity) cannot be taxed. Yet those same fuels, when used by other industries as part of their production processes, *are* often taxed. From an environmental perspective, it is the combustion of the fuel, regardless of the stage of production, which causes damage.[9] If the subsequent consumption of the energy products resulting from this type of energy transformation process is subject to taxation (*e.g.* in the case of an electricity tax at the point of distribution), it might be logical to exempt from tax the fuel inputs (*e.g.* natural gas) that are transformed into energy outputs (*e.g.* electricity) in order to avoid double taxation. On the other hand, coverage of all fuel consumed as energy would require either taxation of the energy consumed in the transformation process (*i.e.* the amount by which energy inputs to the transformation process exceeds outputs) or a grossing-up of the tax on the energy outputs (*e.g.* the electricity) to account for the energy use in the production process.

Tax expenditures relating to the production of fossil fuels

Industries engaged in the extraction of hydrocarbons and mineral resources are unique from other businesses in that the key input to their production – the natural resource in the ground – is commonly publicly owned, there is often significant uncertainty about its exact extent and quality, and its value often depends significantly on the cost of production in the particular location. The production of such resources has the potential to generate super-normal profits.[10] Therefore, in addition to levying the regular corporate

---

8   It is recognised that if, by contrast, tax rates were applied uniformly, international competitiveness concerns could create pressure to set a lower uniform tax rate, which could result in a lower level of internalisation of external costs.

9   This is generally true for pollutants such as carbon dioxide. Other pollutants, such as nitrogen oxides (NO_X), are highly dependent on the method of combustion.

10   Unlike manufacturing, many of the costs of production in natural-resource extraction depend on the location and geological characteristics of the resource being extracted. Given that market prices are determined by the marginal producer (usually the

income tax on profits earned in resource extraction, governments typically levy additional charges that may be seen as representing the "sale price" for the publicly-owned resource. These charges may take various forms such as royalties, additional income taxes, and state participation.

At the same time, many fossil fuel-producing countries have corporate tax expenditures that are targeted at the extraction or production of fossil fuels (and their transformation into usable inputs to intermediate and final consumption). These are often premised on concerns relating to risk and uncertainty, energy security, capital-intensity, high costs, and long project timelines. The tax expenditures reduce the costs of extraction, putting downward pressure on the final price to consumers.

Box 1.4. Supporting the extraction of fossil fuels in the United States and Canada

In the United States, one of the largest tax expenditures is the *excess of percentage over cost depletion* option. Outside of the natural resource sector, taxpayers are normally limited to deducting only their actual expenses from their income. For the minerals sector, producers (with the exception of integrated oil and gas firms) are allowed to deduct a fixed percentage of gross income from the mineral property to account for depletion in reserves (oil, coal, gold, *etc.*) instead of the value of the actual depletion. This fixed percentage is highly favourable and can even exist well after the expenses to acquire and develop a property have been recovered. It is estimated that this tax expenditure would provide a USD 980 million subsidy to fossil-fuel production in 2010 (US Office of Management and Budget, 2011). As part of the budgets for FY2011 and FY2012, the executive branch proposed to eliminate this benefit for coal mines, as well as for oil and gas wells (in addition to other tax expenditures).

Much of Canada's oil production comes from so-called oil sands, where oil and sand are naturally combined, requiring additional processing steps to produce marketable oil. This requires extra capital and additional water and energy use. Such oil-sands development receives a tax benefit through the use of an accelerated capital cost allowance. This provisions allows firms to deduct expenditures on capital assets at a faster rate than other businesses and faster than what economic rates of depreciation would suggest, providing a financial advantage. The cost of this measure in nominal cash-flow terms was estimated at the time of the 2007 federal budget to be on the order of CAD 300 million annually (0.02% of GDP) for the 2007-11 period. The 2007 federal budget announced the phase-out of this measure over the 2011-15 period.

Tax expenditures in this area are commonly provided through the corporate income tax (CIT) system and may be targeted to fossil fuels or to resource extraction more generally. Such tax expenditures are provided through, among other features of the tax code, accelerated depreciation allowances for capital, investment tax credits, additional

---

highest-cost producer supplying the market at any given time), the normal operation of the market can give rise to profits that are much larger (*i.e.* "super-normal") than those which would have been the minimum to justify investment in a particular well or mine. However, much of the investment in a well or mine is immobile: it cannot be used to produce another product or transferred to another location if prices fall below production costs. In addition, any economic rent going to those producers with lower costs may eventually be capitalised in the resource mineral rights, provided the relevant market is competitive enough. In that case, it is the owners of the resource (as opposed to the firm extracting the resource) that may end up receiving most of the long-run producer surplus.

deductions for exploration and production, and preferential capital gains treatment for particular fields. Tax expenditures on production can also take less visible forms such as the special treatment of income from state-owned enterprises, tax relief for income earned on industry sinking funds (*e.g.* for site remediation), tax-exempt bonds, the use of foreign tax credits for what may be considered royalty payments, and exemptions from restrictions on passive losses[11] (Box 1.4).

The effect of these tax benefits is to lower the cost of production and (since many are related to capital) provide an incentive for more investment, and potentially greater production, than would otherwise be the case, which would generally be at the cost of reduced economic output elsewhere because of the diversion of investment. This can affect both firm profitability and the price of fuels to be sold (depending, among other things, on the degree to which the price is set internationally). For firms with marginally profitable production, such schemes may not only have incremental effects on production, but can have a bearing on whether or not the firm continues producing at all. In other situations, such as where supply is constrained (by factors such as regulatory restrictions or limitations on labour or materials), tax benefits may simply increase firm profitability or contribute to inflation of input costs.

Tax-expenditure features may also be found in royalty systems, resource-rent taxes, and other specialised fiscal instruments that apply to resource extraction. Such features must be considered in the context of the particular fiscal system of which they form a part.

Measurement and interpretation of tax expenditures

Unlike direct expenditures, where outlays can usually be readily measured, tax expenditures are estimates of revenue that is foregone due to a particular feature of the tax system that reduces or postpones tax relative to some benchmark tax system. There are a number of important caveats concerning both the interpretation and comparability of tax expenditure estimates, however. These affect both: *(i)* what constitutes a tax expenditure, and *(ii)* how its size should be gauged. A number of these caveats are discussed below.

The data on tax expenditures that are provided in this inventory reflect estimates generated by national and sub-national governments themselves, and as such reflect the benchmark against which the governments chose to make these comparisons.

Defining a benchmark

A key challenge in determining or assessing tax expenditures is to identify the standard or benchmark tax regime against which the nature and extent of any concession is judged. A number of different approaches to deciding on the benchmark regime are possible, and these vary among countries.

- Many countries base their tax-expenditure estimates on a conceptual view about what constitutes "normal" taxation of income and consumption. Typically, the

---

[11]   A passive loss is a loss incurred through a rental property, limited partnership, or other enterprise in which a corporation or individual does not have a working interest. A working interest in an oil and gas property is one by a party that is expected to contribute to the cost of developing and operating the property. Parties merely holding rights to royalties and production payments are not considered to have working interests.

benchmark is defined to include structural features of the tax system, while special features intended to address objectives other than the basic function of the tax (*e.g.* raising revenues, or internalising externalities) may be considered to be deviations from the benchmark. The line between what is structural and what is special, however, is often not a clear one.

- Some countries take a reference-law approach and identify only concessions which appear as such on the face of the law as tax expenditures. Under this approach, a tax credit would likely be identified as a tax expenditure, while differential tax rates on two products within a broader category might not be.

- A few countries restrict their tax-expenditure estimates to those tax reliefs (*e.g.* refundable income-tax credits) that are clearly analogous to public expenditure.

Even in a relatively straightforward case, such as reduced VAT rates, the different approaches could lead to different results. Some countries take their standard rate of VAT as the baseline for measuring the revenue forgone from taxation of some goods and services at lower rates, while others regard such lower rates as an intrinsic part of their VAT and would therefore report no tax expenditure. Where countries have many different rates, it may not be clear which rate should be considered the benchmark.

Another approach is not to look at the current or normal tax regime but rather an "optimal" tax regime, something more often done as an analytic exercise than in practice. This is of particular relevance when investigating tax expenditures related to fossil fuels, given the presence of externalities – the cost imposed on others in society by a private action. When externalities are introduced, the issue of a baseline level against which to measure tax expenditures can change significantly. Harmful air emissions is one of the important reasons why countries implement environmentally related taxes, though other externalities, like traffic congestion[12] and noise pollution, also sometimes motivate taxes (supplementing their motivation as a means to raise revenue for public purposes). Through excise taxes, countries can place a price on environmental damage, thereby encouraging a more socially optimal level of emissions, which would be lower than without taxation. Under this approach, such taxes are levied in addition to taxes needed for general revenue raising.

In practice, the pursuit of optimal taxation (that is, the level of taxation that accounts for all externalities, efficiency effects, the revenue raising needs of government, and the interaction of these effects on the overall economy) is complicated. Quite apart from essentially normative issues such as determining revenue needs, countries would need extensive analytical work to determine optimal tax rates, which would vary significantly over time, and across users, locations and fuels. A further complicating factor is that the externalities may vary in scale among uses of fossil fuels, as many of them may be unrelated to the emission of greenhouse gases (*e.g.* local air pollution such as emissions of particulate matter or NO_X). For these reasons, in practice externalities are not commonly considered in establishing tax-expenditure baselines. Nevertheless, it is an important concept to consider as work continues on consideration of how tax systems can influence market decisions regarding the production and consumption of fossil fuels.

---

12. Excise taxes on fuel are, at best, an indirect way to reduce congestion, which is a phenomenon that has more to do with the time of day when a vehicle is being driven, and where it is being driven, than with the act of consuming fuel in a vehicle *per se.*

Importance of tax system context

Whatever baseline is chosen against which to measure tax expenditures, it is important to consider the overall taxation system. Since most countries do not have theoretically pure tax systems, there are sometimes tax features that may seem to subsidise fossil fuels, but which are in fact a mechanism to compensate or correct for other features of the system. Similarly, a feature of the tax system that may be considered a tax expenditure in one country may not be a tax expenditure in another country, given differing overarching systems in which fossil fuels are taxed.

On the production side, for example, the taxation of natural resource extraction is, as noted, a complex area that goes beyond normal corporate taxation. Countries use varying approaches, such as royalty systems, resource-rent taxes, and cash-flow taxes to tax the super-normal profits that can be associated with resource extraction and ensure a fair return to the public when publicly-owned resources are sold. All of these issues must be taken into account when assessing any particular feature of a tax system.

- For example, immediate expensing of capital expenses for an oil company may be a tax expenditure under a standard corporate income tax, but would likely not be considered a tax expenditure under a cash-flow based tax regime, where immediate expensing of capital and non-deductibility of financing charges (such as interest payments) would be considered neutral.

- Again, lower royalty rates on less productive or more costly fields may arguably be "tax expenditures" in that they represent a concession relative to standard rates. On the other hand, they may be rough ways of taking into account higher costs and lower margins in systems that otherwise would over-tax (and therefore potentially render uneconomic) economically marginal projects (which generate little or no economic rent). In a fiscal system designed for rent capture, varying royalty rates may be the norm.

- As with tax expenditures, resource royalty concessions are not indicative of the overall level of royalties in a country. For example, a country could increase resource royalty rates across the board, while simultaneously introducing a special credit to reflect cost increases in a particular subsector. Assuming the credit were reported as a royalty concession (equivalent to a tax expenditure), it would be included in the inventory of support even though the two changes together resulted in an increase in the overall level of royalties. This treatment is consistent with the purpose of the inventory in highlighting cases where more favourable treatment is provided for one sector or group relative to the norm under a specifically identifiable concession. It is intended to facilitate discussion about the purpose and impact of such concessions. As with relief from excise duties and carbon taxes, the support provided by particular royalty concessions needs to be considered in the broader context of the fiscal system of which is forms a part.

As with relief from excise duties and carbon taxes, this is an area in which detailed knowledge of the tax regime is needed to establish whether there are indeed tax expenditures and, if so, how they should be quantified.

The hypothecation or ear-marking of taxes to fund specific public expenditures – making the tax a kind of user charge – is an issue that involves similar complexity. Other complications can arise where countries have allowed some reductions in a tax on fossil-fuel inputs to a production process and the scale of these rebates reflects the degree of exposure of an industry to international competition or the deployment of other policy instruments to reduce emissions (as has occurred with some carbon taxes and emission-trading systems).

Measuring tax expenditures

Even when the baseline is clear, countries use different ways to measure the extent of the tax expenditure.

- The *revenue foregone* method, the most straightforward, looks at the rate of the tax concession multiplied by the base or uptake. For example, a reduced rate of EUR 0.25 per litre of diesel for taxis from a normal tax rate of EUR 0.45 per litre would yield annual tax expenditures of EUR 180 million if taxi drivers used 900 million litres of fuel a year.

- The *revenue gain* method estimates the increase in government revenues expected to be realised if the tax expenditure were eliminated, thereby incorporating anticipated behavioural changes. Using the same example, the tax expenditure under this method would be the difference in tax rates – EUR 0.20 as before – multiplied by the expected use of fuel by taxi drivers. Under this method, the use will be below 900 million litres, since raising the tax rate will likely encourage some people to no longer take taxis, assuming at least some of the cost is passed through to the users. Therefore, the quantity may only be 800 million litres, leading to a lower tax-expenditure estimate. In the context of climate-change discussions, the extent of the behavioural change is in fact of considerable interest, since the impact of reforming tax expenditures relating to fossil fuels on greenhouse-gas emissions is a key motivation of the exercise. However, such behavioural changes can also be incorporated at a later stage in the analysis, but require the use of models.

- The *expenditure equivalent* method estimates the level of funding that would be needed to meet the same outcome using a spending programme. In the previous example, it would estimate what level of direct subsidy would be needed to maintain the level of taxi drivers' income if the tax expenditure were eliminated. Since most direct government payments are taxed (whereas some benefits provided through preferential tax rates are not), the expenditure equivalent will tend to be larger than the tax expenditure measured by either the revenue foregone or the revenue gain method.

Measures that defer payment of tax without changing the ultimate nominal tax liability are another source of valuation differences across tax expenditure accounts. A common example is accelerated depreciation allowances for capital investments. By allowing the cost of capital assets to be deducted more quickly than they would under the benchmark system, these provisions result in higher deductions and lower taxes in the early years in the life of a particular investment, but lower deductions and higher taxes in the later years of the investment. There are two main approaches to estimating the tax expenditure associated with such measures. The *nominal cash flow approach* measures the extent to which taxes in a particular year are higher or lower as a result of the accelerated allowance than they would have been in its absence. This measure is normally negative in the early years of an investment (indicating a positive tax expenditure) and higher in the later years. In contrast, the *present value approach* measures the discounted value of the time series of annual cash-flow tax expenditures, normally estimated from the time at which the asset is purchased. The two approaches both provide useful information, but they are quite distinct and not directly comparable.

Whichever valuation approach is used, countries typically calculate the value of each tax expenditure on the assumption that all other provisions remain unchanged. Due to interactions and behavioural responses, the revenue impact of eliminating multiple measures is not necessarily equal to the sum of the individual values. Great caution is therefore required in adding together estimates of multiple measures.

International comparability

Tax-expenditure accounting was not designed with international comparability in mind. The estimates reported in this document provide useful information about the relative treatment of different products *within* a national tax system and the economic incentives created for actors in that system. In the absence of a common benchmark, however, tax-expenditure estimates are not readily comparable across countries. Even where countries have adopted broadly the same methodological approach, the way in which they have implemented it in response to practical issues, such as how far a relief should be regarded as a structural part of the tax regime, may well differ (*e.g.* depreciation allowances used in calculating taxable profits).

A fundamental limitation on comparability is differences among countries in the definition of the benchmark tax system. For this reason, a simple cross-country comparison of tax expenditures can lead to a misleading picture of the relative treatment of fossil fuels.

- For example, assume that Country X and Country Y both consider their tax rate on petrol to be the benchmark rate for transportation fuel. Country X taxes petrol at EUR 1.0/L and diesel at EUR 0.6/L, resulting in a EUR 0.4/L tax expenditure for diesel. In contrast, Y taxes both petrol and diesel at EUR 0.4/L. X therefore reports a significant tax expenditure relating to diesel, while Y reports no tax expenditure, even though Y's tax rate on diesel is significantly lower than X's.

In light of these factors, tax-expenditure estimates must be used carefully. The fact that a particular country reports higher tax expenditures relating to fossil fuels than another does not necessarily mean that the first country effectively provides a higher level of support. The higher tax expenditures may simply be due to factors such as:

- higher benchmark tax rates against which tax expenditures are measured;

- a stricter definition of the benchmark tax system that results in more features being singled out as tax expenditures; or

- a more complete set of tax-expenditure accounts.

Higher reported tax expenditures for some countries thus may reflect higher levels of taxation or greater transparency in reporting rather than a higher level of 'support'.

Figure 1.2.   Taxes on petrol (P) and diesel (D) in OECD countries (excluding VAT)

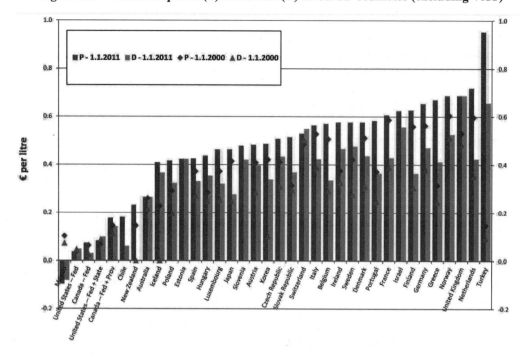

Source: OECD/EEA database on instruments for environmental policy, accessible at www.oecd.org/env/policies/database.

The bottom line is that national tax expenditure estimates can only be considered in the broader context of the particular tax system of the country in question. With this in mind, the OECD has work underway that aims to place national tax expenditures related to fossil-fuel consumption in context by illustrating the structure of fuel taxation in each OECD country. This work will facilitate dialogue about energy use in each country, the objectives of fuel taxation, and how the structure and rates of taxes on different fuels and users of fuel may be influencing consumption decisions.

Meanwhile, given differences among countries in levels of reporting with respect to tax expenditures, the OECD encourages all countries to be open and transparent in the reporting of tax-system features that may encourage the production or consumption of fossil fuels. Greater transparency will facilitate ongoing analysis and dialogue about how government policies, including those with respect to taxation, affect the production and use of fossil fuels.

References

Australian Government (2009), "Budget Strategy and Outlook: Budget Paper No. 1, 2009-10," Available at:
    http://www.budget.gov.au/2009-10/content/bp1/downloads/bp_1.pdf.

British Columbia Ministry of Finance (n.d.), "Harmonized Sales Tax: Rebates and Exemptions," Available at http://www.gov.bc.ca/hst/rebates_exemptions.html. Also see http://www.gov.bc.ca/hst/faq.html.

European Commission (2010), "Emission Trading System: Auctioning," Available at: http://ec.europa.eu/environment/climat/emission/auctioning_en.htm.

French Ministry of the Budget, Public Accounts, Public Service and Reform of the State (2010), "Projet de Loi de Finances pour 2010: Évaluation de Voies et Moyens, Tome II: Dépenses Fiscales," Available at: http://www.performance-publique.gouv.fr/farandole/2010/pap/pdf/VMT2-2010.pdf

French Ministry of Economy, Industry and Labour (n.d.), "Fiche technique – particularités fiscales en Corse," Available at: http://www10.minefi.gouv.fr/transfert/20/Fiscal_Corse.pdf.

G20 (2009), "Leaders' Statement: The Pittsburgh Summit, September 24 – 25 2009".

German Federal Environment Agency (2010), *Environmentally Harmful Subsidies in Germany*, originally published in German in 2008, Available (in English) at: http://www.umweltdaten.de/publikationen/fpdf-l/3896.pdf.

IEA: International Energy Agency (2009a), *Energy Prices and Taxes*, 2009, 4th Quarter, IEA: Paris.

IEA (2009b), *Energy Statistics of OECD Countries: 2009 Edition*, IEA: Paris.

OECD (2009a), *Declaration on Green Growth*, Adopted at the Meeting of the Council at Ministerial Level on 25 June 2009, Paris, Accessible at http://www.oecd.org/dataoecd/58/34/44077822.pdf.

OECD (2009b), OECD's Producer Support Estimate and Related Indicators of Agricultural Support: Concepts, Calculations, Interpretation and Use (The PSE Manual), OECD Trade and Agriculture Directorate, Paris. Available at: http://www.oecd.org/document/43/0,3343,en_2649_33773_41106667_1_1_1_1,00.html.

OECD (2010), *Tax Expenditures in OECD Countries*, OECD Publications, Paris.

OECD/EEA database on instruments for environmental policy, Accessible at: http://www2.oecd.org/ecoinst/queries/.

Nova Scotia Department of Finance (n.d.), "HST Rebates," available at http://www.gov.ns.ca/finance/en/home/taxation/harmonizedsalestax/hstrebates.aspx.

United Kingdom's Her Majesty's Treasury (2009), *Budget 2009: Building Britain's Future*, Available at: http://www.hm-treasury.gov.uk/d/bud09_completereport_2520.pdf. For more complete information on tax expenditures, refer to Her Majesty's Revenue and Customs statistics, Available at: http://www.hmrc.gov.uk/stats/tax_expenditures/menu.htm.

United States Office of Management and Budget (2011), *Analytical Perspectives: Budget of the US Government, Fiscal Year 2012*, Available at: http://www.gpoaccess.gov/usbudget/fy12/pdf/BUDGET-2012-PER.pdf.

Chapter 2

Australia

This chapter identifies, documents, and provides estimates of the various budgetary transfers and tax expenditures that relate to the production or use of fossil fuels in *Australia*. An overview of *Australia's* energy economy is first given to place the measures listed into context. A data-documentation section then describes those measures in a systematic way. Whenever possible, the description details a measure's formal beneficiary, its eligibility criteria and functioning, and the fuels whose production or use stand to benefit from the measure. The chapter ends with a set of charts and tables that provide, subject to availability, quantitative information and estimates for the various measures listed.

2. AUSTRALIA

Energy resources and market structure

Coal mining dominates Australia's energy production, with almost three-quarters of coal output going to export. Australia holds the fifth-largest coal reserve base in the world. It also produces and exports significant volumes of natural gas, the proven reserves of which have grown significantly in recent years with the discovery of large volumes of unconventional gas. The country is less well-endowed with oil resources; just under half of the country's oil is currently imported. Coal is the leading primary fuel in Australia's energy mix, accounting for 42% of total energy use; it is used mainly for power generation. Oil, with 31% and natural gas, with 22%, meet most of the rest of the country's energy needs, while biomass, hydro-electric power and other sources of renewable energy make only a minor contribution. Well over half of the country's total energy production is exported.

Australia was a pioneer of energy market liberalisation in the 1990s. Early reforms involved the deregulation of its downstream oil sector and the coal-mining industry, the lifting of export controls on coal, the introduction of regulated third-party access to gas and electricity networks, and the privatisation of some utilities owned by federal and state governments. Structural and regulatory reforms in electricity and gas have continued in recent years with the aim of creating efficient wholesale and retail markets.

Over 90% of Australian coal production is anthracite and bituminous (black) coal. The industry is located almost entirely in the states of New South Wales (NSW) and Queensland, with close to three-quarters of production coming from open-cast mines. The industry is wholly in private hands. Four major coal mining companies – Rio Tinto, BHP Billiton, Xstrata and Anglo American – together account for well over half of total Australian black-coal production. Lignite (brown coal) is produced exclusively in the state of Victoria, almost all of it by three mines in the Latrobe Valley.

The oil industry is also entirely privately owned. The upstream sector is made up of small, medium and large companies, many of which are foreign-based. Refining is in the hands of four vertically integrated refiner-marketers: BP, Caltex, Mobil and Shell. There are also independent fuel retailers, including supermarkets, some of which have established alliances with the refiners.

The natural-gas sector has undergone considerable change as a result of market expansion and reform. Many of the vertically integrated public gas utilities have been structurally disaggregated and the separated entities privatised. Energex, in Queensland, is the only major gas-distribution company still in state ownership. Retail competition is being progressively introduced in most jurisdictions.

The electricity sector has been unbundled into separate generating, transmission, distribution and marketing companies. There is a mixture of state-owned and private companies in power generation, transmission and distribution, while all marketers are privately owned. In South Australia, state-owned assets are privately managed under long-term leases. The Snowy Mountains Hydro Electric Scheme, co-owned by the NSW and Victoria states, is the only company in which the Federal government holds a stake. Electricity transmission in Australia is open access. The Australian Energy Market Commission (AEMC) is responsible for determining rules and giving policy advice covering the national electricity market (NEM). The Australian Energy Regulator (AER) is responsible for rule enforcement for the NEM as well as economic regulation of transmission and distribution networks. Prices for most transmission assets in the NEM are set by AER, subject to a revenue cap, but it is also possible for new assets to be unregulated and earn market rates.

Prices, taxes and support mechanisms

With the exception of electricity and natural gas, energy prices are completely deregulated in Australia. Despite the introduction of contestability in retail markets, the electricity and gas for households and for small businesses that have not chosen to switch to a new supplier continue to be regulated on a cost-of-service basis. Victoria is the only state to have abolished retail price controls, in 2008. The other states plan to eliminate retail price regulation only when competition is well-established.

Upstream taxes include federal taxes on petroleum production and royalties on the production of petroleum from the North West Shelf. The states and territories also impose royalties on petroleum production. Downstream taxes comprise mainly the general Goods and Services Tax (GST) and excise taxes on motor fuels. GST – a type of VAT charged at each stage of production and distribution, currently at a rate of 10% – is applicable to sales of nearly all final energy products. All motor fuels are subject to a flat per-litre federal excise tax, though there are some exemptions. Liquefied petroleum gas (LPG), as well as liquefied and compressed natural, receives a complete exemption from the excise tax. In addition, domestic producers of biofuels (both ethanol and biodiesel) receive excise-tax rebates, which are also available to imported biodiesel.

There are no longer any significant support measures in the upstream sector in Australia, following the removal in 2008 of a partial exemption from an excise tax normally levied on crude oil for condensate – a low-density mixture of hydrocarbon liquids contained in gaseous form in the raw natural gas produced from some gas fields. In the downstream sector, the principal support measure at the federal level other than differential taxation, is the Fuel Tax Credits for Heavy Diesel Vehicles programme, which provides businesses operating heavy trucks a partial or full rebate on the fuel excise tax depending on the type of vehicle they drive and the sector in which they operate. Eligibility for the tax credit is conditional on satisfying certain environmental criteria. The federal government also runs a grant scheme for consumers who convert their gasoline cars to LPG, though the government recently announced that it would cap the number of grants to be issued for three years. Some states also provide support to some forms of energy use. Western Australia has a diesel subsidy programme for on-road trucks. Queensland runs a Home Energy Emergency Assistance Scheme, which provides low-income households with emergency assistance if they prove unable to pay their electricity and gas bills, as well as a Reticulated Natural Gas Rebate programme, which provides the elderly in need with annual rebates on their gas bills.

Data documentation

General notes

The fiscal year in Australia runs from 1 July to 30 June. Following OECD convention, data are allocated to the starting calendar year so that data covering the period July 2005 to June 2006 are allocated to 2005.

Since Australia is a federal country, the data collection exercise was also conducted for a sample of three states. Those three states are: Western Australia (WA), Queensland (QLD), and Victoria (VIC).

Producer Support Estimate

The offshore extraction of oil and natural gas in Australia is subject to a particular tax regime that combines a resource tax and the regular corporate income tax. The Petroleum Resource Rent Tax (PRRT) was introduced with the Petroleum Resource Rent Tax Assessment Act of 1987. It is project-based and applies to taxable profits at the rate of 40%.[13] PRRT rules allow for the full deduction of exploration, development, and decommissioning expenditures. Financing costs are, however, not deductible for PRRT purposes. Unclaimed deductions can be carried forward and compounded every year at varying rates. Some of these deductions can also be transferred to other projects within the same company or group.

The general corporate income-tax rate in Australia is 30% and deductions are allowed for PRRT payments, business expenses, and exploration costs related to mining (including coal) and oil and gas extraction. Some expenses related to mine rehabilitation and the removal of offshore platforms are also deductible for income-tax purposes. Royalties are only levied when production is not subject to the PRRT (or its onshore equivalent, the Resource Rent Royalty).

The immediate write-off of both capital and exploration-and-development expenditures is normally considered under the systems in many countries to amount to a preferential tax treatment. The reason is that in calculating taxable profits in most income-tax systems, capital expenses are allocated over the period to which they contribute to earnings. Allowing the immediate writing-off these types of expenditure therefore provides companies with something akin to a zero-interest loan from the government since it delays the collection of taxes. A present-value calculation would indeed show a positive transfer from the government to the companies benefiting from such provisions.

However, when combined with an impossibility for companies to deduct interest costs and other financing charges, the immediate write-off of both capital and exploration-and-development expenditures may not be considered a preferential tax treatment. This is due to the fact that this particular combination of tax provisions may approximate what is known as a "cash-flow" tax system. Cash-flow tax systems can be theoretically equivalent to the more common imputed-income tax systems where the objective is to levy a neutral business tax (Boadway and Bruce, 1984). For that reason, provisions such as the expensing of exploration and development costs may not be preferential tax provisions in the particular case of the Australian PRRT.

---

[13] Some offshore areas like the North West Shelf remain subject to the old royalty and crude-oil excise regime or to production-sharing contracts.

The Australian government recently confirmed that it would introduce changes to its resource taxation regime effective on 1 July 2012. These changes include the creation of a new Mineral Resource Rent Tax (MRRT) that will apply to both iron ore and coal, and the extension of the PRRT regime to all onshore and offshore oil and gas projects.

Cleaner Fuels Grants Scheme (data for 2005-09)

This programme was initially designed to support biodiesel only but was then extended to ultralow-sulphur diesel and premium unleaded petrol starting in FY 2005/06. A breakdown by fuel is available from the Australian Taxation Office so that only payments related to premium unleaded petrol and ultralow-sulphur diesel are being reported. Support for premium unleaded petrol stopped on 31 December 2007.

Sources: Australian Taxation Office (various years).

Tag: AUS_dt_03

North West Shelf Gas Financial Assistance (data for 1997-2000)

Not much information is available regarding this item. It appears several times in Western Australia's State Budget under the *Grants, Subsidies and other Transfer Payments* heading, but the specifics of the scheme are not described. North West Shelf Gas is, however, a major gas supplier in Western Australia.

The FY 2000/01 budget reports annual amounts up to FY 2003/04 while that for FY 2001/02 seems to suggest that payments stopped around FY 2000/01. Assuming that recent reporting tends to be more reliable, and in order to ensure consistency across programmes and countries, the measure is deemed phased-out following FY 2000/01.

Sources: Western Australian Government (various years).

Tag: AUS_dt_05

Dampier to Bunbury Gas Pipeline Sale Assistance (data for 2004)

The Dampier to Bunbury gas pipeline is a major source of supply to Western Australia. It was initially state-owned but was sold in 1998 to a private company, Epic Energy. In turn, the latter sold it to another private consortium in 2004. That particular sale seems to have benefited from state assistance according to Western Australian budget papers.

Sources: Western Australian Government (various years).

Tag: AUS_dt_08

Accelerated Depreciation for Mining Buildings (data for 1994-2008)

The programme is reported as having started in 1982 and was phased out in 2001. It was, however, still giving rise to a significant positive tax expenditure in 2009 as assets acquired years ago kept on depreciating faster relative to their effective life. The concession allows companies to depreciate buildings used in the mining and quarrying sector over ten years or the life of the project, whichever is shorter.

Because the measure applies to both mining and quarrying, for this and similar measures, we deduct from the annual amounts reported in official tax expenditure documents the estimated share associated with mining output that is not concerned with fossil fuels. This is done using gross output data from the EU KLEMS database on the assumption that the tax expenditure is evenly distributed across sub-sectors according to output. The remaining amounts are then allocated to the various types of fossil fuels (*i.e.* crude oil, natural gas, and coal) using production data from the IEA.

Sources: Australian Treasury (various years), EU KLEMS, IEA.

Tag: AUS_te_02

Capital Expenditure Deduction for Mining, Quarrying and Petroleum Operations (data for 1994-2010)

The programme dates back to 1921 and was phased out in 2001. It was very similar to the concession on accelerated depreciation for mining buildings (see above), the only difference being that it applied to certain types of capital expenditure.

Since the measure applies to the mining sector as a whole, we deduct from the annual amounts reported in official tax expenditure documents the estimated share associated with mining output that is not concerned with fossil fuels. This is done using gross output data from the EU KLEMS database. The remaining amounts are then allocated to the various types of fossil fuels (*i.e.* crude oil, natural gas, and coal) using production data from the IEA.

Sources: Australian Treasury (various years), EU KLEMS, IEA.

Tag: AUS_te_03

Infrastructure Bonds Scheme – Transport (data for 1996-2008)

This programme started in 1992 under the aegis of the Development Allowance Authority. It was aimed at encouraging investment in infrastructure projects through the issuance of Develop Australia Bonds (*i.e.* Infrastructure Bonds) that provided lenders with tax-deductible interest payments. Although part of the concession targeted water and transport infrastructure, the rest was earmarked for gas and electricity projects, such as co-generation plants or gas pipelines. The programme was terminated in 1997 and replaced with the Infrastructure Borrowings Tax Offset Scheme. However, deductions were still being claimed as of 2008.

Data from the Development Allowance Authority annual reports were used to roughly estimate the shares of the reported annual tax expenditures that are attributable to gas infrastructure and power plants. We treat those two components of the scheme as separate programmes since one relates to the supply side while the other relates to the demand side.

The gas infrastructure part is said to represent around 16% of all projects. Since it is excludable and benefits few gas producers, the programme is included in the PSE and is allocated to natural gas only.

Sources: Development Allowance Authority (various years), Australian Treasury (various years), Parliament of Australia (1997).

Tag: AUS_te_07

Infrastructure Borrowings Tax Offset Scheme – Transport (data for 1997-2007)

The Infrastructure Borrowings Tax Offset Scheme (IBTOS) is very similar to the Infrastructure Bonds Scheme it was meant to replace back in 1997. One major difference is that IBTOS features a lower cap on annual expenditures (AUD 75 million). New infrastructure projects stopped being accepted as of May 2004, however. The estimation method follows that of the Infrastructure Bonds Scheme (see above), meaning that we break IBTOS into two separate programmes using rough project-type shares from the Development Allowance Authority's annual reports.

Sources: Development Allowance Authority (various years), Australian Treasury (various years), Parliament of Australia (1997).

Tag: AUS_te_09

Exemption from Crude-Oil Excise for Condensate (data for 2001-)

This concession was introduced in 1977 and exempts condensate[14] from the excise tax that is normally levied on crude-oil production taking place outside the PRRT framework (*cf.* introductory remark). Although the exemption was abolished in 2008, condensate remains subject to a lower rate than that applied to fields discovered prior to September 1975 (which is the Treasury benchmark). The measure therefore continues to yield positive and significant tax expenditures.

Estimates are not available for the years preceding 2001.

Sources: Australian Treasury (various years).

Tag: AUS_te_11

Exploration and Prospecting Deduction (data for 2006-)

This provision was introduced in 1968 and allows mining and quarrying companies to deduct exploration and prospecting expenses in full in the year in which they are incurred for income-tax purposes. The measure does not pertain to the PRRT regime (*cf.* introductory remark).

Since the measure applies to the mining sector as a whole, we deduct from the annual amounts reported in official tax expenditure documents the estimated share associated with mining output that is not concerned with fossil fuels. This is done using gross output data from the EU KLEMS database. The remaining amounts are then allocated to the various types of fossil fuels (*i.e.* crude oil, natural gas, and coal) using production data from the IEA.

Sources: Australian Treasury (various years), EU KLEMS, IEA.

Tag: AUS_te_13

Increased Deduction for Petroleum Exploration Expenditure (no data available)

This provision was introduced in 2004 to encourage exploration in designated, remote offshore areas. It allowed oil and gas companies to deduct as much as 150%

---

[14]   Condensate is only subject to the petroleum production excise tax when marketed jointly with crude oil.

of the qualifying exploration costs incurred in a given year. The benchmark PRRT deduction for such costs is 100%. This 50% uplift expired in 2009.

No estimates of the revenue foregone due to the cost uplift are available.

Sources: Australian Treasury (various years).

Consumer Support Estimate

Diesel and Alternative Fuels Grants Scheme (data for 2000-02)

The Diesel and Alternative Fuels Grants Scheme (DAFGS) was introduced in 2000 as part of the *A New Tax System* initiative before becoming part of the EGCS (*i.e.* the former version of the Fuel Tax Credits) starting in 2003. For that reason, reporting stops around that time and the EGCS thereupon includes both DFRS and DAFGS payments (see also "Fuel Tax Credits" below). The DAFGS gives certain on-road users a grant aimed at cutting the fuel costs they have incurred.

Although the EGCS is a tax expenditure, only its former DFRS component used to specifically offset fuel excise taxes. The DAFGS is therefore reported as a budgetary transfer.

Sources: Australian Taxation Office (various years), Australian Treasury (2001), Webb (2000, 2001).

Tag: AUS_dt_01

Fuel Sales Grants Scheme (data for 2000-07)

The programme was introduced in 2000 as part of the *A New Tax System* initiative to compensate certain areas of the country for the introduction of a federal, harmonised Goods and Services Tax (the so-called GST). The measure targeted fuel retailers in remote and "regional areas" before being subsequently phased-out in 2006. As a rough approximation, we allocate 90% of the payments to diesel and 10% to gasoline given that the scheme overwhelmingly benefits producers of primary commodities.

Sources: Australian Taxation Office (various years), Australian Treasury (2001), Webb (2000, 2001).

Tag: AUS_dt_02

Queensland Fuel Subsidy Scheme (data for 1999-2009)

This measure started in 1997 and gave rise to significant annual subsidies until it was phased out in July 2009. In essence, it was meant to compensate Queensland fuel users for the introduction of a federal excise tax on petroleum products, following a 1997 High Court decision banning state-level excise taxes (Queensland did not levy a fuel excise tax at the time). Beneficiaries include bulk end users, some off-road diesel users, and retailers who were thus expected to pass on the benefit to final consumers of fuels.

Official data on monthly sales of petroleum products in Queensland suggest that roughly 50% of the subsidy can be allocated to diesel oil, 45% to gasoline, and 5% to LPG. Values for the years 2000 and 2001 were linearly interpolated since the corresponding amounts could not be found in Queensland's budget documents.

Sources: Queensland Government (various years), Department of Resources, Energy and Tourism (various years).

Tag: AUS_dt_04

Western Australian Diesel Subsidy (data for 1997-)

The programme seems to date back to 1997 for the same reasons that led to the creation of the Queensland Fuel Subsidy Scheme (see above). However, its size is much smaller than the Queensland scheme since Western Australia did not have a zero excise tax on diesel at the time. Although the measure initially targeted both off-road and on-road users, the introduction of several federal grants in July 2000 resulted in the programme being restricted to on-road users from that date forward. A Productivity Commission report mentions in a footnote the existence of an older scheme in Western Australia but no additional information regarding it could be found.

Data prior to FY 1997/98 are not available.

Sources: Western Australian Government (various years).

Tag: AUS_dt_06

Home Energy Emergency Assistance Scheme (data for 2007-)

This measure provides low-income households with emergency assistance in case they prove unable to pay their electricity and natural gas bills. It does not, however, give rise to direct transfers to consumers since payments are made to energy companies. We used data from the IEA's Energy Balances for the residential sector to estimate the share of payments that is attributable to natural gas (about 35%).

Sources: Queensland Government (various years), IEA.

Tag: AUS_dt_10

Reticulated Natural Gas Rebate (data for 2007-)

The programme, which was initially called the Gas Pensioner Rebate Scheme, was renamed the Reticulated Natural Gas Rebate in 2007. It provides the elderly in need with annual rebates of about AUD 55. Contrary to the Home Energy Emergency Assistance Scheme, payments are made directly to households and target natural gas specifically.

Sources: Queensland Government (various years).

Tag: AUS_dt_09

Petroleum Products Freight Subsidy Scheme (data for 2001-05)

The programme was put in place in 1965 and granted assistance to those fuel distributors that were selling eligible petroleum products in remote areas of the country. It was then phased out in 2006. Few details are actually available, but it seems that the programme used to provide fixed annual amounts of AUD 3.5 million (at least in the last years). For that reason, we report the same value for every missing year starting at the first observation available (2001).

Eligible fuels include gasoline, diesel, and kerosene-type jet fuel. IEA Energy Balances data for rail, road and domestic aviation suggest the following breakdown: diesel (31%), gasoline (61%), and kerosene-type jet fuel (8%).

Sources: Australian Treasury (2001), IEA.

Tag: AUS_dt_12

Fuel Tax Credits (data for 1994-)

The programme dates from 1982 when the Commonwealth Government decided to replace the old exemption certificate scheme – prone to abuse – with a new Diesel Fuel Rebate Scheme (DFRS). The scheme subsequently went through several changes in terms of coverage and rates, being first renamed the Energy Grants Credit Scheme (EGCS) in 2003, before being given its current name in 2006. It provides eligible users with a partial or full rebate on the fuel excise tax, depending on the type of vehicle they drive and the sector in which they operate.

The mining sector is eligible for the Fuel Tax Credits programme, which makes the latter both a producer subsidy and a consumer subsidy. However, given the relative importance of those two components, only the consumption side is considered. The measure thus forms part of the CSE.

The annual amounts reported under the Fuel Tax Credits also include those reported under the Diesel and Alternative Fuels Grants Scheme starting in 2003, since the programme was at the time merged with the DFRS to become the EGCS programme (see above).

Sources: Australian Taxation Office (various years), Australian Treasury (2001), Webb (2000, 2001).

Tag: AUS_te_01

Reduced Excise Rate on Aviation Fuel (data for 1996-)

Consumers of both aviation gasoline and aviation turbine fuel have benefited from a reduced rate of excise tax since March 1956. The Australian Treasury includes this concession in its annual Tax Expenditures Statement. Only the part that relates to domestic flights is, however, reported.

Though it relates to both aviation gasoline and kerosene-type jet fuel, consumption of the latter dwarfs the use being made of the former according to IEA data. For that reason, we allocate the measure entirely to kerosene-type jet fuel.

Sources: Australian Treasury (various years), IEA.

Tag: AUS_te_04

Exemption from Excise for 'Alternative Fuels' (data for 1994-)

This concession was introduced in 1985 and targets liquefied petroleum gas, liquefied natural gas, and compressed natural gas.

We allocated annual amounts from the Australian Treasury to all three different fuels using data from the IEA's Energy Balances on fuel use in the road transport sector.

Sources: Australian Treasury (various years), IEA.

Tag: AUS_te_05

Reduced Excise Rate on Heating Oil, Fuel Oil and Kerosene (data for 1996-2006)

The Australian Government began levying excise tax on heating oil, fuel oil and kerosene in 1983. However, these fuels remained subject to a much lower rate when used other than in an internal combustion engine. This lasted until 2006, when tax rates were then set high enough to match those applying to regular petroleum products. This rise was, however, paralleled by the introduction of an equivalent rebate that in effect nullifies the incidence of excise. Starting in 2006, annual estimates for this rebate are being reported as part of the Fuel Tax Credits (see above).

We allocated annual amounts from the Australian Treasury to all three different fuels using data from the IEA's Energy Balances on fuel use in both the residential sector and the commercial services sector.

Sources: Australian Treasury (various years), IEA.

Tag: AUS_te_06

Infrastructure Bonds Scheme – Power Generation (data for 1996-2008)

Like the Infrastructure Bonds Scheme for transport (see above), this programme started in 1992 under the aegis of the Development Allowance Authority. It was aimed at encouraging investment in infrastructure projects through the issuance of Develop Australia Bonds (*i.e.* Infrastructure Bonds) that provided lenders with tax-deductible interest payments. Although part of the concession targeted water and transport infrastructure, the rest was earmarked for gas and electricity projects such as co-generation plants or gas pipelines. The programme was terminated in 1997 and replaced with the Infrastructure Borrowings Tax Offset Scheme. However, deductions were still being claimed as of 2008.

Data from the Development Allowance Authority annual reports were used to roughly estimate the shares of the reported annual tax expenditures that are attributable to gas infrastructure and power plants. We treat those two components of the scheme as separate programmes since one relates to the supply side while the other relates to the demand side

The power generation part is said to represent around 23% of all projects. Though it appears under the "Electricity" heading, virtually all examples of power generation projects financed through the scheme are gas-fired cogeneration plants. Taxpayer privacy arrangements make access to a full listing of the projects and the associated costs impossible, hence the entire value of the scheme was allocated to natural gas as a rough approximation.

Sources: Development Allowance Authority (various years), Australian Treasury (various years), Parliament of Australia (1997).

Tag: AUS_te_08

Infrastructure Borrowings Tax Offset Scheme – Power Generation (data for 1997-2007)

The Infrastructure Borrowings Tax Offset Scheme (IBTOS) is very similar to the Infrastructure Bonds Scheme it was meant to replace back in 1997. One major difference is that IBTOS features a lower cap on annual expenditures (AUD 75 million). New infrastructure projects stopped being accepted as of May 2004, however. The estimation method follows that of the Infrastructure Bonds Scheme (see above), meaning we break IBTOS into two separate programmes using rough project-type shares from the Development Allowance Authority annual reports.

Sources: Development Allowance Authority (various years), Australian Treasury (various years), Parliament of Australia (1997).

Tag: AUS_te_10

Diesel Fuel Exemption Certificate Scheme (data for 1995-99)

This programme provided off-road users of diesel in the state of Victoria with an exemption from the fuel excise tax. As for Western Australia's diesel subsidy (see above), the introduction of several federal rebates on off-road use of diesel resulted in the programme being phased-out in 2000.

Sources: Victorian State Government (various years).

Tag: AUS_te_12

General Services Support Estimate

Coal Industry Development (data for 2006-)

Budget documents mention that the measure aims at expanding coal companies' market opportunities overseas.

Lack of details prevents us from allocating it to the PSE so it is allocated to the GSSE. We use production data from the IEA to allocate the annual amounts reported in budget documents to the various types of coal concerned.

Sources: Western Australian Government (various years), IEA.

Tag: AUS_dt_07

Collingwood Park Assistance Package (data for 2008)

This package forms part of a broader tendency to help residents affected by mine subsidence. Normally, the mining industry is held liable for subsidence damage.

The measure is allocated to the GSSE as it does not increase current production or consumption of coal. Estimates prior to 2008 could not be found. We use production data from the IEA to allocate the annual amounts reported to the various types of coal concerned.

Sources: DEEDI (2008), IEA.

Tag: AUS_dt_11

References

Policies or transfers

Australian Taxation Office (various years) *Taxation Statistics*, Available at: http://www.ato.gov.au/corporate/pathway.asp?pc=001/001/009/005&mfp=001/001 &mnu=43433#001_001_009_005.

Australian Treasury (2001) *History of Fuel Taxation in Australia*, Fuel Taxation Inquiry, Background Papers, Available at: http://fueltaxinquiry.treasury.gov.au/content/backgnd/002.asp.

Australian Treasury (various years) *Tax Expenditures Statements*, Available at: http://www.treasury.gov.au/content/taxation.asp?ContentID=343&titl=Taxation.

Boadway, Robin and Neil Bruce (1984) 'A General Proposition on the Design of a Neutral Business Tax', *Journal of Public Economics*, Vol. 24, No. 2, pp. 231-239.

DEEDI (2008) *Budget Papers*, Department of Employment, Economic Development and Innovation, Queensland Government, Available at: http://www.dme.qld.gov.au/corporate_publications_1.cfm.

Department of Resources, Energy and Tourism (various years) *Australian Petroleum Statistics*, Available at: http://www.ret.gov.au/resources/fuels/aps/pages/default.aspx.

Development Allowance Authority (various years), *Annual Report*, Australian Government.

Parliament of Australia (1997) *Bills Digest 146 1996-97*, Information and Research Services, Parliamentary Library, Available at: http://www.aph.gov.au/library/pubs/bd/1996-97/97bd146.htm.

Queensland Government (various years) *Budget Papers*, Queensland State Budget, Available at: http://www.budget.qld.gov.au/previous-budgets/index.shtml.

Victorian State Government (various years) *Budget Papers*, Victorian State Budget, Available at: http://www.dtf.vic.gov.au/CA25713E0002EF43/pages/publications-budget-papers-past-budget-papers.

Webb, Richard (2000) *Petrol and Diesel Excises*, Research Paper No.6 (2000-01), Commerce and Industrial Relations Group, Parliamentary Library, Available at: http://www.aph.gov.au/library/pubs/rp/2000-01/01RP06.htm.

Webb, Richard (2001) *Fuel Price Subsidy Schemes*, Research Note No.24 (2000-01), Information and Research Services, Parliamentary Library, Available at: http://www.aph.gov.au/library/pubs/rn/2000-01/01rn24.pdf.

Western Australian Government (various years) *Budget Statements*, Western Australian State Budget, Available at: http://www.ourstatebudget.wa.gov.au/.

Energy statistics

IEA, *Energy Balances of OECD Countries*, 2010 Edition, International Energy Agency, Paris.

EU KLEMS, *EU KLEMS Growth and Productivity Accounts: November 2009 Release*, Available at: http://www.euklems.net/.

Figure 2.1.   Shares of fossil-fuel support by fuel, average for 2008-10 – Australia

Coal — — Natural Gas

Petroleum —

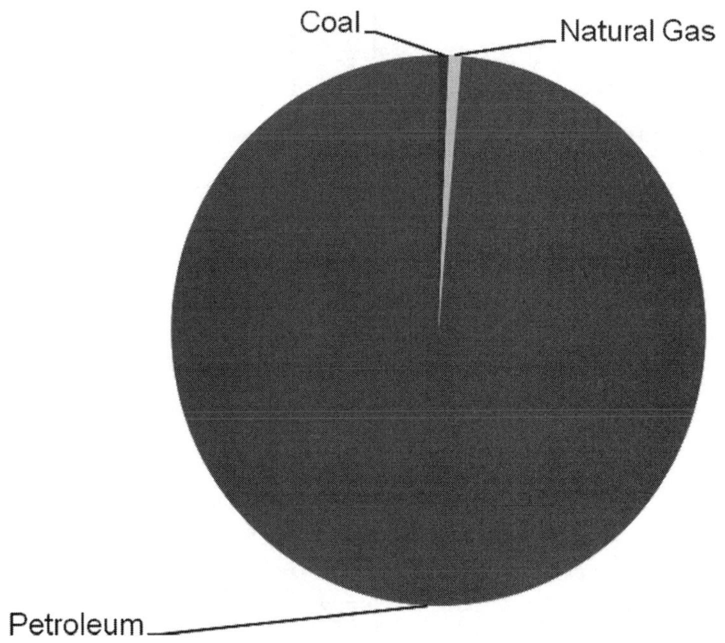

Source: OECD.

Figure 2.2.   Shares of fossil-fuel support by indicator, average for 2008-10 – Australia

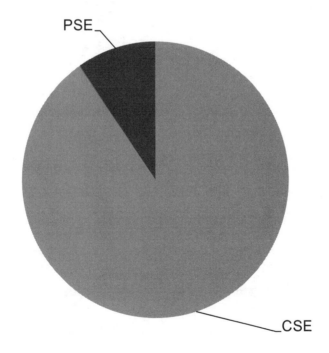

PSE —

— CSE

Source: OECD.

Table 2.1. Summary of fossil-fuel support to coal – Australia

(Millions of Australian dollars, nominal)

Support element	Jurisdiction	Avg 2000-02	Avg 2008-10	2008	2009	2010p
Producer Support Estimate						
Support for capital formation						
Accelerated Depreciation for Mining Buildings	Federal	102.70	n.a.	21.04	n.a.	n.a.
Capital Expenditure Deduction for Mining *et al.*	Federal	7.10	2.49	3.51	2.34	1.64
Exploration and Prospecting Deduction	Federal	n.c.	31.17	28.05	30.39	35.06
Consumer Support Estimate (n.a.)						
General Services Support Estimate						
Collingwood Park Assistance Package	QLD	n.a.	n.a.	10.00	n.a.	n.a.
Coal Industry Development	WA	n.a.	3.41	6.16	4.06	0.02

Note: Tax expenditures for any given country are measured with reference to a benchmark tax treatment that is generally specific to that country. Consequently, the estimates contained in the table above are not necessarily comparable with estimates for other countries. In addition, because of the potential interaction between them, the summation of individual measures for a specific country may be problematic. The allocation of particular measures across fuel types was done by the OECD Secretariat based on the IEA's Energy Balances.

Source: OECD.

Table 2.2. Summary of fossil-fuel support to petroleum – Australia

(Millions of Australian dollars, nominal)

Support element	Jurisdiction	Avg 2000-02	Avg 2008-10	2008	2009	2010p
Producer Support Estimate						
Support to unit returns						
Cleaner Fuels Grants Scheme	Federal	n.a.	n.a.	69.00	0.00	n.a.
Exemption from Crude Oil Excise for Condensate	Federal	165.00	586.67	580.00	600.00	580.00
Support for capital formation						
Accelerated Depreciation for Mining Buildings	Federal	91.72	n.a.	11.93	n.a.	n.a.
Capital Expenditure Deduction for Mining *et al.*	Federal	6.34	1.41	1.99	1.33	0.93
Exploration and Prospecting Deduction	Federal	n.c.	17.68	15.91	17.23	19.89
Consumer Support Estimate						
Consumption						
Diesel and Alternative Fuels Grants Scheme	Federal	706.44	n.a.	n.a.	n.a.	n.a.
Fuel Sales Grants Scheme	Federal	231.73	n.a.	n.a.	n.a.	n.a.
Queensland Fuel Subsidy Scheme	QLD	520.13	n.a.	560.00	28.00	n.a.
Western Australian Diesel Subsidy	WA	4.07	9.43	9.12	9.44	9.72
Petroleum Products Freight Subsidy Scheme	Federal	3.50	n.a.	n.a.	n.a.	n.a.
Fuel Tax Credits	Federal	2 099.12	5 020.73	5 069.75	4 996.23	4 996.23
Reduced Excise Rate on Aviation Fuel	Federal	793.33	983.33	970.00	980.00	1 000.00
Exemption from Excise for 'Alternative Fuels'	Federal	571.30	539.79	565.80	517.02	536.53
Reduced Excise Rate on Heating Oil *et al.*	Federal	249.59	n.a.	n.a.	n.a.	n.a.
General Services Support Estimate (n.a.)						

Note: Tax expenditures for any given country are measured with reference to a benchmark tax treatment that is generally specific to that country. Consequently, the estimates contained in the table above are not necessarily comparable with estimates for other countries. In addition, because of the potential interaction between them, the summation of individual measures for a specific country may be problematic. The allocation of particular measures across fuel types was done by the OECD Secretariat based on the IEA's Energy Balances.

Source: OECD.

INVENTORY OF ESTIMATED BUDGETARY SUPPORT AND TAX EXPENDITURES FOR FOSSIL FUELS © OECD 2011

Table 2.3. Summary of fossil-fuel support to natural gas – Australia

(Millions of Australian dollars, nominal)

Support element	Jurisdiction	Avg 2000-02	Avg 2008-10	2008	2009	2010p
Producer Support Estimate						
Support to unit returns						
Dampier to Bunbury Gas Pipeline Sale Assistance	WA	n.a.	n.a.	n.a.	n.a.	n.a.
Income support						
North West Shelf Gas Financial Assistance	WA	5.36	n.a.	n.a.	n.a.	n.a.
Support for capital formation						
Accelerated Depreciation for Mining Buildings	Federal	79.01	n.a.	19.69	n.a.	n.a.
Capital Expenditure Deduction for Mining et al.	Federal	5.48	2.33	3.28	2.19	1.53
Infrastructure Bonds Scheme Transport	Federal	5.60	n.a.	0.80	n.a.	n.a.
Infrastructure Borrowings Tax Offset Scheme - Transport	Federal	2.93	n.a.	n.a.	n.a.	n.a.
Exploration and Prospecting Deduction	Federal	n.c.	29.17	26.26	28.44	32.82
Consumer Support Estimate						
Reticulated Natural Gas Rebate	QLD	n.a.	2.96	2.96	2.96	2.96
Home Energy Emergency Assistance Scheme	QLD	n.a.	1.05	1.05	1.05	1.05
Exemption from Excise for 'Alternative Fuels'	Federal	23.70	13.55	14.20	12.98	13.47
Infrastructure Bonds Scheme Power Generation	Federal	8.05	n.a.	1.15	n.a.	n.a.
Infrastructure Borrowings Tax Offset Scheme - Power Generation	Federal	4.22	n.a.	n.a.	n.a.	n.a.
General Services Support Estimate (n.a.)						

Note: Tax expenditures for any given country are measured with reference to a benchmark tax treatment that is generally specific to that country. Consequently, the estimates contained in the table above are not necessarily comparable with estimates for other countries. In addition, because of the potential interaction between them, the summation of individual measures for a specific country may be problematic. The allocation of particular measures across fuel types was done by the OECD Secretariat based on the IEA's Energy Balances.

Source: OECD.

Chapter 3

Belgium

This chapter identifies, documents, and provides estimates of the various budgetary transfers and tax expenditures that relate to the production or use of fossil fuels in *Belgium*. An overview of *Belgium's* energy economy is first given to place the measures listed into context. A data-documentation section then describes those measures in a systematic way. Whenever possible, the description details a measure's formal beneficiary, its eligibility criteria and functioning, and the fuels whose production or use stand to benefit from the measure. The chapter ends with a set of charts and tables that provide, subject to availability, quantitative information and estimates for the various measures listed.

3.   BELGIUM

Energy resources and market structure

Belgium has negligible economically recoverable resources of fossil energy and relies heavily on imported energy. Coal was once the main indigenous energy source, but there has been no domestic production of coal since the last mine closed in 1992. Belgium produces very small amounts of oil, but no natural gas. Primary energy supply is relatively diversified, with oil meeting 40% of the country's needs in 2009, natural gas 25% and coal 7%. Nuclear power accounts for over one-fifth of energy supply and well over half of total electricity generation. Renewables account for the remaining 5% of primary energy supply. In aggregate, imports meet almost three-quarters of the country's energy needs (treating nuclear power as indigenous production).

The principal goals of Belgian energy policy are security of supply through the diversification of geographical sources of supply and fuels; energy efficiency; transparent and competitive energy pricing; and environmental protection. The three regions – Wallonia, Brussels-Capital and the Flemish region – have also adopted energy policies covering their areas of competence, prioritising energy efficiency and renewables. Increasingly, policy is driven by EU laws and regulations. At the national level, a key policy objective is the phase-out of nuclear energy. A 2003 law prohibits the construction of new nuclear plants and sets a 40-year limit on the operating lifetime of existing plants. Unless the law is amended, it will require three of the country's seven nuclear power plants to be shut by 2015 at the latest. An agreement was reached in 2009 with the nuclear-power generators to extend the lifetime of these plants to 2025, but this has not yet been made law.

Belgium's energy sector is almost entirely in private hands, though some local distribution of electricity and natural gas is carried out by companies that are wholly or partially owned by municipalities. The gas and electricity markets have been fully opened to competition, as required under EU law, but traditional suppliers, notably GDF Suez in gas and its subsidiary, Electrabel, in electricity, continue to hold dominant positions, especially in the household sector. The national regulator, the Electricity and Gas Regulatory Commission (CREG), is mainly responsible for approving transmission and distribution tariffs and market monitoring. Each of the three regions has its own regulatory body, which are primarily responsible for approving local distribution tariffs.

Prices, taxes and support mechanisms

As required by EU law, there are no price controls on energy as such. However, the central government maintains a system of price ceilings on the main oil products under an agreement with the national oil industry federation. These ceilings are intended to act as a cushion against sudden price spikes; in practice, actual market prices tend to be lower than the agreed price ceilings. The CREG and the regional regulators set network charges for electricity and gas, but do not have the legal means to control electricity or gas prices to most final consumers.

Energy supply attracts VAT at the standard rate of 21%, with the exception of coal for household use, which is taxed at 12%. Excise duties are levied on oil products at different rates. There is also a special levy on household use of gasoline, light heating oil, natural gas, LPG and electricity, which is used to finance various public services, including the CREG. Electricity and gas supplied under social tariffs are exempt from this levy. In 2008, the government introduced a special annual tax on the nuclear power generators in response to concerns that they were making large profits from assets that were depreciated before liberalisation.

There are a small number of tax preferences relating to energy consumption in Belgium. Certain categories of business consumers, notably companies consuming large quantities of energy and those holding an environmental permit, benefit from a reduced rate of excise tax on sales of some petroleum products (diesel fuel, LPG and kerosene). Some off-road vehicles and stationary engines that are operated in the construction and civil-engineering sectors also qualify for tax reductions. There are three measures that directly support household energy use: the Heating Oil Social Fund, which provides low-income and heavily indebted households with grants to help them pay their heating bills; a social tariff for natural gas and electricity for disadvantaged households, set every six months by the CREG on the basis of the lowest commercial tariff in the country, with suppliers receiving the difference between the social tariff and the actual market tariff from a fund managed by the regulator and financed by the federal government; and a special heating grant, in the form of a lump-sum payment, introduced in 2009 to dampen the impact of rising energy prices on the heating bills (electricity, natural gas or heating oil) of households that benefit from either the Heating Oil Social Fund or a social tariff.

Data documentation

General notes

The fiscal year in Belgium coincides with the calendar year. Following OECD convention, amounts prior to 1999 are expressed as 'euro-fixed series', meaning that we applied the fixed EMU conversion rate (1 EUR = 40.339 BEF) to data initially expressed in the Belgian Franc (BEF).

Producer Support Estimate

Belgium supported the production of hard coal until 1992, at which time the last mine still in operation was closed. Since then, it has not supported the production of any fossil fuel.

Consumer Support Estimate

Fuel-Tax Reduction for Certain Professional Uses (data for 1997-)

This provision provides certain professional users with a reduced rate of excise tax on sales of petroleum products. Eligible users include those companies that consume large quantities of such fuels and those that possess a Permis Environnemental or Vergunning Milieudoelstelling (Environmental Permit).

This tax reduction applies mainly to diesel fuel (containing both low and high levels of sulphur) but recent budget documents also provide estimates for LPG and kerosene starting in 2004. Data are not available prior to 1997.

Sources: Chambre des Représentants de Belgique (various years [a]).

Tag: BEL_te_01

Fuel-Tax Exemption for Regional Bus Transport (data for 1997-2008)

This measure exempted providers of regional bus transport services from the excise tax that is normally levied on sales of petroleum products. It was initially capped at BEF 2 000 (EUR 50) per 1 000 litres, but was then phased out in June 2008.

Sources: Chambre des Représentants de Belgique (various years [a]).

Tag: BEL_te_02

Fuel-Tax Reduction for Certain Industrial Uses (data for 1997-)

Certain industrial and commercial activities undertaken in Belgium can benefit from a reduced rate of excise tax applied to petroleum products. Eligible uses include some off-road vehicles and stationary engines that are operated in the construction and civil-engineering sectors.

The provision applies to both diesel fuel and kerosene. Accordingly, we allocate the annual amounts reported in official budget documents to diesel fuel and kerosene on the basis of the IEA's Energy Balances for the construction and commercial and public services sectors.

Sources: Chambre des Représentants de Belgique (various years [a]), IEA.

Tag: BEL_te_03

Fuel-Tax Exemption for Agriculture (data for 1997-2004)

This provision exempts agriculture, horticulture, and forestry from the excise tax that is normally levied on sales of petroleum products. The measure applied only to diesel fuel and kerosene until 2004, at which time coverage was extended to heavy fuel, LPG, natural gas, electricity, hard coal, coke, and lignite.

Data are only available up to 2004 for both diesel fuel and kerosene. Consequently, we allocated the annual amounts reported in official budget documents to diesel fuel and kerosene on the basis of the IEA's Energy Balances for the agriculture and forestry sector.

Sources: Chambre des Représentants de Belgique (various years [a]), IEA.

Tag: BEL_te_04

Fonds Social Mazout (data for 2007-)

The Fonds Social Mazout or Sociaal Verwarmingsfonds (Heating Oil Social Fund) is a programme that provides low-income and heavily indebted households with grants to help them pay their heating bills. The fund operates all year long and is specifically tied to consumption of heating oil.

Funding comes from both the industry and the Belgian government. Thus, we only report here the amounts attributable to government funding.

Sources: Directorate General Statistics and Economic Information, Chambre des Représentants de Belgique (various years [b]).

Tag: BEL_dt_01

Social Tariff for Natural Gas (data for 2004-)

Certain households in Belgium are entitled to a reduced tariff for both natural gas and electricity. This "social tariff" was introduced in 2004. It is set once every six months by the Commission de Régulation de l'Électricité et du Gaz or Commissie voor de Regulering van de Elektriciteit en het Gas (Regulatory Commission for Electricity and Natural Gas) on the basis of the lowest commercial tariff in the country.

Payments are made to suppliers out of the federal budget to compensate them for the difference between the reduced tariff and the market price. This means that the Social Tariff for Natural Gas is not a cross-subsidy *per se*. Eligible households include those that are entitled to welfare programmes, disabled persons, and the elderly.

Only those amounts that pertain to natural gas are here being reported.

Sources: Directorate General Statistics and Economic Information, Chambre des Représentants de Belgique (various years [b]).

Tag: BEL_dt_02

Special Heating Grant (data for 2010-)

This programme was introduced in 2009 to dampen the impact of rising energy prices on poor households. It provides eligible consumers with a lump-sum discount on their heating bills worth EUR 105 a year. The measure applies to heating in general, irrespective of whether it comes from electricity, natural gas or heating oil (so-called mazout). To be eligible, households must not already benefit from either the Fonds Social Mazout or the Social Tariff for Natural Gas (see above).

We use the IEA's Energy Balances for the residential sector to allocate the amounts reported in official budget documents to heating oil, natural gas, and electricity. Only those amounts that pertain to heating oil and natural gas are here being considered. Data are not available prior to 2010.

Sources: Chambre des Représentants de Belgique (various years [b]), IEA.

Tag: BEL_dt_03

References

Policies or transfers

Chambre des Représentants de Belgique (various years [a]) *Annexe – Inventaire des Exonérations, Abattements et Réductions qui Influencent les Recettes de l'État, Budget des Voies et Moyens,* Available at: http://docufin.fgov.be/intersalgfr/thema/stat/Stat_fiscale_uitgaven_fed.htm.

Chambre des Représentants de Belgique (various years [b]) *Projet de Budget Général des Dépenses,* Available at: http://www.lachambre.be/kvvcr/showpage.cfm?section=|pri|budget&language=fr&rightmenu=right_pri&story=2010-2011.xml.

Energy statistics

IEA, *Energy Balances of OECD Countries*, 2010 Edition, International Energy Agency, Paris.

Figure 3.1. **Shares of fossil-fuel support by fuel, average for 2008-10 – Belgium**

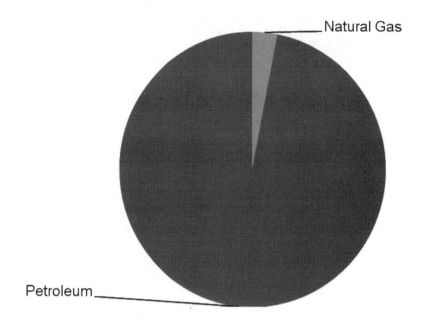

Source: OECD.

Figure 3.2. **Shares of fossil-fuel support by indicator, average for 2008-10 – Belgium**

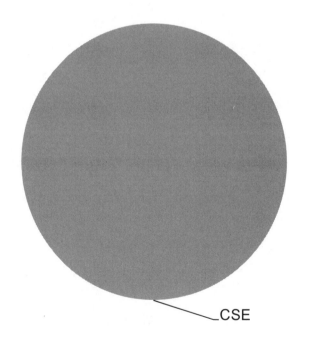

Source: OECD.

Table 3.1.Summary of fossil-fuel support to petroleum – Belgium

(Millions of euros, nominal)

Support element	Jurisdiction	Avg 2000-02	Avg 2008-10	2008	2009	2010p
Producer Support Estimate (n.a.)						
Consumer Support Estimate						
Consumption						
Fonds Social Mazout	Federal	n.a.	13.25	33.33	0.00	6.42
Special Heating Grant	Federal	n.a.	n.a.	n.a.	n.a.	3.90
Fuel Tax Reduction for Certain Professional Uses	Federal	1 592.16	1 563.54	1 652.11	1 519.25	1 519.25
Fuel Tax Exemption for Regional Bus Transport	Federal	5.63	n.a.	4.19	n.a.	n.a.
Fuel Tax Reduction for Certain Industrial Uses	Federal	124.30	110.11	109.33	110.50	110.50
Fuel Tax Exemption for Agriculture	Federal	35.92	n.c.	..	..	..
General Services Support Estimate (n.a.)						

Note: Tax expenditures for any given country are measured with reference to a benchmark tax treatment that is generally specific to that country. Consequently, the estimates contained in the table above are not necessarily comparable with estimates for other countries. In addition, because of the potential interaction between them, the summation of individual measures for a specific country may be problematic. The allocation of particular measures across fuel types was done by the OECD Secretariat based on the IEA's Energy Balances.

Source: OECD.

Table 3.2. Summary of fossil-fuel support to natural gas – Belgium

(Millions of euros, nominal)

Support element	Jurisdiction	Avg 2000-02	Avg 2008-10	2008	2009	2010p
Producer Support Estimate (n.a.)						
Consumer Support Estimate						
Consumption						
Social Tariff for Natural Gas	Federal	n.a.	51.19	52.40	34.13	67.06
Special Heating Grant	Federal	n.a.	n.a.	n.a.	n.a.	4.01
General Services Support Estimate (n.a.)						

Note: Tax expenditures for any given country are measured with reference to a benchmark tax treatment that is generally specific to that country. Consequently, the estimates contained in the table above are not necessarily comparable with estimates for other countries. In addition, because of the potential interaction between them, the summation of individual measures for a specific country may be problematic. The allocation of particular measures across fuel types was done by the OECD Secretariat based on the IEA's Energy Balances.

Source: OECD.

Chapter 4

Canada

This chapter identifies, documents, and provides estimates of the various budgetary transfers and tax expenditures that relate to the production or use of fossil fuels in *Canada*. An overview of *Canada's* energy economy is first given to place the measures listed into context. A data-documentation section then describes those measures in a systematic way. Whenever possible, the description details a measure's formal beneficiary, its eligibility criteria and functioning, and the fuels whose production or use stand to benefit from the measure. The chapter ends with a set of charts and tables that provide, subject to availability, quantitative information and estimates for the various measures listed.

4. CANADA

Energy resources and market structure

Canada has substantial and diversified fossil-energy resources, and the energy sector makes a significant contribution to the economy. It is a net exporter of oil, natural gas and coal, as well as uranium (being the world's largest producer) and electricity (the majority of it hydropower-based). Canada has the second-largest proven oil reserves in the world, most of which are in oil sands. Production from oil sands has grown rapidly in recent years, broadly offsetting a decline in output of conventional oil. Proven natural gas reserves have risen in the last few years, mainly thanks to shale gas and other unconventional types of gas, though overall production and exports (entirely to the United States) have declined. Oil and gas together account for two-thirds of the country's primary energy use, with hydro-based electricity (12%) and nuclear power (9%) accounting for most of the rest. Overall, Canada exports about one-third of its energy production.

Canadian energy policy relies on competitive markets for determining supply, demand, prices and trade. The federal government no longer has any ownership stake in any major energy company, other than Atomic Energy of Canada Limited (AECL) – a Crown corporation responsible for managing Canada's national nuclear energy research and development programme, including the marketing of CANDU reactor technology. The privatisation of Petro-Canada, previously the main state-owned energy company, was completed in 2004. By contrast, all but one of the ten provinces still have Crown corporations in energy, notably in hydropower production.

In general, the provinces have jurisdictional responsibility for the resources that lie within their boundaries and are therefore responsible for oversight of the industry within their boundaries. Four provinces – British Columbia, Alberta, Saskatchewan and Newfoundland and Labrador – account for a large majority of Canada's oil-and-gas production. Production in British Columbia, Alberta and Saskatchewan is regulated by the provinces, but in Newfoundland and Labrador (as in Nova Scotia) the federal government and the province jointly regulate offshore production activities. In addition, federal government jurisdiction applies to Crown and some private lands north of 60 degrees latitude in the territories, reserve lands and offshore frontier areas. However, territorial governments are provided with the authority to exercise most onshore-land and natural-resource responsibilities where devolution or administrative agreements are in place. The upstream oil and gas industry in Canada is highly competitive, with hundreds of exploration and production firms.

The natural gas gathering and transmission pipeline network is owned and operated by several private companies. The main exceptions are TransGas and Swan Valley Gas Corporation, which are provincial Crown corporations, owned by SaskEnergy in Saskatchewan and Manitoba Hydro in Manitoba. Gas distribution assets are typically owned and operated by private companies that have exclusive rights to distribute gas in a given regional or local area. Distribution companies are provincially regulated and most are the only retailer in their concession area with the exception of the provinces of Alberta and Ontario, where some retail competition exists. Regulation of the gas industry is primarily in the hands of the provincial authorities, with the National Energy Board responsible for regulating interprovincial and international gas trade and pipelines.

In most provinces, the electricity industry is highly integrated, and the bulk of generation, transmission and distribution services are provided by a few dominant utilities. Although some of these are privately owned, most are Crown corporations owned by the provincial governments. In some cases, small generators also exist, but rarely compete directly with a Crown corporation. In many cases, the previously integrated utilities are increasingly becoming functionally unbundled to accommodate the introduction of wholesale competition, and in some provinces, generation, transmission and distribution/retail activities are structurally distinct. In several places, notably in Alberta, some municipalities have maintained ownership of their local distribution utility facilities, while also setting up municipally owned generating companies to compete in the open wholesale market. Only two provinces – Ontario and Alberta – have moved to full retail competition. Generation, transmission and distribution services are regulated largely by provincial regulatory agencies.

Prices, taxes and support mechanisms

Most energy commodity prices are unregulated in Canada. Nonetheless, some retail oil price controls remain in place in Québec, New Brunswick, Nova Scotia, Prince Edward Island and Newfoundland and Labrador. These provincial controls set a maximum retail price or a minimum price, or (in the case of Prince Edward Island and Nova Scotia) both. Natural gas and electricity prices are regulated in most provinces by a quasi-judicial board or commission on a cost-of-service basis. In Alberta and Ontario, prices are set by the market, although households and smaller commercial consumers have the option of subscribing to a regulated rate.

Income tax treatment of the oil, gas and mining sectors in Canada has been undergoing fundamental reforms. Royalties are now fully deductible from income for corporate income-tax purposes, and the resource allowance, a special deduction permitted in lieu of royalty deductibility, has been phased out. Also, corporate tax rates for the oil, gas and mining sectors, which had been higher than those for other industries for a number of years, have been brought into line with the general corporate rate. The accelerated capital cost allowance for oil-sands projects (which permitted companies a fast write-off of certain kinds of assets) is being phased out over the period 2011-15. In its 2011 budget, the Canadian government announced that in order to make the system more neutral, deduction rates for oil sands resource rights and certain intangible development costs of oil sands projects would be reduced to the rates applicable in the conventional oil and gas sector. However, several other tax measures that support energy production remain in place. These include: accelerated depreciation for physical assets in mines (including coal mines, but not oil sands mines) and for successful oil, gas and mineral exploration expenses; flow-through shares, which allow a corporation to transfer unused exploration and development expenses to their shareholders; and the ability for small oil and gas companies to reclassify some development expenses as exploration expenses under the flow-through share scheme. In addition, Alberta offers several royalty-reduction programmes that target specific types of oil and gas projects. Federal excise taxes are imposed on leaded and unleaded gasoline, diesel and aviation fuels used on domestic flights. Since April 2008, renewable fuels (ethanol and biodiesel) are subject to the same federal excise taxes as the motive fuels (gasoline and diesel fuel) with which they are blended. Diesel used as heating oil is exempt for excise tax. Diesel used in the generation of electricity is also exempt, except where the electricity so generated is used primarily in the operation of a vehicle. A federal goods and services tax (GST) is levied on all fuels and energy services. In all provinces except Alberta and the territories of Yukon, Northwest Territories, and Nunavut, a provincial sales tax is also generally levied, in several cases combined with the GST into a Harmonized Sales Tax (HST).

The provinces also levy taxes on fuels. Some provinces have programmes or fiscal features that support the consumption of certain types of energy. For example, in Alberta, a farm fuel distribution allowance provides farmers with a direct budgetary transfer to compensate them for the federal component of the excise tax levied on sales of petroleum products; another provision exempts farmers from the province component of the tax. The province of Saskatchewan exempts marked diesel fuel sold to valid Fuel-Tax Exemption Permit holders for use in unlicensed farm, unlicensed primary production (*i.e.* commercial fishing, commercial trapping, commercial logging and commercial peat harvesting) machinery, and licensed farm vehicles. Nova Scotia provides households with a sales-tax rebate on their heating bills.

Canada has traditionally provided support to northern communities to assist with the high cost of living in remote communities, including issues relating to access to energy. Support has been provided to First Nations communities in northern Ontario, for example, to upgrade infrastructure for power generation and alleviate the impact of high diesel fuel costs on generating and distributing electricity.

Data documentation

General notes

The fiscal year in Canada runs from 1 April to 31 March. Following OECD convention, data are allocated to the starting calendar year so that data covering the period April 2005 to March 2006 are allocated to 2005.

Since Canada is a federal country, the data collection exercise was also conducted for a sample of three provinces. Those three provinces are: Alberta (AB), Saskatchewan (SK), and Nova Scotia (NS). For this reason, coverage of reported Canadian measures cannot be considered complete.

The inventory includes a number of provincial tax expenditures within resource royalty systems. These are included because they are explicitly defined as quantified departures from the general royalty rules. As noted in the opening section of the document (see sections in Chapter 1 on "*Tax expenditures relating to fossil fuels as inputs to production*" and "*Defining a benchmark*"), however, it is important that such measures, including their objectives and impacts, be considered (in a parallel way with income tax and consumption tax measures) within the context of the broader royalty system of which they form a part.

Producer Support Estimate

Several features of Canada's tax system that indirectly support production of fossil fuels – including coal and oil sands – apply to the mining sector as a whole. While our definition of support stresses specificity as a requisite, we consider those measures that apply to mining in general as being specific enough to warrant their inclusion in the database. In the absence of data on the actual sector distribution of the usage of these measures, as in other countries, the OECD has presumed based on relative output levels that the majority of the usage relates to fossil-fuel extraction. This should not be interpreted, however, as reflecting the views of the responsible governments. [15]

A counter-example of a measure that we have not considered specific enough would be the Atlantic Investment Tax Credit, which provides a 10% income tax credit for tangible capital investments in a particular region of Canada by corporations in certain sectors. Because this tax provision applies to a range of goods-producing sectors including mining (including oil and gas extraction), logging, farming, fishing and manufacturing, we have not included it in the database.

Earned Depletion Allowance (data for 1991-)

This tax provision allowed oil and gas and mining corporations to claim additional deductions against their income tax base. Those additional deductions could generally equal up to 25% of the company's resource profits and were specifically meant to encourage further exploration and development. In practice, oil and gas and mining companies investing in the exploration and development of mineral resources in Canada were able to claim depletion allowances in addition to other available deductions such as those for Canadian Exploration Expense and Canadian Development Expense (see below), thereby obtaining overall deductions in excess of the total amounts actually spent on exploration and development (*e.g.* for as much as 133% of these amounts). Unclaimed depletion allowances could be accumulated in a pool to be carried forward indefinitely. Although the measure was phased out on 1 January 1990, unclaimed allowances from the pool were still giving rise to limited annual tax expenditures on a cash-flow basis as of 2010.

Because the measure applies to the mining sector as a whole (*cf.* introductory remark), for this and similar measures, we deduct from the annual amounts reported in official tax expenditure documents the estimated share associated with mining output that is not concerned with fossil fuels. This is done using gross output data from the OECD's STAN database on the assumption that the tax expenditure is evenly distributed across sub-sectors according to output. The remaining amounts are then allocated to the various types of fossil fuels (*i.e.* crude oil, natural gas, and coal) using production data from the IEA.

Sources: Department of Finance Canada (various years), Natural Resources Canada (2010[a]), IEA, OECD.

Tag: CAN_te_01

---

[15] An estimated allocation based on gross-output shares is used here to provide readers with a sense of the magnitudes involved. Since these allocations are not from government sources and are based on general volume and value ratios, they might not always correlate well with actual distributions, if such information were available. These assumptions have been made by the OECD and should not be interpreted as reflecting the views of the responsible government.

Excess of Resource Allowance over Non-Deductibility of Royalties (data for 1993-2006)

Starting in 1976, oil and gas and mining companies operating in Canada were able to deduct a fixed percentage (25%) of their annual resource profits from their taxable income. This provision was meant to compensate companies for the non-deductibility of government royalties (which in Canada are primarily levied at the province level) that had been in place since 1974. In practice, the resource allowance sometimes exceeded the amount of royalties paid to the provinces. It was decided to phase out this provision over a five-year period starting in 2003. Government royalties, therefore, are now once again deductible from the income tax base.

Because royalties are often treated as operating expenses and in order to ensure a consistent reporting across countries, we consider here the net fiscal cost of the resource allowance. This is consistent with the Canadian tax expenditure accounts, which subtract from the total revenue foregone the revenues that arise due to the non-deductibility of provincial royalties. This yields positive tax expenditures for most of the period under consideration.

Since the measure applies to the mining sector as a whole (*cf.* introductory remark), we deduct from the annual amounts reported in official tax expenditure documents the estimated share associated with mining output that is not concerned with fossil fuels. This is done using gross output data from the OECD's STAN database. The remaining amounts are then allocated to the various types of fossil fuels (*i.e.* crude oil, natural gas, and coal) using production data from the IEA.

Sources: Department of Finance Canada (various years), Natural Resources Canada (2010[a]), IEA, OECD.

Tag: CAN_te_02

Canadian Exploration Expense (no data available)

The Canadian Exploration Expense (CEE) provision allows oil and gas and mining companies to deduct exploration expenses in full in the year in which they are incurred. Exploration expenses include the costs of geological surveys and exploratory drilling, whether successful or unsuccessful. For the mining sector (including oil sands mines and coal mines, but not including conventional oil and gas), CEE also includes intangible costs incurred for the purpose of bringing a mine into production, such as clearing land or removing overburden, described as "pre-production development costs". Unclaimed deductions can be carried forward indefinitely.

The notes to Canada's tax expenditure accounts remark that the costs of development, of successful exploration and, potentially, of some unsuccessful exploration would not be immediately deductible in the benchmark tax system. Canada does not, however, produce annual estimates of the revenue foregone due to the CEE.

In its 2011 budget, the Canadian government announced that development expenses incurred for the purpose of bringing a new oil-sands mine into production, currently immediately deductible as CEE, will in future be treated as Canadian development expenses (CDE), deductible at a rate of 30% per year. This will align the deduction rates for pre-production development costs in oil-sands mines with the rates applicable to *in situ* oil-sands projects and the conventional oil and gas sector. The change will be phased in over the 2013-16 period.

Sources: Department of Finance Canada (various years), Government of Canada (2011), Natural Resources Canada (2010[a]).

Canadian Development Expense – Oil Sands Property (no data available)

In the conventional oil and gas sector, the cost of acquiring rights to explore for, drill or extract oil or natural gas, or to acquire an oil or natural-gas well or other resource property, is treated for tax purposes as Canadian oil and gas property expense (COGPE). COGPE is deductible at the rate of 10% per year on a declining balance basis. By contrast, the cost of acquiring oil sands leases and other oil sands resource property generally could be treated as Canadian development expense (CDE), which is deductible at the rate of 30 per cent per year on a declining balance basis.

In its 2011 budget, the government of Canada announced a reduction in the deduction rate for resource rights in the oil sands sector to the 10% rate that applies to resource rights in the conventional oil and gas sector(COGPE). This change was cited as one that would "improve fairness and neutrality of the taxation of oil sands relative to other sectors". The government estimates that this change, together with the change described above in respect of development costs for oil-sands mines, will save an amount of revenues rising to CAD 75 million per year in 2015-16, and generate total savings of CAD 220 million over the next five years.

Sources: Department of Finance Canada (various years), Government of Canada (2011), Natural Resources Canada (2010[a]).

Flow-Through Share Deductions (data for 1996-)

Flow-through shares were introduced in some form as early as the 1950s to help finance the production of oil, gas, and other minerals. Under current rules, companies that have incurred exploration and development expenses (see "Canadian Exploration Expense" and "Canadian Development Expense" above) can issue flow-through shares to transfer to investors deductions in respect of those expenses up to the value of the share. Investors thus acquire both an equity interest in the issuing company and a tax deduction. This makes it easier for resource companies to attract capital, and thus favours investment in exploration and development of resources. A tax expenditure arises to the extent that the deduction is taken earlier than it otherwise would have been taken, or is claimed at a higher rate (*e.g.* because the investor is subject to a tax rate higher than the issuing company).

The amount of benefit provided to producers by this measure is indirect and depends on the degree to which it attracts incremental capital investment to the sector. The tax-expenditure estimates for this measure are the cost to the government of allowing investors (individuals and corporations, not necessarily engaged in the fossil-fuel sector) to deduct, in calculating their taxable income, expenses renounced by corporations. They represent the cost to the government of providing the support, rather than the value of the benefit received by corporations in the sector.

Canada's Department of Finance changed the way it estimates and reports the annual revenue foregone due to this tax provision in the 2008 and 2010 editions of its tax expenditure report. This results in a break in the time series in terms of how the information is reported in 2003 and again in 2005. The reports caution that the figures for years before 2003 over-state the tax expenditure in that they include resource deductions claimed by individuals other than via flow-through shares, while the figures for years before 2005 do not take into account the special rules that apply to the taxation of gains on the disposition of flow-through shares.

Because the measure applies to the mining sector as a whole (*cf.* introductory remark), we deduct from the annual amounts reported in official tax expenditure documents the estimated share associated with mining output that is not concerned with fossil fuels. This is done using gross output data from the OECD's STAN database. The remaining amounts are then allocated to the various types of fossil fuels (*i.e.* crude oil, natural gas, and coal) using production data from the IEA.

Sources: Department of Finance Canada (various years), Government of Canada (2011), Natural Resources Canada (2010[a]), IEA, OECD.

Tag: CAN_te_03

Reclassification of Expenses Under Flow-Through Shares (data for 1996-)

Starting in 1992, junior oil and gas companies (having less than CAD 15 million worth of taxable capital employed in Canada) have been able to reclassify a limited amount each year of development expenses as exploration expenses when they are transferred to investors under flow-through shares (see "Flow-Through Share Deductions" above). Exploration expenses can be deducted in full in the year in which they are incurred while development expenses can be deducted at 30% per year. This has the effect of accelerating the tax deductions obtained by investors who acquire flow-through shares, thereby making it easier for oil and gas companies to raise capital. The amount of development expenses that can be reclassified as exploration expenses is currently capped at CAD 1 million per company.

The benefit provided to producers by this measure is indirect and depends on the degree to which it attracts incremental capital investment to the sector. The tax-expenditure estimates for this measure are the cost to the government of allowing investors (individuals and corporations, not necessarily engaged in the fossil-fuel sector) to deduct, in calculating their taxable income, Canadian exploration expenses instead of Canadian development expenses. They represent the cost to the government of providing the support, rather than the value of the benefit received by corporations in the sector.

Canada's Department of Finance changed the way it estimates and reports the annual revenue foregone due to this tax provision in the 2008 edition of its tax expenditure report. This results in a break in the time series in terms of how the information is reported around 2003, at which time the new data become available.

We use production data from the IEA to allocate the annual amounts reported in tax expenditure reports to oil and natural gas extraction.

Sources: Department of Finance Canada (various years), Natural Resources Canada (2010[a]), IEA, OECD.

Tag: CAN_te_04

Accelerated Capital Cost Allowance (limited data for 2007-)

Most machinery, equipment and structures used to produce income from a mine or an oil-sands project, are eligible to be deducted at a capital cost allowance (CCA) rate of 25% per year under CCA Class 41. This rate also applies to assets owned by a mineral-resource owner that are used in the initial processing of ore from the mineral resource or in the upgrading of bitumen (the oil-sands product) from the mineral resource into synthetic crude oil. In addition to the regular CCA deduction, an accelerated CCA has been provided since 1972 for assets acquired for use in new mines, including oil-sands mines, and major mine expansions (*i.e.* those that increase the capacity of a mine by at least 25%). This provision allows a company to deduct as early as the year the asset is available for use up to the full amount of the remaining capital cost, not exceeding the taxpayer's income for the year from the project (calculated after deducting the regular CCA deductions). In 1996, this accelerated CCA was extended to in-situ oil sands projects (which use oil wells rather than mining techniques to extract bitumen). The 1996 changes also extended the accelerated CCA to expenditures on eligible assets acquired in a taxation year for use in a mine or oil-sands project, to the extent that the cost of those assets exceeds 5% of the gross revenue for the year from the mine or project.

The Canadian 2007 budget announced the phase-out of the accelerated CCA for oil-sands projects – leaving in place the regular 25% CCA rate for these assets. To ensure a stable investment climate, the existing accelerated CCA was grandfathered for oil sands assets acquired before 2012 in project phases that commenced major construction prior to the Budget announcement. For other assets, companies maintained the ability to claim accelerated CCA until 2010, with the rate being gradually reduced between 2011 and 2015. The accelerated CCA for mines other than oil sands mines is not affected by this phase-out.

The government of Canada does not produce annual estimates of the revenue foregone due to the accelerated capital cost allowance for mines and oil sands projects. It has stated, however, that the estimated cost of the provision in the oil sands sector (which is being phased out), was forecast at the time of the announcement to be on the order of CAD 300 million per year over the period 2007 to 2011, before the beginning of the phase-out. The government noted, however, that the value can vary considerably from one year to another based on project and industry factors.

Sources: Department of Finance Canada (various years), Department of Finance Canada (2007), Department of Finance Canada (2008), Natural Resources Canada (2010[a]).

Tag: CAN_te_06

Syncrude Remission Order (data for 1991-2005)

The Syncrude project is a joint venture set up in the 1970s to exploit some of the oil sands that are located in the province of Alberta. The Syncrude Remission Order was enacted in 1976 to allow investors participating in the Syncrude project to deduct both royalties and the resource allowance from their income-tax base (see also "Excess of Resource Allowance over Non-Deductibility of Royalties" above). This initial agreement had a built-in phase-out mechanism through which deductions would cease when cumulative production reaches 2.1 billion barrels or on 31 December 2003 at the latest.

We allocate the measure entirely to oil sands. Data come from Canada's Department of Finance up to 1995 and from the Public Accounts of Canada thereafter. Because the Syncrude Remission Order expired in 2003, positive cash transfers in following years could be related to delays in filing, assessing and processing remissions to the venture participants.

Sources: Department of Finance Canada (various years), Natural Resources Canada (2010[a]), Public Accounts of Canada (various years).

Tag: CAN_te_05

Energy Industry Drilling Stimulus (data for 2009-)

The province of Alberta introduced this initiative in 2009 on a temporary basis to support the production of oil and natural gas. It comprises two different programmes, both of which reduce the amounts of provincial royalties that are to be paid by producers. The Drilling Royalty Credit for new oil and gas wells provides them with a CAD 200 royalty credit per metre drilled. A cap is, however, set on the amount of credit a company can receive, with the limit being contingent on the production levels from the preceding year. In addition, the New Well Incentive Program sets a maximum royalty rate of 5% for the first 50 000 barrels of oil produced (500 000 thousand cubic feet for natural gas). While the Energy Industry Drilling Stimulus was initially designed to last one year only, the government of Alberta announced in 2009 that the initiative would be further extended.

Some fiscal measures related to oil and gas production may not constitute tax expenditures under an alternative baseline where royalties (or severance taxes) vary with market conditions and production costs. We include here the annual amounts of negative revenues as reported by Alberta Energy (various years).

We use production data from the IEA to allocate the annual amounts reported in budget documents to oil and natural gas extraction.

Sources: Alberta Energy (various years), IEA.

Tag: CAN_te_07

Alberta Royalty Tax Credit (data for 1997-2007)

The Alberta Royalty Tax Credit (ARTC) was introduced in 1974 at the time when provincial royalties were made non-deductible for income-tax purposes (see also "Excess of Resource Allowance over Deductibility" above). It provided all Alberta Crown royalty payers with a royalty credit, calculated at a specified percentage of the lesser of Crown royalties paid to the province of Alberta in the year or a specified annual maximum amount of qualifying royalties. The ARTC was eliminated in 2007 when Crown royalties again became fully deductible for federal and provincial income-tax purposes.

Some fiscal measures related to oil and gas production may not constitute tax expenditures under an alternative baseline where royalties (or severance taxes) vary with market conditions and production costs. We include here the annual amounts of negative revenues as reported by Alberta Energy (various years).

We use production data from the IEA to allocate the annual amounts reported in budget documents to oil and natural gas extraction.

Sources: Alberta Energy (various years), IEA.

Tag: CAN_te_08

Alberta Crown Royalty Reductions (data for 2001-)

The province of Alberta offers several royalty-reduction programmes that target specific types of oil and gas projects. Although a detailed breakdown by programme is not available, this item includes measures for enhanced oil recovery projects and low-productivity and reactivated wells. The Ministry of Energy's Annual Report for FY2009/10 mentions that the province of Alberta features seven such programmes (excluding the Energy Industry Drilling Stimulus described above).

Some fiscal measures related to oil and gas production may not constitute tax expenditures under an alternative baseline where royalties (or severance taxes) vary with market conditions and production costs. We include here the annual amounts of negative revenues as reported by Alberta Energy (various years).

We use production data from the IEA to allocate the annual amounts reported in budget documents to oil and natural gas extraction.

Sources: Alberta Energy (various years), IEA.

Tag: CAN_te_09

Saskatchewan Petroleum Research Incentive (data for 2004 and 2006)

This programme was introduced in FY1998/99 and has been periodically renewed since then. Its latest renewal was decided in FY2010/11 for a period of five years, with automatic expiry on 31 March 2015. The Saskatchewan Petroleum Research Incentive (SPRI) provides a credit against royalties and production taxes that would otherwise be payable in order to cover a portion of the eligible costs of enhanced oil recovery projects and projects involving new technology in the oil and natural-gas industries. Over the five-year renewal period, a total of CAD 30 million is made available (*i.e.* the tax expenditure is estimated at an average of CAD 6 million per year). Maximum credits per project are: 50% of eligible research costs incurred with the Petroleum Technology Research Centre, up to a maximum credit of CAD 1 million; and 30% of eligible field pilot research costs, up to a maximum credit of CAD 3 million. The programme is designed to encourage companies to field-test recovery technologies on a pilot scale, and does not apply to full-scale commercial projects.

Readers are advised that some fiscal measures related to oil and gas production may not constitute tax expenditures under an alternative baseline where royalties (or severance taxes) vary with market conditions and production costs.

The government of Saskatchewan does not produce annual estimates on a regular basis of the royalties foregone due to this programme. For that reason, the database only contains data for two years.

Sources: Saskatchewan Energy and Resources (various years).

Tag: CAN_te_15

Support to SaskEnergy for the La Ronge Project (data for 2006)

The government of Saskatchewan provided SaskEnergy with a one-time grant for FY2006/07 to help finance the completion of a natural-gas distribution project in the area of La Ronge. SaskEnergy is the sole distributor of natural gas in the province of Saskatchewan.

Sources: Saskatchewan Finance (various years).

Tag: CAN_dt_04

Consumer Support Estimate

Alberta Farm Fuel Distribution Allowance (data for 1999-)

This programme provides farmers in the province of Alberta with a 6 Canadian-cent-per-litre grant on their purchases of marked (*i.e.* dyed) diesel and heating fuel. It is generally provided upfront at time of sale.

Sources: Government of Alberta (various years), Alberta Agriculture and Rural Development (various years).

Tag: CAN_dt_02

Alberta Tax Exempt Fuel Use Program (data for 2009-)

Sales of marked fuel to be used in eligible, unlicensed off-road vehicles in the province of Alberta are exempted from the provincial fuel tax usually levied on sales of petroleum products (9 Canadian cents per litre in Alberta). This tax exemption is generally provided upfront at time of sale. In 2011, the government of Alberta narrowed the range of exempted uses to unlicensed vehicles.

Annual estimates are not reported but the government of Alberta mentioned in its 2011 Budget that the programme would cost CAD 160 million for FY2009/10.

Sources: Government of Alberta (various years).

Tag: CAN_te_10

Alberta Farm Fuel Benefit (no data available)

The Alberta Farm Fuel Benefit exempts fuel purchased by farmers in the province of Alberta from the provincial fuel tax. As set out by the Fuel Tax Act and the Fuel Tax Regulations, marked tax-exempt fuel can be used by farmers for farming operations in Alberta if all the specified criteria are met. Fuel may be used in licensed (*e.g.* farm trucks) and unlicensed vehicles.

Annual estimates are not reported for this programme.

Sources: Government of Alberta (various years).

Fuel-Tax Exemption for Farm Activity, Heating and Mining (data for 1999-)

Marked diesel fuel may be sold exempt of tax (normally 15 Canadian cents per litre) to valid Fuel-Tax Exemption Permit holders for use in unlicensed farming, unlicensed primary production (*i.e.* commercial fishing, commercial trapping, commercial logging and commercial peat harvesting) machinery, and licensed farm vehicles. Unmarked gasoline may be sold by bulk fuel dealers at an 80% reduced tax rate to farmers for use in eligible farming activities. Prior to 2000, the Fuel-Tax Rebate for farm-use gasoline was capped at a maximum of CAD 900 per year.

Marked diesel fuel sold for eligible heating uses in the province of Saskatchewan may be sold exempt of tax if identified as heating fuel or fuel oil at the time of sale.

Fuel used in unlicensed machinery and equipment used in mineral exploration in the province of Saskatchewan may be eligible for a full rebate of fuel-tax. Fuel consumed in licensed vehicles or equipment is not eligible for a rebate, regardless of its use. Mineral exploration does not include processing, developing or producing minerals from the site beyond those activities which are by necessity part of exploring or prospecting for minerals.

For farming activity, we use data from Natural Resources Canada on energy use in Saskatchewan's farming sector to allocate the annual amounts reported in budget documents to diesel fuel and gasoline. The amounts reported for heating and mining are entirely allocated to diesel fuel.

Sources: Saskatchewan Finance (various years), Natural Resources Canada (2010[b]).

Tag: CAN_te_11

Sales-Tax Exemption for Natural Gas (limited data for 1999-)

Saskatchewan's Provincial Sales Tax (PST) exempts the retail sale of motive fuels, all natural-gas consumption, and the residential consumption of electricity.

Electricity, natural gas, and propane used in the processing of minerals are not subject to PST either. The power exemption typically begins when the raw materials enter the mill and ends when the final product is moved to storage. Electricity consumed for any other purpose, including lighting of premises, underground extraction of minerals, shaft hoist and elevators, movement of raw materials prior to processing, water pumping, ventilation, and movement of finished product to storage, is subject to tax. Natural gas and propane used to produce steam that is used in the milling process is not subject to tax. Natural gas and propane used for other heating purposes is also exempt.

Electricity, diesel fuel, domestic fuel oil, coke and gas used in a direct manufacturing process are not subject to PST. The exemption for manufacturing electricity applies only to the electricity which is consumed by equipment and machinery used in a direct manufacturing process. Electricity consumed for any other purpose, including lighting of premises, ventilation, refrigeration and elevators, is subject to tax.

Due to data constraints, we only report here the portion of the exemption that is concerned with the consumption of natural gas.

Sources: Saskatchewan Finance (various years).

Tag: CAN_te_14

Home Heating Assistance for Alternative Fuels (data for 2005)

This initiative is a one-time appropriation for FY2005/06 which was meant to provide eligible households and businesses in Saskatchewan with a CAD 200 grant for heating purposes. Eligibility required that heating be provided using either fuel oil or propane.

We allocate this item entirely to heating oil given the lack of data and the very low share of propane in overall residential heating.

Sources: Saskatchewan Finance (various years).

Tag: CAN_dt_05

Your Energy Rebate (data for 2006-)

> This programme was introduced in 2006 by the government of Nova Scotia to provide households with a sales-tax rebate on their heating bills (8%). The measure applies irrespective of whether heating comes from electricity, heating oil, propane, firewood, or coal. It is also not tied to income.

> We use data from Natural Resources Canada on energy use in Nova Scotia's residential sector to allocate the annual amounts reported in budget documents to electricity, heating oil, coal, propane, and wood. We only report, however, the amounts attributable to heating oil, propane, and coal.

> Sources: Nova Scotia Finance (various years), Natural Resources Canada (2010[b]).

> Tag: CAN_te_16

General Services Support Estimate

Orphan Well Fund (data for 2009-2010)

> This one-off Alberta programme was introduced in 2009 along with the Energy Industry Drilling Stimulus (see above). It provided funding for the cleaning up of old, "legacy" oil and gas wells on the grounds that this would free up industry resources. The measure applied primarily to those sites where no distinct party can be held liable, *i.e.* orphan wells. Funds were administered by the Orphan Well Association which normally levies a fee on the upstream oil and gas industry to pay for the cleaning up and reclamation of sites. The present item only covers additional funding from the government of Alberta.

> Estimates are based on a single CAD 30 million appropriation that we split evenly between 2009 and 2010. This comes from the fact that the appropriated sum had to be spent no later than 31 March 2011. We use production data from the IEA to allocate the annual amounts reported in budget documents to oil and natural gas extraction. The measure is attributed to the GSSE as it does not increase current production or consumption of oil and natural gas.

> Sources: Alberta Energy (various years), Orphan Well Association (2010), IEA.

> Tag: CAN_dt_01

Petroleum Technology Research Centre (data for 1999-)

> The Petroleum Technology Research Centre (PTRC) was set up in 1998 to conduct research connected to enhanced oil recovery techniques and carbon capture and storage. The Centre is primarily funded on a project basis by the government of Saskatchewan, Natural Resources Canada (a federal department), the U.S. Department of Energy, and the industry.

> We report here public funding coming from all levels of government. We use production data from the IEA to allocate the annual amounts reported in budget documents to oil and natural gas extraction. The measure is attributed to the GSSE as it does not increase current production or consumption of oil and natural gas. It also benefits the oil and gas industry as a whole. Data for the year 2006 are not available.

> Sources: Petroleum Technology Research Centre (various years), IEA.

> Tag: CAN_dt_03

References

Policies or transfers

Alberta Agriculture and Rural Development (various years) *Ministry of Agriculture and Rural Development Annual Reports*, Government of Alberta, Available at: http://www.agric.gov.ab.ca/app21/ministrypage?cat1=Ministry&cat2=Reports.

Alberta Energy (various years) *Ministry of Energy Annual Reports*, Government of Alberta, Available at: http://www.energy.alberta.ca/About_Us/1001.asp.

Department of Finance Canada (2007) *The Budget Plan 2007*, Available at: http://www.budget.gc.ca/2007/pdf/bp2007e.pdf.

Department of Finance Canada (2008) *Letter from the Minister of Finance dated 28 March 2008*, Available at:
http://www.oag-bvg.gc.ca/internet/English/pet_222_e_30317.html.

Department of Finance Canada (various years) *Tax Expenditures and Evaluations*, Government of Canada, Available at: http://www.fin.gc.ca/purl/taxexp-eng.asp.

Government of Alberta (various years) *Budget Documents & Quarterlies*, Available at: http://www.finance.alberta.ca/publications/budget/index.html#01_02.

Government of Canada (2011) *A Low-Tax Plan for Jobs and Growth*, Available at: http://www.budget.gc.ca/2011/plan/Budget2011-eng.pdf.

Natural Resources Canada (2010[a]) *Mining-Specific Tax Provisions*, Available at: http://www.nrcan.gc.ca/mms-smm/busi-indu/mtr-rdm/mst-rps-eng.htm.

Natural Resources Canada (2010[b]) *National Energy Use Database*, Office of Energy Efficiency, Available at:
http://www.oee.nrcan.gc.ca/corporate/statistics/neud/dpa/data_e/databases.cfm.

Nova Scotia Finance (various years) *Budget Documents*, Government of Nova Scotia, Available at:
http://www.gov.ns.ca/finance/en/home/budget/budgetdocuments/default.aspx.

Orphan Well Association (2010) *Orphan Well Association 2009/10 Annual Report*, Alberta Oil and Gas Orphan Abandonment and Reclamation Association, Available at: http://www.orphanwell.ca/pg_reports.html.

Petroleum Technology Research Centre (various years) *Annual Report*, Available at: http://www.ptrc.ca/news.php.

Public Accounts of Canada (various years) *Additional Information and Analyses*, Prepared by the Receiver General for Canada, Government of Canada, Available at: http://epe.lac-bac.gc.ca/100/201/301/public_accounts_can/index.html.

Saskatchewan Energy and Resources (various years) *Annual Report*, Government of Saskatchewan, Available at:
http://www.publications.gov.sk.ca/deplist.cfm?d=22&c=870.

Saskatchewan Finance (various years) *Provincial Budget*, Government of Saskatchewan, Available at: http://www.finance.gov.sk.ca/budget/.

Energy statistics

IEA, *Energy Balances of OECD Countries*, 2010 Edition, International Energy Agency, Paris.

OECD, *STAN STructural ANalysis Database*, Available at:
http://www.oecd.org/document/62/0,3746,en_2649_34445_40696318_1_1_1_1,00.html.

Figure 4.1.   Shares of fossil-fuel support by fuel, average for 2008-10 – Canada

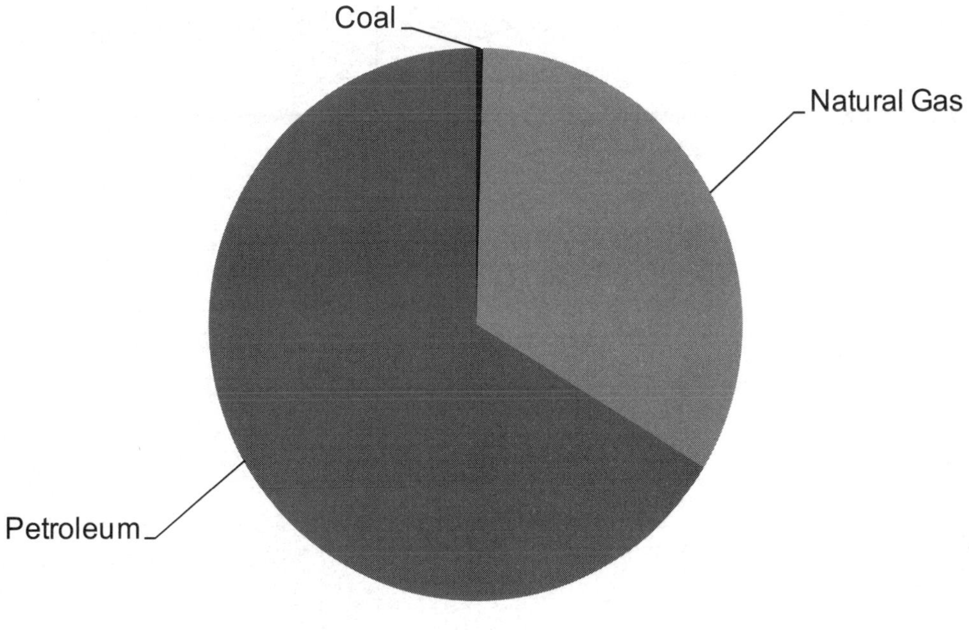

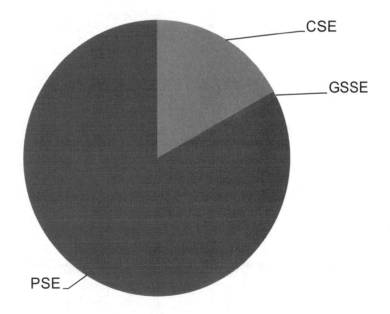

Source: OECD.

Figure 4.2.   Shares of fossil-fuel support by indicator, average for 2008-10 – Canada

Source: OECD.

Table 4.1.Summary of fossil-fuel support to coal – Canada

(Millions of Canadian dollars, nominal)

Support element	Jurisdiction	Avg 2000-02	Avg 2008-10	2008	2009	2010p
Producer Support Estimate						
Support for land (e.g. royalty concessions)						
Excess of Resource Allowance over Non Deductibility of Royalties	Federal	6.53	n.a.	n.a.	n.a.	n.a.
Support for capital formation						
Earned Depletion Allowance	Federal	0.66	0.11	0.10	0.11	0.11
Flow Through Share Deductions	Federal	2.31	4.93	5.25	4.20	5.34
Consumer Support Estimate						
Consumption						
Your Energy Rebate	NS	n.a.	3.24	2.42	3.03	4.27
General Services Support Estimate (n.a.)						

Note: Tax expenditures for any given country are measured with reference to a benchmark tax treatment that is generally specific to that country. Consequently, the estimates contained in the table above are not necessarily comparable with estimates for other countries. In addition, because of the potential interaction between them, the summation of individual measures for a specific country may be problematic. The allocation of particular measures across fuel types was done by the OECD Secretariat based on the IEA's Energy Balances.

Source: OECD.

Table 4.2. Summary of fossil-fuel support to petroleum – Canada

(Millions of Canadian dollars, nominal)

Support element	Jurisdiction	Avg 2000-02	Avg 2008-10	2008	2009	2010p
Producer Support Estimate						
Support for land (e.g. royalty concessions)						
Excess of Resource Allowance over Non Deductibility of Royalties	Federal	135.16	n.a.	n.a.	n.a.	n.a.
Syncrude Remission Order	Federal	130.85	n.a.	n.a.	n.a.	n.a.
Energy Industry Drilling Stimulus	AB	n.a.	n.a.	n.a.	590.17	386.04
Alberta Royalty Tax Credit	AB	51.99	n.a.	n.a.	n.a.	n.a.
Alberta Crown Royalty Reductions	AB	n.c.	239.65	353.91	182.52	182.52
Saskatchewan Petroleum Research Incentive	SK	n.c.	n.c.	::	::	::
Support for capital formation						
Earned Depletion Allowance	Federal	13.76	2.52	2.23	2.67	2.67
Flow Through Share Deductions	Federal	46.81	114.99	122.41	97.93	124.64
Reclassification of Expenses Under FTS	Federal	13.65	-6.86	-7.38	-7.91	-5.27
Accelerated Capital Cost Allowance[1]	Federal	n.c.	300.00	300.00	300.00	300.00
Consumer Support Estimate						
Consumption						
Alberta Farm Fuel Distribution Allowance	AB	31.14	31.69	29.39	33.17	32.50
Home Heating Assistance for Alternative Fuels	SK	n.a.	n.a.	n.a.	n.a.	n.a.
Alberta Tax Exempt Fuel Use Program[2]	AB	n.c.	n.c.	::	160.00	160.00
Fuel Tax Exemption for Farm Activity Heating and Mining	SK	143.57	129.10	130.00	132.10	125.20
Your Energy Rebate	NS	n.a.	27.77	20.78	25.95	36.59
General Services Support Estimate						
Orphan Well Fund	AB	n.a.	n.a.	n.a.	7.91	7.91
Petroleum Technology Research Centre	SK	0.75	3.02	2.65	3.20	3.20

Note: Tax expenditures for any given country are measured with reference to a benchmark tax treatment that is generally specific to that country. Consequently, the estimates contained in the table above are not necessarily comparable with estimates for other countries. In addition, because of the potential interaction between them, the summation of individual measures for a specific country may be problematic. The allocation of particular measures across fuel types was done by the OECD Secretariat based on the IEA's Energy Balances. ([1]) The government of Canada does not produce annual estimates of the revenue foregone due to the accelerated capital cost allowance for mines and oil sands projects. It has stated, however, that the estimated cost of the provision in the oil sands sector (which is being phased out), was forecast at the time of the announcement to be on the order of CAD 300 million per year over the period 2007 to 2011, before the beginning of the phase-out. The government noted, however, that the value can vary considerably from one year to another based on project and industry factors. ([2]) The government of Alberta estimated the cost of the Tax Exempt Fuel Use Program at CAD 160 million for FY2009/10. Estimates are not available on a calendar-year basis. The provisional CAD 160 million value for 2010 is reported by the OECD and may not reflect the views of the government of Alberta (see also "General notes").

Source: OECD.

INVENTORY OF ESTIMATED BUDGETARY SUPPORT AND TAX EXPENDITURES FOR FOSSIL FUELS © OECD 2011

Table 4.3. Summary of fossil-fuel support to natural gas – Canada

(Millions of Canadian dollars, nominal)

Support element	Jurisdiction	Avg 2000-02	Avg 2008-10	2008	2009	2010p
Producer Support Estimate						
Support for land (e.g. royalty concessions)						
Excess of Resource Allowance over Non Deductibility of Royalties	Federal	155.16	n.a.	n.a.	n.a.	n.a.
Energy Industry Drilling Stimulus	AB	n.a.	n.a.	n.a.	528.89	345.96
Alberta Royalty Tax Credit	AB	59.87	n.a.	n.a.	n.a.	n.a.
Alberta Crown Royalty Reductions	AB	n.c.	214.77	317.16	163.57	163.57
Saskatchewan Petroleum Research Incentive	SK	n.c.	n.c.	:	:	:
Support for capital formation						
Support to SaskEnergy for the La Ronge Project	SK	n.a.	n.a.	n.a.	n.a.	n.a.
Earned Depletion Allowance	Federal	15.88	2.26	1.99	2.39	2.39
Flow Through Share Deductions	Federal	53.70	103.05	109.70	87.76	111.69
Reclassification of Expenses Under FTS	Federal	15.68	-6.14	-6.62	-7.09	-4.73
Consumer Support Estimate						
Consumption						
Sales Tax Exemption for Natural Gas	SK	31.90	29.50	28.20	35.10	25.20
General Services Support Estimate						
Orphan Well Fund	AB	n.a.	n.a.	n.a.	7.09	7.09
Petroleum Technology Research Centre	SK	0.86	2.71	2.38	2.87	2.87

Note: Tax expenditures for any given country are measured with reference to a benchmark tax treatment that is generally specific to that country. Consequently, the estimates contained in the table above are not necessarily comparable with estimates for other countries. In addition, because of the potential interaction between them, the summation of individual measures for a specific country may be problematic. The allocation of particular measures across fuel types was done by the OECD Secretariat based on the IEA's Energy Balances.

Source: OECD.

Chapter 5

Chile

This chapter identifies, documents, and provides estimates of the various budgetary transfers and tax expenditures that relate to the production or use of fossil fuels in *Chile*. An overview of *Chile's* energy economy is first given to place the measures listed into context. A data-documentation section then describes those measures in a systematic way. Whenever possible, the description details a measure's formal beneficiary, its eligibility criteria and functioning, and the fuels whose production or use stand to benefit from the measure. The chapter ends with a set of charts and tables that provide, subject to availability, quantitative information and estimates for the various measures listed.

5. CHILE

Energy resources and market structure

Chile, being a mountainous country, has significant hydroelectric resources, contributing to 41% of its electricity supply. However, annual output is variable, as droughts are frequent, and generation remains concentrated in the central-southern zones of the country. Biomass in the form of firewood, mostly used for heating and cooking, accounts for more than half of the final energy consumption in Chile's residential sector. Nevertheless, fossil fuels account for almost 80% of the country's total primary energy supply (TPES), where petroleum products are the dominant form (55%), followed by coal (13%) and natural gas (10%). With little indigenous production of fossil fuels, Chile imports close to 75% of its TPES in the form of oil, natural gas and coal. And, until the arrival of liquefied natural gas (LNG) in July 2009, it depended almost exclusively on one supplier of piped gas: Argentina. LNG is now imported through two terminals located at Quinteros and Mejillones.

In 2007 and 2008, Chile lost most of its gas imports from Argentina, at a time when its hydroelectric production was severely affected by drought. Chile was faced with an immediate challenge to find additional energy supplies to fuel in order to continue its economic growth and replace the costly diesel oil that had to be used in power stations that had been originally built to run on natural gas from Argentina. The domestic production of coal accounts for 9% of Chile's total coal consumption and this resource is expected to play a larger part in the power sector's energy supply over the longer term.

Chile produces a small amount of gas from the Magallanes Basin in the far south. In 2008, an international tender for hydrocarbon exploration in the Magallanes Region was launched, under the supervision of the Ministry of Mining. Of the ten blocks on offer, nine were awarded; six will be operated exclusively by independent companies and consortia. In the three remaining blocks, the winning bidders will operate in partnership with the national oil company, ENAP.

Under the Chilean Constitution, the exploration for, and extraction of, crude oil and natural gas can be carried out either directly by ENAP or by private companies through exploration and exploitation contracts established with the Chilean state. Private companies can also participate in imports, refining, storage, and distribution activities. Currently, ENAP dominates not only oil extraction but also refining (it owns the country's three refineries), importing, storage and maritime transport, as well as pipeline transport in partnership with other companies. It does not compete directly in the retail sector, however.

ENAP is also active in natural-gas transmission, and owns six pipelines in the far south of the country. Other companies, all privately owned, operate the four major pipelines in the populous centre of the country, and the three pipelines in the northern region. Seven of all those pipelines are international and connect Chile to Argentina. Natural gas is distributed through networks owned by seven companies in various cities.

The pioneering privatisation and liberalisation of Chile's electricity sector, starting in the 1980s, was completed in 1998 with the sale of the last state-owned utility, Edelaysen. The SIC, which supplies electricity to more than 90% of the country's population of 17 million, is the country's main electrical system. The northern system, SING, comprises one-third of the country's total installed capacity and covers an area equivalent to 25% of Chile's continental territory, but it serves only 6% of the population. Generation, transmission and distribution are unbundled horizontally in both the SIC and the SING. However, generators in the SIC also own transmission assets and distribution networks in the SIC since a single holding company can own assets in more than one of these sectors through companies with independent legal status. Thirty-five generation companies currently operate in the SIC. Almost 90% of the capacity belongs to three large holding companies.

Prices, taxes and support mechanisms

Prices for petroleum-based fuels are freely set by the refiner and throughout the distribution chain, including retail sales at service stations. A specific excise tax (IEC) is levied on transport fuels (*i.e.* gasoline, diesel, LPG and compressed natural gas). Gasoline is taxed at a fixed rate of UTM[16] 6 per m^3 (USD 0.5 per litre), diesel at a fixed rate of UTM 1.5 per m^3 (USD 0.12 per litre), and LPG and compressed natural gas are taxed at a rate of 1.4 UTM per m^3 (USD 0.12 per litre) and 1.93 UTM per 1 000 m^3 (USD 0.16 per m^3) respectively.

There is, however, an explicit government policy to reduce price volatility for those final consumers that are subject to the IEC. The Consumers' Protection System for IEC taxpayers (SIPCO) was established in February 2011 and covers all the transport fuels mentioned above (*i.e.* gasoline, diesel, LPG and compressed natural gas). The use of those fuels for other purposes than transport is not covered by SIPCO since it is not subject to the IEC. In practice, for each fuel subject to SIPCO, a price band is established around the fuel's average of past and future prices over a five-month window. Every week, the National Energy Commission (CNE) estimates an import parity price based on prices in the two previous weeks. If this estimated price exceeds the price-band ceiling, a reduction in the rate of IEC tax is applied to benefit final fuel consumers. Conversely, if the import parity price of the week is below the price-band floor, an increase in the rate of IEC tax is applied to make up the difference, paid for by final consumers. SIPCO thus aims to be revenue-neutral over the medium-term.

Before SIPCO was implemented, two other price-stabilisation mechanisms existed which had similar objectives but were designed differently. The Petroleum Price Stabilisation Fund (FEPP) was the first of these mechanisms. It was established in 1991 and initially covered a wide range of petroleum products. Its scope is now restricted to domestic kerosene. The second of these mechanisms was the Fuel Price Stabilisation Fund (FEPC). It operated from 2005 to 2010 and is thus no longer active. Both FEPP and FEPC shared SIPCO's objective, which is to insulate consumers of fuels from price volatility. They were, however, designed differently since both mechanisms were funds while SIPCO varies rates of tax.

---

[16] The UTM (*unidad tributaria mensual*, or monthly tax unit) is an inflation-tracking currency unit. The UTM was valued at CLP 38 173 in May 2011, equivalent to approximately USD 81.

All fuels and electricity are charged the normal value-added tax (VAT) of 19%. In addition, imported fuels attract a most-favoured-nation import duty of 6%; imports from countries that have signed a trade agreement with Chile enter duty-free.

Data documentation

General notes

The Chilean tax system relies on the use of the UTM (*Unidad Tributaria Mensual*). The UTM is a unit of account used exclusively for tax purposes. Its exchange rate vis-à-vis the Chilean peso is adjusted monthly on the basis of the consumer price index, thereby keeping its real value more or less constant.

Consumer Support Estimate

Consumers' Protection System (SIPCO) (no data available)

The Consumers' Protection System for IEC taxpayers (SIPCO) was established in February 2011 to smooth fluctuations in fuel prices. It applies to the use of gasoline, diesel, LPG and compressed natural gas for transport purposes only.

Fuel taxation occurs at the point of first sale (or import) of the relevant product. It relies on the use of an import parity price (IPP) and an intermediate reference price (iRP), both of which are set on a weekly basis and measured in USD per m^3. The former – the IPP – is obtained by averaging, over the last two weeks, the c.i.f. price of the relevant fuel plus a mark-up to account for various elements such as customs duties, exchange-rate fluctuations, logistics and the importer margin. This price tries to replicate the import price in a competitive market since Chile is a small producer of fossil fuels and relies extensively on imports to meet its energy needs. The iRP stands for the average price of the relevant fuel over the recent past and in the near future. The Comision Naciónal de Energia (CNE) calculates its value on the basis of the following formula:

$$iRP = (1 - a).HP(n) + a.FP(m) + CS(s)$$

where "HP(n)" is a historical average of oil prices over the past "n" weeks, "FP(m)" is an average of anticipated oil prices over the future "m" months, and "CS(s)" is the average crack spread[17] over the past "s" weeks. The parameter "a" varies between 0 and 0.50, "n" and "s" between 8 and 30 weeks, and "m" between 3 and 6 months. A 12.5% price-band is then established around each side of the iRP. If the IPP exceeds the band's ceiling (drops below the band's floor) a reduction (increase) in the rate of IEC tax is applied.

It follows that the domestic price of each transport fuel in Chile is determined by:

$$P^{Dom} = (P^{Int} + DM) . (1 + VAT) + IEC^{Tot}$$

---

[17]   The term "crack spread" is commonly used in the oil industry to refer to the difference between the price of crude oil and that of refinery output.

where "P^{Dom}" stands for the domestic price, "P^{Int}" is the international reference price, "DM" is the distribution margin, "VAT" is Chile's rate of value-added tax, and "IEC^{Tot}" is the total rate of Specific Excise (IEC) Tax on transport fuels. The latter is in turn equal to:

$$IEC^{Tot} = IEC + IEC^{Var}$$

where "IEC" is the basic component of the IEC tax and "IEC^{Var}" is its variable component, which is in turn calculated based on the difference between iRP and IPP.

Sources: Ley Chile (various years).

Law n. 20493, 14/02/2011 http://www.leychile.cl/Navegar?idNorma=1022962

Transitory Reduction on Gasoline Tax (no data available)

This measure was adopted in 2008 and ended in 2010. It provided consumers with a temporary reduction (24 months) in the fuel tax usually levied on gasoline. The tax break was designed to increase with the world price of crude, as measured by the West Texas Intermediate (WTI) reference index. More specifically, the size of the reduction was to increase progressively from UTM 1.5 per m^3 to UTM 3.5 per m^3 whenever the WTI would exceed USD 80, though it never reached the UTM 3.5 maximum authorised by law.

Legal Sources: Ley Chile (various years).

Law n. 20259, 01/07/2009 (FV) http://www.leychile.cl/Navegar?idNorma=270070

Law n. 20360, 30/06/2009 http://www.leychile.cl/Navegar?idNorma=1003771

Law n. 20291, 12/09/2008 http://www.leychile.cl/Navegar?idNorma=277774

Law n. 20259, 25/03/2008 (OV) http://www.leychile.cl/Navegar?idNorma=270070&tipoVersion=0

Petroleum Price Stabilisation Fund (FEPP) (no data available)

Since 1991, the government of Chile has introduced two different price-stabilisation funds for petroleum products. One is the Fondo de Estabilización de Precios del Petróleo (FEPP) and the other is the Fondo de Estabilización de Precios de los Combustibles (FEPC). Their shared objective was to partially cushion the Chilean economy against fluctuations in the world price of oil. Both funds thus worked in a countercyclical way. This means that when world prices are high, previously accumulated revenues are used to lower domestic prices, thereby subsidising consumption of petroleum products. When world prices are low, however, revenues are raised by levying a tax on sales of the same petroleum products.

The FEPP is the first of Chile's two funds, having been established in 1991. It was initially designed to smooth final prices for a wide range of petroleum products such as gasoline, diesel, naphtha, kerosene, fuel oil, and liquefied petroleum gas (LPG). This changed with the introduction of the FEPC in 2005, when it was decided to restrict the range of products to fuel oil and LPG only. Termination of the FEPC in 2010 then brought all those products back under the aegis of the FEPP. Starting with the introduction of SIPCO in February 2011, the FEPP now only covers domestic kerosene.

Price intervention occurs at the point of first sale (or import) of the relevant product. It relies on the use of an import parity price (IPP) and an intermediate reference price (iRP), both of which are set on a weekly basis and measured in USD per m³. The former – the IPP – is obtained by adding to the c.i.f. price of crude oil a mark-up to account for various elements such as customs duties, exchange-rate fluctuations, logistics, and the importer margin. The iRP stands for the expected price of oil over the medium-term. The Comision Naciónal de Energia (CNE) calculates its value on the basis of the following formula:

$$iRP = 0.4\ HP + 0.25\ STF + 0.35\ LTF$$

where "HP" is a historical weighted average of the IPP, and "STF" and "LTF" are short-term and long-term forecasts of IPP prices respectively. The formula is therefore both backward- and forward-looking. The CNE then adds a fixed margin on each side of the iRP to define a price band inside which the domestic price is to fluctuate. A tax is levied or a subsidy granted whenever the IPP falls outside that band.

The initial version of the FEPP (1991-2000) had a built-in asymmetry in the direction of lower prices. This stemmed from a bigger weight ascribed to overshooting of the target price, meaning that subsidies would always be higher than taxes for a given equal variation on each side of the target. The asymmetry resulted in the government having to provide more than USD 463 million in nominal terms to keep the programme in place over the years.

The rapid exhaustion of the fund's resources prompted the government to reform the scheme in 2000. Among the many changes brought about by the reform, the formula for setting the iRP was made public and some degree of flexibility was introduced in the determination of the band's margins. The government also disaggregated the fund at the product level, thereby establishing separate balances for each type of fuel. Last, the formulae were modified to make FEPP transfers contingent on the fund's available resources and the CNE was asked to update the scheme on a weekly basis, thereby allowing a better transmission of world prices to final consumers. Since February 2011, the FEPP has been restricted to domestic kerosene only. This reform (law n. 20.493) also provided for a USD 5.4 million recapitalisation of the fund.

Legal Sources: Ley Chile (various years).

Law n. 19030, 21/10/2004 (FV) http://www.leychile.cl/Navegar?idNorma=30397

Decree 26/2004 Min. Mineria http://www.leychile.cl/Navegar?idNorma=231595

Decree 23/2003 Min. Mineria http://www.leychile.cl/Navegar?idNorma=211022

Law n. 19681, 19/07/2000 http://www.leychile.cl/Navegar?idNorma=172961

Law n. 19660, 02/02/2000 http://www.leychile.cl/Navegar?idNorma=154114

Law n. 19030, 15/01/1991 (OV) http://www.leychile.cl/Navegar?idNorma=30397&tipoVersion=0

Law n. 20493, 14/02/2011 http://www.leychile.cl/Navegar?idNorma=1022962

Fuel Price Stabilisation Fund (FEPC) (no data available)

The FEPC operated between 2005 and 2010 and has since been phased out. It was the second of Chile's price-stabilisation funds (see "FEPP" and "SIPCO"). After the FEPC stopped operating in 2010, all petroleum products were once again allocated to the FEPP until the latter was in turn replaced by SIPCO. Funding for the FEPC was provided using resources from the national copper fund (*Fundo de Compensación de los Ingresos del Cobre*), with the initial endowment amounting to about USD 10 million. This resulted in the FEPP scheme being temporarily suspended for the relevant range of commodities (*i.e.* gasoline, diesel, kerosene, and since 2007, LPG) while keeping a residual role for the other products (fuel oil, and LPG up to 2007).

The FEPC programme was initially supposed to operate until June 2006 and was meant to counterbalance a sharp increase in fuel prices that the FEPP alone could not address. Although being quite similar to the FEPP in terms of its basic design, the FEPC possessed a much smaller margin of fluctuation (5%). Also, calculation of the import parity price (IPP) was not based on the c.i.f. price of crude oil, but instead on the standard West Texas Intermediate (WTI).

As was already the case with the FEPP, the FEPC did not prove self-financing. Over the 2.5 years from January 2007 to July 2009, credits outweighed taxes in the FEPC by USD 288 million. To maintain a positive balance in the fund in the face of these outflows, the government injected more than USD 760 million, of which only USD 362 million remained when the fund effectively ceased to operate in September 2010. After that, the FEPP resumed its earlier functioning, covering all products previously under the FEPC's umbrella until it was in turn replaced by SIPCO in February 2011.

Legal Sources: Ley Chile (various years).

Law n. 20063, 01/02/2010 (FV) http://www.leychile.cl/Navegar?idNorma=242411

Law n. 20402, 01/02/2010 http://www.leychile.cl/Navegar?idNorma=1008692

Law n. 20.339, 03/04/2009 http://www.leychile.cl/Navegar?idNorma=288597

Law n. 20246, 24/01/2008 http://www.leychile.cl/Navegar?idNorma=268805

Law n. 20197, 22/06/2007 http://www.leychile.cl/Navegar?idNorma=26203

Law n. 20115, 01/07/2006 http://www.leychile.cl/Navegar?idNorma=250922

Law n. 20063, 29/09/2005 (OV)
http://www.leychile.cl/Navegar?idNorma=242411&tipoVersion=0

References

Policies or Transfers

Ley Chile (various years) Biblioteca del Congreso Nacional de Chile, Available at: http://www.leychile.cl/.

Energy Statistics

Ministerio de Energía, *Balances Energéticos*, 2009 Edition, Santiago.

Chapter 6

France

This chapter identifies, documents, and provides estimates of the various budgetary transfers and tax expenditures that relate to the production or use of fossil fuels in *France*. An overview of *France's* energy economy is first given to place the measures listed into context. A data-documentation section then describes those measures in a systematic way. Whenever possible, the description details a measure's formal beneficiary, its eligibility criteria and functioning, and the fuels whose production or use stand to benefit from the measure. The chapter ends with a set of charts and tables that provide, subject to availability, quantitative information and estimates for the various measures listed.

6. FRANCE

Energy resources and market structure

France has very limited fossil-energy resources and imports most of its oil and natural gas and all of its coal. Since even before the oil crises of the 1970s, France has pursued a policy of developing its nuclear energy industry to reduce its dependence on fossil energy imports, though almost all of the uranium needed to fuel its nuclear power plants is imported. In 2009, nuclear power accounted for more than three-quarters of France's electricity generation and 42% of its total primary energy supply. Oil accounts for 29% of energy use, having dropped steadily from nearly two-thirds in the 1970s. Natural gas accounts for 15% and hydro-electric power and other renewable energy sources (including municipal waste) for most of the rest. Treating nuclear power as domestic supply, indigenous production meets just over half of the country's energy use.

Historically, France has had a strong tradition of state involvement in the energy sector. In recent years, however, government ownership of energy companies has diminished somewhat. The oil industry is now entirely in private hands. The privatisation of the previously partially state-owned international oil company, Total, which merged with the former state-owned company Elf in 2000, was completed in the late 1990s. A number of other private companies, many of them foreign-based multinationals, are active in the French refining, distribution and marketing businesses.

The state retains substantial ownership stakes in electricity and natural gas. In November 2004, the two incumbent monopoly companies, Electricité de France (EDF) and Gaz de France, both of which were 100% state-owned, became limited companies with a board of directors. The next year, minority stakes in the two companies were sold to private investors. The state retains an 85% stake in EDF, and holds a 36% stake in GDF Suez as a consequence of the merger of Gaz de France with Suez in 2008. AREVA, the primary manufacturer of nuclear-power systems in France, remains majority-owned by the state (primarily though the Commissariat à l'énergie atomique et aux énergies alternatives) although private investors can now hold up to 4% of the capital. The government has created Pluri-annual Investment Plans to evaluate investment choices and to ensure that they align with objectives for desired future developments in the energy sector.

France has liberalised its electricity and gas sectors progressively to comply with EU directives, eliminating the monopoly rights of the two state companies. Transmission and distribution of natural gas and electricity have been unbundled; negotiated third-party access to underground storage of natural gas introduced; and a regulator, the Commission de Regulation de l'Énergie (CRE), and a mediator to protect electricity and gas consumers, were established.

Despite recent moves to liberalise the sector, EDF still accounts for the bulk of power generation. The French transmission network is 100% owned and operated by the French transmission system operator, RTE, or *Gestionnaire du réseau*, a subsidiary of EDF. The distribution network is owned by local authorities (*collectivités territoriales*). RTE is mandated to ensure connection and non-discriminatory access to transmission networks to third parties. Eligibility to choose supplier was first offered in France in 2000 to the largest consumers. Since July 2007, all electricity consumers in France are eligible to choose their supplier. However, EDF still has a dominant market position, and consumer switching rates are very low: In 2010, 95% of residential customers and 86% of business customers (by number of sites supplied) were still supplied by EDF.

GDF Suez is similarly still the dominant player in the natural-gas sector, importing the bulk of the country's gas needs and operating, through GRTgaz, a 100% subsidiary, the national transmission system which covers most of the country. In the south-west, there is a separate network operated by Total Infrastructures Gaz France, which is a 100% subsidiary of Total. GDF Suez also owns the majority of the local distribution networks; the remainder are owned by local authorities. GDF Suez and the other incumbent gas suppliers have retained most of the retail market (93% of residential customers and 81% of business customers).

Prices, taxes and support mechanisms

The prices of all forms of energy other than electricity and gas are set freely by the market. Electricity and gas customers have a choice of supply from incumbent suppliers at regulated tariffs or from alternative suppliers at market rates. Social tariffs for electricity and natural gas are available to residential customers on low incomes. The social tariff for electricity only applies to rates offered by EDF and local, non-nationalised distributors; the social rate for gas is to be applied by all natural-gas suppliers (including new entrants). The CRE is responsible for proposing changes to regulated tariffs, but the government still has the final say over whether to approve or refuse the change (but not modify it). The CRE is also responsible for regulating tariffs for access by third parties to gas and electricity infrastructure.

Energy products and services are subject to VAT at the rate of 19.6%, with the exception of the fixed component of contracts for the distributed supply of electricity, natural gas and liquefied petroleum gas, for which the rate is 5.5%. Excise duties are payable on all sales of oil products (at varying rates according to the fuel, the sector, and the *région*) and a domestic consumption tax is levied on deliveries of coal and natural gas to non-residential consumers. Biofuels benefit, under certain conditions, from a lower rate of excise duty than conventional petroleum transport fuels. The General Tax on Polluting Activities, established in 1999, was extended in 2005 to distributors of automotive fuels that do not meet annual biofuel targets. At the national level, electricity tariffs include a tax called CSPE (*contribution au service public de l'électricité*), which aims to offset the additional costs resulting from electricity production by co-generation, contract purchases of renewable energy, charges resulting from the application of uniform tariffs in areas that are not interconnected, and social provisions. In recent years, the revenues raised by the CSPE tax have not been sufficient to fully offset the additional costs.

There are a number of different mechanisms and arrangements for directing support at some specific fuels and categories of end user. These mainly take the form of partial or full exemptions or refunds on VAT or excise duties on oil products. Examples include a reduced rate of excise duty on fuel used by taxis and specific types of machinery used in farming and construction, and a tax exemption on fuel used by fishing boats. In addition, grants are available under certain conditions for upgrading service stations and for converting old gasoline-fuelled vehicles to run on liquefied petroleum gas (LPG). Other incentives to encourage LPG-fuelled cars include total or partial exemptions on car registration fees and company car taxes. In most cases, the total monetary value of the different forms of support annually is modest.

Data documentation

General notes

The fiscal year in France coincides with the calendar year. Following OECD convention, amounts prior to 1999 are expressed as 'euro-fixed series', meaning that we applied the fixed EMU conversion rate (1 EUR = 6.559 FRF) to data initially expressed in the French Franc (FRF).

Producer Support Estimate

France used to support production of coal through Charbonnages de France (CdF), a state-owned enterprise. Support was at the time deemed necessary owing to the low competitiveness of the French coal industry. By 1990, production had already ceased in the North of the country. An agreement between trade unions and CdF, the "Pacte Charbonnier", was therefore concluded in October 1994 to organise the progressive dismantling of the remaining production sites. The agreement provided for the end of all production by 2005. This was to be achieved through a series of measures meant to address the social costs associated with mine closures. One such measure, the "congé charbonnier de fin de carrière", allowed coal miners to stop working at the age of 45 while remaining entitled to payments worth 80% of their previous wages.

The last remaining mine was closed in 2004, ahead of schedule. CdF was liquidated in 2007 and its debt transferred to the French state, along with the responsibility for all inherited social and environmental liabilities. France does not produce coal any more.

Residual Financial Charges of CdF (data for 1990-96)

This measure provided Charbonnages de France (CdF) with annual payments aimed at relieving the company from some residual financial charges it had inherited in the past. Not much information is available regarding this item but we allocate it to the 'capital' incidence category as suggested by the measure's title.

Sources: Cour des Comptes (2000), Charbonnages de France (various years), Sénat (various years).

Tag: FRA_dt_04

General Research & Development Grant CdF (data for 1990-96)

Charbonnages de France (CdF) used to receive annual Research & Development grants whose object remains unclear given the lack of details found in official documents. The fact that the subsidy is, however, firm-specific directs it to the PSE category rather than the GSSE category.

Sources: Cour des Comptes (2000), Charbonnages de France (various years), Sénat (various years).

Tag: FRA_dt_05

Direct State Aid to CdF (data for 1990-96)

Charbonnages de France (CdF) had been receiving income support from the French government since the aftermath of the Second World War before the company was eventually liquidated in 2007. This item comprises direct aid that was not earmarked for any specific purpose. Such aid stopped in the late 1990s after which it was replaced by annual capital contributions.

Sources: Cour des Comptes (2000), Charbonnages de France (various years), Sénat (various years).

Tag: FRA_dt_06

Interest Payments on 1997-99 Debt of CdF (data for 2000-07)

This item comprises annual payments made to Charbonnages de France (CdF) in order to cover the interest payments on debt the company contracted in the years 1997 to 1999. Reporting ends with CdF's liquidation in 2007.

Sources: Cour des Comptes (2000), Charbonnages de France (various years), Sénat (various years).

Tag: FRA_dt_07

Capital Contribution to CdF (data for 1997-2007)

Following the end of direct state aid to Charbonnages de France (CdF) back in 1997, it was decided to provide the company with annual capital grants meant to cover for insufficient equity. Payments went on until CdF's liquidation in 2007.

This item is allocated to the "income" incidence category because it does not require additional investment on the part of the company. As such, its actual effect is more to support income rather than to finance capital investment.

Sources: Cour des Comptes (2000), Charbonnages de France (various years), Sénat (various years).

Tag: FRA_dt_08

Partial Tax Deduction for Exploration Costs (data for 1999-)

This tax provision is known as the Provisions pour reconstitution des gisements d'hydrocarbures (Provisions for reconstituting oil and gas fields) and dates back to 1953. It allows oil and gas companies operating in France to deduct a fixed percentage of their revenues from their income tax base, provided this amount is later reinvested in exploration. Given that France does not possess abundant petroleum and natural gas resources, the amounts reported are fairly small. Recipients are very few, ranging between five and ten per year.

We use production data from the IEA to allocate the annual amounts reported in budget documents to oil and natural gas extraction.

Sources: Ministère du Budget (various years), IEA.

Tag: FRA_te_02

Excise-Tax Exemption for Natural Gas Producers (data for 2007-)

Natural gas extraction and production are exempted from paying any excise tax on the energy products they use as process energy (*i.e.* not as feedstock). This tax concession is quite recent since it was introduced in 2007. The scale of oil and gas production being small in France, the reported amounts do not add up to significant annual tax expenditures, but we nonetheless include the concession for the sake of completeness. Moreover, the very small number of beneficiaries makes transfers per recipient quite significant (two recipients only in 2009).

Sources: Ministère du Budget (various years).

Tag: FRA_te_11

Excise-Tax Exemption for Refiners (data for 1999-)

Petroleum products used by refiners as process-energy (*i.e.* not as feedstock) are exempted from the energy tax usually levied on such products. This measure dates back to 1956.

The annual amounts reported in budget documents are allocated to the different fuels on the basis of the IEA's Energy Balances for the petroleum refining sector.

Sources: Ministère du Budget (various years), IEA.

Tag: FRA_te_24

Consumer Support Estimate

Prime à la Cuve (data for 2005-09)

This programme was created in 2005 to provide low-income households with grants to help pay for their heating bills. Only those households whose income is not taxable were eligible for the subsidy. Following submission of their heating fuel bills, recipients would receive a lump-sum transfer ranging between EUR 75 and EUR 200. The measure being only transient, it was phased-out in 2009 after the last round of payments was made.

No payments were made in the year 2007 so that a zero value for that particular year is reported.

Sources: DG Trésor.

Tag: FRA_dt_01

Aid to Gas Stations (data for 1999-)

This programme provides gas stations with annual subsidies aimed at upgrading infrastructure and helping small, declining businesses. It is managed by an *ad hoc* committee – the Comité Professionnel de la Distribution des Carburants (Professional Committee for Fuel Retailing) – that was set up in March 1991 to oversee applications and payments. The measure has been allocated to the CSE as it most directly benefits consumers rather than producers.

Data could not be found for the years prior to 1999. We allocate the annual amounts reported in budget documents to the different fuels sold in French gas stations on the basis of the IEA's Energy Balances for the road transport sector. That excludes biofuels but includes gasoline, diesel (which gets the lion's share), and LPG.

Sources: Ministère du Budget (various years), IEA.

Tag: FRA_dt_09

Overseas VAT Exemption for Petroleum Products (data for 1999-)

Petroleum products consumed in certain French overseas *départements* (Guadeloupe, Martinique, and La Réunion) have been exempted since 1951 from the VAT that is normally levied on such products. The concession is meant to help those territories that are both geographically and economically disadvantaged.

Because the measure applies to a few other goods in addition to petroleum products, tax expenditures may overestimate the part of the exemption that effectively benefits fossil fuels. We allocate the annual amounts reported in budget documents to gasoline and diesel fuel on the basis of data contained in Bellec et al. (2009).

Sources: Ministère du Budget (various years), Bellec et al. (2009).

Tag: FRA_te_03

VAT Reduction for Petroleum Products in Corsica (data for 2007-)

A reduced rate of VAT (13%) applies to those petroleum products that are consumed in Corsica, whereas most other goods and services remain subject to the standard continental rate of 19.6%.

Data prior to 2007 are not available.

Sources: Direction Générale des Douanes et des Droits Indirects.

Tag: FRA_te_04

Reduced Rate of Excise for Taxi Drivers (data for 1999-)

Since 1982, taxi drivers in France have been granted a reduced rate of excise tax on petroleum products. The concession takes the form of an annual, capped refund which is based on the amounts of fuel effectively consumed. No other details regarding the specifics of the measure could be found.

We allocate the annual amounts reported in budget documents to gasoline and diesel on the basis of the IEA's Energy Balances for the road transport sector.

Sources: Ministère du Budget (various years), IEA.

Tag: FRA_te_05

Excise-Tax Exemption for Certain Merchants (data for 1999-2008)

This tax concession applied to those merchants that operate from a fixed selling point (*i.e.* that are not itinerant) located in a town counting less than 3 000 inhabitants, while also engaging in small-scale deliveries. The concession was capped at 1 500 litres a year and was phased out at the end of 2008 following a request to this effect by the European Commission.

We allocate the annual amounts reported in budget documents to gasoline and diesel on the basis of the IEA's Energy Balances for the road transport sector.

Sources: Ministère du Budget (various years), IEA.

Tag: FRA_te_06

Excise-Tax Exemption for Co-generation (data for 1999-)

This measure exempts both mineral oils and natural gas burnt for the purpose of co-generation from the excise tax that is normally levied on fuel consumption. It applies only to those plants that were built before 31 December 2007, and for no more than five years. Very few other details are available. Accordingly, we allocate the annual amounts reported in budget documents to mineral oils and natural gas on the basis of the IEA's Energy Balances for the combined heat and power generation sector.

Sources: Ministère du Budget (various years), IEA.

Tag: FRA_te_07

Excise-Tax Exemption for the Ministry of Defence (data for 2006-09)

The French Ministry of Defence was until recently exempted from paying the excise tax on petroleum products. The measure proved short-lived, since it was introduced in 2006 and phased out in 2009. Given that the measure applied for the most part to heavy ground-vehicles such as tanks and trucks, we allocate it entirely to diesel.

Sources: Ministère du Budget (various years).

Tag: FRA_te_08

Excise-Tax Exemption for Local Administrations (data for 2007)

This one-off measure exempted some local and regional administrations from paying the excise tax on natural gas that normally applies in such cases.

Sources: Ministère du Budget (various years).

Tag: FRA_te_09

Excise-Tax Exemption for Biomass Producers (data for 2007-)

This measure is fairly small and exempts some biomass producers (*e.g.* producers of alfalfa) from paying the regular excise tax on coal. The latter is apparently used for dehydrating biomass. We allocate the measure entirely to bituminous coal.

Sources: Ministère du Budget (various years).

Tag: FRA_te_10

Excise-Tax Exemption for Households (data for 2007-)

Under this measure, households are exempted from paying the excise tax that normally applies to consumption of natural gas. Budget documents report that the concession was introduced in 2007 and is meant to avoid distortions between those households that are directly provided with natural gas and those that receive reticulated heat.

Sources: Ministère du Budget (various years).

Tag: FRA_te_12

Reduced Rate for Fuel Oil Used as Diesel Fuel (data for 1999-)

This concession allows farmers and fishermen to benefit from the lower rate of excise tax that applies to heating oil when using the latter in diesel engines. Those two types of fuel are indeed very close and can sometimes be used interchangeably. This measure dates back to 1970 and is specifically described as being meant to help the agriculture and fisheries sectors.

Sources: Ministère du Budget (various years).

Tag: FRA_te_13

Reduced Rate for NGLs Used as Fuel (data for 1999-)

A reduced rate of excise tax is applied to butane and propane when used as transport fuels under certain unspecified conditions. This measure was created in 1993 and is meant to promote energy savings.

Sources: Ministère du Budget (various years).

Tag: FRA_te_14

Reduced Rate for Natural Gas Used as Fuel (data for 2007-)

A 100% reduction in the rate of excise tax is applied to natural gas when used as a transport fuel. Budget documents indicate that the concession was introduced in 2007 but no other details are provided.

Sources: Ministère du Budget (various years).

Tag: FRA_te_15

Reduced Rate of Excise for LPG (data for 2007-)

Liquefied petroleum gas has been subject to a reduced rate of excise tax since 2007. Budget documents report that this tax concession aims at promoting the use of LPG.

Sources: Ministère du Budget (various years).

Tag: FRA_te_16

Reduced Rate for Certain Types of Machines (data for 2007-)

Certain types of machines that function using a diesel-fired engine are not subject to the regular excise tax on diesel fuel. The sectors concerned by this measure are agriculture and construction.

Sources: Ministère du Budget (various years).

Tag: FRA_te_17

Reduced Rate for Petroleum Products in Corsica (data for 1999-)

Diesel fuel and gasoline consumed in Corsica are subject to a reduced rate of excise tax. This reduction applies on top of an existing arrangement that allows regional authorities (*Conseils Régionaux* and the *Assemblée de Corse*) to vary the rate of excise within agreed limits. Only the former provision is reported in order to be consistent with federal countries that apply varying rates of excise tax among sub-national units.

We allocate the annual amounts reported in budget documents to gasoline and diesel on the basis of the IEA's Energy Balances for the road transport sector.

Sources: Ministère du Budget (various years), IEA.

Tag: FRA_te_18

Refund for Public Transportation and Garbage Collection (data for 1999-2008)

This measure was created in 1997 and used to provide public transportation and garbage collection with a capped refund (40 000 litres per year and vehicle) on the excise tax paid for their respective consumption of natural gas and liquefied petroleum gas used as fuels. It was phased out in 2008, following a request to this effect by the European Commission.

We allocate the annual amounts reported in budget documents to natural gas and liquefied petroleum gas on the basis of the IEA's Energy Balances for the road transport sector.

Sources: Ministère du Budget (various years), IEA.

Tag: FRA_te_19

Refund for Diesel Used in Road Transport (data for 1999-)

Excise tax levied on diesel fuel used in road vehicles weighing at least 7.5 tonnes and involved in the transport of freight is, under this tax provision, partly refunded to targeted users. This concession was allegedly introduced in 1999.

Sources: Ministère du Budget (various years).

Tag: FRA_te_20

Refund for Diesel Used in Public Transportation (data for 2001-)

This measure gives certain providers of public road transportation a partial refund on the excise tax usually levied on diesel fuel. Budget documents indicate that it was created in 2001, but no other details are provided.

Sources: Ministère du Budget (various years).

Tag: FRA_te_21

Refund for Fuel Oil Used in Agriculture (data for 2006-)

Farmers have been eligible since 2004 to a partial refund on the excise tax levied on fuel oil. This adds to the fact that fuel oil is often used as diesel fuel in agriculture, and that, as such, farmers already benefit from a lower rate of excise tax than would otherwise be the case (see above). The present measure explicitly aims at helping the agricultural sector cope with high energy prices. Although the refund was meant to be both discretionary and transitory, it has been reinstated every year since its first inception in 2004.

Data for the years 2004 and 2005 are unfortunately not available.

Sources: Ministère du Budget (various years).

Tag: FRA_te_22

Excise-Tax Exemption for Certain Boats (data for 1999-)

This tax concession exempts the fuel used in certain boats from the excise tax that normally applies to consumption of petroleum products. The boats concerned by the exemption are those that are engaged into maritime navigation while not being used for private, leisure purposes. The definition thus mostly encompasses fishing vessels. Since boats rely heavily on diesel fuel (or, in some cases, on fuel oil which is very close to diesel fuel), this item is entirely allocated to diesel.

Sources: Ministère du Budget (various years).

Tag: FRA_te_23

Excise-Tax Exemption for Domestic Aviation (data for 2000-)

Domestic aviation in France is exempted from the excise tax that is normally levied on sales of petroleum products. This provision does not apply to aircraft used for private, leisure purposes, nor does it include flights between mainland France and its overseas *départements* (*DOM*).

We allocate the measure entirely to kerosene-type jet fuel.

Sources: Commissariat Général au Développement Durable based on data from CITEPA.

Tag: FRA_te_25

General Services Support Estimate

Benefits to Former Miners CdF (data for 1990-2004)

Charbonnages de France (CdF) used to receive annual grants meant to help the company pay for benefits to former miners. The latter mostly consisted of benefits related to housing and heating. Responsibility over their payment was transferred to the Agence Nationale pour la Garantie des Droits des Mineurs (ANGDM) following the closure of the last mine in 2004. Given that CdF was the sole producer of hard coal in France, subsequent payments by the ANGDM are not included in the database.

Sources: Cour des Comptes (2000), Charbonnages de France (various years), Sénat (various years).

Tag: FRA_dt_02

Management of Old Mining Sites CdF (data for 1990-2000)

This item consists of annual grants to Charbonnages de France (CdF) that were meant to finance the company's management of its old mining sites. Payments are allocated to the GSSE as they do not increase current production or consumption of hard coal.

Sources: Cour des Comptes (2000), Charbonnages de France (various years), Sénat (various years).

Tag: FRA_dt_03

References

Policies or transfers

Bellec, Gilles, Anne Bolliet, Thomas Cazenave, Jean-Guy de Chalvron, Nicolas Clouet, and Thibaut Sartre (2009) *Rapport sur la Fixation des Prix des Carburants dans les départements d'outre-mer*, March 2009, Secrétariat d'État à l'outre-mer, Available at: http://www.ladocumentationfrancaise.fr/rapports-publics/094000153/index.shtml.

Charbonnages de France (various years) *Statistique Charbonnière Annuelle*, Archives Nationales du Monde du Travail, Roubaix

Cour des Comptes (2000) *La Fin des Activités Minières*, Rapport au Président de la République, Rapports Publics Thématiques, Available at: http://www.ccomptes.fr/fr/CC/Publications-RPT.html.

Ministère du Budget (various years) *Documentation Budgétaire*, Available at: http://www.performance-publique.gouv.fr/?id=24.

Sénat (various years) *Rapports d'Information*, Available at: http://www.senat.fr/.

Energy statistics

IEA, *Energy Balances of OECD Countries*, 2010 Edition, International Energy Agency, Paris.

Figure 6.1.   Shares of fossil-fuel support by fuel, average for 2008-10 – France

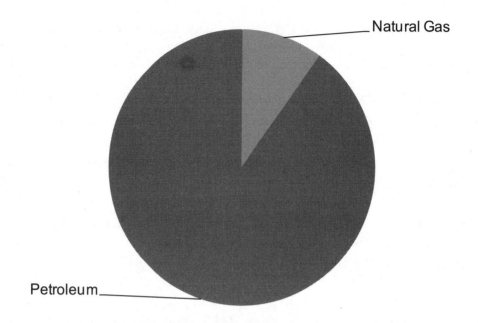

Source: OECD.

Figure 6.2.   Shares of fossil-fuel support by indicator, average for 2008-10 – France

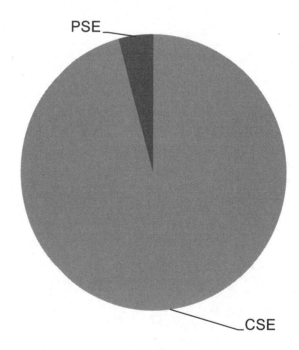

Source: OECD.

Table 6.1.Summary of fossil-fuel support to coal – France

(Millions of euros, nominal)

Support element	Jurisdiction	Avg 2000-02	Avg 2008-10	2008	2009	2010p
Producer Support Estimate						
Income support						
Capital Contribution to CdF	–	345.53	n.a.	n.a.	n.a.	n.a.
Support for capital formation						
Interest Payments on 1997-99 Debt of CdF	–	32.51	n.a.	n.a.	n.a.	n.a.
Consumer Support Estimate						
Consumption						
Excise-Tax Exemption for Biomass Producers	–	n.a.	2.00	0.00	3.00	3.00
General Services Support Estimate						
Management of Old Mining Sites CdF	–	11.20	n.a.	n.a.	n.a.	n.a.
Benefits to Former Miners CdF	–	421.47	n.a.	n.a.	n.a.	n.a.

Note: Tax expenditures for any given country are measured with reference to a benchmark tax treatment that is generally specific to that country. Consequently, the estimates contained in the table above are not necessarily comparable with estimates for other countries. In addition, because of the potential interaction between them, the summation of individual measures for a specific country may be problematic. The allocation of particular measures across fuel types was done by the OECD Secretariat based on the IEA's Energy Balances.

Source: OECD.

Table 6.2. Summary of fossil-fuel support to petroleum – France

(Millions of euros, nominal)

Support element	Jurisdiction	Avg 2000-02	Avg 2008-10	2008	2009	2010p
Producer Support Estimate						
Income support						
Partial Tax Deduction for Exploration Costs	–	2.73	2.03	0.00	6.10	0.00
Support for intermediate inputs						
Excise–Tax Exemption for Refiners	–	61.00	105.00	105.00	105.00	105.00
Consumer Support Estimate						
Consumption						
Prime à la Cuve	–	n.a.	n.a.	124.59	190.75	n.a.
Aid to Gas Stations	–	10.77	7.33	8.00	6.38	7.61
Overseas VAT Exemption for Petroleum Products	FR97	124.67	70.00	80.00	65.00	65.00
VAT Reduction for Petroleum Products in Corsica	FR20	n.c.	13.92	13.58	13.99	14.19
Reduced Rate of Excise for Taxi Drivers	–	63.67	19.33	17.00	15.00	26.00
Excise-Tax Exemption for Certain Merchants	–	4.27	n.a.	3.00	n.a.	n.a.
Excise-Tax Exemption for Co-generation	–	0.00	1.43	1.43	1.43	1.43
Excise-Tax Exemption for the Ministry of Defense	–	n.a.	n.a.	30.00	10.00	n.a.
Reduced Rate for Fuel Oil Used as Diesel Fuel	–	993.33	1 100.00	1 100.00	1 100.00	1 100.00
Reduced Rate for NGLs Used as Fuel	–	5.67	6.00	6.00	6.00	6.00
Reduced Rate of Excise for LPG	–	n.a.	40.33	39.00	41.00	41.00
Reduced Rate for Certain Types of Machines	–	n.a.	25.00	0.00	0.00	75.00
Reduced Rate for Petroleum Products in Corsica	–	1.57	1.00	1.00	1.00	1.00
Refund for Public Transportation and Garbage Collection	–	0.60	n.a.	1.19	n.a.	n.a.
Refund for Diesel Used in Road Transport	–	257.67	297.00	295.00	288.00	308.00
Refund for Diesel Used in Public Transportation	–	n.a.	26.00	26.00	26.00	26.00
Refund for Fuel Oil Used in Agriculture	–	n.c.	138.67	165.00	101.00	150.00
Excise-Tax Exemption for Certain Boats	–	202.67	99.00	101.00	98.00	98.00
Excise-Tax Exemption for Domestic Aviation	–	368.43	305.23	315.10	300.30	300.30
General Services Support Estimate (n.a.)						

Note: Tax expenditures for any given country are measured with reference to a benchmark tax treatment that is generally specific to that country. Consequently, the estimates contained in the table above are not necessarily comparable with estimates for other countries. In addition, because of the potential interaction between them, the summation of individual measures for a specific country may be problematic. The allocation of particular measures across fuel types was done by the OECD Secretariat based on the IEA's Energy Balances.

Source: OECD.

INVENTORY OF ESTIMATED BUDGETARY SUPPORT AND TAX EXPENDITURES FOR FOSSIL FUELS © OECD 2011

Table 6.3. Summary of fossil-fuel support to natural gas – France

(Millions of euros, nominal)

Support element	Jurisdiction	Avg 2000-02	Avg 2008-10	2008	2009	2010p
Producer Support Estimate						
Income support						
Partial Tax Deduction for Exploration Costs	–	2.24	1.63	0.00	4.90	0.00
Support for intermediate inputs						
Excise-Tax Exemption for Natural Gas Producers	–	n.a.	1.67	1.00	2.00	2.00
Consumer Support Estimate						
Consumption						
Excise-Tax Exemption for Co-generation	–	25.33	8.57	8.57	8.57	8.57
Excise-Tax Exemption for Local Administrations	–	n.a.	n.a.	37.00	n.a.	n.a.
Excise-Tax Exemption for Households	–	n.a.	227.33	200.00	237.00	245.00
Reduced Rate for Natural Gas Used as Fuel	–	n.a.	7.00	3.00	9.00	9.00
Refund for Public Transportation and Garbage Collection	–	0.06	n.a.	0.81	n.a.	n.a.
General Services Support Estimate (n.a.)						

Note: Tax expenditures for any given country are measured with reference to a benchmark tax treatment that is generally specific to that country. Consequently, the estimates contained in the table above are not necessarily comparable with estimates for other countries. In addition, because of the potential interaction between them, the summation of individual measures for a specific country may be problematic. The allocation of particular measures across fuel types was done by the OECD Secretariat based on the IEA's Energy Balances.

Source: OECD.

Chapter 7

Germany

This chapter identifies, documents, and provides estimates of the various budgetary transfers and tax expenditures that relate to the production or use of fossil fuels in *Germany*. An overview of *Germany's* energy economy is first given to place the measures listed into context. A data-documentation section then describes those measures in a systematic way. Whenever possible, the description details a measure's formal beneficiary, its eligibility criteria and functioning, and the fuels whose production or use stand to benefit from the measure. The chapter ends with a set of charts and tables that provide, subject to availability, quantitative information and estimates for the various measures listed.

7.   GERMANY

Energy resources and market structure

Germany's proven reserves of oil and natural gas are modest and have been dwindling in recent years after decades of production. Recent technological advances hold out the prospect of new discoveries of unconventional gas, which could lead to a revival of production. Indigenous production currently meets 14% of the country's gas use and less than 3% of its oil use. Hard-coal mining began in earnest in the 18th century and the country still produces hard coal, meeting almost one quarter of its total hard-coal needs. But hard-coal mining is uneconomic and the remaining mines will close by 2018 as subsidies are phased out. Lignite is produced from opencast mines that do not attract direct support measures. Germany has a relatively balanced mix of fuels in its primary energy mix, with oil making up the largest share of primary supply, at more than one-third, followed by natural gas (22%), coal (12%), lignite (11%) and nuclear power (11%). Compared with other OECD countries, Germany has a very high share of renewables in its energy mix, accounting for about 9% of primary supply, with more than 80%-coming from combustible renewables and waste. Germany relies on imports for over 60% of its overall energy needs.

The German energy industry has traditionally been mainly privately owned, though there are still a large number of small electricity and gas distribution companies that are either wholly or partially owned by municipalities. The oil industry is fully liberalised, with no government ownership. Despite the takeovers of DEA Mineralöl AG by Shell in Germany and Veba Oel AG by German BP in 2002, creating two dominant players, Germany's oil-refining and retail sectors retain a relatively large number of operators.

All production of hard coal is carried out by RAG Deutsche Steinkohle, a wholly owned subsidiary of Ruhrkohle AG (RAG).. In 2007, the shareholders, including E.ON and RWE, transferred their shares for a symbolic EUR 1 to the RAG Stiftung (foundation). In 2011, RAG Deutsche Steinkohle operated five deep coal mines at sites in the Ruhr and Saar regions and in Ibbenbüren in North Rhine-Westphalia. As production costs remain well above revenues, the company gets substantial government subsidies. Lignite is produced from opencast mines, primarily by five companies, including Vattenfall and RWE.

Germany has implemented market reforms in the electricity and gas sectors in line with EU directives. Grid operators are now subject to regulation by the newly established Federal Network Agency (Bundesnetzagentur, BNetzA) and by regulatory authorities in the individual German states (Länder), some of whom have elected to transfer these powers to the BNetzA. The Federal Cartel Office (Bundeskartellamt) has responsibility for approving mergers and monitoring anti-competitive behaviour. Despite these reforms, the incumbent operators in the wholesale and retail markets have retained large market shares. E.ON and RWE are among the dominant players in both the gas and the electricity markets.

A central pillar of German energy policy is the phase-out of nuclear power, which was decided by the government in 1999. A 2001 agreement between the German government and energy utilities, as well as resulting amendments to the Nuclear Power Act in 2002, sets out the terms of the planned phase-out. Changes to the Atomic Energy Act enshrined the nuclear phase-out in German law. The legislation sets a time limit for commercial electricity generation for each existing power station based on an average 32-year lifetime. The nuclear law was changed in 2011 as a result of the Fukushima nuclear power plant accident in Japan. All nuclear-power stations in Germany will now be placed out of service by 2022.

Prices, taxes and support mechanisms

The prices of all forms of energy are set freely by the market, as required by EU competition law. Electricity and natural gas supply is regulated by the BNetzA. In principle, suppliers are allowed to pass through all costs, including the wholesale cost of buying the gas and network-related costs and charges.

All forms of energy are subject to value-added tax at 19%. Excise tax and a special tax to fund the emergency storage fund (EBV) are applied (at different rates) to oil products. An ecological tax, introduced in 1999, is levied on oil products, natural gas and electricity. The eco-tax is levied at different rates according to the fuel and the customer category (households pay a higher charge than industry). The "eco-tax" refers in this context only to the tax increase since April 1999, in addition to the mineral-oil tax from before that time. One of the reasons put forward for introducing the eco-tax in Germany was that the increase in the costs of energy products would have a steering effect, encouraging the efficient use of natural resources.

By far the most important subsidy in Germany is the financial assistance to the hard-coal industry. The cost of producing coal in Germany is far higher than the price of imported coal; the difference is made up by a subsidy to RAG. RAG also receives support for closing down its mines. The cost of these combined subsidies stood at EUR 1.7 billion in 2010, even though both production and support measures had been declining for many years (as reflected for hard coal in Figure 7.1). In mid-2007 the federal government, the governments of the states with mines, the unions and RAG agreed on a detailed road map to end all subsidies in a socially acceptable manner by the end of 2018. Under the deal, production is being gradually scaled back, limited by the retirement dates of miners. Subsidies for production will continue to be paid jointly by the federal government and North Rhine-Westphalia until 2014, after which time the federal government will assume payment of all production subsidies. Subsidies for closing down mines will be paid jointly until 2018. Mining costs that remain after the closure of the pits will primarily be paid out of a fund, which will be filled with the proceeds of a public sale of the equity-investment assets of RAG, now directly owned by the RAG Stiftung. If financing by the foundation falls short, the states of North Rhine-Westphalia and Saarland will guarantee two-thirds of the costs, and the federal government one-third. In addition, another programme provides older coal miners with early retirement payments until they become eligible for regular pension payments. Funding is split between the federal government and the states that possess mines.

Figure 7.1. Total Producer Support Estimate for hard coal, Germany (1999-2009)

(Million EUR, nominal)

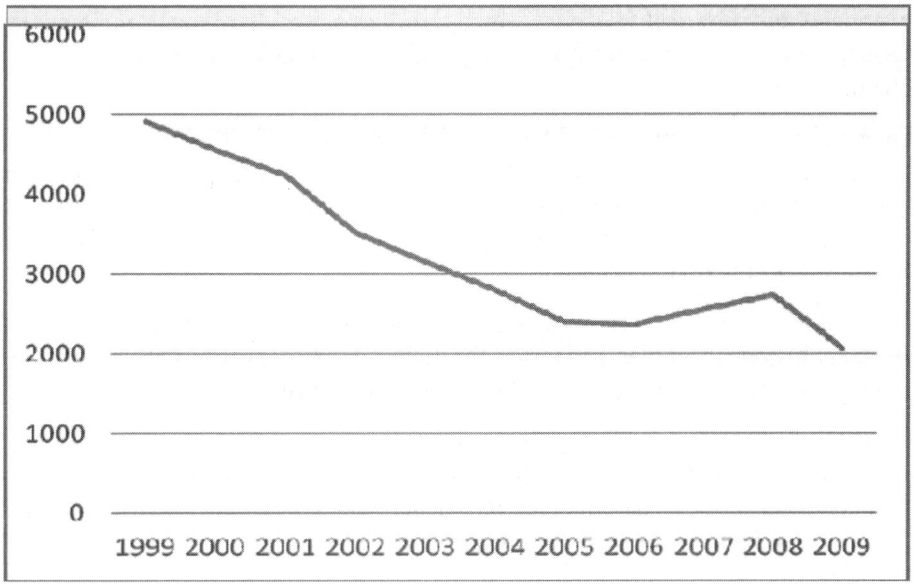

Sources: OECD.

The main features of the tax code relating to energy consumption involve tax exemptions, reductions, rebates and (partial) refunds for particular fuels and sectors. These include an exemption from energy taxes normally applied to the use of electricity, coal, natural gas, and petroleum products enjoyed by energy companies that use energy for processing purposes; tax privileges on heating oil, natural gas and LPG for certain users in the agriculture, forestry and manufacturing sectors; tax relief on diesel used in agriculture; an energy-tax exemption on fuels used in power stations of more than 2 MW and in efficient co-generation plants, as well in commercial aviation and in barges carrying freight on inland waterways; reduced energy taxes on fuels used in public transport; and reduced rates of eco-tax on fuels used in energy-intensive processes and techniques, mainly in the steel and chemical industries to protect their competitiveness. Those tax exemptions do not reduce energy prices below world-market prices.

Data documentation

General notes

The fiscal year in Germany coincides with the calendar year. Following OECD convention, amounts prior to 1999 are expressed as 'euro-fixed series', meaning that we applied the fixed EMU conversion rate (1 EUR = 1.956 DEM) to data initially expressed in the Deutsche Mark (DEM). In a few cases[18], the conversion into EUR was already made in official government documents.

Since Germany is a federal country, the data collection exercise was also conducted for two states (*Länder*), North Rhine-Westphalia (NW) and Saarland (SR)

---

[18]   This applies to the support measures tagged as DEU_dt_13, DEU_dt_14, DEU_dt_15, DEU_dt_16, DEU_dt_17, and DEU_dt_18.

Producer Support Estimate

Hard-coal mining in Germany has traditionally attracted support for geological, historical and political reasons. Since production of hard coal remains largely uneconomic, most mines are due to close by 2018 when subsidies to the industry are planned to be removed.

Over the years, production of hard coal has been scaled back through numerous government policies. In the 1990s, the industry underwent various capacity adjustment plans. Funding for these programmes was usually provided jointly by the coal-mining Land and the federal government, with the former accounting for two-thirds of the total.

The industry also received substantial government aid to remain in operation. Hard-coal production was supported through a combination of debt relief schemes, mining-royalty exemptions, and reduced pension contributions for miners.

Germany follows European Commission regulations regarding state aid. The federal government does not provide subsidies to coal-mining under article 5-3 (current production aid). In preparation for the closure of mines, most of the subsidies are now early-retirement schemes for coal workers.

RAG Debt Claims in North Rhine-Westphalia (data for 1991-98)

This item comprised annual payments made to *Ruhrkohle AG* (RAG) in order to cover part of its debt. RAG is Germany's biggest hard coal producer. Funding was split between the federal government and the North Rhine-Westphalia Land, with the former accounting for two-thirds of the total.

Sources: Bundesministerium der Finanzen (various years), Finanzministerium des Landes Nordrhein-Westfalen (various years).

Tag: DEU_dt_02

Adjustment Aid to EBV in North Rhine-Westphalia (data for 1991-93)

This item comprised annual payments made to *Eschweiler Bergwerks-Verein* (EBV) in order to help the company adjust its production capacity. Funding was split between the federal government and the North Rhine-Westphalia Land, with the former accounting for two-thirds of the total.

Sources: Bundesministerium der Finanzen (various years), Finanzministerium des Landes Nordrhein-Westfalen (various years).

Tag: DEU_dt_03

Adjustment Aid to RAG in North Rhine-Westphalia (data for 1991-94)

This item comprised annual payments made to *Ruhrkohle AG* (RAG) in order to help the company adjust its production capacity. Funding was split between the federal government and the North Rhine-Westphalia Land, with the former accounting for two-thirds of the total.

Sources: Bundesministerium der Finanzen (various years), Finanzministerium des Landes Nordrhein-Westfalen (various years).

Tag: DEU_dt_04

Aid to Cover Revenue Losses in Certain Areas in North Rhine-Westphalia (data for 1991-98)

This programme formed part of the so-called *Kohlepfennig* (Coal Penny) which was Germany's largest coal subsidy. The *Revierausgleich* component that is reported here was meant to compensate certain producers for revenue shortfalls arising from the sale of high-cost or low-quality coal to thermal power stations. Funding was split between the federal government and the North Rhine-Westphalia Land, with the former accounting for two-thirds of the total. Payments seem to have stopped in 1998.

Sources: Bundesministerium der Finanzen (various years), Finanzministerium des Landes Nordrhein-Westfalen (various years).

Tag: DEU_dt_05

Coking Coal Aid in North Rhine-Westphalia (data for 1991-97)

This programme – otherwise known as the *Kokskohlenbeihilfe* – was created in 1967 and allowed the steel industry to buy domestic coking coal at a price equal to that of imported coal. The entire gap between production prices and market prices was thus funded by both the federal and the Land government. Payments went on for several decades until they eventually ceased in 1998. Funding was split between the federal government and the North Rhine-Westphalia Land, with the former accounting for two-thirds of the total.

Since data from the Land budget are less disaggregated than are federal data, annual amounts mentioned under the heading "683 20 – 631" in the Land budget papers are allocated to Coking Coal Aid before 1998 and to Combined Aids after that. This approach yields numbers that are consistent with those reported in Storchmann (2005).

Sources: Bundesministerium der Finanzen (various years), Finanzministerium des Landes Nordrhein-Westfalen (various years).

Tag: DEU_dt_06

Third Power Generation Act (data for 1991-2002)

This programme formed the bulk of what was otherwise known as the *Kohlepfennig* (Coal Penny). Under this agreement, power plants were required to burn fixed amounts of domestic coal in exchange for financial compensation covering the cost difference between domestic coal and oil (or imported coal depending on the quantities of input). Such compensation was paid out of a separate federal fund called the *Ausgleichsfonds zur Sicherung des Steinkohleneinsatzes*, which in turn was financed through a levy imposed on electricity consumers (the so-called *Kohlepfennig*). The whole scheme was eventually abolished in the late 1990s.

The amounts we report are those appearing as *Zuschüsse an Kraftwerksunternehmen* in the federal fund's annual report to the Bundestag.

Sources: Deutscher Bundestag (various years).

Tag: DEU_dt_09

Fifth Power Generation Act (data for 1996-97)

This measure proved short-lived in that it was introduced in 1996 before being phased out in 1998, at which time it was replaced by a package of Combined Aids (see below). It was meant to maintain the provision of subsidies to domestic coal usage during the transition from the Third Power Generation Act to the new system of combined aids that subsequently gathered several old programmes into one overarching budgetary framework.

Sources: Bundesministerium der Finanzen (various years).

Tag: DEU_dt_10

Combined Aids in North Rhine-Westphalia (data for 1998-)

This aid package has been replacing and combining previous programmes such as the different versions of the Power Generation Act (see above) since 1998. It provides general support to the hard coal industry in order to ease its gradual decline. The programme still gives rise to significant federal and state annual payments.

Since data from the Land budget are less disaggregated than are federal data, annual amounts mentioned under the heading "683 20 – 631" in the Land budget papers are allocated to Coking Coal Aid before 1998 and to Combined Aids after that. This approach yields numbers that are consistent with those reported in Storchmann (2005).

Sources: Bundesministerium der Finanzen (various years), Finanzministerium des Landes Nordrhein-Westfalen (various years).

Tag: DEU_dt_11

Aids for Capacity Reduction in North Rhine-Westphalia (data for 1997-2001)

This programme started in 1997 to provide income support to coal-mining companies affected by the decline of the industry. It was meant to help firms adjust their production capacities. Funding was split between the federal government and the North Rhine-Westphalia Land, with the former accounting on average for about two thirds of the total. Since the measure was only a temporary one, payments ended following 2001.

Sources: Bundesministerium der Finanzen (various years), Finanzministerium des Landes Nordrhein-Westfalen (various years).

Tag: DEU_dt_12

Aid to Cover Revenue Losses in Certain Areas in Saarland (data for 1995-2000)

In the years between 1995 and 2000, Saarland provided *Saarbergwerke AG* with compensation for the revenue shortfalls arising from the sale of high-cost or low-quality coal (for a similar scheme in North Rhine-Westphalia, see DEU_dt_05).

Sources: Landtag des Saarlandes (2005).

Tag : DEU_dt_14

Aid to Saarbergwerke AG (data for 1997-2001)

In 1992, Saarland decided to provide financing for the management of *Saarbergwerke AG* in five installments over the years between 1997 and 2001.

Sources: Landtag des Saarlandes (2005).

Tag : DEU_dt_15

Capital Injections into Saarbergwerke AG (data for 1996-1998)

Saarland committed to "cleaning up" *Saarbergwerke*'s debt due to the fact that the state participated in the *Kokskohlebeihilfe* programme (see DEU_dt_06) for the years 1995 – 1997. *Saarbergwerke AG* was injected with capital in three installments in the years 1996 – 1998.

Sources: Landtag des Saarlandes (2005).

Tag : DEU_dt_16

Miners' Bonus (data for 1991-2008)

This measure provides miners with an income-tax deduction, thereby making wages in the mining industry more attractive. Although it targets labour inputs, the miners' bonus is specifically aimed at boosting hard coal production and therefore constitutes a production subsidy. Its creation dates back to 1956 and payments seem to have stopped around 2008.

Sources: Bundesministerium der Finanzen (various years).

Tag: DEU_te_03

Mining Royalty Exemption for Hard Coal (data for 1982-)

German mining companies are subject to a two-layered royalty system in which the federal government sets a guideline that *Länder* can decide to follow or not. The Federal Mining Act (BBergG) of 1982 sets the said guideline at 10% of the market value of production. The state of North-Rhine Westphalia which accounts for about 90% of Germany's hard coal production maintains royalties on hard coal at 0%.

Even though sub-national royalty rates vary between 0 and 40%, we use the federal guideline (10%) as the benchmark for our subsequent calculations. Production data at market value were not readily available so that we use coal-import prices from the IEA to estimate the market value of North-Rhine Westphalia's production of hard coal. Production data at the subnational level, however, do not distinguish between the different types of hard coal that are extracted. We therefore apply a weighted average of prices for coking coal and steam coal, with the former accounting for approximately 60% of hard coal production in Germany. It follows that our estimate is on the lower side for at least two reasons: (i) it relies on a low benchmark for royalty rates; and (ii) import prices for coal may well be lower than domestic prices.

Sources: Statistik der Kohlenwirtschaft e.V., UBA (2008).

Tag: DEU_te_06

Manufacturer Privilege (data for 1991-)

Coal, natural gas, and petroleum products used by energy companies as process energy (*i.e.* not as feedstock) are, under this measure, exempted from the energy tax that normally applies to final consumption of fossil fuels.

We use data from the IEA's Energy Balances for the transformation sector (excluding extraction and the nuclear industry) to allocate annual amounts reported in the *Subventionsbericht* (Subsidy Report) to the different fuels. These are predominantly refinery gas and fuel oil.

Sources: Bundesministerium der Finanzen (various years), UBA (2008).

Tag: DEU_te_07

Mining Royalty Exemption for Lignite (data for 1982-)

Coal-mining companies in Germany are subject to a two-layered royalty system in which the federal government sets a guideline that *Länder* can decide to follow or not. The Federal Mining Act (BBergG) of 1982 sets the said guideline at 10% of the market value of production. Most of Germany's *Länder* do not, however, levy such a charge on production of lignite

Even though sub-national royalty rates vary between 0 and 40%, we use the federal guideline (10%) as the benchmark for our subsequent calculations. Production data at market value were not readily available so that we use production volumes from *Statistik der Kohlenwirtschaft*. Obtaining prices for lignite is complex since it is not openly traded. Hence, there is no market price for it. We thus take the average of the prices reported by *Rheinbraun Brennstoff GmbH* and in both *Lausnitz* and *Mitteldeutschland*. This yields price estimates of about EUR 10 per tonne that are consistent with the values reported in UBA (2008). Data are not available after 2008.

Sources: Statistik der Kohlenwirtschaft e.V., UBA (2008).

Tag: DEU_te_14

Consumer Support Estimate

Energy-Tax Breaks for Agriculture and Manufacturing (data for 1999-)

This programme provides certain users in the agriculture, forestry and manufacturing sectors with a lower rate of tax on heating fuels. The latter include heating oil, natural gas and LPG. The measure was introduced in 1999 along with the so-called *Ökologische Steuerreform* (Ecological Tax Reform) and has since gone through some changes regarding the rates that apply to each fuel.

We use data from the IEA's Energy Balances for the agricultural and manufacturing sectors to allocate annual amounts reported in the Subventionsbericht (Subsidy Report) to all three fuels. Since both this measure and the "Tax Relief for Fuels Used in Power Generation" were reported under the same budget line prior to 2005, we use their respective shares of the total budgetary amount in 2005 to separate them into two different items.

Sources: Bundesministerium der Finanzen (various years), UBA (2008).

Tag: DEU_te_01

Peak Equalisation Scheme (data for 2001-)

This measure is closely related to the Energy Tax Breaks for Agriculture and Manufacturing (see above) in that it targets the same fuels and sectors. Following the introduction of a new "ecotax" in 1999, pension contributions were reduced as a way to compensate German companies for the higher taxes paid on energy inputs. The measure therefore provides certain companies with an additional refund on their energy tax bills in cases where the decrease in pension contributions does not prove large enough to offset the new tax burden. We only consider here the refunds that pertain to heating fuels as opposed to those that pertain to electricity, that is, we report the *Mineralölsteuer* (or the *Energiesteuer*) part and not the *Stromsteuer* part.

We use data from the IEA's Energy Balances for the agricultural and manufacturing sectors to allocate annual amounts reported in the *Subventionsbericht* (Subsidy Report) to all three fuels. Tax expenditures data prior to 2001 are not available.

Sources: Bundesministerium der Finanzen (various years), UBA (2008).

Tag: DEU_te_02

Tax Relief for Fuels Used in Power Generation (data for 1999-)

This measure, introduced in 1999, exempts fuels used in power generation from the regular energy tax which applies elsewhere. Power plants with an output of more than 2 megawatts and CHP plants with an efficiency rate of at least 70% are concerned.

We use data from the IEA's Energy Balances for both power and CHP plants to allocate annual amounts reported in the *Subventionsbericht* (Subsidy Report) to the different fuels. Prior to 2007, the measure encompassed all fuels used for power generation. From 2007, however, the measure has been applied to coal only. We allocate annual amounts accordingly which results in coal getting the lion's share with about 90% of the total on average for the period between 1999 and 2006 and 100% for the period between 2007 and 2010. Since both this measure and the "Energy Tax Breaks for Agriculture and Manufacturing" were reported under the same budget line prior to 2005, we use their respective shares of the total budgetary amount in 2005 to separate them into two different items.

Sources: Bundesministerium der Finanzen (various years), UBA (2008).

Tag: DEU_te_04

Tax Relief for Energy-Intensive Processes (data for 2006-)

This tax expenditure exempts certain energy-intensive processes and techniques from the energy tax that has been levied since 1999. The measure itself was, however, only introduced in August 2006 as part of the *Energiesteuergesetz* (Energy Tax Act). It applies mostly to particular processes in the steel and chemical sectors and is meant to maintain the competitiveness of those industries. We only consider here the refunds that pertain to fossil fuels as opposed to those that pertain to electricity, that is, we report the *Mineralölsteuer* (or the *Energiesteuer*) part and not the *Stromsteuer* part).

We use detailed IEA estimates (unpublished) to allocate annual amounts reported in the Subventionsbericht (Subsidy Report) to all different fuels. These are mostly natural gas and coal.

Sources: Bundesministerium der Finanzen (various years), UBA (2008).

Tag: DEU_te_05

Fuel-Tax Exemption for Commercial Aviation (data for 1991-)

Since 1953, commercial air carriers in Germany have been exempted from the energy tax that is usually levied on consumption of mineral fuels. The concession is explicitly listed in the Ministry of Finance's *Subventionsbericht* (Subsidy Report) and refers only to domestic flights given that international aviation remains subject to the Chicago convention of 1956 restricting taxation of jet fuel.

Sources: Bundesministerium der Finanzen (various years), UBA (2008).

Tag: DEU_te_08

Fuel-Tax Exemption for Internal Waterway Transportation (data for 1991-)

This concession exempts internal waterway transportation from paying the fuel tax that normally applies to consumption of diesel. The measure in its current version dates back to 1962 and is still active as of 2010.

Sources: Bundesministerium der Finanzen (various years), UBA (2008).

Tag: DEU_te_09

Tax Relief for Public Transportation (data for 2000-)

Not much information is available in the Subventionsbericht (Subsidy Report) for this measure. It was introduced in 2000 and apparently reduces the fuel tax levied on public passenger transportation. The legal basis for it can be found in *EnergieStG §
56* where it is stated that the measure applies not only to motor fuels but also to natural gas and LPG.

Accordingly, we allocated the annual amounts on the basis of the IEA's Energy Balances for the road transport sector.

Sources: Bundesministerium der Finanzen (various years), UBA (2008).

Tag: DEU_te_10

Tax Relief for LPG and Natural Gas (data for 1996-)

Consumption of LPG and natural gas in the transport sector is, under this measure, subject to relief from the fuel tax. Although the concession was introduced in 1995 and initially targeted vehicles used in public transportation only, it was subsequently broadened in April 1999 to include all vehicles.

We allocated the measure entirely to LPG given the very low share of natural gas used as fuel. Indeed, natural gas does not even enter the IEA's balances for road transport.

Sources: Bundesministerium der Finanzen (various years), UBA (2008).

Tag: DEU_te_11

Refund for Diesel Used in Agriculture and Forestry (data for 1991-)

This measure was created in 1951 and provides both agriculture and forestry with a tax rebate on diesel fuel. It was renamed in 2001 when it was moved from the transfers category (*Gasölverbilligung*) to the tax expenditure category (*Agrardieselvergütung*) in the *Subventionsbericht* (Subsidy Report). Since 2005, refunds have been capped at 10 000 litres and a maximum refund of EUR 350 per year, thereby limiting annual payments. It is also important to note that the energy tax in Germany is distinct from the road tax.

Sources: Bundesministerium der Finanzen (various years), UBA (2008).

Tag: DEU_te_12

Fuel-Tax Rebate for Horticultural Work (data for 2001-04)

This measure was introduced for a period of four years only, starting in 2001 and ending in 2004. It provided the German horticultural sector with a fuel tax rebate on the heating fuel used in greenhouses.

Sources: Bundesministerium der Finanzen (various years).

Tag: DEU_te_13

General Services Support Estimate

Aid for Water Contamination (data for 1991-99)

This programme started in 1969 and earmarked significant annual expenditure for undertaking rehabilitation works at old mining sites. These mainly aimed at treating contaminated ground-water. Funding was split between the federal government and the North Rhine-Westphalia Land; contributions from the latter were growing over time from about a third in the first three years to about half of the total by the time the scheme ended. Reporting in budget documents stops after 1999. The measure is allocated to the GSSE as it does not increase current production or consumption of coal.

Sources: Bundesministerium der Finanzen (various years), Finanzministerium des Landes Nordrhein-Westfalen (various years).

Tag: DEU_dt_01

Early Retirement Payments in North Rhine-Westphalia (data for 1991-)

This programme provides older, unemployed coal miners with early retirement payments until they become eligible for regular pension payments. It goes back to 1972 and is still giving rise to significant annual expenditure. Funding is split between the federal government and the North Rhine-Westphalia Land, with the former accounting for two-thirds of the total. The measure is, however, allocated to the GSSE as it does not increase current production or consumption of coal.

Sources: Bundesministerium der Finanzen (various years), Finanzministerium des Landes Nordrhein-Westfalen (various years).

Tag: DEU_dt_07

Re-Adaptation Aid, Art. 56 ECSC (data for 1991-2006)

This measure was introduced in 1960 to help workers affected by the decline of the coal industry (along with the ore and steel industry) in the context of Art. 56 of the European Coal and Steel Community (ECSC) Treaty of Paris. It aims at reallocating the workforce away from these declining sectors through the use of training programmes and various allowances. Payments from the federal government ceased a few years after the Treaty of Paris had expired back in 2002. We allocated the measure to the GSSE as it does not increase current production or consumption of coal.

Sources: Bundesministerium der Finanzen (various years).

Tag: DEU_dt_08

Rehabilitation of Lignite Mining Sites in East Germany (data for 1993-)

Rehabilitation of lignite mining sites (*Braunkohlesanierung*) began in 1990 and was undertaken together by the federal government and East-German "Lignite states" (*Braunkohleländer*) – Saxony, Brandenburg, Saxony-Anhalt, and Thüringen – which all provided substantial financial resources for the programme.

The programme will be in operation at least until the end of 2012, as stipulated by the current federal document regarding the financing of rehabilitation of lignite mining sites in the years between 2008 and 2012 (*VA IV Braunkohlesanierung*). The scheme encompasses a wide range of activities, including rehabilitating over 200 mining pits in 31 lignite mining areas, the vast majority of which were turned into lakes; securing over 1 000 km of embankment; liquidating the assets of briquette factories, power plants and industrial boilers; restoring water balances in regions affected by mining; dealing with the consequences of mine flooding; collecting and evaluating information on about 1 230 potentially contaminated mining sites, and undertaking necessary remedial measures.

As stated by the federal government, the total cost of running the rehabilitation of lignite mining sites programmes in the years between 1991 and 2007 amounted to over EUR 8 billion paid jointly by the federal government and the abovementioned East-German *Länder*. The federal government and the "Lignite states" committed to securing over EUR 1 billion for the programme for the years between 2008 and 2012.

Aggregate data estimates for *Braunkohlesanierung* are available for the years between 1993 and 2012. Data estimates for the period between 2008 and 2012 are appropriations. In 1993, financing came solely from spending earmarked for job creation (*Arbeitsbeschaffugsmaßnahmen*). Estimates for the period between 1993 and 2007 cover the total cost of running the rehabilitation programme, whereas the appropriations are computed excluding the cost of labour (*Lohnkostenzuschüsse*) as it is said to be difficult to forecast. Since this measure does not increase current production or consumption of coal, we allocate it to the GSSE.

Sources: Bundesregierung (2008), Bundesregierung (2009).

Tag: DEU_dt_13

Reimbursement of "Legacy Payments" in Saarland (data for 1995-1998)

Until 1998, Saarland committed to financing the "legacy payments" of its hard-coal mines. Such payments comprised the costs of rehabilitation of mining sites and water-retention measures.

Since this measure does not increase current production or consumption of coal, we allocate it to the GSSE.

Sources: Landtag des Saarlandes (2005).

Tag: DEU_dt_17

Early Retirement Payments in Saarland (data for 1995-2004)

Saarland committed to covering one-third of early retirement payments for miners who suffered from mine decommissioning and capacity-adjustment measures. Saarland is expected to continue financing this share of early-retirement payments until 2012. The federal government has already committed to covering the full cost of the measure from the beginning of 2012.

Saarland also participates in financing retraining of laid-off workers from the mining sector. Since this measure is co-financed by the European Social Fund, we do not include it in the inventory. Total spending for this item in the years 1995-2004 amounted to about EUR 11 million.

Data are available for the period 1995-2004. Since social payments for laid-off workers do not increase current production or consumption of coal, we allocate this item to the GSSE.

Sources: Landtag des Saarlandes (2005).

Tag: DEU_dt_18

References

Policies or transfers

Bundesministerium der Finanzen (various years) *Subventionsberichte*, Available at: http://www.bundesfinanzministerium.de/.

Bundesregierung (2008) *Antwort der Bundesregierung auf eine Kleine Anfrage von der Fraktion Die Linke zur Fortführung der Braunkohle-Sanierung in den Ländern Brandenburg, Sachsen- Anhalt, Sachsen und Thüringen in den Jahren 2008 bis 2012, BT-Drs. 16/8969 vom 24.04.2008*, Available at: http://dip21.bundestag.de/dip21/btd/16/089/1608969.pdf.

Bundesregierung (2009), *Information zur Sanierung der Altlasten des Braunkohlebergbaus in den neuen Ländern, Stand: 20.05.2009*, Available at: http://www.bmu.de/files/pdfs/allgemein/application/pdf/braunkohle_lang.pdf.

Bundesregierung (2010) *Antwort der Bundesregierung auf eine Kleine Anfrage von der Fraktion Die Linke zur Zukunft der Braunkohlesanierung in den Ländern Brandenburg, Sachsen, Sachsen- Anhalt und Thüringen ab dem Jahr 2013, BT-Drs. 17/469 vom 19.01.2010*, Available at: http://dip21.bundestag.de/dip21/btd/17/004/1700469.pdf.

Deutscher Bundestag (various years) *Rechnungslegungen über das Sondervermögen des Bundes "Ausgleichsfonds zur Sicherung des Steinkohleneinsatzes"*, Available at: http://www.bundestag.de/.

Finanzministerium des Landes Nordrhein-Westfalen (various years) *Haushaltspläne*, Available at: http://www.fm.nrw.de/.

Landtag des Saarlandes (2005), *Antwort zu der Anfrage de Abgeordneten Christoph Hartmann (FDP), Betr.: Landeszuwendungen für den Bergbau,* Available at: http://www.landtag-saar.de/dms13/Aw0335.pdf.

Storchmann, Karl (2005) 'The rise and fall of German hard coal subsidies', *Energy Policy*, Vol. 33, No. 11, pp.1469-1492.

UBA (2008), Environmentally Harmful Subsidies in Germany, UmweltBundesAmt, Available at: http://www.umweltdaten.de/publikationen/fpdf-l/3896.pdf.

Energy statistics

IEA, *Energy Balances of OECD Countries*, 2010 Edition, International Energy Agency, Paris.

Figure 7.2.   Shares of fossil-fuel support by fuel, average for 2008-10 – Germany

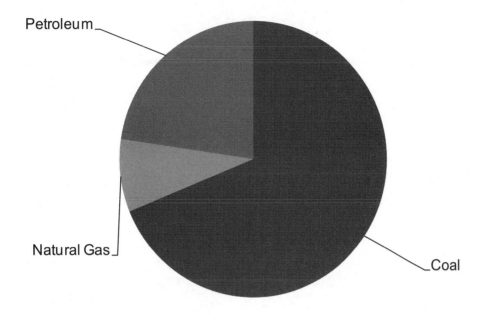

Source: OECD.

Figure 7.3.   Shares of fossil-fuel support by indicator, average for 2008-10 – Germany

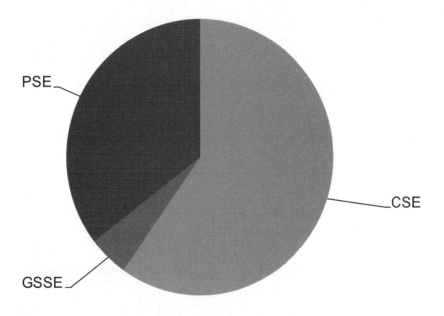

Source: OECD.

Table 7.1. Summary of fossil-fuel support to coal – Germany

(Millions of euros, nominal)

Support element	Jurisdiction	Avg 2000-02	Avg 2008-10	2008	2009	2010p
Producer Support Estimate						
Support to unit returns						
Third Power Generation Act	Federal	14.47	n.a.	n.a.	n.a.	n.a.
Income support						
Combined Aids	NW	3 824.33	1 953.69	2 332.32	1 781.27	1 747.48
Aids for Capacity Reduction	NW	n.a.	n.a.	n.a.	n.a.	n.a.
Aid to Saarbergwerke AG	SR	n.a.	n.a.	n.a.	n.a.	n.a.
Support for intermediate inputs						
Manufacturer Privilege	Federal	6.09	8.90	8.29	9.21	9.21
Support for land (*e.g.* royalty concessions)						
Mining Royalty Exemption for Hard Coal	NW	100.42	320.96	410.45	276.22	276.22
Mining Royalty Exemption for Lignite	NW SR	185.46	198.51	198.51	198.51	198.51
Support for labour						
Miners' Bonus	Federal	34.67	n.a.	1.00	n.a.	n.a.
Consumer Support Estimate						
Consumption						
Tax Relief for Fuels Used in Power Generation	Federal	654.15	2 266.33	2 196.00	2 303.00	2 300.00
Tax Relief for Energy-Intensive Processes	Federal	n.a.	204.64	204.17	204.17	205.56
General Services Support Estimate						
Early Retirement Payments	NW	180.38	165.08	171.61	163.72	159.91
Re-Adaptation Aid Art. 56 ECSC	Federal	22.10	n.a.	n.a.	n.a.	n.a.
Early Retirement Payments in SR	SR	7.68	n.c.	..	..	..

Note: Tax expenditures for any given country are measured with reference to a benchmark tax treatment that is generally specific to that country. Consequently, the estimates contained in the table above are not necessarily comparable with estimates for other countries. In addition, because of the potential interaction between them, the summation of individual measures for a specific country may be problematic. The allocation of particular measures across fuel types was done by the OECD Secretariat based on the IEA's Energy Balances.

Source: OECD.

INVENTORY OF ESTIMATED BUDGETARY SUPPORT AND TAX EXPENDITURES FOR FOSSIL FUELS © OECD 2011

Table 7.2. Summary of fossil-fuel support to petroleum – Germany

(Millions of euros, nominal)

Support element	Jurisdiction	Avg 2000-02	Avg 2008-10	2008	2009	2010p
Producer Support Estimate						
Support for intermediate inputs						
Manufacturer Privilege	Federal	225.54	247.51	230.44	256.04	256.04
Consumer Support Estimate						
Consumption						
Energy Tax Breaks for Agriculture and Manufacturing	Federal	24.44	33.36	33.19	33.40	33.50
Peak Equalisation Scheme	Federal	2.05	16.89	17.07	15.38	18.23
Tax Relief for Fuels Used in Power Generation	Federal	6.14	0.00	0.00	0.00	0.00
Tax Relief for Energy-Intensive Processes	Federal	n.a.	142.92	142.59	142.59	143.57
Fuel Tax Exemption for Commercial Aviation	Federal	357.33	660.00	640.00	660.00	680.00
Fuel Tax Exemption for Internal Waterway Transportation	Federal	195.00	147.00	118.00	157.00	166.00
Tax Relief for Public Transportation	Federal	31.45	64.43	62.87	63.81	66.62
Tax Relief for LPG and Natural Gas	Federal	20.00	156.67	120.00	160.00	190.00
Refund for Diesel Used in Agriculture and Forestry	Federal	298.37	283.33	135.00	320.00	395.00
Fuel Tax Rebate for Horticultural Work	Federal	n.a.	n.a.	n.a.	n.a.	n.a.
General Services Support Estimate (n.a.)						

Note: Tax expenditures for any given country are measured with reference to a benchmark tax treatment that is generally specific to that country. Consequently, the estimates contained in the table above are not necessarily comparable with estimates for other countries. In addition, because of the potential interaction between them, the summation of individual measures for a specific country may be problematic. The allocation of particular measures across fuel types was done by the OECD Secretariat based on the IEA's Energy Balances.

Source: OECD.

Table 7.3. Summary of fossil-fuel support to natural gas – Germany

(Millions of euros, nominal)

Support element	Jurisdiction	Avg 2000-02	Avg 2008-10	2008	2009	2010p
Producer Support Estimate						
Support for intermediate inputs						
Manufacturer Privilege	Federal	7.83	13.06	12.16	13.51	13.51
Consumer Support Estimate						
Consumption						
Energy Tax Breaks for Agriculture and Manufacturing	Federal	153.36	283.30	281.81	283.60	284.50
Peak Equalisation Scheme	Federal	12.95	143.44	144.93	130.62	154.77
Tax Relief for Fuels Used in Power Generation	Federal	50.91	0.00	0.00	0.00	0.00
Tax Relief for Energy-Intensive Processes	Federal	n.a.	223.18	222.68	222.68	224.20
General Services Support Estimate (n.a.)						

Note: Tax expenditures for any given country are measured with reference to a benchmark tax treatment that is generally specific to that country. Consequently, the estimates contained in the table above are not necessarily comparable with estimates for other countries. In addition, because of the potential interaction between them, the summation of individual measures for a specific country may be problematic. The allocation of particular measures across fuel types was done by the OECD Secretariat based on the IEA's Energy Balances.

Source: OECD.

Chapter 8

Hungary

This chapter identifies, documents, and provides estimates of the various budgetary transfers and tax expenditures that relate to the production or use of fossil fuels in *Hungary*. An overview of *Hungary's* energy economy is first given to place the measures listed into context. A data-documentation section then describes those measures in a systematic way. Whenever possible, the description details a measure's formal beneficiary, its eligibility criteria and functioning, and the fuels whose production or use stand to benefit from the measure. The chapter ends with a set of charts and tables that provide, subject to availability, quantitative information and estimates for the various measures listed.

8.   HUNGARY

Energy resources and market structure

Hungary has modest resources of oil and gas, but production has peaked and is expected to continue to decline. Well over 80% of the country's requirements of oil, and almost 80% of its natural gas, are imported, with virtually all of these imports coming from Russia. Over 60% of the coal used in Hungary is produced indigenously, though coal accounts for only 10% of the country's total primary energy supply. Natural gas is the leading fuel in the energy mix, accounting for 37%, followed by oil (27%) and nuclear power (16%). Combustible renewables account for another 6%; modern renewable technologies, such as wind and solar energy, make a negligible contribution. Nuclear energy and gas each account for over one-third of Hungary's electricity generation, and gas for another quarter. Over 15% of the country's electricity supply is imported, mainly from Slovakia.

There is a mixture of public and private ownership of energy assets in Hungary. MOL, the former national oil company, which was privatised in the 1990s, dominates the upstream oil and gas industry and operates the national gas transmission system. Natural-gas sales to captive customers are undertaken by five regional monopolies, all of which are foreign-owned (by E.On, Gaz de France and Italgas). The municipality of Budapest owns half of the Budapest Supply Company, while the other half is owned by RWE.

MVM, a fully state-owned company, is the central institution in the Hungarian electricity market. It controls approximately 80% of electricity production and sales in Hungary, either directly or indirectly. It also holds 99.95% of Paks NPP, which operates the country's sole nuclear power plant; 99.7% of the former transmission system operator, National Powerline; 100% of the system operator and transmission network owner and operator, MAVIR; and 80% of the Vértes power plant, of which local authorities hold the remaining shares. MVM also owns 25% plus one share of all power-generating companies privatised in the mid-1990s; is the majority owner of several co-generation companies and, through a subsidiary, operates the reserve power plants to ensure reliable power. An MVM subsidiary is also one of the leading trading companies on the competitive power market.

The government has transposed all relevant EU directives on opening up electricity and gas markets to competition, but has done little to restrict the power of the incumbents in electricity and gas. As a result, the development of effective competition in both sectors is below that which would be possible under the changed legislation.

Prices, taxes and support mechanisms

Oil product and coal prices in Hungary are deregulated and are set by the market. The regulator, the Hungarian Energy Office, sets prices for transportation tariffs in electricity and natural gas networks, regulated retail prices for electricity, gas and heat to households and small business consumers, and wholesale electricity prices paid to generators operating under a long-term power purchase agreement or eligible for feed-in tariffs. Small consumers are allowed to move back and forth between the regulated and the open market. Regulated natural gas end-user prices are the same throughout the country, regardless of distance from the main supply points. They are set according to a formula that takes account of import prices plus 8.5% for the operation of the system and other non-gas-supply costs. This effectively keeps regulated prices well below those in the open market.

All fuels and energy services are subject to value-added tax (VAT). Excise taxes are levied on sales to industry of transport fuels, natural gas and electricity; households pay excise taxes on transport fuels and LPG.

Gas and heat prices to end-users are subsidised both through the regulated pricing formula and an explicit subsidy paid to public gas suppliers who must credit it explicitly on the bills to households they supply directly, or credit it to the account of district heat suppliers who supply heat to households, in proportion to the number of households served. The subsidy is paid on a per-household basis, with no consideration for the actual financial situation of the household, or the status of occupancy.

Since 2000, no direct government aid has been extended to coal production. However, indirect aid was given to hard-coal production through a very favourable power purchase agreement, under which the Oroszlány power station was operating. Until 2006, these subsidies were implicit in the power prices paid to the station's owner, which also operates the Márkushegy mine that supplies coal to the station. In 2005, the European Commission authorised a restructuring package under which grants to coal mines would be phased out by 2010. A direct support system for coal is now in operation, under which the funds are paid by electricity consumers through the electricity tariff, and a levy modelled on the former German "Coal Penny" was added to the transmission tariff on 6 January 2006. In addition, direct government assistance continues to be given to support mine closures and rehabilitate mining areas.

Data documentation

General notes

The fiscal year in Hungary coincides with the calendar year.

Producer Support Estimate

Coal Pennies (data for 2008-)

Price support is provided to coal producers through a mechanism similar to the German "Coal Penny". The scheme consists of levies that are paid by final electricity consumers to finance purchases of coal-generated power by electricity companies. Coal-generated power is generally more expensive owing to the low competitiveness of the coal-mining industry.

We allocate the measure entirely to lignite.

Sources: Government of Hungary, Government Decisions No. 3329/1990, 3530/1992, 3439/1993.

Tag: HUN_dt_01

Consumer Support Estimate

Fuel-Tax Refund for Railways (data for 2007-)

Railways operating in Hungary are being refunded the excise tax paid on purchases of diesel fuel.

Sources: Ministry of Finance (various years).

Tag: HUN_te_01

Fuel-Tax Refund for Agriculture (data for 1990-)

The off-road use of diesel in the agricultural sector in Hungary is subject to refunds from the excise tax normally levied on sales of petroleum products.

Sources: Ministry of Finance (various years), OECD.

Tag: HUN_te_02

Household Natural-Gas and Heat Subsidies (data for 2008-)

This programme was created in 2003 to subsidise the consumption of natural gas by households. Since most district heating in Hungary makes an extensive use of natural gas, it was decided at the time that the programme would also cover the residential consumption of heat. Starting in 2010, support is now restricted to heat only.

We allocate the measure entirely to natural gas for the years prior to 2010. Starting in 2010, we then use data from the IEA's Energy Balances (for the heat generation sector) to allocate the amounts reported to the different fuels involved in heat generation.

Sources: Government of Hungary, Government Orders No. 113/2003, 289/2007, 238/2008, Hungarian Energy Office Order No. 238/2008, IEA.

Tag: HUN_dt_02

Reduced Rate of VAT for District Heating (data for 2009-)

Sales of district heat are subject to a lower rate of VAT. Since about 98% of heat in Hungary comes from fossil fuels, we consider this measure as supporting consumption.

We allocate the amounts reported to the different types of fuel on the basis of the IEA's Energy Balances for the heat generation sector.

Sources: Ministry of Finance (various years), IEA.

Tag: HUN_te_03

General Services Support Estimate

Support for Mine Decommissioning (no data available)

Support is provided by the government of Hungary for the decommissioning of certain state-owned coal mines. Direct budgetary transfers range between HUF 1 and 2 billion a year.

We allocate this measure to the GSSE since it does not support current production or consumption of coal. No detailed annual estimates are available for this programme.

Sources: Ministry of Finance (various years).

Early-Retirement Payments for Miners (no data available)

Coal miners in Hungary are entitled to receive social transfers like early-retirement payments and "coal emolument supplements". These transfers are meant to alleviate the social costs associated with the closure of several coal-mining sites.

We allocate this measure to the GSSE since it does not support current production or consumption of coal. No detailed annual estimates are available for this programme but the 2007 State Budget Act mentions a number close to HUF 6.55 billion (USD 31.5 million).

Sources: Ministry of Finance (various years).

References

Policies or transfers

Ministry of Finance (various years), Government of Hungary, Available at:
http://www.kormany.hu/hu/nemzetgazdasagi-miniszterium.

OECD, *Producer and Consumer Support Estimates database*, Monitoring Farm Support and Evaluating Policy, Available at:
http://www.oecd.org/topic/0,3699,en_2649_33797_1_1_1_1_37401,00.html.

Energy statistics

IEA, *Energy Balances of OECD Countries*, 2010 Edition, International Energy Agency, Paris.

Figure 8.1.   Shares of fossil-fuel support by fuel, average for 2008-10 – Hungary

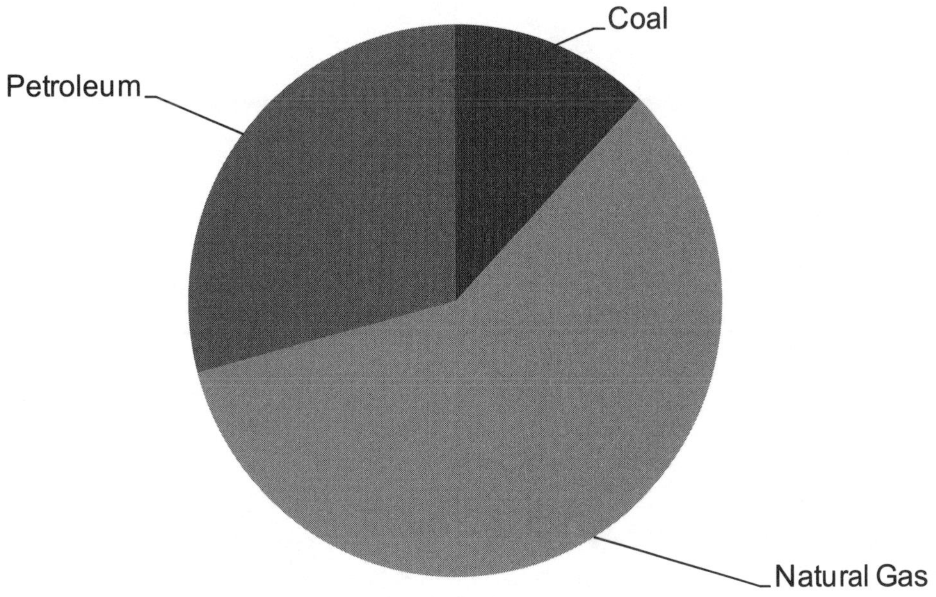

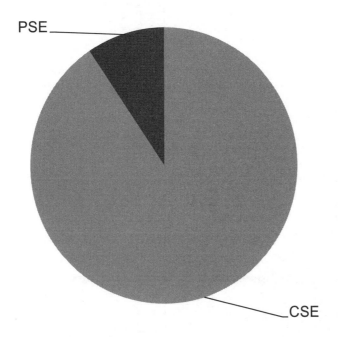

Source: OECD.

Figure 8.2.   Shares of fossil-fuel support by indicator, average for 2008-10 – Hungary

Source: OECD.

Table 8.1. Summary of fossil-fuel support to coal – Hungary

(Millions of Hungarian forints, nominal)

Support element	Jurisdiction	Avg 2000-02	Avg 2008-10	2008	2009	2010p
Producer Support Estimate						
Support to unit returns						
Coal Pennies	–	n.c.	9 266.67	10 000.00	8 900.00	8 900.00
Consumer Support Estimate						
Consumption						
Household Natural Gas and Heat Subsidies	–	n.a.	1 477.25	0.00	0.00	4 431.75
Reduced Rate of VAT for District Heating	–	n.a.	n.a.	n.a.	443.17	3 013.59
General Services Support Estimate (n.a.)						

Note: Tax expenditures for any given country are measured with reference to a benchmark tax treatment that is generally specific to that country. Consequently, the estimates contained in the table above are not necessarily comparable with estimates for other countries. In addition, because of the potential interaction between them, the summation of individual measures for a specific country may be problematic. The allocation of particular measures across fuel types was done by the OECD Secretariat based on the IEA's Energy Balances.

Source: OECD.

Table 8.2. Summary of fossil-fuel support to petroleum – Hungary

(Millions of Hungarian forints, nominal)

Support element	Jurisdiction	Avg 2000-02	Avg 2008-10	2008	2009	2010p
Producer Support Estimate (n.a.)						
Consumer Support Estimate						
Consumption						
Household Natural Gas and Heat Subsidies	–	n.a.	851.33	0.00	0.00	2 553.98
Fuel Tax Refund for Railways	–	n.c.	7 000.00	7 000.00	7 000.00	7 000.00
Fuel Tax Refund for Agriculture	–	16 313.00	20 367.67	17 601.00	21 465.00	22 037.00
Reduced Rate of VAT for District Heating	–	n.a.	n.a.	n.a.	255.40	1 736.71
General Services Support Estimate (n.a.)						

Note: Tax expenditures for any given country are measured with reference to a benchmark tax treatment that is generally specific to that country. Consequently, the estimates contained in the table above are not necessarily comparable with estimates for other countries. In addition, because of the potential interaction between them, the summation of individual measures for a specific country may be problematic. The allocation of particular measures across fuel types was done by the OECD Secretariat based on the IEA's Energy Balances.

Source: OECD.

Table 8.3. Summary of fossil-fuel support to natural gas – Hungary

(Millions of Hungarian forints, nominal)

Support element	Jurisdiction	Avg 2000-02	Avg 2008-10	2008	2009	2010p
Producer Support Estimate (n.a.)						
Consumer Support Estimate						
Consumption						
Household Natural Gas and Heat Subsidies		–	53 780.54	82 000.00	62 000.00	17 341.63
Reduced Rate of VAT for District Heating		–	n.a.	n.a.	1 734.16	11 792.31
General Services Support Estimate (n.a.)						

Note: Tax expenditures for any given country are measured with reference to a benchmark tax treatment that is generally specific to that country. Consequently, the estimates contained in the table above are not necessarily comparable with estimates for other countries. In addition, because of the potential interaction between them, the summation of individual measures for a specific country may be problematic. The allocation of particular measures across fuel types was done by the OECD Secretariat based on the IEA's Energy Balances.

Source: OECD.

Chapter 9

Iceland

This chapter identifies, documents, and provides estimates of the various budgetary transfers and tax expenditures that relate to the production or use of fossil fuels in *Iceland*. An overview of *Iceland's* energy economy is first given to place the measures listed into context. A data-documentation section then describes those measures in a systematic way. Whenever possible, the description details a measure's formal beneficiary, its eligibility criteria and functioning, and the fuels whose production or use stand to benefit from the measure. The chapter ends with a set of charts and tables that provide, subject to availability, quantitative information and estimates for the various measures listed.

9. ICELAND

Energy resources and market structure

Iceland is a mountainous island straddling the mid-Atlantic ridge. These geographic features have endowed it with an abundance of renewable energy. Currently, around 85% of its primary energy supply, and almost 100% of its electricity, is obtained from hydro-electric power or geothermal heat. The country produces no fossil fuels, and hence imports all its petroleum-derived transport fuels. Only a small amount of fossil fuels are used for industrial processes.

Iceland converted from oil to geothermal district heating during the period 1940 to 1975. Today, 87% of space heating comes from geothermal resources and most of the rest is provided by renewable electricity. The government continues to support the increased direct use of geothermal heat for district heating in small communities (some 130 of which operate outdoor swimming pools), through long-term, low-interest loans.

Private companies supply Iceland with petroleum products; state-owned companies dominate the rest of Iceland's energy economy. Landsvirkjun (the National Power Company), the largest electricity producer in Iceland, is owned by the Icelandic State (50%) and two of the country's largest municipalities, Reykjavík (45%) and Akureyri (5%). The company sells its production wholesale to local utilities and directly to power-intensive industries. It also owns and operates the national grid. Reykjavík Energy, which is municipally owned, provides hot water to half of Iceland's population, and also generates electricity using turbines powered by geothermal steam.

At 50 000 kWh a year, Iceland's per-capita electrical consumption is by far the highest in the world. More than 85% of this consumption is by industry, dominated by aluminium smelting. Less than one-fifth of Iceland's economically and environmentally viable potential for electrical production from renewable energy resources (estimated at over 50 TWh/year) is currently being harnessed, however. A major aim of the government is to displace fossil fuels used for transport with electrical energy, either directly (through, for example, battery-powered vehicles) or indirectly through the production of hydrogen. In 1998 the Icelandic Parliament set a specific target of converting the country's vehicle and fishing fleets to hydrogen produced from renewable energy by no later than 2050. (In 2011 the target date was moved forward, to 2020.) With this aim in mind, Icelandic New Energy (INE), was founded in 1999 to promote the use of hydrogen fuel in Iceland. The company is 51% owned by VistOrka – a consortium of investment funds, the Ministry of Industry and Commerce, Iceland's major energy companies, and the University of Iceland – with the remainder owned by Daimler, Norsk Hydro and Shell Hydrogen.

Prices, taxes and support mechanisms

With the exception of petroleum products, energy prices are set by government-owned utilities in Icleand. Electricity for general users is sold by licensed traders (of which there are currently seven), who are selected by the users and buy the energy from production companies, most on fixed agreement of 1 to 12 years duration from Landsvirkjun, or from their own production companies. Electricity contracts for power-intensive projects are concluded on a long-term basis (frequently of 20 years duration or more), and in many cases the price component of such contracts indexes the price of electricity to the price of the output of the business in question, *e.g.* the price of aluminium. These contracts are frequently structured on a "take-or-pay" basis, and a special tariff applies to the fee for transmitting electricity to power-intensive industries. Energy prices for power-intensive industries are not publicly available but all power contracts with such industries are notified to the EFTA (European Free Trade Association) Surveillance Authority, which in 2010 concluded that the contracts were in line with the market investor principle and did not involve state aid.

The use of petroleum fuels in transport is taxed directly and indirectly through several taxes. Motor vehicles are charged an excise duty at the port of import. The excise duty levied on private cars is based on the engine capacity, measured in cubic centimetres: 30% for vehicles with an engine capacity up to 2000 cm^3, and 45% for vehicles with larger engines. Reduced rates are levied on vehicles intended for use as taxis and rental cars, and for cars that are capable of being partially fuelled with electricity or methane. Excise taxes are completely waived for most large buses, goods trucks and off-road vehicles; cars exclusively used for motor sport and for rescue operations; and cars exclusively fuelled with electricity or hydrogen. Owners of all vehicles, no matter how fuelled, also pay a semi-annual weight tax and disposal charge. The weight tax is ISK 6.83 for the first 1 000 kg of vehicle weight, ISK 9.21 for the next 2 000 kg and ISK 2 277 for each tonne above 3 000 kg. A disposal charge of ISK 350 is levied on each vehicle twice a year, payable for fifteen years from the date of the first registration of the vehicle in the country. Once the vehicle is delivered for scrap, a ISK 15 000 refund is paid to the owner. There is also a weight-distance tax on large vehicles.

All motor fuels used by road vehicles are subject to a road tax (*þungaskattur*), which is ISK 42.23 per litre for gasoline and ISK 45 per litre for diesel, as well as the normal VAT (*virðisaukaskattur*) of 24.5%. Off-road use, and diesel fuel used for space heating is exempt from this tax. Liquefied petroleum gas (LPG), as well as liquefied and compressed natural gas, receives a complete exemption from the excise tax. Aviation fuel and kerosene also benefit from lower rates of duty.

A reduced rate of VAT applies to most foodstuffs and a number of other items, hot water delivered by pipes, electricity, oil for space heating, and water for swimming pools. As of 1 March 2007, this lower rate was reduced to 7%.

Data documentation

General notes

The fiscal year in Iceland coincides with the calendar year.

Consumer Support Estimate

Lower VAT Rate on Oil for Space Heating (no data available)

A reduced rate of VAT is applied to oil for space heating. The difference (7% compared with the normal rate of 24.5% is) applied to the annual value of heating oil consumed by households, and allocated to diesel.

No data estimates are available for this scheme.

Source: Principal tax rates 2009.

Lower Excise-Tax Rate on Diesel for Space Heating (no data available)

An excise-tax rate of ISK 45 per litre is applied to diesel used as fuel for motor vehicles (this tax was temporarily reduced by ISK 4 per litre from 1 July 2005 until 1 July 2006). Diesel fuel for used for other purposes (mainly space heating) is exempt from this tax.

No data estimates are available for this scheme.

Source: Taxes and duties on motor vehicles and fuel.

References

Policies or transfers

Principal tax rates 2009, Ministry of Finance. Available at:
http://eng.fjarmalaraduneyti.is/customs-and-taxes/principaltaxrates/nr/11977.

Taxes and duties on motor vehicles and fuel, Ministry of Finance. Available at:
http://eng.fjarmalaraduneyti.is/customs-and-taxes/nr/1764.

Chapter 10

Ireland

This chapter identifies, documents, and provides estimates of the various budgetary transfers and tax expenditures that relate to the production or use of fossil fuels in *Ireland*. An overview of *Ireland's* energy economy is first given to place the measures listed into context. A data-documentation section then describes those measures in a systematic way. Whenever possible, the description details a measure's formal beneficiary, its eligibility criteria and functioning, and the fuels whose production or use stand to benefit from the measure. The chapter ends with a set of charts and tables that provide, subject to availability, quantitative information and estimates for the various measures listed.

10. IRELAND

Energy resources and market structure

Ireland has few fossil-energy resources and is highly dependent on energy imports. The only indigenously produced energy sources are peat, combustible renewables and waste, and small volumes of natural gas. Oil accounts for half of the country's primary energy supply, all of which is imported, while gas contributes another 31%. All but 7% of the gas consumed is imported via an interconnector with the United Kingdom; domestic production has been declining for several years with the depletion of mature fields and delays to the start-up of the Corrib field, which was discovered in 1997. Imported coal meets 9% of the country's energy needs, and indigenously produced peat, which is used for electricity generation and heating purposes, for 6%. The share of renewable energy is currently relatively small, but the government plans to increase production substantially to reduce dependence on imported energy and lower greenhouse-gas emissions.

The energy sector is characterised by a mixture of private and public ownership. The oil industry, which is fully deregulated, is entirely in private hands, with several companies competing in the retail sector. For several decades, the state-owned Irish National Petroleum Company operated Ireland's sole petroleum refinery, in Cork. In 2001, however, the 75 000 bpd Whitegate refinery, and the associated oil terminal on Whiddy Island, were sold to Tosco Corporation (now a subsidiary of Conoco-Phillips) for $100 million. As part of the deal, the company promised to maintain or expand production at the refinery through 2016, and to keep on all the staff with no redundancies. The refinery today supplies around 35% of the Republic's demand for petroleum products.

State-owned companies dominate the electricity, gas and peat sectors. The Electricity Supply Board (ESB) holds two-thirds of generating capacity, though its share has been falling as new power producers have entered the market. It also owns the transmission system, the operation of which is the responsibility of another state-owned body, EirGrid, as well as the distribution network. Bord Gáis Éireann (BGE) owns the gas transmission and distribution network, operating the transmission system through a subsidiary company. Retail competition has developed to only a relatively small degree. Bord na Móna, a partially state-owned company, is the country's main peat producer.

Prices, taxes and support mechanisms

The prices of all forms of energy are deregulated, with the exception of electricity and gas. All customers can opt to switch supplies from incumbent to competing suppliers, who offer prices freely determined by the market. The electricity and gas tariffs of ESD and BGE for small and medium-sized customers, as well as network charges, are regulated by the Commission for Energy Regulation (CER) on a cost-of-service basis. Fuels and energy services are subject to VAT at a special rate of 13.5%, with the exception of gasoline and diesel fuel for road use, for which the standard rate of 21% is applied. Excise taxes (including a national oil reserve levy) are levied on all oil products. There are no excise taxes on natural gas, peat, coal or electricity.

The main form of public support to fossil energy other than the low rate of VAT is a subsidy to peat production. This takes the form of a Public Service Obligation (PSO) levy to support the higher cost of ESB's purchases of electricity generated from peat, which are mandated by the government. The mechanism has been approved by the European Commission through to 2019. The costs recovered through the PSO levy, calculated by the CER, equate to the additional costs of the power purchases over and above the cost of electricity purchased at market prices.

Data documentation

General notes

The fiscal year in Ireland coincides with the calendar year. Following OECD convention, amounts prior to 1999 are expressed as 'euro-fixed series', meaning that we applied the fixed EMU conversion rate (1 EUR = 0.788 IEP) to data initially expressed in the Irish Pound (IEP).

Producer Support Estimate

Public Service Obligation for Peat (data for 2004-)

The Public Service Obligation (PSO) is a levy charged on all final electricity consumers to finance purchases of peat-generated power by the Electricity Supply Board (ESB). The costs of generating electricity using peat usually exceed the market price. ESB is therefore compensated through PSO-financed transfers for its mandatory purchases of peat-generated electricity. The value of the PSO is set on an annual basis by the Commission for Energy Regulation (CER) to meet the additional costs incurred by ESB. The legal basis for the PSO scheme is set out in the Electricity Regulation Act of 1999. Support to peat-fired power plants is expected to cease by 2020.

Although the PSO scheme applies to certain renewable energy sources too, we only report here the part that concerns peat-fired power plants such as the Lough Ree and Edenderry plants.

We allocate this measure to the PSE since it guarantees demand for peat produced in Ireland, thereby providing higher returns to peat producers. While the fiscal year in Ireland matches the calendar year, PSO periods run from 1 October to 30 September of the following year. Accordingly, data allocated to 2010 cover the period running from 1 October 2009 to 30 September 2010. The PSO levy was exceptionally set to zero for the period running from October 2008 to September 2009.

Sources: CER (various years).

Tag: IRL_dt_01

Expensing of Exploration and Development Costs (no data available)

The upstream oil and gas sector in Ireland attracts a specific corporate income-tax rate of 25%, as compared to the 12.5% rate that applies to most other sectors. Full deductions are, however, allowed for exploration, development, and field abandonment costs in the year in which they are incurred. Unclaimed deductions can be carried forward for an unlimited amount of time. In addition, the Irish government does not levy any royalties, nor does it participate in projects.

Starting in January 2007, licenses issued after that date are now also subject to a Petroleum Resource Rent Tax (PRRT) as provided for in the 2008 Finance Act. The PRRT is a progressive tax on the profits from oil and gas extraction.

No estimates of the revenue foregone due to this provision are available.

Sources: Department of Communications, Energy and Natural Resources (2011).

Consumer Support Estimate

Reduced VAT Rate for Certain Energy Products (no data available)

A reduced rate of VAT (13.5%) is applied to sales of certain fuels in Ireland. Eligible products include coal, peat, natural gas, electricity, kerosene-type jet fuel, dyed diesel, and hydrocarbon oils used for domestic or industrial heating purposes. The on-road use of gasoline, diesel, and LPG remains taxed at the standard 21% rate.

No estimates of the revenue foregone due to the reduced rate of VAT are available.

Sources: Revenue (2008).

References

Policies or transfers

CER (various years) *Public Service Obligation Levy – Decision Paper*, Commission for Energy Regulation, Available at:
http://www.cer.ie/en/renewables-decision-documents.aspx#PSODecisions.

Department of Communications, Energy and Natural Resources (2011) *Petroleum Taxation in Ireland*, Government of Ireland, Available at:
http://www.dcenr.gov.ie/NR/rdonlyres/E226421F-47B6-42DB-9458-C5EF0EE619 30/0/PetroleumTaxationinIreland.pdf.

Revenue (2008) *VAT Guide*, Indirect Taxes Division, Irish Tax and Customs, Available at: http://www.revenue.ie/en/tax/vat/leaflets/index.html.

Figure 10.1.   Shares of fossil-fuel support by indicator, average for 2008-10 – Ireland

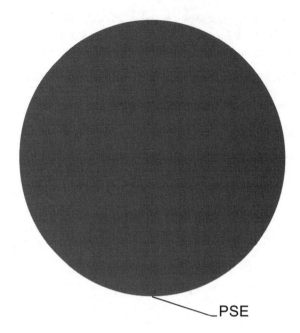

Source: OECD.

Table 10.1.   Summary of fossil-fuel support to coal – Ireland

(Millions of euros, nominal)

Support element	Jurisdiction	Avg 2000-02	Avg 2008-10	2008	2009	2010p
Producer Support Estimate						
Support to unit returns						
Public Service Obligation for Peat	–	n.a.	46.72	46.64	0.00	93.52
Consumer Support Estimate (n.a.)						
General Services Support Estimate (n.a.)						

Note: Tax expenditures for any given country are measured with reference to a benchmark tax treatment that is generally specific to that country. Consequently, the estimates contained in the table above are not necessarily comparable with estimates for other countries. In addition, because of the potential interaction between them, the summation of individual measures for a specific country may be problematic. The allocation of particular measures across fuel types was done by the OECD Secretariat based on the IEA's Energy Balances.

Source: OECD.

Chapter 11

Israel

This chapter identifies, documents, and provides estimates of the various budgetary transfers and tax expenditures that relate to the production or use of fossil fuels in *Israel*. An overview of *Israel's* energy economy is first given to place the measures listed into context. A data-documentation section then describes those measures in a systematic way. Whenever possible, the description details a measure's formal beneficiary, its eligibility criteria and functioning, and the fuels whose production or use stand to benefit from the measure. The chapter ends with a set of charts and tables that provide, subject to availability, quantitative information and estimates for the various measures listed.

The statistical data for Israel are supplied by and under the responsibility of the relevant Israeli authorities. The use of such data by the OECD is without prejudice to the status of the Golan Heights, East Jerusalem and Israeli settlements in the West Bank under the terms of international law.

11. ISRAEL

Energy resources and market structure

Apart from the 5% of its total primary energy that is obtained from renewable energy sources, Israel depends almost totally on fossil fuels for its energy supply. Around 35% of its energy comes from imported coal, which is used entirely to generate electricity. About half of its energy comes from imported crude oil and products. The rest comes from natural gas which is both imported via a pipeline from Egypt and produced domestically. The gas is mainly used to generate electricity. Small amounts of natural gas are also used for water desalinisation.

Israel's consumption of natural gas is expected to triple by 2020, to 15 billion cubic meters a year. In 2004, Israel began producing natural gas from deposits in the Yam Tethys field, from which around 17 billion cubic metres have already been extracted and around 10-15 billion cubic metres remain. More recently exploration has revealed significant additional deposits. Another field (Tamar) contains 250 billion cubic metres of confirmed reserves and is expected to begin production in 2013; this field could supply all of Israel's current domestic requirements for at least 20 years. A potentially larger field (Leviathan) is estimated to have 450 billion cubic metres of gas, although these have yet to be confirmed as "proven" reserves. Therefore in total, the undersea gas fields explored to date are estimated to contain about 700 billion cubic metres of gas. The potential for further discoveries is considerable: the US Geological Survey estimates that there are 3.5 trillion cubic meters of gas in the whole Levant Basin, approximately two-thirds of which lies within Israel's jurisdiction. Geologically, it is likely that there are oil resources in the vicinity of the natural gas fields but at the time of writing there had been no significant findings.

Oil shale is another resource being explored in Israel. The World Energy Council reported in November 2010 that Israel's underground oil shale (marinite) deposits, which underlay some 15% of the country at a depth of about 300 meters, could yield the equivalent of 4 billion barrels of oil using traditional open-cast mining techniques. Most of Israel's shale resources are located in the Rotem basin region of the northern Negev desert, near the Dead Sea. According to Israel's Ministry of National Infrastructures, the total geological endowment of the country's oil shale may well exceed several hundred billion barrels, but mineable reserves form only a tiny fraction of that figure. Traditionally, mining oil-shale requires tremendous amounts of water and energy, inputs not available in Israel in abundance.

Israel's energy sector is yet to become fully competitive. Electricity production and distribution remain dominated by the state-owned *Israel Electricity Corporation.* Progress in reforming this sector has been slow. Private-sector production is set to expand but the 'network' component is yet to be separated from other activities and distribution remains fully operated by the incumbent. Development of the offshore gas fields is being conducted by the private sector, much of it by a consortium of companies headed by a

U.S. oil company (Noble Energy). The transmission of natural gas, however, is carried out by the Israel Natural Gas Lines Company (INGL), a government subsidiary established in 2004 to construct and operate a national high-pressure gas transmission system. Currently, INGL operates purely as a transmission carrier, serving large customers.

Prices, taxes and support mechanisms

Over the last decade, Israel has advanced reforms to deregulate its oil sector, particularly the gasoline industry. Among other changes, a cost-plus basis system was abolished, some price controls for end users of petroleum products were eliminated and the two oil refineries have been privatised. The retail price of gasoline (excluding tax and excise) remains based on a formula linked to crude oil prices but this does not appear to result in markedly different (ex-tax) prices from elsewhere. However, relatively high excise duties mean the full price of vehicle fuels is similar to that in a number of European countries; at the beginning of 2011 the price for a litre of 95 octane fuel was approximately ILS 7.10 (about USD 2). Transport fuels are subject to both a VAT of 16% and excise taxes of ILS 2.89 (USD 0.84) per litre for gasoline and ILS 2.76 (USD 0.80) per litre for diesel. The government raised the excise tax on gasoline by ILS 0.20 (USD 0.06) per litre on 1 January 2011, but removed it a month later in the face of public protest at rising fuel prices. Plans remain to add ILS 0.20 per litre to the excise in January 2012.

In September 2009, a four-year fuel tax reform was concluded, as a result of which the excise-tax rates on diesel and gasoline were matched and the diesel annual car licensing fee was reduced to match the fee on gasoline engine cars. The reform intended to reduce economic distortions influencing the choice between diesel- and gasoline-powered cars. As of April 2011, the tax on diesel, at ILS 2.76 per litre, was only 5% lower than the excise tax on gasoline. However, large businesses and industries that depend on diesel fuel for income generation (including agriculture, construction, and fishing) are entitled to apply for diesel tax refunds. Buses and taxies are also included in this refund scheme.

Excise duties are also imposed on fuels used for stationary purposes. The tax on coal, which was increased at the beginning of 2011 from ILS 8.6 (USD 2.50) to ILS 43.3 (USD 12.60) per tonne, is now substantially higher than the excises on heavy oil and natural gas – respectively, ILS 13.9 and ILS 15.8 per tonne – and may further encourage a shift away from coal-fired electricity production.

In August 2009 Israel approved a tax reform which seeks to improve vehicle efficiency and reduce emissions. The purchase tax on private cars in Israel, at 83% plus VAT is one of the highest in developed countries. The reform set tax rebates according to the degree of reduced vehicular air pollution emissions, taking into account local pollutants (CO, HC, NO_X, and PM) as well as CO_2 emissions. Vehicles in the lowest emission category, after the refund, pay a 45% tax; hybrid-electric cars are charged only 30% and totally electric vehicles 10% (in all cases plus VAT).

The prices of electricity are regulated by the Electricity Authority, and are not directly subsidised. Israel's natural-gas market is relatively immature, and gas prices are set by long term supply contracts for large customers, dominated by the contracts between the pipeline importer, domestic producers and the IEC. Future prices for natural gas in Israel are expected to be set by what independent power producers can afford to pay, and by the fuel-substitution possibilities of the major consumers. It is expected that natural gas will become the dominant fuel used in new power plants (mainly CCGTs) and in existing steam turbines converted from heavy fuel oil. Energy security and flexibility considerations are likely to ultimately constrain expansion of gas-fired electricity production.

Israel's concession-based regime for taxing hydrocarbon production, dating from 1952, was revised in April 2011. The new law provides that royalties on hydrocarbon discoveries will remain at 12.5%, while a special profit levy (in addition to regular corporate tax) will begin after the developers have paid back investment outlays plus a return allowance. The tax will start at 20% of taxable income after a payback of 150% on the investment has been reached, and will rise in incremental steps, reaching 50% after a return of 230% on the investment. The total take by the state (including the 12.5% royalty) will therefore not exceed 62.5%. Any change in the rate of corporate income tax will trigger a corresponding change in the profits tax. The new regime is being applied to existing development projects and in these cases transitional provisions have been made to soften the tax burden and encourage production and development. The Tamar field is notably expected to benefit from these concessions. In broad terms the new fiscal regime has raised the effective tax on resources significantly to a level that is much closer to those typical elsewhere.

Data documentation[19]

General notes

Israel's fiscal year coincides with the calendar year.

Producer Support Estimate

The oil and gas industry in Israel is regulated by a system of fees, royalty payments and tax deductions developed in the 1950s. The fiscal provisions that are unique to the oil and gas industry are the *Oil Law* (1952), *Oil Regulations* (1953), *Income Tax Ordinance* (1961) and some parts of the income tax legislation, especially the *Deductions from the Income of Holders of Oil Rights* (1956) and the *Rules for Calculating Tax for the Holding and Sale of Participation Units in an Oil Exploration Partnership* (1988).

Israel started producing natural gas in 2004. As this is a relatively recent development, the issues of producer taxation and royalty payments are currently under review by the government (*Knesset*), the Ministry of Finance and participants representing the civil society. In April 2010, the Minister of Finance appointed a committee to examine the fiscal framework for the oil and gas resources in Israel, headed by Professor Eytan Sheshinski. The Sheshinski Committee submitted its final conclusions in January 2011. It recommended that the 12.5% rate of royalty payments should remain unchanged since increasing it could have a negative impact on the development of relatively less profitable gas fields. The depletion deduction, however, should be cancelled as it leads to a considerable reduction of the amount of

---

[19]   The statistical data for Israel are supplied by and under the responsibility of the relevant Israeli authorities. The use of such data by the OECD is without prejudice to the status of the Golan Heights, East Jerusalem and Israeli settlements in the West Bank under the terms of international law.

taxable income which has no economic justification, the Committee concluded. The Committee also instituted a progressive oil and gas levy on profits. Its initial rate will be 20% and it will gradually rise to 50% according to the amount of the excess profits. The new levy-calculation formula will give incentives for increasing exploration expenditure. Costs that accumulated during the lease stage of the oil-and-gas-asset development will be awarded accelerated depreciation at a rate of 10%. Investments made by the end of 2013 will be given a maximum of amount of accelerated depreciation rate of 15%.

Reduced Royalty Payments (data for 2004-)

The *Oil Law* (1952) stipulates that the rate of royalty payments that the holder of a lease is required to pay is 12.5% of gross income.[20] The value of natural gas produced from the Tethys concession (operated by a consortium of Noble Energy and the Delek Group) is calculated by taking into account 70% of the expenses for the construction of the production platform, 60% of the operating expenses and 100% of the expenses for the gas pipeline and other facilities not connected to the platform. For the 2004-10 period, total royalty payments amounted to 10.6% of gross income.

Data are available for the 2004-09 period from the *Sheshinski Report.* They comprise calculations of the amounts of total tax breaks (the sum of the reduction in royalty payments and the depletion deduction) and the total royalty payments. In order to estimate both the reduction in royalty payments and the depletion deduction, we compute the amounts of royalties that should be paid according to the Oil Law. We then calculate the amounts that constitute the reduction in royalty payments as the difference between the royalty payments that ought to have been paid and those that were actually paid. The difference between the total tax breaks and the reduction in royalty payments is the depletion deduction.

We use production data from the IEA to allocate the annual amounts reported in the Sheshinski report to oil and natural gas extraction.

Sources: Sheshinski Report (2011), IEA.

Tag: ISR_te_01

Depletion Deduction (data for 2004-)

Tax arrangements for the oil and gas industry are detailed in the *Deductions from the Income of Holders of Oil Rights Act of 1956* which allow for special deductions that reduce the taxable income of companies operating in the sector. In 1988, the benefits were expanded and the state allowed for the transfer of the tax breaks listed in the abovementioned document to the outside investors through the trading of securities. Eligible tax benefits include the following items: depletion deduction, recognition of exploration and development expenses as operating expenses, deductions due to the

---

[20]   Gross income is the market value of the oil at the wellhead. If a market price for the price of oil at the wellhead is not available at the time of royalty-payment calculation, costs of the resource transportation from the wellhead to the selling point should be deducted from the selling price. When it comes to royalty payments for gas based on offshore deposits, there is uncertainty as to the definition of the wellhead and the costs that should be attributed to the selling point. Hence, it is difficult to determine the exact amount of the royalty

abandonment of an oil asset, depreciation in respect of the acquisition of land, and exemption from the payment of customs duty and other import taxes.

The *Deductions from the Income of Holders of Oil Rights Act* grants the holder of oil rights an annual imputed deduction that amounts to 27.5% of gross income[21] in a given tax year but no more than 50% of net income.[22] *The Sheshinski Report* states that the rationale behind the depletion deduction is that its amount should reflect the depletion of the resource in the deposit and, as such, the impairment in the value of an asset. Since no payment has been made for the resource in the deposit in first place and the depleted asset is owned by the state, this depletion deduction constitutes a producer-support measure, Report concludes.

Data are available for the 2004-09 period. See "Reduced Royalty Payments" for explanation of the calculation method. We use production data from the IEA to allocate the annual amounts reported in the Sheshinski report to oil and natural gas extraction.

Sources: Sheshinski Report (2011), IEA.

Tag: ISR_te_02

Consumer Support Estimate

Excise-Tax Exemptions on Diesel (data for 2007-)

The *Excise Tax on Fuel Order of 2005* provides for tax rebates on diesel fuel if used for income-generation purposes in the following commercial vehicles: buses, taxis, fishing boats, and working vehicles such as tractors. The tax rebate for commercial vehicles varies between 45% and 50% on a capped amount of diesel equivalent to the "average consumption" for a given use.

In September 2009, the excise tax on diesel was set to match the excise tax on gasoline as a result of a four-year government reform aiming at reducing economic distortions influencing the choice between diesel- and gasoline-powered cars. However, large businesses and industries that depend on diesel fuel for income generation, can still apply for diesel tax rebates.Sources: Customs Authority, Ministry of Environment, Ministry of Finance (2005), Ministry of National Infrastructures.

Tag: ISR_dt_01

---

[21]   Gross income is defined as the amount received from the sale at the wellhead of the crude oil produced and utilised from the benefit or income less royalties. The *Sheshinski Report* states that there is another method of calculating the depletion deduction but since this method is only applicable if an acquisition of an asset had been affected, we do not discuss it here.

[22]   Net income is defined as gross income less the deductions that may be attributed to the production of oil and gas, with the exception of the depletion allowance.

General Services Support Estimate

National Coal Ash Board Funding (no data available)

The National Coal Ash Board (NCAB) is a governmental agency was established in 1993 by the Ministry of Energy and Infrastructures (now the Ministry of National Infrastructures), in co-operation with the Ministry of the Environment, the Interior Ministry, the Israel Electric Company (IEC), and the National Coal Supply Company (NCSC). Its aim is to promote more economic uses for coal ash accumulating at Israel's coal-fired power stations through investing state resources in research and development related to economic and environmental issues concerning coal-fired power stations, through co-operative initiatives with potential users.

No estimates are available for this programme.

Sources: NCAB (2011).

References

Policies or transfers

Ministry of Finance (2005) *Excise Tax on Fuel Order of 2005*, Government of Israel, Available at: http://www.finance.gov.il/customs/tsav_solar2005.pdf.

NCAB (2011) *Israeli National Coal Ash Board, NCAB Mission,* Available at: http://www.coal-ash.co.il/english/about.html.

Sheshinski Report (2011) *Conclusions of the Committee to Examine the Policy on Oil and Gas Resources in Israel, Headed by Professor Sheshinski*, State of Israel, January 2011, Available at: *http://mof.gov.il/Budg+etSite/Reform/Lists/List11/Attachments/1/shashinskiFullReport_n.pdf*.

Energy statistics

IEA, *Energy Balances of OECD Countries*, 2010 Edition, International Energy Agency, Paris.

Figure 11.1. Shares of fossil-fuel support by fuel, average for 2008-10 – Israel

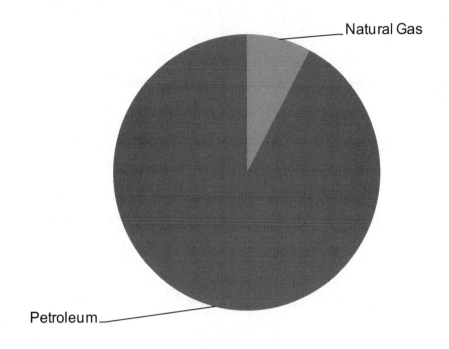

Source: OECD.

Figure 11.2. Shares of fossil-fuel support by indicator, average for 2008-10 – Israel

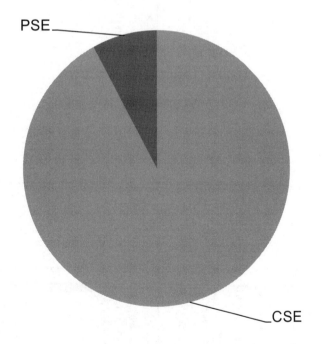

Source: OECD.

Table 11.1. Summary of fossil-fuel support to petroleum – Israel

(Millions of Israeli shekels, nominal)

Support element	Jurisdiction	Avg 2000-02	Avg 2008-10	2008	2009	2010p
Producer Support Estimate						
Support to unit returns						
Reduced Royalty Payments		–	n.c.	0.03	0.02	0.03	0.03
Income support						
Depletion Deduction		–	n.c.	0.11	0.12	0.11	0.11
Consumer Support Estimate						
Consumption						
Excise-Tax Exemption on Diesel		–	n.a.	1 733.33	1 500.00	1 700.00	2 000.00
General Services Support Estimate (n.a.)						

Note: Tax expenditures for any given country are measured with reference to a benchmark tax treatment that is generally specific to that country. Consequently, the estimates contained in the table above are not necessarily comparable with estimates for other countries. In addition, because of the potential interaction between them, the summation of individual measures for a specific country may be problematic. The allocation of particular measures across fuel types was done by the OECD Secretariat based on the IEA's Energy Balances.

Source: OECD.

Table 11.2. Summary of fossil-fuel support to natural gas – Israel

(Millions of Israeli shekels, nominal)

Support element	Jurisdiction	Avg 2000-02	Avg 2008-10	2008	2009	2010p
Producer Support Estimate						
Support to unit returns						
Reduced Royalty Payments	–	n.c.	26.86	25.79	27.40	27.40
Income support						
Depletion Deduction	–	n.c.	120.00	123.07	118.46	118.46
Consumer Support Estimate (n.a.)						
General Services Support Estimate (n.a.)						

Note: Tax expenditures for any given country are measured with reference to a benchmark tax treatment that is generally specific to that country. Consequently, the estimates contained in the table above are not necessarily comparable with estimates for other countries. In addition, because of the potential interaction between them, the summation of individual measures for a specific country may be problematic. The allocation of particular measures across fuel types was done by the OECD Secretariat based on the IEA's Energy Balances.

Source: OECD.

Chapter 12

Italy

This chapter identifies, documents, and provides estimates of the various budgetary transfers and tax expenditures that relate to the production or use of fossil fuels in *Italy*. An overview of *Italy's* energy economy is first given to place the measures listed into context. A data-documentation section then describes those measures in a systematic way. Whenever possible, the description details a measure's formal beneficiary, its eligibility criteria and functioning, and the fuels whose production or use stand to benefit from the measure. The chapter ends with a set of charts and tables that provide, subject to availability, quantitative information and estimates for the various measures listed.

12. ITALY

Energy resources and market structure

Italy produces small volumes of natural gas and oil and virtually no coal, so most of the country's fossil-fuel supplies – as well as a significant share of its electricity – are imported. They are augmented by local production of energy from renewable sources. Import dependence has been increasing in recent years. Oil and natural gas each account for around 40% of Italy's total primary energy supply, the rest coming from coal (8%), combustible renewables and waste (4%), hydro and geothermal energy (both 3%) and imported electricity (2%). In total, indigenous production meets only 16% of the country's primary energy needs.

The role of the state in the Italian energy sector has been greatly reduced by a programme of privatisation that was launched in the 1990s. Until 1995, Eni, the dominant oil and gas company in Italy, was fully state-owned; by 2001, the state's share of the company had been reduced to just over 30%. The company has retained a dominant position in the Italian upstream oil and gas sector, although a number of privately owned Italian and foreign companies have also established a significant presence. Eni remains the leading refining and marketing company, with about 30% of the market. The Italian oil market is fully liberalised. The government intervenes only to protect competition and to avoid abuse of dominant position.

Eni is also a leading player in the downstream gas market, through its 50% ownership of the main gas group, Snam Rete Gas, which controls most of the physical gas infrastructure in Italy. This includes almost the entire transmission network (Snam Rete Gas), a liquefied natural gas import business (GNL Italia), almost all the underground gas storage capacity in Italy (Stogit), and the leading local distribution network operator (Italgas). These businesses are functionally and legally unbundled.

The state has retained a 31% stake (21% directly and 10% through the majority state-owned bank, Cassa Depositi e Prestiti) in the former national electricity company, Enel, which continues to enjoy a dominant position in the national market. Despite government measures to encourage wholesale competition, the company is still Italy's largest power generator, controlling just over half of total capacity, and is among Europe's largest generators measured by installed capacity. The other leading generators are Edison (in which the French company, EDF, has a majority stake), E.On Produzione (formerly Endesa Italia, majority owned by Germany's E.On) and Enipower (a subsidiary of Eni). Terna, in which Cassa Depositi e Prestiti holds a near-30% stake, is the primary owner and operator of the national high-voltage transmission grid. There are a large number of distribution companies, many of them owned by municipalities. Enel remains by far the largest distribution network operator, distributing approximately 86% of total distributed volumes.

Italy has liberalised its electricity and gas sectors progressively in conformance with EU directives. Transmission and distribution of natural gas and electricity have been unbundled and a regulator, Autorità per l'Energia Elettrica e il Gas (AEEG), set up to supervise access to networks and regulate tariffs. Since July 2007, all electricity consumers are free to choose their supplier, while retaining the right to be supplied at regulated prices. Switching rates are low among household customers: Enel and Eni still account for the bulk of electricity and gas sales.

Prices, taxes and support mechanisms

The prices of all forms of energy other than electricity are set freely by the market. Electricity consumers have a choice of supply from incumbent suppliers at regulated tariffs or from alternative suppliers at market rates. There are no regulated tariffs for gas, but the AEEG has put in place a public service reference price for gas for all domestic customers and small businesses, based on the actual price of gas at entry points to the Italian transmission system.

Italy applies different rates of VAT and excise tax on energy at the national level. Oil products are subject to excise tax and VAT (at a rate of 20%) for gasoline, diesel, light fuel oil and LPG. Natural gas is subject to excise tax and VAT, as well as additional taxes at the regional level. A lower rate of VAT, currently 10%, is applied to sales of natural gas up to 480 cubic metres a year, and 20% for the remaining consumption. Different rates of excise tax are levied on gas according to whether the consumer is a business or a household and to the level of consumption (higher taxes are applied to higher consumption levels for households and vice versa for industry). The household tax rates are lower in the south of the country. For electricity, households pay a 10% rate of VAT; excise tax is not charged on the first 150 kWh per month of consumption (where capacity is up to 3 kW). For consumption above that volume, excise tax is charged at a fixed rate, which is slightly higher for secondary residences. For industrial consumers, excise tax is charged at a fixed rate on consumption over 200 MWh per month; provincial taxes, which vary by province, are levied on sales up to 200 MWh per month.

There are a number of excise-tax exemptions, reductions and rebates for specific fuels and sectors. These include (but are not limited to) shipping (inland and maritime); rail transport; certain end users in the agriculture, horticulture, aquaculture and forestry sectors; diesel fuel used in public passenger transportation and by ambulances; fuel used by trucking companies; and LPG and heating oil sold in certain regions, such as those not served by a natural-gas distribution network. There is also an excise-tax rebate on automotive fuels for people living in oil-producing areas.

Support to energy production includes cheap loans and grants to encourage natural gas production in depressed regions and relief from royalty payments on the first tranche of production of oil and gas.

Data documentation

General notes

Following OECD convention, amounts prior to 1999 are expressed as "euro-fixed series", meaning that we applied the fixed EMU conversion rate (1 EUR = 1 936.27 ITL) to data initially expressed in the Italian Lira (ITL).

The fiscal year in Italy runs from 1 July to 30 June. Following OECD convention, data are allocated to the starting calendar year so that data covering the period July 2005 to June 2006 are allocated to 2005.

Producer Support Estimate

Royalty-Free Thresholds (no data available)

Italy's royalty regime is set out in a legal act which was adopted in November 1996 (Decreto Legge No.625) but rates have recently been increased for onshore production (10% as of January 2009). The additional revenues thus collected are meant to finance a reduction in fuel prices for those consumers living in areas where oil and gas extraction takes place. Meanwhile, the overall royalty framework remains characterised by lower rates applicable to offshore production (4% for oil and 7% for natural gas). Royalty revenues are generally divided between different jurisdictions with the central government retaining between 30% and 45% of the total.

The 1996 act also provides for a royalty relief on the first 20 000 tonnes of oil produced onshore per year (50 000 tonnes in the case of offshore production). A similar provision applies to natural gas for the first 25 million cubic meters (80 million cubic meters in the case of offshore production).

No estimates of the revenue foregone due to the royalty relief are available.

Sources: Ministero dello Sviluppo Economico (2011), Parlamento Italiano (1996).

Consumer Support Estimate

Fuel-Tax Exemption for Shipping (data for 2010-)

This provision exempts the use of fuel for navigation purposes from the excise tax that is normally levied on sales of petroleum products. It applies specifically to transportation of goods and passengers along national waterways and within EU waters. The measure also encompasses the use of fuel in the fisheries sector.

We allocated the annual amounts reported in tax expenditure documents to diesel and heavy fuel on the basis of the IEA's Energy Balances for the fisheries and domestic navigation transport sectors.

Sources: Dipartimento delle Finanze, IEA.

Tag: ITA_te_01

Fuel-Tax Reduction for Rail Transport (data for 2010-)

Rail transport in Italy benefits from a 70% reduction in the rate of excise tax that normally applies to sales of diesel fuel.

Sources: Dipartimento delle Finanze.

Tag: ITA_te_02

Energy Tax Breaks for Agriculture (data for 2010-)

The agriculture, horticulture, forestry, and aquaculture sectors in Italy benefit from a reduced rate of excise tax for their use of diesel and gasoline. The reduction with respect to the benchmark rate amounts to 78% for diesel and 51% for gasoline.

Data from the IEA's Energy Balances for the agriculture and forestry sectors indicate that the use of diesel dwarfs that of gasoline, with the latter accounting for less than 1% of total energy use. For that reason, we allocate the measure entirely to diesel fuel.

Sources: Dipartimento delle Finanze.

Tag: ITA_te_03

Tax Relief for Public Transport (data for 2010-)

This measure provides public transportation in Italy with a 60% reduction in the rate of excise tax normally levied on sales of petroleum products. The reduction also applies in a few instances to boat transfers whenever road transport is not available. Rail transport is, however, excluded (see "Fuel-Tax Reduction for Rail Transport" above). Various caps are set on the amounts of fuel to which the reduction applies, with these caps depending on population density on a regional basis.

We allocate the measure entirely to diesel fuel.

Sources: Dipartimento delle Finanze.

Tag: ITA_te_04

Tax Relief for Ambulances (data for 2010-)

This provision grants ambulances providing assistance or first-aid a 60% reduction in the excise tax levied on sales of petroleum products. We allocate the measure entirely to diesel fuel.

Sources: Dipartimento delle Finanze.

Tag: ITA_te_05

Tax Relief for Certain LPG Users (no data available)

The use of LPG in certain industrial plants and buses used for public transportation purposes is subject to a 90% reduction in the excise tax levied on sales of petroleum products.

No estimates of the revenue foregone due to this reduction are available.

Sources: Dipartimento delle Finanze.

Tax Relief for Trucking Companies (data for 2010-)

Trucking companies operating in Italy can obtain partial refunds on the amount of excise tax paid for their fuel purchases. Refunds usually correspond to a fixed amount of fuel.

We allocate the measure entirely to diesel fuel.

Sources: Dipartimento delle Finanze.

Tag: ITA_te_06

Tax Relief for Industrial Users of Natural Gas (data for 2010-)

Large industrial users of natural gas can benefit from a reduction in the rate of excise tax usually levied on sales of natural gas. The reduction equals 60% and applies to those users whose consumption volumes exceed 1.2 million cubic meters per year.

Sources: Dipartimento delle Finanze.

Tag: ITA_te_07

Tax Relief for Users Living in Disadvantaged Areas (data for 2010-)

This provision is meant to benefit those users of fuel who reside in poor, remote areas where provision of natural gas can prove challenging. Relief is provided by means of a set of reductions on the excise tax that normally applies to sales of petroleum products.

Because the measure applies to both LPG and diesel, we allocated the annual amounts reported in tax expenditure documents to both fuels on the basis of the IEA's Energy Balances for the residential sector.

Sources: Dipartimento delle Finanze, IEA.

Tag: ITA_te_08

References

Policies or transfers

Ministero dello Sviluppo Economico (2011) *Gettito Royalties Anno 2010*, Direzione Generale per le Risorse Minerarie ed Energetiche, Available at: http://unmig.sviluppoeconomico.gov.it/unmig/royalties/royalties.asp.

Parlamento Italiano (1996) *Decreto Legislativo 25 novembre 1996, n. 625*, Leggi, Available at: http://www.parlamento.it/parlam/leggi/deleghe/96625dl.htm.

Energy statistics

IEA, *Energy Balances of OECD Countries*, 2010 Edition, International Energy Agency, Paris.

Figure 12.1.   Shares of fossil-fuel support by fuel, average for 2008-10 – Italy

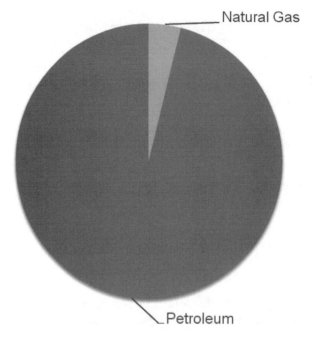

Source: OECD.

Figure 12.2.   Shares of fossil-fuel support by indicator, average for 2008-10 – Italy

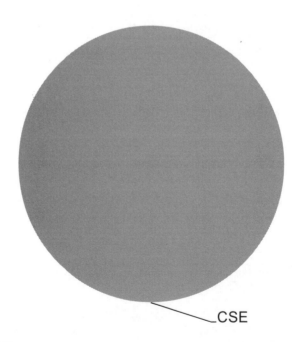

Source: OECD.

Table 12.1. Summary of fossil-fuel support to petroleum – Italy

(Millions of euros, nominal)

Support element	Jurisdiction	Avg 2000-02	Avg 2008-10	2008	2009	2010p
Producer Support Estimate (n.a.)						
Consumer Support Estimate						
Consumption						
Fuel Tax Exemption for Shipping		–	492.00	..		492.00
Fuel Tax Reduction for Rail Transport		–	1.40	..		1.40
Energy Tax Breaks for Agriculture		–	816.80	..		816.80
Tax Relief for Public Transport		–	14.20	..		14.20
Tax Relief for Ambulances		–	4.10	..		4.10
Tax Relief for Trucking Companies		–	95.00	..		95.00
Tax Relief for Users Living in Disadvantaged Areas		–	51.90	..		51.90
General Services Support Estimate (n.a.)						

Note: Tax expenditures for any given country are measured with reference to a benchmark tax treatment that is generally specific to that country. Consequently, the estimates contained in the table above are not necessarily comparable with estimates for other countries. In addition, because of the potential interaction between them, the summation of individual measures for a specific country may be problematic. The allocation of particular measures across fuel types was done by the OECD Secretariat based on the IEA's Energy Balances.

Source: OECD.

Table 12.2.   Summary of fossil-fuel support to natural gas – Italy

(Millions of euros, nominal)

Support element	Jurisdiction	Avg 2000-02	Avg 2008-10	2008	2009	2010p
Producer Support Estimate (n.a.)						
Consumer Support Estimate						
Consumption						
Tax Relief for Industrial Users of Natural Gas	–	n.a.	60.00	:	:	60.00
General Services Support Estimate (n.a.)						

Note: Tax expenditures for any given country are measured with reference to a benchmark tax treatment that is generally specific to that country. Consequently, the estimates contained in the table above are not necessarily comparable with estimates for other countries. In addition, because of the potential interaction between them, the summation of individual measures for a specific country may be problematic. The allocation of particular measures across fuel types was done by the OECD Secretariat based on the IEA's Energy Balances.

Source: OECD.

Chapter 13

Japan

This chapter identifies, documents, and provides estimates of the various budgetary transfers and tax expenditures that relate to the production or use of fossil fuels in *Japan*. An overview of *Japan's* energy economy is first given to place the measures listed into context. A data-documentation section then describes those measures in a systematic way. Whenever possible, the description details a measure's formal beneficiary, its eligibility criteria and functioning, and the fuels whose production or use stand to benefit from the measure. The chapter ends with a set of charts and tables that provide, subject to availability, quantitative information and estimates for the various measures listed.

13. JAPAN

Energy resources and market structure

Japan has negligible fossil-energy resources and relies almost entirely on imported fuels and domestically produced nuclear power. The energy mix is reasonably well diversified. Oil is the leading fuel, accounting for just under half of total primary energy supply. Coal provides one-fifth, while nuclear power and natural gas each contribute about 15%. Renewables and combustible waste together account for the remaining 3%. The share of oil has fallen steadily since the 1970s, largely in favour of nuclear power and natural gas, virtually all of which is imported as LNG. Only 16% of the country's energy needs are met from indigenous sources (including nuclear power). Japan is the third-largest oil consumer in the world behind the United States and China, the third-largest net importer of crude oil and the largest importer of both LNG and coal.

Japan's energy sector is dominated by private, domestic companies, with public-sector ownership largely limited to some municipal gas and electricity utilities, most of which are small. Oil exploration and development are conducted by private-sector companies with the support of the Japan Oil, Gas and Metals National Corporation (JOGMEC) – a government agency set up in 2004 to, among other things, promote exploration and development of oil and natural gas deposits for use in Japan, taking over part of the operations of the now-defunct Japan National Oil Corporation (JNOC). New companies were formed out of the rest of JNOC's assets, including Inpex and Japex, and were then privatised, though the Japanese government maintains a small equity stake in each firm. All of Japan's oil refineries are privately owned. Distribution of oil products is conducted solely by private-sector companies, including foreign companies. The latter's share of the market has grown in recent years with the easing of regulatory restrictions.

The natural gas industry is also largely in private hands. The majority of gas is imported by Japan's electricity companies for power generation. These utilities, and some large industrial users, import their gas independently from the city gas industry. Electric utilities also supply LNG to other new entrants to the gas market. The city gas industry is fragmented into more than 200 vertically integrated regional companies, the bulk of which are privately owned. The four major gas utilities – Tokyo Gas, Osaka Gas, Toho Gas and Saibu Gas – supply about three-quarters of the total gas market. There are also over 1 600 small, community gas utilities. Although most pipelines in Japan are owned by gas utilities, some power utilities and domestic gas producers own pipelines as service providers.

Japan's electricity sector is comprised of ten vertically integrated electricity utilities (VIUs) covering all the geographic regions of Japan, one large wholesale supplier, J-Power, and numerous other wholesale suppliers, municipal utilities and auto-generators. The biggest generators are Tokyo Electric Power Company (TEPCO), Kansai, Chubu, Kyushu, Tohoku and J-Power.

Market reforms have been implemented progressively in the Japanese gas and electricity sectors since the mid-1990s, though at a slow pace compared with most other OECD countries. At present, around 60% of both markets have been liberalised, *i.e.* sales to final consumers who are free to choose their supplier. But actual switching rates remain very low, especially among medium-sized customers. There are some legal requirements on VIUs to unbundle their networks and system operation from other activities, but full structural unbundling is not required. Responsibility for governance of the electricity and gas sectors lies with the Ministry of Economy, Trade and Industry (METI); the Electric Power System Council of Japan (ESCJ) – an independent, private and non-profit body made up of the VIUs, independent power producers and suppliers (PPS), other wholesale electricity companies and representatives from the academic world – is responsible for establishing rules for access to the transmission grid and to enhance market transparency.

Prices, taxes and support mechanisms

There are no price controls on oil products or coal in Japan. Electricity and gas prices in the non-liberalised sector are regulated, as are network charges to suppliers in the liberalised sector. All fuels and energy services are subject to a general consumption tax (akin to a value-added tax) at a flat rate of 5% (4% national, and 1% prefectural), as well as excise and other taxes at different rates according to the fuel.

A general petroleum excise tax is levied on crude oil refined in Japan. A petroleum and coal tax is levied on all final sales of oil products, natural gas and coal (Table 13.1). Gasoline, diesel and LPG are subject to additional excise taxes; a local road tax is also levied on gasoline, the revenues from which are used to finance road construction and maintenance. In the case of diesel fuel, the consumption tax is applied to the price before excise and road taxes are added. Domestic aviation fuel is also taxed to finance airport construction. Electricity sales to households and businesses carry a Power Source Development Tax, which is intended to finance measures to support new sources of power generation, nuclear power research and development and other activities. Tax rates on fossil fuels have remained unchanged in nominal terms since 2001, except for natural gas and LPG, and coal. Exemptions apply to many end uses.

The government funds directly the costs of maintaining publicly owned emergency oil stocks, which are managed by JOGMEC. There is no levy on oil sales or on the oil industry to cover these costs.

Japan has long been a world leader in energy research and development. The government provides direct and indirect support to this activity, which is seen as a vital element in increasing the country's energy security and reducing carbon-dioxide emissions. Direct public spending on energy research as a percentage of its GDP is the largest in the OECD. The bulk of this funding goes to nuclear power.

Table 13.1. Energy-related taxes in Japan, 2001 and 2009

Fuel	Formal incidence	Units	2001	2009	Exemptions
Tax on unleaded gasoline	National gasoline tax	per litre	48.6	48.6	Aviation, diplomats, heating, gasoline used as solvent
	Local gasoline tax	per litre	5.2	5.2	
Delivery tax	Light oil	per litre	32.1	32.1	Agriculture, forestry, fishing, mining.
	Heavy oil	per litre	32.1	32.1	
LPG tax	LPG used for transport	per kg	17.5	17.5	Exports; LPG used as heating fuel or in manufacturing.
Petroleum and coal tax	Natural gas and imported LPG	per kg	0.72	1.08	Exports; fuel oil used in agriculture, forestry or fishing;
	Crude oil, imported petroleum products	per litre	2.04	2.04	naphtha and gaseous hydrocarbons used as raw materials for production
	Coal	per kg	–	0.70	of petrochemicals and ammonia.
Aviation fuel tax	Domestic use	per litre	26	26	Central and local governments, international air transport
Power-resource development tax	Sales of electricity	per kWh	0.445	0.375	None

Source: OECD, Environmental Performance Review – Japan, OECD Publications, Paris, November 2010, based on data from the Government of Japan.

Data documentation

General notes

The Japanese fiscal year runs from 1 April through 31 March of the following year. Following OECD convention, fiscal-year data are assigned to the closest calendar year; hence data covering the period April 2009 through March 2010 are reported as "2009" in the database.

Producer Support Estimate

Price Support on Sales to Electricity and Non-Ferrous Industries (data for 1982-99)

For many years, large Japanese consumers of domestic thermal coal paid a price for that coal well above the world market price.

The value of the associated transfer was estimated by the IEA by multiplying the quantity of domestic thermal coal consumed (expressed in thermal-equivalent terms) by the difference between the imported thermal-coal price (obtained from customs statistics) and the average delivered price of domestic thermal coal delivered to electric power stations. We allocate the full value of the transfer to bituminous coal.

Sources: IEA (1988), IEA (various years).

Tag: JPN_dt_05

Price Support on Sales to Steel and Coke Industries (data for 1982-90)

For many years, through 1990, large Japanese consumers of domestic coking coal paid a price for that coal well above the world market price.

The value of the associated transfer was estimated by the IEA by multiplying the quantity of domestic coking coal consumed (expressed in thermal-equivalent terms) by the difference between the imported coking-coal price (obtained from customs statistics) and the average delivered price of domestic coking coal delivered to steelmakers. We allocate the full value of the transfer to bituminous coal.

Sources: IEA (1988), IEA (various years).

Tag: JPN_dt_06

Grants for Modernising Coal Pits (data for 1982-99)

These grants were given generally to help improve the efficiency and general working conditions in underground mines.

We allocate the value of the grants entirely to bituminous coal.

Sources: IEA (1988), IEA (various years).

Tag: JPN_dt_01

Grants for Stabilising the Coal Industry (data for 1982-99)

These were given generally to help stabilise individual coal-mining companies' accounts, thereby smoothing contraction of the industry.

We allocate the value of the grants entirely to bituminous coal.

Sources: IEA (1988), IEA (various years).

Tag: JPN_dt_02

Grants to Improve Safety Conditions (data for 1982-99)

These grants were given to coal-mining companies' to help them finance safety improvements in underground mines.

We allocate the value of the grants entirely to bituminous coal.

Sources: IEA (1988), IEA (various years).

Tag: JPN_dt_03

Grants for Paying Off Interest on Loans (data for 1987-97)

These grants were given to coal-mining companies to help them meet the interest charges on loans used to finance stockpiles of surplus coal.

We allocate the value of the grants entirely to bituminous coal.

Sources: IEA (1988), IEA (various years).

Tag: JPN_dt_04

Natural-Gas Exploration Subsidy (data for 2007-)

>   This measure aims at promoting natural gas exploration by mining companies.

>   Sources: IEA (2008), OECD.

>   Tag: JPN_dt_11

Oil-Prospecting Subsidy (data for 2007-)

>   This measure supports geological surveys abroad.

>   Sources: IEA (2008), OECD.

>   Tag: JPN_dt_12

Oil-Refining Rationalisation Subsidy (data for 2007-)

>   This programme assists the development of advanced oil-refining technologies.

>   Sources: IEA (2008), OECD.

>   Tag: JPN_dt_13

Oil Product Quality Assurance Subsidy (data for 2007-)

>   This measure supports the analysis of petroleum products and development of analytical techniques.

>   Sources: IEA (2008), OECD.

>   Tag: JPN_dt_14

Large-Scale Oil Disaster Prevention Subsidy (data for 2007-)

>   This programme supports the construction and maintenance of oil fences and their transport in emergencies.

>   Sources: IEA (2008), OECD.

>   Tag: JPN_dt_15

Consumer Support Estimate

Promotion of Natural-Gas Use Subsidy (data for 2007-)

>   This programme helps private firms convert coal-burning facilities to natural gas-burning ones.

>   Sources: IEA (2008), OECD.

>   Tag: JPN_dt_16

General Services Support Estimate

Regional Aid to Coal-Mining Districts (data for 1982-99)

>   These grants were intended to help general economic development in depressed coal-mining districts.

>   We allocate the value of the grants entirely to bituminous coal.

Sources: IEA (1988), IEA (various years).

Tag: JPN_dt_07

Grants for Worker Retraining (data for 1982-99)

These grants helped to pay for the retraining of coal miners made redundant by reductions in coal output.

We allocate the value of the grants entirely to bituminous coal.

Sources: IEA (1988), IEA (various years).

Tag: JPN_dt_08

Grants to Offset Costs of Closing Collieries (data for 1982-99)

These refer to payments made to workers who were made redundant as a result of the closing of coal mines.

We allocate the value of the grants entirely to bituminous coal.

Sources: IEA (1988), IEA (various years).

Tag: JPN_dt_09

Grants to Help Pay for Subsidence Damage (data for 1982-99)

These grants were given to the Coal Mine Damage Corporation for the purpose of dealing with the restoration of environmental damage arising from coal mining undertaken in the past.

We allocate the value of the grants entirely to bituminous coal.

Sources: IEA (1988), IEA (various years).

Tag: JPN_dt_10

Subsidy for Oil-Refining Technology Programmes (data for 2007-)

This measure promotes joint research with oil-producing countries on oil-refining technologies.

Sources: IEA (2008), OECD.

Tag: JPN_dt_17

Subsidy for Structural Reform Measures (data for 2007-)

This programme assists business diversification and other structural reform measures by oil distributors.

Sources: IEA (2008), OECD.

Tag: JPN_dt_18

References

Policies or transfers

IEA (various years) *Coal Information*, OECD Publications, Paris.

IEA (1988) *Coal Prospects and Policies in IEA Countries: 1987 Review*, OECD Publications, Paris.

IEA (2008) *Energy Policies of IEA Countries: Japan 2008 Review*, OECD Publications, Paris.

Figure 13.1. Shares of fossil-fuel support by fuel, average for 2008-10 – Japan

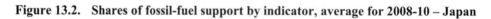

Natural Gas

Petroleum

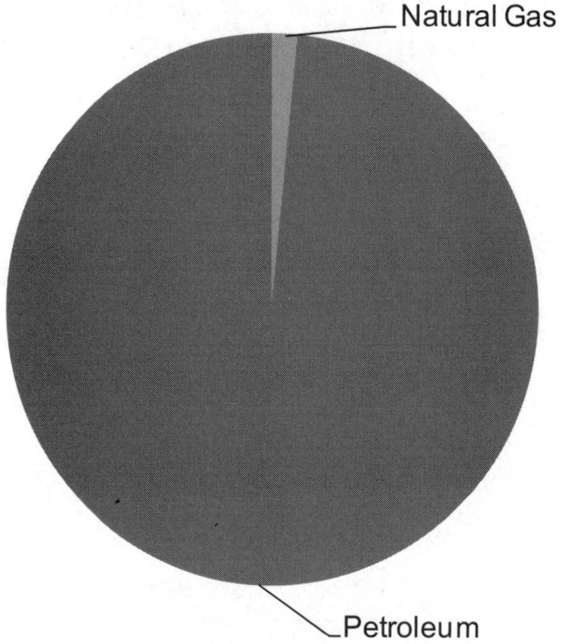

Source: OECD.

Figure 13.2. Shares of fossil-fuel support by indicator, average for 2008-10 – Japan

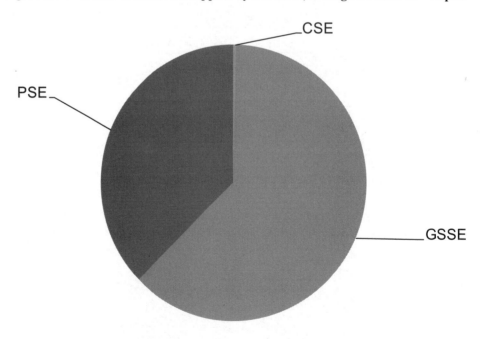

CSE

PSE

GSSE

Source: OECD.

Table 13.2. Summary of fossil-fuel support to petroleum – Japan

(Millions of Japanese yen, nominal)

Support element	Jurisdiction	Avg 2000-02	Avg 2008-10	2008	2009	2010p
Producer Support Estimate						
Support for intermediate inputs						
Large-Scale Oil Disaster Prevention Subsidy	–	n.c.	743.54	::	777.08	710.00
Support for knowledge creation						
Oil Prospecting Subsidy	–	n.c.	700.85	::	1 100.91	300.79
Oil Refining Rationalisation Subsidy	–	n.c.	10 269.40	::	10 942.02	9 596.78
Oil Product Quality Assurance Subsidy	–	n.c.	1 675.03	::	1 700.05	1 650.00
Consumer Support Estimate (n.a.)						
General Services Support Estimate						
Subsidy for Structural Reform Measures	–	n.c.	12 200.49	::	15 206.88	9 194.09
Subsidy for Oil Refining Technology Programmes	–	n.c.	11 309.15	::	10 760.95	11 857.34

Note: Tax expenditures for any given country are measured with reference to a benchmark tax treatment that is generally specific to that country. Consequently, the estimates contained in the table above are not necessarily comparable with estimates for other countries. In addition, because of the potential interaction between them, the summation of individual measures for a specific country may be problematic. The allocation of particular measures across fuel types was done by the OECD Secretariat based on the IEA's Energy Balances.

Source: OECD.

Table 13.3.   Summary of fossil-fuel support to natural gas – Japan

(Millions of Japanese yen, nominal)

Support element	Jurisdiction	Avg 2000-02	Avg 2008-10	2008	2009	2010p
Producer Support Estimate						
Support for capital formation						
Natural Gas Exploration Subsidy		–	600.06	..	800.11	400.02
Consumer Support Estimate						
Consumption						
Promotion of Natural Gas Use Subsidy		–	412.12	..	699.97	124.26
General Services Support Estimate (n.a.)						

Note: Tax expenditures for any given country are measured with reference to a benchmark tax treatment that is generally specific to that country. Consequently, the estimates contained in the table above are not necessarily comparable with estimates for other countries. In addition, because of the potential interaction between them, the summation of individual measures for a specific country may be problematic. The allocation of particular measures across fuel types was done by the OECD Secretariat based on the IEA's Energy Balances.

Source: OECD.

Chapter 14

Korea

This chapter identifies, documents, and provides estimates of the various budgetary transfers and tax expenditures that relate to the production or use of fossil fuels in *Korea*. An overview of *Korea's* energy economy is first given to place the measures listed into context. A data-documentation section then describes those measures in a systematic way. Whenever possible, the description details a measure's formal beneficiary, its eligibility criteria and functioning, and the fuels whose production or use stand to benefit from the measure. The chapter ends with a set of charts and tables that provide, subject to availability, quantitative information and estimates for the various measures listed.

14. KOREA

Energy resources and market structure

Korea has minimal fossil-fuel resources and imports all but 2% of its coal supplies, 1% of its oil and 1% of its natural gas. Korea is the world's second-largest importer of liquefied natural gas (LNG), after Japan, and is the fifth-largest importer of oil. The country relies heavily of fossil energy, with oil accounting for 40% of primary energy supply, coal 28% and gas 13%. Nuclear power accounts for 17% and renewables for the rest. The share of oil has fallen sharply over the last decade, as supplies of coal, gas and nuclear power have increased. Overall, over 80% of Korea's energy is imported, even treating nuclear power as indigenous production (all its uranium fuel needs are imported).

There is significant state ownership in Korea's energy industry. While the downstream oil industry and coal mining have been largely privatised, the gas, electricity and district heating sectors remain primarily under public ownership. The state-owned Korea National Oil Corporation (KNOC) is responsible for Korea's strategic oil reserves, as well as for the exploration, development and production of oil and natural gas within and outside of the country. Private companies dominate refining, wholesale imports, distribution and retailing. The leading oil companies are SK, GS Caltex, Inchon Oil Refinery, S-Oil and Hyundai Oil Bank.

Five of the country's eight anthracite mines (all bituminous coal is imported) are privately owned. The remaining three mines are run by the state-owned Korea Coal Corporation (KCC), which is also responsible for managing the supply of domestic anthracite and supporting the development of the domestic coal market, including the workforce and new technologies. Private-sector and other government-owned companies import coal from the world market for their own needs directly or through a private intermediary, mostly under medium- or long-term contracts. In support of the government's policy of developing overseas energy projects, private Korean companies and the Korea Resources Corporation (KORES) are currently involved in more than a dozen overseas bituminous coal projects.

The Korea Gas Corporation (KOGAS), a state-owned and operated company, holds a monopoly on gas imports, transmission and wholesale supply, though some companies are allowed to import gas directly for their own use. The retail market is made up of more than 30 city gas companies. The central government oversees the wholesale market; local governments and provinces oversee the retail market. Moves to privatise and deregulate the sector and open up the wholesale and retail markets to competition have largely stalled.

Korea's electricity industry is dominated by the Korea Electric Power Corporation (KEPCO), a 50% state-owned vertically integrated utility. In 2001, KEPCO was reorganised into six power-generation subsidiaries (gencos): Korea Hydro and Nuclear Power (KHNP), which owns the nation's nuclear plants and large hydroelectric dams, and five companies with thermal generation assets. KEPCO also retained the national transmission and distribution grids. At the same time, a power market, the state-owned Korea Power Exchange (KPX), was established. Currently the six power-generation companies, which control about four-fifths of capacity, and independent producers sell their output into a power pool, while KEPCO is the sole buyer. Plans in the early 2000s for the five thermal generation companies to be privatised have been shelved. The state-owned Korea District Heating Corporation (KDHC) supplies about 60% of all heat sales in Korea; the rest of the market is supplied by around 20 other companies, approximately 15% of which are privately owned.

Prices, taxes and support mechanisms

The wholesale and retail prices of oil and bituminous coal are completely deregulated. The wholesale prices of domestically produced anthracite coal and briquettes are set by the government as part of a subsidy to support uneconomic mining. Gas and heat prices are controlled directly by the Ministry of Commerce, Industry and Energy (MOCIE). The Korea Electricity Commission (KOREC), a quasi-autonomous body within MOCIE, is responsible for regulating KPX and final electricity prices. Final decisions are made by MOCIE following the rulings or deliberations of KOREC; in practice, the minister does not usually overrule KOREC.

Korea imposes import duties on crude oil and refined products; the latter are taxed more heavily, providing a tax advantage for Korean refineries relative to product importers. Bituminous-coal imports also carry a duty. A flat-rate VAT of 10% is levied on all sales of fuels and energy services. Excise taxes are levied on oil products and gas sales to both households and businesses; transport fuels are also subject to additional taxes, including an education tax and an array of transport taxes (so-called traffic, energy, and environmental taxes).

Government support to fossil-energy production concerns mainly coal. Support to producers of anthracite coal has been in place for several decades, involving price support, subsidies for acquiring capital equipment, subsidies for exploration, and support of a more general nature. The price-support component was repealed at the end of 2010. Direct investments made by the government and public funding related to research and development by KCC and KORES were halted earlier. The government also provides support to the production of anthracite briquettes mainly by setting the price below cost (to protect low-income households) and paying the difference to producers. Support is due to be phased out progressively and terminated by the end of 2020, though a scheme to provide vouchers to subsidy consumption is expected to be expanded to offset the impact of higher prices.

The government is also planning to introduce funding for a project to develop clean coal-technologies that is planned by SK Energy (Korea's largest oil refiner) and Pohang Iron and Steel Co (a domestic steel maker). The government already provides funding for research and development projects related to exploration technologies for oil and other mineral resources, as well as to integrated coal gasification combined-cycle (ICGCC) technology as part of its renewable-energy research programme. The Korean government also encourages private exploration and production overseas through tax benefits and the extension of credit lines to domestic companies by the Korea Export-Import bank.

Consumption subsidies concern mainly excise-tax exemptions for various fuels and categories of consumer. These include exemptions for farmers, fishing boats and certain types of coastal passenger ships from the various taxes that are usually levied on sales of oil products; exemptions on sales of anthracite coal and briquettes from VAT (as well as price controls as described above); and grants to disabled persons and so-called "state meritorious persons" to cover the increase in fuel prices since 2001.

Data documentation

General notes

The fiscal year in Korea coincides with the calendar year.

Producer Support Estimate

Support to Coal Production (data for 1989-)

The Korean government has been providing support to producers of anthracite coal for several decades. This support is usually provided in different ways and reporting a complete breakdown is not practical. For that reason, several items are here bundled together under the same general heading of "Support to Coal Producers". This includes price support, subsidies for acquiring capital equipment, subsidies for exploration, and support of a more general nature. The price-support component was repealed at the end of 2010 though.

We aggregate available data for this programme by category of statutory incidence (returns, capital, income, and knowledge). "Direct Support" thus includes bounties, defficiency payments, and subsidies covering freight costs. The "Capital and Facilities" category is composed of support to exploration, mining enlargement, tunnelling, mining mechanisation, and acquisition of safety facilities. "Government Injection" refers to investments made by the government, and "Research Fund" contains funding related to company-specific R&D (the two beneficiaries were Korea Coal Corporation and Resources Corporation). Support provided through the last two categories (government injection and R&D) stopped earlier than 2009.

We allocate the entire programme to anthracite coal.

Sources: MIRECO (2010).

Legal Sources: Price Stabilisation Act, Article 2; Coal Industry Act, Article 29.

Tag: KOR_dt_07 to KOR_dt_10

Support to Briquette Production (data for 1989-)

Support to production of coal briquettes in Korea is provided in different ways and reporting a complete breakdown is not practical. For that reason, several items are here bundled together under the same general heading of "Support to Briquette Production". These include mostly subsidised inputs and capital upgrades. Support is expected to be phased out progressively and terminated by the end of 2020 as indicated in the 2010 Annex on country submissions for the G-20.

We aggregate available data for this programme by category of statutory incidence (inputs and capital). "Costs of Intermediates" thus includes subsidies covering various manufacturing and freight costs (maritime and road) while "Facilities" refers to capital upgrades. Support provided through the latter category (Facilities) stopped earlier than 2009.

Sources: MIRECO (2010).

Tag: KOR_dt_13 to KOR_dt_14

Funding for Clean Coal R&D (no data available)

SK Energy (Korea's largest oil refiner) and Pohang Iron and Steel Co (a domestic steel maker) are planning to develop jointly clean coal technologies at a total cost of KRW 3 350 billion (about USD 2.9 billion). The two companies envisage developing a manufacturing process for synthetic natural gas and the production of synthetic crude oil. The Korean government is to provide funding for KRW 25 billion (USD 21.6 million) in support of these initiatives.

No data are available yet given the very recent nature of the project.

Sources: KETEP (2009).

Tag: KOR_dt_19

Consumer Support Estimate

Fuel Tax Exemption for Agriculture (data for 2004-)

This tax provision was introduced in 1972 but the exemptions were only granted starting in 1986. It exempts farmers from the various taxes that are usually levied on sales of petroleum products such as gasoline, diesel, heavy oil, kerosene, and LPG. The final price of motor fuels in Korea comprises several layers of taxes such as the regular VAT (10%), the education tax, and an array of transport taxes (the so-called traffic, energy, and environmental taxes). In the case of heavy oil, kerosene, and LPG, an "individual consumption" tax is levied in lieu of the transport taxes.

Because a breakdown by type of tax could not be found, the exemptions for agriculture are being reported as a single item. Fuel-specific data were, however, available so that no further manipulation proved necessary. Time coverage becomes consistent starting in 2004 with only the years 1990, 1995, and 2000 being available before that.

Sources: MIFAFF (2010).

Legal Sources: Restriction of Special Taxation Act, Article 106-2.

Tag: KOR_te_01

Fuel Tax Exemption for Fisheries (data for 2004-)

This item dates back to 1972 and is similar to the exemption for agriculture (see above) except that it was seemingly introduced earlier and that it applies to the fisheries sector. Certain coastal passenger ships are also eligible for the exemption provided that fuel is being supplied directly to the Korea Shipping Association.

Because a breakdown by type of tax could not be found, the exemptions for fisheries are being reported as a single item. Fuel-specific data were, however, available so that no further manipulation proved necessary. The amounts reported under this heading do not include the exemption for coastal passenger ships.

Sources: MIFAFF (2010).

Legal Sources: Restriction of Special Taxation Act, Article 106-2.

Tag: KOR_te_02

VAT Exemption for Briquettes (data for 2001-)

The Value-Added Act exempts sales of coal briquettes from the value-added tax, which normally amounts to 10% of the pre-tax sale price. This exemption was introduced in 1976 and is meant to benefit low-income households through lower prices.

We estimate the cost of this exemption using the revenue-foregone method, meaning that we apply the standard rate of VAT (10%) to the total value of briquettes sold in a given year.

Sources: KEI (2007), KEEI (2010).

Legal Sources: Value-Added Tax Act, Article 12, 1-3.

Tag: KOR_te_03

VAT Exemption for Anthracite Coal (data for 2001-)

Sales of anthracite coal are exempted from the standard rate of value-added tax (10%). This exemption is meant to benefit low-income households through lower prices.

As for the VAT exemption on sales of briquettes, we estimate the cost of this provision using the revenue-foregone method, meaning that we apply the standard rate of VAT (10%) to the total value of coal sold in a given year. Data are only available for the 2001-06 period.

Sources: KEI (2007), KEEI (2010).

Legal Sources: Value-Added Tax Act, Article 12, 1-3.

Tag: KOR_te_04

Fuel Subsidy for Certain Users (data for 2001-)

This measure provides buses, taxis, freight transport, and passenger ships operating in coastal waters with direct grants covering 50% of the increase in the price of fuel between 2001 and 2002, and 100% of the increase that followed 2003. Support is also provided to disabled persons and so-called "State meritorious persons" for the entire price increase since 2001.

Available data allow a distinction to be made between types of fuels and users so that we break the programme into six different items (one for each type of recipient).

Sources: KEI (2007).

Legal Sources: Passenger Transport Service Act, Article 43 & 50.

Tag: KOR_dt_01 to KOR_dt_06

General Services Support Estimate

Stockpiling of Coal Briquettes (data for 1989-98)

This measure was meant to guarantee an adequate supply of coal briquettes during the cold winter season in Korea. Available sources indicate that funding stopped following 1998.

Because the measure benefits the briquette sector as a whole and – depending on the value of the relevant elasticities – may also benefit consumers, we allocated it to the GSSE.

Sources: MIRECO (2010).

Tag: KOR_dt_15

Coal Mining - Inherited Environmental Liabilities (data for 1989-)

This item comprises funding for environmental protection and reclamation of mining areas. The measure is allocated to the GSSE as it does not increase current production or consumption of coal.

Sources: MIRECO (2010).

Tag: KOR_dt_11

Coal Mining - Inherited Social Liabilities (data for 1989-)

This item includes funding for welfare programmes, treatment of pneumoconiosis (*i.e.* the "black lung disease" that affects coal miners), accident compensation insurance, and elementary education and scholarship funds for miners' children. Support is also provided to address the consequences of mine closures.

The measure is allocated to the GSSE as it does not increase current production or consumption of coal.

Sources: MIRECO (2010).

Tag: KOR_dt_12

Funding for CCS and Clean-Fuel R&D (data for 2000-)

The Korean government provides funding for R&D activities connected to carbon capture and storage as well as cleaner fuels.

The measure is added to the GSSE since it benefits the fossil-fuel sectors as a whole. It also does not increase current production or consumption of such fuels. We allocated the annual amounts reported in official publications to natural gas, hard coal, and heavy fuel oil on the basis of the IEA's Energy Balances for the generation sector.

Sources: KETEP (2009), IEA.

Tag: KOR_dt_16

Funding for Resources Technologies R&D (data for 2000-)

This programme provides funding supporting R&D projects connected to exploration technologies for oil and other mineral resources.

The measure is allocated to the GSSE since it benefits the oil and gas sectors as a whole. It also does not increase current production or consumption of such fuels. We split the annual amounts reported in official publications between crude oil and natural gas on the basis of the IEA's Energy Balances (Total Primary Energy Supply).

Sources: KETEP (2009), IEA.

Tag: KOR_dt_17

Funding for Renewable Energy R&D (data for 2000-)

The Korean government contributes to funding R&D projects connected to Integrated Gasification Combined Cycle (IGCC) as part of its renewable energy research programme.

Because the measure benefits the coal sector as a whole, we allocated it to the GSSE. It also does not increase current production or consumption of coal.

Sources: KETEP (2009), IEA.

Tag: KOR_dt_18

References

Policies or transfers

Coal Industry Act; Passenger Transport Service Act; Price Stabilisation Act; Restriction of Special Taxation Act, Value-Added Tax Act. Available at: http://elaw.klri.re.kr

MIFAFF (2010) *Statistical Yearbook*, Ministry for Food, Agriculture, Forestry and Fisheries, Available at: http://english.mifaff.go.kr.

MIRECO (2010) *Yearbook of MIRECO Statistics*, Mine Reclamation Corporation, Available at: http://www.mireco.or.kr.

KEEI (2010) *Yearbook of Energy Statistics*, Korea Energy Economics Institute, Available at: http://www.keei.re.kr.

KEI (2007) *The Environmentally Friendly Reform and its Effect of Subsidies in the Energy and Electric Power Sectors (I)*, Korea Environment Institute.

KETEP (2009) *Energy R&D Statistics*, Korea Institute of Energy Technology Evaluation and Planning, Available at: http://ketep.re.kr.

Energy statistics

IEA, *Energy Balances of OECD Countries*, 2010 Edition, International Energy Agency, Paris.

Figure 14.1.   Shares of fossil-fuel support by fuel, average for 2008-10 – Korea

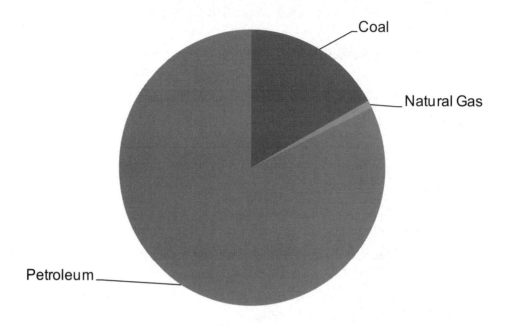

Source: OECD.

Figure 14.2.   Shares of fossil-fuel support by indicator, average for 2008-10 – Korea

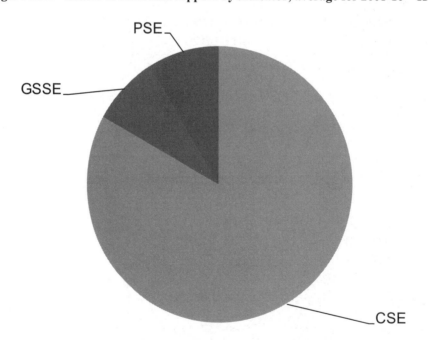

Source: OECD.

Table 14.1. Summary of fossil-fuel support to coal – Korea

(Millions of Korean won, nominal)

Support element	Jurisdiction	Avg 2000-02	Avg 2008-10	2008	2009	2010p
Producer Support Estimate						
Support to unit returns						
Support to Coal Production - Direct Support	–	122 830.34	36 020.33	59 595.00	24 233.00	24 233.00
Income support						
Support to Coal Production - Government Injection	–	n.a.	n.a.	n.a.	n.a.	n.a.
Support for intermediate inputs						
Support to Briquette Production - Costs of Intermediates	–	48 340.67	145 376.33	133 687.00	151 221.00	151 221.00
Support for capital formation						
Support to Coal Production - Capital and Facilities	–	1 567.00	10 821.67	9 685.00	11 390.00	11 390.00
Consumer Support Estimate						
Consumption						
VAT Exemption for Briquettes	–	6 226.00	20 536.33	19 393.00	21 108.00	21 108.00
VAT Exemption for Anthracite Coal	–	39 635.50	n.c.	:	:	:
General Services Support Estimate						
Coal Mining - Inherited Environmental Liabilities	–	31 255.00	0.00	0.00	0.00	0.00
Coal Mining - Inherited Social Liabilities	–	108 529.00	143 696.67	165 320.00	132 885.00	132 885.00
Funding for CCS and Clean-Fuel R&D	–	9 238.38	13 891.55	13 658.08	14 008.29	14 008.29
Funding for Renewable Energy R&D	–	5 666.67	3 866.67	10 600.00	500.00	500.00

Note: Tax expenditures for any given country are measured with reference to a benchmark tax treatment that is generally specific to that country. Consequently, the estimates contained in the table above are not necessarily comparable with estimates for other countries. In addition, because of the potential interaction between them, the summation of individual measures for a specific country may be problematic. The allocation of particular measures across fuel types was done by the OECD Secretariat based on the IEA's Energy Balances.

Source: OECD.

Table 14.2.   Summary of fossil-fuel support to petroleum – Korea

(Millions of Korean won, nominal)

Support element	Jurisdiction	Avg 2000-02	Avg 2008-10	2008	2009	2010p
Producer Support Estimate (n.a.)						
Consumer Support Estimate						
Consumption						
Fuel Subsidy for Certain Users - Buses		n.a.	n.c.	..	..	..
Fuel Subsidy for Certain Users - Taxis		n.a.	n.c.	..	..	..
Fuel Subsidy for Certain Users - Freight Transport		n.a.	n.c.	..	..	..
Fuel Subsidy for Certain Users - Passenger Ships		n.a.	n.c.	..	..	..
Fuel Subsidy for Certain Users - Disabled Persons		n.a.	n.c.	..	..	..
Fuel Subsidy for Certain Users - Meritorious Persons		n.a.	n.c.	..	..	..
Fuel Tax Exemption for Agriculture		557 872.00	1 131 696.00	1 153 530.00	1 120 779.00	1 120 779.00
Fuel Tax Exemption for Fisheries		n.c.	694 200.00	579 600.00	751 500.00	751 500.00
General Services Support Estimate						
Funding for CCS and Clean-Fuel R&D		2 574.60	952.24	936.24	960.25	960.25
Funding for Resources Technologies R&D		1 588.26	1 229.34	1 219.43	1 234.30	1 234.30

Note: Tax expenditures for any given country are measured with reference to a benchmark tax treatment that is generally specific to that country. Consequently, the estimates contained in the table above are not necessarily comparable with estimates for other countries. In addition, because of the potential interaction between them, the summation of individual measures for a specific country may be problematic. The allocation of particular measures across fuel types was done by the OECD Secretariat based on the IEA's Energy Balances.

Source: OECD.

Table 14.3.   Summary of fossil-fuel support to natural gas – Korea

(Millions of Korean won, nominal)

Support element	Jurisdiction	Avg 2000-02	Avg 2008-10	2008	2009	2010p
Producer Support Estimate (n.a.)						
Consumer Support Estimate (n.a.)						
General Services Support Estimate						
Funding for CCS and Clean-Fuel R&D	–	2 553.70	4 989.54	4 905.68	5 031.47	5 031.47
Funding for Resources Technologies R&D	–	11 078.40	15 303.99	15 180.57	15 365.70	15 365.70

Note: Tax expenditures for any given country are measured with reference to a benchmark tax treatment that is generally specific to that country. Consequently, the estimates contained in the table above are not necessarily comparable with estimates for other countries. In addition, because of the potential interaction between them, the summation of individual measures for a specific country may be problematic. The allocation of particular measures across fuel types was done by the OECD Secretariat based on the IEA's Energy Balances.

Source: OECD.

Chapter 15

Luxembourg

This chapter identifies, documents, and provides estimates of the various budgetary transfers and tax expenditures that relate to the production or use of fossil fuels in *Luxembourg*. An overview of *Luxembourg's* energy economy is first given to place the measures listed into context. A data-documentation section then describes those measures in a systematic way. Whenever possible, the description details a measure's formal beneficiary, its eligibility criteria and functioning, and the fuels whose production or use stand to benefit from the measure. The chapter ends with a set of charts and tables that provide, subject to availability, quantitative information and estimates for the various measures listed.

15. LUXEMBOURG

Energy resources and market structure

Luxembourg produces no fossil fuels, refines no petroleum, and half of its electricity is imported. Imported oil accounts for some 61% of its total primary energy supply, followed by natural gas (28%) and coal (2%). Net imports of electricity supply 7% of the country's energy needs, and the remaining 2% came from renewable energy sources, mostly biofuels for transport and other biomass-based fuels, but also small amounts of hydro-electricity and wind power.

Oil's dominance in Luxembourg's energy supply is explained in large part by sales of diesel and gasoline to foreign drivers – truckers crossing Luxembourg and cross-border commuters – who take advantage of the country's lower excise taxes on these fuels compared with the taxes applied by neighbouring EU Member States. Domestic transport fuel use is estimated to account for only one-fifth of total sales volume in Luxembourg.

Luxembourg meets its minimum oil stockholding obligations as a member of the IEA and the EU by obliging all oil importers to maintain stocks of petroleum products equivalent to at least 90 days of deliveries into domestic consumption during the previous calendar year. However, some 85% of this storage capacity is located outside of the country. The government is currently considering whether to create a national stockholding agency and to expand domestic storage capacity.

Luxembourg's natural-gas market is dominated by a small number of vertically integrated companies. Creos Luxembourg S.A. (formerly SOTEG) owns and operates the transmission system, and it supplies the majority of the market. Most of Creos's shares are owned by various private utilities, though the State maintains minority ownership. Creos also operates one of the two main electricity-transmission systems in the country. The State of Luxembourg owns about 40% of the company, via direct shareholdings and through the Société Nationale de Crédit et d'Investissement. The other main electricity grid operator is the Société de Transport de l'Electricité (SOTEL). Most of the electricity-distribution companies are owned by municipalities.

Prices, taxes and support mechanisms

Luxembourg maintains a price-setting mechanism for oil products through a signed agreement with oil-importing companies. This sets a maximum price for oil products sold to the end-consumer, including gasoline, automotive diesel, heating oil and liquefied petroleum gas (LPG). The pricing formula is based on the published price of oil products (Platt's Antwerp CIF product prices), to which the government adds a standard cost of transport from Antwerp to Luxembourg, a standard distribution margin covering the profits of the importers and the filling stations, and the cost of compulsory storage. These different costs are determined by the government after discussion with the oil companies' association (Groupement Pétrolier Luxembourgeois) and the retailers. The government decides when to change the maximum price according to market price variations in Antwerp, and there is a four-day delay between the time prices are quoted and the time retailers are able to adjust to a new maximum rate. Roughly two-thirds of fuel is sold at the maximum level, with the rest sold by small independent retailers which set prices below this level.

Both Luxembourg's natural gas and electricity markets are regulated by the Institut Luxembourgeois de Régulation (ILR), whose responsibilities include monitoring competition and preventing the abuse of dominant position. ILR also sets the network tariffs and the conditions for access to the network, based on rate-of-return regulation. The ILR is funded by the network operators.

Electricity prices before taxes are higher than in almost any other OECD country, especially for smaller companies and households. These high ex-tax prices are partly explained by the small market size and the large share of costly underground distribution cables. To compensate for the high ex-tax prices, Luxembourg applies an average ad valorem excise tax of 10.4% on household electricity prices, which is lower than that applied by its neighbours.

Luxembourg charges a reduced rate of VAT on for solid mineral fuel and mineral oil – 12%, compared with the normal VAT of 15% (which is below the rate of all three of its bordering countries: 21%, 19.6% and 19% respectively in Belgium, France and Germany in 2008). An even lower VAT rate, 6%, is applied to natural gas (liquid or gaseous) suitable for heating, lighting and motor fuel; electric current; heat supplied by a heating network. The government raised its excise duties on diesel in 2008, to EUR 0.302 per litre, in line with the EU directive setting minimum levels of taxation on energy products. This now puts Luxembourg's excise duties on diesel closer to Belgium's (EUR 0.32 per litre), while still significantly below those of France and Germany (EUR 0.43 and EUR 0.47 per litre, respectively), which maintain levels well above the European minimum. Agricultural use of petroleum fuels is exempted from excise tax.

Data documentation

General notes

The fiscal year in Luxembourg coincides with the calendar year. Following OECD convention, amounts prior to 1999 are expressed as "euro-fixed series", meaning that we apply the fixed EMU conversion rate (1 EUR = 40.339 LUF) to data initially expressed in the Luxembourg franc (LUF).

Consumer Support Estimate

Reduced Rate of VAT for Solid Mineral Fuel and Mineral Oil (no data available)

The standard VAT rate in Luxembourg is 15%. Since 1 January 2007, a 12% VAT rate has been applied to the supply of certain items, including solid mineral fuel and mineral oil.

No estimates of the revenue foregone due this provision are available.

Sources: Administration de l'Enregistrement et des Domaines (2011).

Reduced Rate of VAT for Natural Gas and Electricity (no data available)

The standard VAT rate in Luxembourg is 15%. Since 1 January 2007, a 6% VAT rate has been applied to natural gas and electricity (as well as plants and flowers). From 1 January 2009, heat and wood used for heating have also been subject to this reduced VAT rate.

No estimates of the revenue foregone due this provision are available.

Sources: Administration de l'Enregistrement et des Domaines (2011).

Reduced Rate of Excise for Certain Uses of Petroleum Fuels (no data available)

Sales of certain petroleum products (diesel, LPG, kerosene) in the Luxembourg are subject to a zero rate of excise duty when used in agriculture, horticulture, or for heating purposes.

No estimates of the revenue foregone due this provision are available.

Sources: Administration des Douanes et Accises (2011).

Reduced Rate of Excise for Coal and Natural Gas (no data available)

The use of coal, coke, and natural gas in the Luxembourg is subject to a zero rate of excise duty.

No estimates of the revenue foregone due this provision are available.

Sources: Administration des Douanes et Accises (2011).

References

Policies or transfers

Administration des Douanes et Accises (2011) *Tableau des taux d'accise applicables au Luxembourg*, Le Gouvernement du Grand-Duché de Luxembourg, Available at: http://www.do.etat.lu/acc/taux_et_timbres/taux_nationaux.htm.

Administration de l'Enregistrement et des Domaines (2011) *Loi TVA*, Le Gouvernement du Grand-Duché de Luxembourg, Available at: http://www.aed.public.lu/tva/loi/index.html.

Chapter 16

Mexico

This chapter identifies, documents, and provides estimates of the various budgetary transfers and tax expenditures that relate to the production or use of fossil fuels in *Mexico*. An overview of *Mexico's* energy economy is first given to place the measures listed into context. A data-documentation section then describes those measures in a systematic way. Whenever possible, the description details a measure's formal beneficiary, its eligibility criteria and functioning, and the fuels whose production or use stand to benefit from the measure. The chapter ends with a set of charts and tables that provide, subject to availability, quantitative information and estimates for the various measures listed.

16. MEXICO

Energy resources and market structure

Mexico has substantial resources of oil and natural gas. It is the world's seventh-leading producer of oil, though production has fallen sharply in the last five years or so as a result of declining output at the country's main producing field, Cantarell. Just over one-third of Mexico's oil production is exported. Natural gas production has been rising rapidly, but has not kept pace with demand, such that net imports – mainly piped from the United States, but now supplemented by increasing volumes of LNG – have grown from less than a tenth of supply in 2000 to almost one-fifth in 2009. Mexico's energy mix is dominated by oil and gas: oil accounts for 56% of total primary energy supply and natural gas 28%; most of the rest comes from a mixture of coal (half domestically produced and half imported), combustible renewables and waste, and geothermal energy, with a single nuclear plant contributing 2%. The share of oil has continued to fall steadily in recent years, while that of gas has grown briskly. National coal production peaked at 13.8 million tonnes in 2007, and has declined since then. Roughly one-fifth of the country's total production of energy is exported.

The energy sector is almost entirely run by state-owned companies. The national oil and gas company, Petroleos Mexicanos (Pemex), enjoys a monopoly on hydrocarbons production, oil refining and the marketing of oil products in the country. Pemex is the largest company in Mexico and one of the largest oil companies in the world. It has four operating subsidiaries: exploration and production, gas and basic petrochemicals, petrochemicals, and refining. In 2008, Mexico enacted new legislation that sought to reform the country's oil sector, with the aim of curbing the slide in crude-oil production. The measures included several administrative and institutional changes, including the establishment of a new hydrocarbons agency to regulate the sector. The reforms fell short of opening up exploration and production to competitors, but allow Pemex to create incentive-based service contracts with private companies. Pemex was also granted greater autonomy, including the ability to establish more flexible mechanisms for procurement and investment.

Pemex is also the dominant, but not the sole, company active in natural gas distribution and retailing. The Mexican government opened the downstream gas sector to private operators in 1995, though no single company may participate in more than one industry function (transportation, storage, or distribution). It also created the Energy Regulatory Commission (CRE) to monitor and regulate the sector. Nonetheless, Pemex still operates all the country's high-pressure gas pipelines and all 12 gas-processing plants, as well as most of the country's gas-distribution network. The two LNG import terminals currently in operation in Mexico are owned by foreign companies: Altamira, which started up in 2006, is a joint venture of Royal Dutch Shell, Total and Mitsui, while the Costa Azul terminal, which began receiving LNG in 2008, is operated by Sempra. A third plant is being built at Manzanillo by a consortium of Mitsui, KOGAS, and Samsung.

The structure of the coal-mining industry in Mexico has undergone tremendous change over the last 50 years. The 1961 mining code placed the control of capital in Mexican hands (a process known as the "Mexicanización" of the industry). A reform of the code in 1975 opened up foreign investment to a maximum 34% of the share of total capital in coal mines, and the 1992 Mexican Mining Law allowed 100% control of coal-mining properties not only by private Mexican interests, but also by foreign mining companies, subject to a standard concession-based process. Today, the major players in the industry are a mix of Mexican and foreign companies, some subsidiaries of diversified mining conglomerates.

State-owned Comision Federal de Electricidad (CFE) is the dominant player in power generation, controlling about two-thirds of installed generating capacity. CFE also holds a monopoly on electricity transmission and distribution. In 2009, CFE absorbed the operations of Luz y Fuerza del Centro (LFC), a state-owned company that managed distribution of electricity in Mexico City. The Comision Reguladora de Energia (CRE) has principle regulatory oversight of the electricity sector, but does not have direct jurisdiction over CFE. Changes to Mexican law in 1992 opened the generation sector to private participation. Any company seeking to establish private electricity generating capacity, or begin importing or exporting electric power, must obtain a permit from CRE. Most of the independent power producers operate combined-cycle gas turbines fuelled with natural gas.

Prices, taxes and support mechanisms

All energy prices are controlled in Mexico. The current legal framework, which dates back to 2000, allows the government to set retail prices of gasoline, diesel and LPG. Traditionally, pre-tax prices have been set well below the cost of imports, generally lagging any rise in import prices, with the government paying Pemex (the monopoly importer) the difference. Excise taxes are levied on transport fuels. VAT is levied on all fuels and energy services to non-commercial consumers.

All electricity tariffs are approved by the Ministry of Finance and Public Credit (SHCP); a tariff proposal is prepared once a year by an interagency group composed of the SHCP, CFE, LFC, CRE, the Ministry of Energy (SENER) and the national Water Commission (CAN). Average electricity tariffs in Mexico for small businesses and households have generally been held well below average cost, resulting in large subsidies, though – with the exception of the agricultural sector – they have trended upwards over the past decade.

The bulk of support to the consumption of fossil fuels in Mexico appears to be provided through tax provisions. There are fuel-tax credits available for the agriculture and fisheries sectors, for commercial vessels, for commuters, and for certain uses of diesel for other purposes than in a vehicle. Most of these credits benefit diesel fuel. They are also provided on top of the regulated prices that are set below import prices.

Data documentation

General notes

The fiscal year in Mexico coincides with the calendar year.

Consumer Support Estimate

General Diesel Tax Credit (data for 2003-06)

The Mexican government provides a tax credit applicable to purchases of diesel fuel at service stations for final consumption. The measure is generally available for automotive use in vehicles providing public and private transport of people or cargo through roads and highways.

This item also includes the diesel tax credits for the agriculture, forestry, and fisheries sectors for the years prior to 2007, at which time more disaggregated data become available.

Sources: Secretaría de Hacienda y Crédito Público (various years).

Tag: MEX_te_01

Diesel Tax Credit for Commuters (data for 2003-)

This measure helps commuters by providing them with a tax credit applicable to purchases of diesel fuel. No additional details could be found.

Sources: Secretaría de Hacienda y Crédito Público (various years).

Tag: MEX_te_02

Tax Credit for Marine Diesel (data for 2003-)

This measure provides a tax credit to certain final users of "marine" diesel fuel. The credit applies mostly to commercial shipping and related activities.

Sources: Secretaría de Hacienda y Crédito Público (various years).

Tag: MEX_te_03

Tax Credit for Purchased Diesel (data for 2008-)

This tax credit was introduced in 2008 and targets the use of diesel fuel for other purposes than in a vehicle. Eligible uses include most commercial activities (with the notable exception of mining) and certain marine and ground vehicles which have a low speed.

Sources: Secretaría de Hacienda y Crédito Público (various years).

Tag: MEX_te_04

Fuel-Tax Credit for Agriculture and Fisheries (data for 2007-)

This measure provides the agriculture, forestry, and fisheries sectors with a fuel-tax credit on their purchases of diesel fuel. Prior to 2007, this tax credit was comprised in the broader "General Diesel Tax Credit" (see above).

Sources: Secretaría de Hacienda y Crédito Público (various years).

Tag: MEX_te_05

Petroleum Revenue Stabilisation Fund (data for 2007-)

The Fondo de Estabilización de los Ingresos Petroleros (FEIP) was created in 2000 to smooth the impact of fluctuations in the price of oil on government revenues. As in Chile, the FEIP works in a countercyclical way, with the domestic sales price of petroleum products being either taxed or subsidised depending on variations in a benchmark import price.

The prices of petroleum products such as diesel, gasoline, and LPG are determined on a monthly basis by a governmental body. Where the Chilean FEPP uses a pre-determined formula, the Mexican FEIP relies on internal price forecasts. Gaps between those forecasts and actual reference prices result in either taxes or subsidies, depending on whether benchmark prices overshoot or undershoot the forecasts.

Starting in 2007, we report here the estimates of FEIP subsidies as they appear in Mexico's tax expenditure reports under "Impuesto negativo por enajenación de gasolinas y diesel" (Negative tax on the sale of gasoline and diesel). Since those estimates are understood as deviations from a benchmark import price, they may overlap with the IEA's subsidy estimates which rely on a price-gap approach. The latter approach compares the domestic price of petroleum products to an international reference price to infer the magnitude of support to the consumption of fuels.

Sources: Secretaría de Hacienda y Crédito Público (various years).

Tag: MEX_te_06.

References

Policies or transfers

Secretaría de Hacienda y Crédito Público (various years) *Presupuesto de Gastos Fiscales*, Government of Mexico, Available at:
http://www.shcp.gob.mx/INGRESOS/Paginas/presupuestoGastos.aspx.

Figure 16.1. Shares of fossil-fuel support by indicator, average for 2008-10 – Mexico

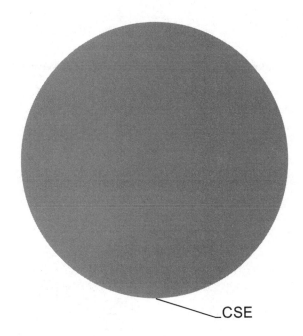

CSE

Source: OECD.

Table 16.1. Summary of fossil-fuel support to petroleum – Mexico

(Millions of Mexican pesos, nominal)

Support element	Jurisdiction	Avg 2000-02	Avg 2008-10	2008	2009	2010p
Producer Support Estimate (n.a.)						
Consumer Support Estimate						
Consumption						
General Diesel Tax Credit	Federal	n.c.	n.a.	n.a.	n.a.	n.a.
Diesel Tax Credit for Commuters	Federal	n.c.	2 032.07	0.00	3 048.10	3 048.10
Tax Credit for Marine Diesel	Federal	n.c.	57.00	0.00	85.50	85.50
Tax Credit for Purchased Diesel	Federal	n.a.	155.00	0.00	465.00	0.00
Fuel Tax Credit for Agriculture and Fisheries	Federal	n.c.	410.33	1 077.70	101.80	51.50
Petroleum Revenue Stabilisation Fund	Federal	n.c.	68 934.23	195 503.91	5 649.40	5 649.40
General Services Support Estimate (n.a.)						

Note: Tax expenditures for any given country are measured with reference to a benchmark tax treatment that is generally specific to that country. Consequently, the estimates contained in the table above are not necessarily comparable with estimates for other countries. In addition, because of the potential interaction between them, the summation of individual measures for a specific country may be problematic. The allocation of particular measures across fuel types was done by the OECD Secretariat based on the IEA's Energy Balances.

Source: OECD.

Chapter 17

Netherlands

This chapter identifies, documents, and provides estimates of the various budgetary transfers and tax expenditures that relate to the production or use of fossil fuels in the *Netherlands*. An overview of the *Netherland's* energy economy is first given to place the measures listed into context. A data-documentation section then describes those measures in a systematic way. Whenever possible, the description details a measure's formal beneficiary, its eligibility criteria and functioning, and the fuels whose production or use stand to benefit from the measure. The chapter ends with a set of charts and tables that provide, subject to availability, quantitative information and estimates for the various measures listed.

17. NETHERLANDS

Energy resources and market structure

The Netherlands has substantial but dwindling resources of natural gas, having been a major producer and exporter of gas to the rest of Europe since the super-giant Groningen field – the 11th largest ever discovered and the fourth-largest by peak production – was first developed in the early 1960s. Production has been in decline for several years, as Groningen edges closer to exhaustion and as smaller fields are reaching maturity. Oil resources are smaller, with output meeting only two-thirds of the country's own needs (additional volumes of crude oil are imported and refined for export markets). Unsurprisingly, gas is the single largest fuel in the Dutch primary energy mix, accounting for 40% of the country's energy use, closely followed by oil (38%). Coal contributes 10%, with the remainder coming from a mixture of nuclear power (from one reactor) and renewables (mainly biomass and wind power). In total, indigenous production meets over four-fifths of the country's primary energy needs.

For the most part, the Dutch energy industry is in private hands, but there is significant ownership of assets by the state, the provinces and municipalities in the gas and electricity sectors. The upstream oil and gas industry is entirely private and liberalised. NAM, owned jointly by Shell and ExxonMobil, operates Groningen and is, hence, the largest gas producer; several other oil and gas producers operate small fields onshore and offshore in the North Sea. All the refineries and distribution and retailing networks are privately owned.

Gasunie, a wholly state-owned company, owns and operates the gas transportation network through its affiliate Gas Transport Services (GTS). A trading and supply company, GasTerra, which is half owned by the state (10% directly and 40% through EBN, a state-owned company) and half by Shell and Exxon (25% each), sells domestically produced gas in the Netherlands. It is the major player in the wholesale market, with a share of nearly 60%. Four supply companies – Essent, Eneco, Nuon and Delta, which are mainly owned by provincial and municipal governments – dominate the retail market. Under a 2006 law mandating ownership unbundling of distribution companies, distribution assets must be fully separated from supply activity, and cannot be sold to private companies or investors. Gas competition is well developed, with a relatively large proportion of small consumers having switched away from the incumbent suppliers, in contrast with the situation in most other EU countries.

Electricity generating assets are partly privately owned and partly owned by provincial or municipal governments. Some major players have been overtaken by foreign energy companies over the last years. These foreign energy companies are partly or wholly owned by other states. The five largest generators – Electrabel, Essent, Nuon, E.ON Benelux and Delta – together hold more than two-thirds of installed capacity. Most of the remaining capacity is in combined heat and power plants operated by industrial firms, municipalities and the horticultural sector. The country's transmission system operator, TenneT, is fully owned by the state. There are more than 30 supply companies, of which the largest are Essent, Nuon and Eneco. The fourth-largest, Oxxio, was first owned by the UK firm, Centrica, but it has been taken over by Eneco.

Prices, taxes and support mechanisms

There are no wholesale or retail price controls on any fuel or energy service in the Netherlands. However, a so-called safety net exists for retail electricity and gas prices. The national regulator, the Office of Energy Regulation (Energiekamer) within the Competition Authority, is responsible for approving all tariffs and for ensuring that prices charged to consumers are reasonable; where this is not the case, the regulator can impose a tariff on the supplier, though this has never been necessary in practice.

In addition to VAT, excise taxes and a special compulsory storage fee (COVA) are levied on the sale of oil products, and an energy tax is levied on sales of electricity and gas (with tax rates decreasing with the level of consumption). As in many other countries, jet fuel is exempt from excise taxes when it is used for the purpose of commercial air navigation. There are some tax breaks aimed at encouraging exploration and production of hydrocarbons. For example, in order to promote the development of offshore marginal gas fields, a 25% deduction of investment costs can be applied to the calculation of the base for royalties.

Data documentation

General notes

The fiscal year in the Netherlands coincides with the calendar year. Following OECD convention, amounts prior to 1999 are expressed as 'euro-fixed series', meaning that we applied the fixed EMU conversion rate (1 EUR = 2.204 NLG) to data initially expressed in the Dutch Guilder (NLG).

Producer Support Estimate

The taxes and fees that apply to exploration and production of oil and gas are described in the 2003 Mining Act. Profits from production of hydrocarbons are subject to a 25.5% corporation tax (*Vennootschapsbelasting*) rate and royalty payments (*Winstaandeel*) at a 50% rate. These payments are, however, reduced by a cost uplift that allows for an extra 10% of the costs to be deducted from the income for royalty purposes.

Small Fields Policy (no data available)

This measure was introduced in 1974 to encourage gas producers to exploit small fields. Many such fields have been discovered in the Netherlands since the 1970s. Their volume is about a third of the super-giant Groningen field, which acts as a 'swing producer', balancing fluctuations in supply and demand in the gas market.

The *1998 Gas Act* stipulates that the trading and supply company, Gas Terra, must act as a guaranteed buyer of gas from small fields. Although gas companies can sell their output from small fields to other parties, Gas Terra has an obligation to immediately buy their gas at the prevailing market price. Gas Terra thus removes all uncertainties related to demand. Since Gas Terra is half-state-owned, this purchase agreement constitutes a measure encouraging exploration and production of gas.

No estimates are available for this item.

Sources: EBN, Gas Act (1998), Small Fields Policy.

Aid for Exploration of Offshore Marginal Gas Fields (no data available)

This measure provides a deduction from the base for calculating royalty payments to gas companies that explore offshore marginal (*i.e.* insufficiently profitable) gas fields. This policy was approved by the European Commission in 2010. Gas producers exploring offshore marginal gas fields can deduct up to 25% of their investment costs from their profit when calculating their amount of taxable income.

No estimates are available for this item.

Sources: Small Fields Policy.

Consumer Support Estimate

Tax-expenditure estimates between 2001 and 2009 were provided by the Ministry of Finance. All other data estimates come from publicly available government sources.

Reduced Energy-Tax Rate in Horticulture (data for 2001-)

At the introduction of the energy tax in 1996, the government decided to apply a zero energy-tax rate to fuels used in the horticultural sector, under the condition that those benefitting from the scheme would participate in voluntary agreements to improve their energy efficiency. The European Commission approved this exemption until the end of 1999.

In 2000, the exemption was replaced by a tax reduction that was to be diminished over time. In particular, the European Commission stipulated that the reduced energy-tax rate granted to the horticultural sector in the Netherlands had to be raised both in 2002 and 2005 by 10% in comparison with the benchmark, which was the rates of the energy tax that applied to other energy-intensive businesses.

This tax expenditure applies mainly to natural gas (virtually all horticultural enterprises are connected to the natural-gas grids) and, hence, the amount of this tax expenditure is allocated to natural gas only. Those very few horticultural enterprises that are not connected to the natural-gas grids can obtain a partial refund for mineral oils used for heating.

Sources: Information on 2008-11 Tax Expenditures (2011), Ministry of Finance (various years).

Tag: NLD_te_01

Energy-Tax Rebate for Religious Institutions (data for 2001-.)

Since 2000, users of buildings that are primarily used for public religious services or for philosophical reflection can apply for a 50% energy-tax rebate for both natural gas and electricity. Those very few religious institutions that are not connected to the natural-gas grids can obtain a partial refund for mineral oils used for heating.

We use the IEA's Energy Balances for the residential sector to allocate the amounts reported in official budget documents to natural gas and electricity. Only those amounts that pertain to natural gas are considered.

Sources: IEA, Ministry of Finance (various years), Information on 2008-11 Tax Expenditures (2011).

Tag: NLD_te_02

Energy-Tax Rebate for Non-Profit Organisations (data for 2001-)

The 50% energy-tax rebate mentioned above also applies to the heating of buildings of non-profit organisations. The sport sector is (partially) compensated by the Ministry of Health, Welfare and Sport. Since 2006, community buildings used by non-profit organisations for over 70% of the time could also apply for the rebate.

We use the IEA's Energy Balances for the residential sector to allocate the amounts reported in official budget documents to natural gas and electricity. Only those amounts that pertain to natural gas are considered.

Sources: IEA, Ministry of Finance (various years).

Tag: NLD_te_03

Differentiated Tax Rate on Gas Oil (data for 2001-)

A differentiated tax rate applies to gas oil, depending on its use. A higher rate applies when it is used as transport fuel. A lower rate applies to uses other than as transport fuel, *e.g.* when used for heating or in off-road machinery. Sources: Ministry of Finance (various years), Information on 2008-11 Tax Expenditures (2011).

Tag: NLD_te_05

References

Policies or transfers

Government Budget (2009), Available at: http://www2.miljoenennota.prinsjesdag2009.nl/downloads/Internetbijlagen.pdf.

EBN, *Oil and Gas*, Available at: http://www.ebn.nl/en/activities_oil-and-gas.php.

European Commission (2007), *State Aid / The Netherlands, Aid No N 396/07, Energy green tax, reduction for the glasshouse horticulture sector*, Available at: http://ec.europa.eu/agriculture/stateaid/decisions/n39607_en.pdf.

Gas Act (1998), Available at: http://www.energiekamer.nl/engels/gas/Index.asp.

NL Oil and Gas Portal (2009), *Fees and Taxation Related to Exploration and Production Licenses in the Netherlands and Its Continental Shelf*, Available at: http://www.nlog.nl/resources/procedures/NLOG_Taxation_Nov2009.pdf.

Parliamentary Note (2002), *Notitie fiscaliteit, landbouw- en natuurbeleid, Kamerstuk 28 207 nr. 1, Tweede Kamer der Staten-Generaal*, Available at: http://cdn.ikregeer.nl/pdf/kst-28207-1.pdf.

Small Fields Policy, *Kleine Gasvelden, Rijksoverheid*, Available at: http://www.rijksoverheid.nl/onderwerpen/gas/gasexploratie-en-productie/kleine-gasvelden.

Information on 2008-11 Tax Expenditures (2011), Available at: http://www.rijksoverheid.nl/bestanden/documenten-en-publicaties/brochures/2010/12/27/informatieblad-belastingtarieven-2008-2011/informatieblad-belastingtarieven-2008-2011.pdf.

Energy statistics

IEA, *Energy Balances of OECD Countries*, 2010 Edition, International Energy Agency, Paris.

Figure 17.1.   Shares of fossil-fuel support by fuel, average for 2008-10 – Netherlands

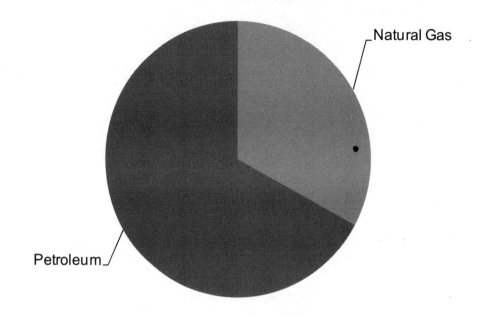

Source: OECD.

Figure 17.2.   Shares of fossil-fuel support by indicator, average for 2008-10 – Netherlands

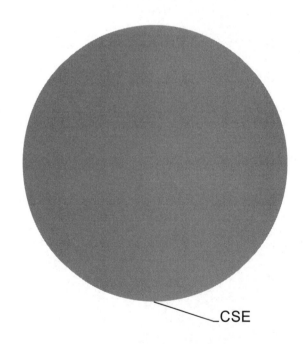

Source: OECD.

INVENTORY OF ESTIMATED BUDGETARY SUPPORT AND TAX EXPENDITURES FOR FOSSIL FUELS © OECD 2011

Table 17.1. Summary of fossil-fuel support to petroleum – Netherlands

(Millions of euros, nominal)

Support element	Jurisdiction	Avg 2000-02	Avg 2008-10	2008	2009	2010p
Producer Support Estimate (n.a.)						
Consumer Support Estimate						
Consumption						
Differentiated Tax Rate on Gas Oil		–	n.c.	225.67	228.00	208.00	241.00
General Services Support Estimate (n.a.)						

Note: Tax expenditures for any given country are measured with reference to a benchmark tax treatment that is generally specific to that country. Consequently, the estimates contained in the table above are not necessarily comparable with estimates for other countries. In addition, because of the potential interaction between them, the summation of individual measures for a specific country may be problematic. The allocation of particular measures across fuel types was done by the OECD Secretariat based on the IEA's Energy Balances.

Source: OECD.

Table 17.2. Summary of fossil-fuel support to natural gas – Netherlands

(Millions of euros, nominal)

Support element	Jurisdiction	Avg 2000-02	Avg 2008-10	2008	2009	2010p
Producer Support Estimate (n.a.)						
Consumer Support Estimate						
Consumption						
Reduced Energy Tax Rate for Horticulture	–	50.50	92.00	98.00	86.00	92.00
Energy Tax Rebate for Religious Institutions	–	2.42	4.36	3.85	4.61	4.61
Energy Tax Rebate for Non Profit Organisations	–	2.81	14.10	11.54	15.38	15.38
General Services Support Estimate (n.a.)						

Note: Tax expenditures for any given country are measured with reference to a benchmark tax treatment that is generally specific to that country. Consequently, the estimates contained in the table above are not necessarily comparable with estimates for other countries. In addition, because of the potential interaction between them, the summation of individual measures for a specific country may be problematic. The allocation of particular measures across fuel types was done by the OECD Secretariat based on the IEA's Energy Balances.

Source: OECD.

Chapter 18

New Zealand

This chapter identifies, documents, and provides estimates of the various budgetary transfers and tax expenditures that relate to the production or use of fossil fuels in *New Zealand*. An overview of *New Zealand*'s energy economy is first given to place the measures listed into context. A data-documentation section then describes those measures in a systematic way. Whenever possible, the description details a measure's formal beneficiary, its eligibility criteria and functioning, and the fuels whose production or use stand to benefit from the measure. The chapter ends with a set of charts and tables that provide, subject to availability, quantitative information and estimates for the various measures listed.

18. NEW ZEALAND

Energy resources and market structure

Relative to the size of its market, New Zealand is reasonably well-endowed with fossil-energy resources. It is a net exporter of coal, but imports the lion's share of its oil; natural gas production is in decline, as the Maui field – the main producing field since the end of the 1970s – nears economic exhaustion, which is forcing down consumption as there are no facilities to import gas. Oil is the leading fuel in the primary energy mix, accounting for almost a quarter of total energy supply, followed by gas, with 20%. Geothermal energy supplies a further 17% – the second-largest share of any OECD country (after Iceland) – hydropower 12%, coal 9% and biomass 8%. On balance, imports account for only 14% of total energy supply.

Despite pioneering moves to liberalise the energy industry in the 1980s and 1990s, the state retains significant ownership stakes, notably in electricity. The oil industry was liberalised in the 1980s, removing price controls, government involvement in refining, licensing requirements for wholesalers and retailers and restrictions on imports of refined products. Upstream oil and gas production is dominated by Shell, which operates the Maui field in partnership with Todd Energy through Shell Todd Oil Services. BP, Caltex, Mobil and Z Energy own about three-quarters of New Zealand's only refinery at Marsden Point; the remaining shares are owned by outside and institutional investors. Together with Gull Petroleum, these companies are responsible for wholesaling and retailing. The natural gas market was deregulated in the 1980s and 1990s, though the government still holds an interest in downstream retailers through two state-owned enterprises (SOEs), Genesis Energy and Mighty River Power, which have started to move into upstream activities.

Meridian, another SOE, together with Genesis and Mighty River, hold the bulk of power generation capacity. The SOE, Transpower, is responsible for transmission, while close to 30 companies own and operate local distribution networks. The ownership of distribution companies is a mix of public listings, shareholder co-operatives, community trusts and local bodies; most are owned by trusts. Distribution and retailing are structurally unbundled and the retail market is completely contestable. There is a high degree of vertical integration between generation and retail activities, with the five main generation companies controlling almost all retail sales.

Prices, taxes and support mechanisms

There are no price controls on any fuel or energy service in New Zealand. A goods and services tax (GST), which is generally refundable for commercial users, is payable on all fuels and energy services. Gasoline, LPG and compressed natural gas are subject to excise taxes and various special levies. There are also road-user charges and other fees imposed on commercial diesel vehicles. The government refunds the excise duty and the GST on automotive fuels consumed in off-road uses. An Energy Resources Levy is applied to natural gas produced from fields discovered before 1986 and on some opencast coal production. Some tax breaks and royalty reductions were put in place as part of a suite of measures to encourage exploration for new oil and gas reserves (also offshore) but the royalty reductions expired at the end of 2009. There are also special levies on gas and electricity to fund safety-related regulatory activities. There are no subsidies on gas or electricity for low-income consumers.

Data documentation

General notes

The fiscal year in New Zealand runs from 1 July to 30 June. Following OECD convention, data are allocated to the starting calendar year so that data covering the period July 2005 to June 2006 are allocated to 2005.

Producer Support Estimate

Tax Deductions for Petroleum-Mining Expenditures[23] (no data available)

The current taxation scheme for petroleum mining has been in place since 1991.[24] It comprises two concessions relating to the treatment of petroleum mining expenditure. Exploration expenditure is fully deductible in the year in which it is incurred, including expenditure of a capital nature. Petroleum exploration expenditure includes exploratory-well expenditure, prospecting expenditure, and expenditure to acquire an existing privilege, a prospecting permit for petroleum, or an exploration permit for petroleum.

Petroleum development expenditure is deductible in equal amounts over an accelerated seven-year period. Petroleum development expenditure means expenditure incurred by a petroleum miner that directly concerns a permit area, and is for acquiring, constructing, or planning petroleum mining assets. While income from a petroleum field with a life shorter than seven years may be over-taxed as a result of this provision, income from a petroleum field with a life of more than seven years may end up being under-taxed.

In 2008, a number of additional concessions were granted. Petroleum asset owners have been given the option of using a reserve depletion method for calculating tax depreciation on petroleum development expenditure, in addition to the standard seven-year straight-line option. The reserve depletion options allows for tax recovery of development expenditure to be made in line with the field's production profile. It was introduced to deal with a concern that petroleum miners may be discouraged under the previous regime from investing in projects that have a life

---

[23] There is also a concessionary tax regime in place for the mining of "specified minerals" such as gold, silver, alumina minerals and silica, whereby a mining company can deduct all exploration and development expenditure in the year it is incurred, irrespective of whether or not it is paid for the acquisition of an asset. However, the list of specified minerals *does not* include coal, which is taxed under the same rules as ordinary companies.

[24] In the Crown Minerals Act of 1991, petroleum is defined as any naturally occurring hydrocarbon (other than coal), or mixtures of, whether in a gaseous, liquid, or solid state.

span of less than seven years. This option, which applies from 1 April 2008, is not available for fields already in production at 1 April 2008.

Another 2008 amendment allows the deduction for development expenditure to begin from the date at which the expenditure is incurred. Previously this had been only available to offshore petroleum development, with onshore development expenditure deductible only from the date that commercial production starts. This distinction has been removed. Petroleum mining companies have also been given the ability to deduct any unallocated expenditure when a production well stops producing when a taxpayer is depreciating development expenditure under the reserve depletion method.

The New Zealand government does not collect data on all tax expenditures as the compliance cost of collecting additional data is, in some instances, deemed prohibitive. Uncollected data include the deductions for petroleum mining. The 2010 Tax Expenditure Statement was the first time New Zealand has released tax expenditure data since 1984.

Legal Sources: Sections DT 1, DT 5, and EJ 12 of the Income Tax Act of 2007 (*www.legislation.govt.nz/*).

Sources: New Zealand Treasury (2010), AUPEC (2009), McDouall Stuart (2009).

Reduction in Royalty Payments for Petroleum (no data available)

To provide the Crown with a fair financial return, all petroleum exploration and mining permits are granted subject to conditions that require the permit holder to calculate and pay royalties to the Crown.[25] Since 1995 the standard royalty regime for petroleum comprises:

- an *ad valorem* royalty (AVR) component of 5% payable on the basis of either a sales price received or, where there has been no sale or no arm's length sale, the deemed sales price; and

- an accounting profits royalty (APR) component of 20% payable on the difference between revenue received from the sale of products and the costs of extracting, processing and selling those products up to the point of sale.

In respect of an exploration permit, the permit holder is liable to pay only the AVR. For all mining permits with net sales above NZD 1 million, the permit holder is required to calculate for each period for which a royalty return must be provided both the AVR and the APR, and pay whichever is the higher. Typically, AVR is paid in the early years of production as prior costs are netted against revenue and at the end of the field's life, as production falls. APR is typically paid during the peak years of production of non-marginal fields.

In 2004, as part of a suite of measures to encourage exploration for new gas reserves, the government announced that royalty payments would be reduced. In

---

[25]   Under the Crown Minerals Act 1991, the Crown owns all in-ground petroleum, gold and silver in New Zealand and approximately half of the coal and other mineral resources. It also has jurisdiction of the petroleum and minerals in New Zealand's exclusive economic zone and continental shelf.

summary, for any discovery made between 30 June 2004 and 31 December 2009, the royalty regime comprised:

- an AVR component of 1% on natural gas and 5% on oil; and

- an APR component of 15% on the first NZD 750 million (cumulative) gross sales from an offshore discovery, the first NZD 250 million (cumulative) gross sales from an onshore discovery, and a 20% accounting profits royalty on any additional production.

In addition, royalty, prospecting and exploration costs incurred anywhere in New Zealand between 30 June 2004 and 31 December 2009 were made deductible for the purposes of calculating the accounting profits. Outside this time frame, prospecting and exploration costs deductible for the purposes of calculating the accounting profits royalty are limited to the area of the mining permit and preceding exploration permit. As such, the measure no longer applied as of 31 December 2009.

While data on the value of total petroleum royalties received by the government are available, estimates of the revenue forgone as a result of the reduction in royalty payments are not calculated.

Sources: New Zealand Government (2005).

Non-Resident Drilling Rig and Seismic Ship Tax Exemption (no data available)

On 1 October 2005, an exemption from income tax on income derived from petroleum exploration and development activities in an offshore permit area in New Zealand by a non-resident company was introduced. The original exemption was for a five-year period, starting at the beginning of the non-resident company's 2005/06 financial year and ending on 31 December 2009. The exemption was, however, recently extended by a further five years to end on 31 December 2014.

Exploration and development activities are here defined as the operation of a ship to provide seismic survey readings or the drilling of an exploratory well or other well. These activities must be undertaken for the purposes of identifying and developing exploitable petroleum deposits or occurrences in an offshore permit area.

This provision was introduced as part of the package announced in June 2004 to boost gas exploration. Prior to this, non-resident drilling rig operators and seismic ship operators were taxed on their income derived from New Zealand operations from the first day of their presence in New Zealand, the same as non-residence operators undertaking other activities.[26]

The change means that non-resident offshore rig operators and non-resident operators of seismic survey ships have been exempt from paying company tax on their profits in New Zealand from 2004. The reason for targeting only non-residents is that only non-residents currently provide the types of services covered by the exemption.

Information on the revenue foregone as a result of this policy measure is not available.

---

[26] An exception is provided under some double-tax agreements, whereby non-resident operators are only taxed on their New Zealand derived income if they are in New Zealand for longer than 183 days.

Legal Sources: Section CW 57 of the Income Tax Act of 2007 (*www.legislation.govt.nz/*).

Consumer Support Estimate

Motor-Spirits Excise Duty Refund (data for 1997-)

A motor-spirits excise duty is charged in New Zealand on the sale of certain types of fuel to final consumers (currently NZD 0.48524 per litre on gasoline as from 1 October 2010). Taxable fuels include gasoline, LPG, and compressed natural gas (CNG). As of 1 October 2008, all the revenue from this excise duty – along with road user charges, motor-vehicle registration, and licensing fees – are paid into the National Land Transport Fund and used for road construction and maintenance purposes only. Prior to this date, the government retained a large proportion of the revenue collected from the excise duty charged on gasoline in the general consolidated account.

In general terms, the government allows a refund of the excise duty and the goods and services tax (GST) charged on motor spirits for fuel consumed in off-road usage. Examples of eligible uses would include agricultural vehicles, commercial vessels, and certain licensed vehicles. Refunds are applied for and verified by the New Zealand Transport Agency. Only those applicants meeting legislative and regulative requirements have their refund applications approved.

In addition, provision has been made for the refund of the Accident Compensation Corporation (ACC) Levy for exempted vehicles and for fuel used for commercial purposes (currently NZD 0.099 per litre). The ACC levy was introduced on 1 October 1991 and goes into the ACC Motor Vehicle Account, which covers the cost of accidents and rehabilitation for victims of accidents. These refunds are automatically added onto the refund of fuel excise duty.

Diesel fuel does not qualify for any refunds since it is not subject to the motor-spirits excise duty. Estimates of the annual fuel-tax refunds are available within the Budget documents. The refunds typically account for around 3 to 4% of the revenue collected through the motor-spirits excise duty.

We allocate the amounts reported to gasoline, LPG and CNG on the basis of the IEA's Energy Balances for the agriculture, fisheries, commercial services, and industrial sectors.

Sources: New Zealand Transport Agency (2007), New Zealand Treasury (various years), IEA.

Tag: NZL_te_01

Risk-Sharing Agreement with Genesis Energy (no data available)

On 12 August 2004, the government agreed with Genesis Power Limited, a State-Owned Enterprise (SOE), to underwrite its fuel-supply risk in developing a gas-fired electricity generation plant at its Huntly site for up to a maximum of 10 years. This government guarantee allowed the company to proceed forward with the project.

This measure is viewed by the government as a one-off agreement to provide certainty in the electricity sector during the transition to the post-Maui environment (see "Energy resources and market structure" above). Under the agreement, the Crown will compensate Genesis in the event it is unable to secure the gas that it needs.

To date, the government has not had to pay any compensation to Genesis under the terms of the deed. Information on the value of the agreement to Genesis is commercially confidential.

Sources: Hodgson (2004), New Zealand Treasury (2004).

General Services Support Estimate

Research and Development (data for 1995-)

The government is funding research and development related to energy on a project-by-project basis through the Foundation from Research Science and Technology (FRST). GNS Science, a Crown Research Institute (CRI), provides most of the oil and gas specific research under multi-year programme contracts to FRST. This work ranges from 'big-picture' research into the tectonic evolution of the New Zealand continent, to detailed laboratory analysis of key geological and geochemical components of petroleum systems. One of the main goals of the research is to reduce the perceived geological uncertainties for petroleum exploration in New Zealand.

In 2010, Crown Minerals contracted GNS Science to deliver a two-year Petroleum Exploration and Geosciences Initiative (PEGI) Project worth NZD 7.6 million. The suite of fourteen individual but broadly inter-related projects feature a range of evaluation and research focusing on Taranaki, New Zealand's only current commercially producing petroleum region. Just over half (NZD 4 million) is funded by the Crown Minerals acquisition of petroleum exploration data fund, with the remaining NZD 3.6 million from current FRST grants. Meanwhile, there appears to be little direct research funding provided for coal.

Estimates of the total annual value of research relating to fossil fuels are not directly available, and have to be compiled by adding up the annual allocations of relevant programmes existing in any one year.

We allocate this programme to the GSSE since it does not increase current production or consumption of fossil fuels. Moreover, it benefits the oil and gas industry as a whole. We use production data from the IEA to allocate the annual amounts reported in budget documents to oil and natural gas extraction. Data are not available for the years 2001 to 2003.

Sources: McDouall Stuart (2009), GNS Science (various years), FRST (various years), IEA.

Tag: NZL_dt_01

Acquisition of Petroleum Exploration Data (data for 2004-)

As part of a suite of measures announced in June 2004, the government committed NZD 15 million over three years (FY2004/05 to FY2006/07) to fund the acquisition and processing of high-quality 2D seismic data in New Zealand's offshore basins. The programme is administered by Crown Minerals in close working relationship with the industry and GNS Science, who is contracted to process the seismic data collected. Seismic surveying is central to the government's strategy of attracting oil majors to explore New Zealand's petroleum potential. Before a new acreage area (block offer) is released, seismic data is collected, processed and interpreted – then made freely available to companies interested in bidding for exploration permits. Following the success of the programme in attracting exploration interest, further government funding has been provided to support seismic data acquisition.

We allocate this programme to the GSSE since it does not increase current production or consumption of fossil fuels. Moreover, it benefits the oil and gas industry as a whole. We use production data from the IEA to allocate the annual amounts reported in budget documents to oil and natural gas extraction.

Sources: New Zealand Treasury (various years), Crown Minerals (various years), IEA.

Tag: NZL_dt_02

Management of IEA Oil Stocks (data for 2006-)

As part of its membership of the International Energy Agency, New Zealand is required to hold, at any one time, emergency reserve oil stocks equivalent to 90 days of market demand. The industry's normal stockholding practices have in the past been relied on to meet this requirement, with no minimum stockholding obligations placed on the industry. In 2004, it became apparent that the requirement was no longer complied with. Consequently, since 2007, the government has been meeting the country's overall minimum 90-day net import obligation by tendering for additional oil stocks using "ticket" contracts (an option to purchase stock in an IEA-declared emergency) with major oil companies overseas. Owing to its growing domestic production in recent years, New Zealand's IEA stockholding obligation has fallen from 3.7 million barrels in 2007 to 0.8 million barrels in 2010.

As in the case of the United States, and as a result of the policy of "ticket" contracts, part of the country's IEA obligations is financed out of the general government budget. The entire programme is allocated to crude oil. Because oil stocks benefit the oil sector as a whole and – depending on the value of the relevant elasticities – may also benefit consumers, we allocated the measure to the GSSE.

Sources: New Zealand Treasury (various years), IEA (2010).

Tag: NZL_dt_03

References

Policies or transfers

AUPEC (2009) *Evaluation of the Petroleum Tax and Licensing Regime of New Zealand,* Report to the Ministry of Economic Development, Available at: www.med.govt.nz/upload/70849/AUPEC-July-2009.pdf.

Crown Minerals (various years) *Annual Report*, Available at: www.crownminerals.govt.nz.

FRST (various years) *Research Abstracts and Reports Databases*, Available at: http://myfrst.frst.govt.nz/Public/ResearchReports/.

GNS Science (various years) *Annual Report*, Available at: www.gns.cri.nz.

Hodgson, Pete (2004) *Genesis e3p risk sharing questions and answers*, Available at: http://www.beehive.govt.nz/node/20632.

IEA (2010) *Energy Policies of IEA Countries – New Zealand*, International Energy Agency, Paris.

McDouall Stuart (2009) *Stepping Up: Options for developing the potential of New Zealand's oil, gas and minerals sector*, Report to the Ministry of Economic Development, Available at: www.med.govt.nz/upload/70851/McDouall-Stuart-June-2009.PDF.

New Zealand Government (2005) *Minerals Programme for Petroleum 2005*, Available at: www.crownminerals.govt.nz/cms/pdf-library/petroleum-publications-1/mins-prog-for-petroleum-2005.pdf.

New Zealand Transport Agency (2007) 'Excise duty: Who can get refunds and how', *Factsheet 14*, Available at: www.nzta.govt.nz/resources/factsheets/14/excise-duty.html.

New Zealand Treasury (2004) *Genesis Energy e3p Risk Sharing Agreement with the Government*, Information Release, Available at: www.treasury.govt.nz/publications/informationreleases/genesis/index.htm.

New Zealand Treasury (2010) *2010 Tax Expenditure Statement*, Available at: www.treasury.govt.nz/budget/2010/taxexpenditure.

New Zealand Treasury (various years) *Budget Documents*, Available at: www.treasury.govt.nz/budget/.

Energy statistics

IEA, *Energy Balances of OECD Countries*, 2010 Edition, International Energy Agency, Paris.

Figure 18.1. Shares of fossil-fuel support by fuel, average for 2008-10 – New Zealand

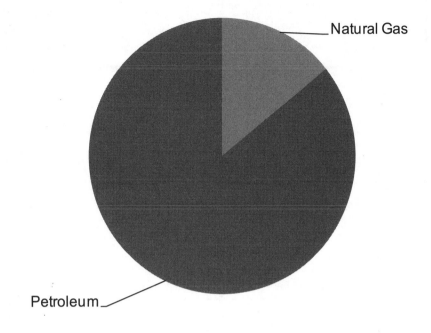

Source: OECD.

Figure 18.2. Shares of fossil-fuel support by indicator, average for 2008-10 – New Zealand

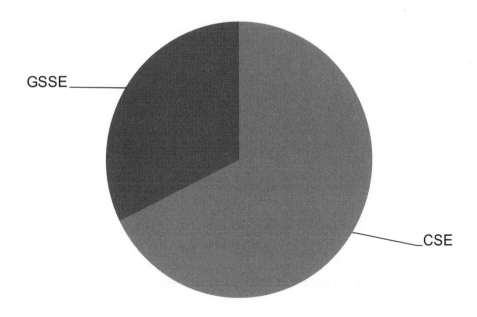

Source: OECD.

Table 18.1. Summary of fossil-fuel support to petroleum – New Zealand

(Millions of New Zealand dollars, nominal)

Support element	Jurisdiction	Avg 2000-02	Avg 2008-10	2008	2009	2010p
Producer Support Estimate (n.a.)						
Consumer Support Estimate						
Consumption						
Motor Spirits Excise Duty Refund	–	24.71	36.46	34.68	36.40	38.31
General Services Support Estimate						
Management of IEA Oil Stocks	–	n.a.	3.29	4.82	2.06	3.00
Research and Development	–	n.c.	2.53	2.78	2.41	2.41
Acquisition of Petroleum Exploration Data	–	n.a.	3.94	2.63	6.44	2.75

Note: Tax expenditures for any given country are measured with reference to a benchmark tax treatment that is generally specific to that country. Consequently, the estimates contained in the table above are not necessarily comparable with estimates for other countries. In addition, because of the potential interaction between them, the summation of individual measures for a specific country may be problematic. The allocation of particular measures across fuel types was done by the OECD Secretariat based on the IEA's Energy Balances.

Source: OECD.

Table 18.2.   Summary of fossil-fuel support to natural gas – New Zealand

(Millions of New Zealand dollars, nominal)

Support element	Jurisdiction	Avg 2000-02	Avg 2008-10	2008	2009	2010p
Producer Support Estimate (n.a.)						
Consumer Support Estimate (n.a.)						
General Services Support Estimate						
Research and Development	–	n.c.	2.99	3.28	2.84	2.84
Acquisition of Petroleum Exploration Data	–	n.a.	4.64	3.10	7.58	3.24

Note: Tax expenditures for any given country are measured with reference to a benchmark tax treatment that is generally specific to that country. Consequently, the estimates contained in the table above are not necessarily comparable with estimates for other countries. In addition, because of the potential interaction between them, the summation of individual measures for a specific country may be problematic. The allocation of particular measures across fuel types was done by the OECD Secretariat based on the IEA's Energy Balances.

Source: OECD.

Chapter 19

Norway

This chapter identifies, documents, and provides estimates of the various budgetary transfers and tax expenditures that relate to the production or use of fossil fuels in *Norway*. An overview of *Noway's* energy economy is first given to place the measures listed into context. A data-documentation section then describes those measures in a systematic way. Whenever possible, the description details a measure's formal beneficiary, its eligibility criteria and functioning, and the fuels whose production or use stand to benefit from the measure. The chapter ends with a set of charts and tables that provide, subject to availability, quantitative information and estimates for the various measures listed.

19. NORWAY

Energy resources and market structure

Norway is the third-leading exporter of oil and natural gas in the world, after Russia and Saudi Arabia. Production increased four-fold in less than two decades, from 1980 to 1997, and has fluctuated since, with declining oil output offset by rising volumes of gas. Most gas is piped to the United Kingdom and continental Europe; LNG exports from a single plant began in 2007. While oil and gas together contribute to 55% of Norway's domestic energy needs, hydropower is the single biggest energy source (Norway is the sixth biggest hydropower producer in the world) accounting for 41% of total primary energy supply. Norway is also involved in a significant power exchange with its neighbours, the magnitude of which depends on precipitation and water inflows to the water reservoirs of the country. Coal has been mined on the Svalbard archipelago since the early 1900s. In 2007 production from the remaining two mines reached a record level of 4.1 million tonnes; by 2009 it had fallen back to 2.6 million tonnes. All but 5% of the coal is now exported, mostly to Germany. A third coal field is undergoing feasibility studies and is planned to commence operations in 2014.

Petroleum forms the backbone of the Norwegian economy, so the government plays a large direct role in the sector. The state holds around one-third of Norway's proven oil and gas reserves. The state direct ownership of these assets is organised into the State's Direct Financial Interest (SDFI) and is managed by the state-owned company, Petoro. The Ministry of Petroleum and Energy (MPE) decides on the SDFI's share of participation when production licences are awarded. The state pays its share of investments and costs, and receives a corresponding share of the income from the production licence. Statoil ASA, an international oil company, 67% of which is owned by the Norwegian state. The company is the biggest player in the upstream sector, operating about 80% of total production on the Norwegian Continental Shelf. Statoil, apart from its own petroleum, is also responsible for marketing of the petroleum owned by the SDFI. The company also has a majority interest in the Mongstad refinery near Bergen. It is the majority shareholder in Statoil Fuel and Retail ASA, which is the leading retailer of oil products in Norway.

Gassco, wholly owned by the state, is the operator of the integrated gas transportation system from the Norwegian Continental Shelf to other European countries. Gassco's responsibilities include planning, monitoring, co-ordinating and administering the transport of gas from the fields to the receiving terminals as well as allocating capacity and developing the transportation system. It also serves as operator for the receiving terminals in Dunkerque (France), Zeebrugge (Belgium), Emden and Dornum (Germany). There are two main domestic natural gas distributors: Gasnor and Lyse Gass.

The Norwegian State, represented by the Ministry of Trade and Industry, also owns 99.9% of the shares in Norske Spitsbergen Kulkompani AS (SNSK), the parent company of Store Norske Spitsbergen Grubekompani AS (SNSG), which carries out coal-mining operations on Svalbard.

Norway was one of the front-runners in electricity-market liberalisation; in 1991 it deregulated its electricity market, which is now fully open for all producers and consumers. All end users are free to choose their electricity supplier. Norwegian electricity-sector legislation is harmonised with EU legislation. The Norwegian power sector comprises a large number of mostly publicly owned participants in various areas of business. The government views hydropower, the source of virtually all the electricity generated, as of strategic value and, as a consequence, it either owns or controls this resource. Around 90% of generating capacity is in public ownership, with local municipalities and county authorities alone owning just over half. The state-owned utility, Statkraft, is the largest generator. There are more than 160 small distribution system operators (DSOs) in Norway, most of them publicly owned. The dominant supplier within a network area is most often a vertically integrated supplier or a supplier within the same corporation as the DSO. By 2010, over a quarter of all household consumers had switched away from the incumbent supplier.

Prices, taxes and support mechanisms

All energy prices in Norway are determined by the market. The Norwegian Water Resources and Energy Directorate (NVE), an agency within MPE, is responsible for regulating electricity network charges (but not electricity tariffs). VAT at a flat rate of 25% is applied to all forms of energy consumption.[27] Excise taxes are levied on oil products and electricity. Several industries are exempt from the excise tax on energy products.

Energy in Norway is subject to several environmental tax measures. An SO_2 tax on mineral oil was introduced in 1971 while taxes on mineral fertilisers, pesticides and lubricant oil were all introduced in 1988. In 1991, the government levied a CO_2 tax on consumption of petrol, auto diesel oil, mineral oil and on the offshore petroleum sector (since CO_2 tax is classified as a deductible operating cost for income tax purposes in paying sectors such as the oil and gas sector, the net amount of the CO_2 tax is lower than its gross amount). Fuels used in the fisheries sector are all exempted from the CO_2 tax. In the past, companies paying the CO_2 tax were all exempted from the Norwegian emissions trading scheme, which ran from 2005-07. Since Norway joined the EU ETS in 2008, however, certain previously ETS-exempted companies are now included in the scheme and they do not pay the CO_2 tax on mineral oil.

Income derived from oil and gas production is subject to a special resource tax of 50%, in addition to the ordinary corporate income tax of 28%. For general income tax purposes, depreciation expenses are calculated according to rules which are unique to the oil and gas industry: expenses incurred in acquiring pipelines and production facilities may be completely written off in straight line over six years, starting from the year when the investment was made, *i.e.* up to $16\frac{2}{3}\%$ annually. The tax base for the purpose of calculating a special resource tax is the ordinary income-tax base, from which cost uplift is deducted. The cost uplift implies that the petroleum industry can write off as much as 30% of the value of depreciable operating assets as of 2005 in straight line over four

---

27   In the northern part of Norway, consumption of electricity and energy produced from alternative energy sources is exempted from VAT. The exemption applies to *e.g.* district heating and bioenergy.

years, starting from the year when the investment was made, *i.e.* up to 7½% annually. If a company incurs losses in a given year, these losses can then be carried forward (with interest, since 2002). If oil and gas companies terminate their activities in Norway with losses, the government reimburses the tax value of those losses. Since 2005, oil and gas companies reporting a loss for tax purposes can also obtain a reimbursement of the tax value (for regular corporate tax and resource tax) of their direct and indirect exploration expenses (excluding financial expenses). In practice, this means a government reimbursement of up to 78% of all the direct and indirect exploration expenses. In this respect, the government shares symmetrically in both profits and losses from exploration and production of petroleum products.

In addition to the regular corporate income tax and special resource tax, petroleum producers must pay taxes on emissions of carbon dioxide and nitrogen oxide.

In the hydropower sector, excess returns in generation are taxed at 30%, in addition to the normal corporate income tax rate of 28%.

Norway in the past subsidised the production of coal at the Norwegian-controlled coal mines in Svalbard. In 2002 ownership of the island's two mines was transferred to SNSG, on the condition that the mining operations would generate an operating profit. Thanks to historically high coal prices and the increased scale of its production in recent years the mines have since 2002 operated without state subsidies.

There are only a few transfers over the Norwegian state budget directly aimed at the upstream oil and gas industry. Direct transfers are limited to funding of petroleum research and budget transfers to the Norwegian Petroleum Directorate for seismic exploration.

Data documentation

General notes

The fiscal year in Norway coincides with the calendar year.

Producer Support Estimate

Operating Subsidy for Store Norske (data for 1999-2001)

For many years, the government of Norway provided operating subsidies to Store Norske, the operator of the Norwegian coal mines in the Spitsbergen archipelago, in order to balance its accounts. The last such annual payment, disbursed in 2001, was worth NOK 136 million.

Data are only available for the 1999-2001 period.

Sources: Store Norske Spitsbergen Grubekompani AS (various years).

Tag: NOR_dt_03

Consumer Support Estimate

Tax expenditures in Norway have been reported in the national budget (*St. meld. nr.1 (Nasjonalbudsjettet)*) since 1999. Those tax expenditures that are related to fossil fuels are listed in the budget in the following two tables: (1) "Estimates of tax expenditures and tax sanctions[28] related to environmental and energy taxes"[29] (*Anslag på skatteutgifter og skattesanksjoner knyttet til miljø- og energirelaterte særavgifter*) and (2) "Tax expenditures and sanctions by sector" (*Skatteutgifter og -sanksjoner for næringslivet*). These tables comprise numerous energy-, CO_2-, NO_x- and SO2-tax exemptions and reductions.[30]

CO_2 Tax Exemption for Fisheries (data for 1999-)

Norway provides the fisheries sector with an exemption from the CO_2 tax that is normally levied on sales of mineral oil (*CO_2-avgift på mineralolje*).

The mineral oil category comprises, among other fuels, diesel oil, kerosene and fuel oil. Since the fisheries sector relies predominantly on diesel, we have allocated this support measure entirely to this particular fuel.

Sources: Ministry of Finance (various years), CO_2 Tax (2011).

Tag: NOR_te_01

CO_2 Tax Exemption for Natural Gas and LPG (no data available)

A CO_2 tax on natural gas and LPG (*CO_2-avgift på naturgass og LPG*) was introduced on 1 September 2010. The tax rate levied on these fuels is in line with the benchmark which is the CO_2-tax rate levied on mineral oil. The tax is mainly imposed on the fuels used for heating and in land transport.

Natural gas and LPG used in domestic shipping and the greenhouse sector are also exempted from the tax. The manufacturing sector benefits from a lower rate on natural gas and a full tax exemption on LPG.

No estimates for 2010 were provided in the budget.

Sources: Ministry of Finance (2011), CO_2 Tax (2011).

NO_x Tax Exemption for the Petroleum Sector (data for 2008-)

A tax on emissions of NO_x was introduced in 2007. An exemption from this tax is granted to those industrial users that participate in the government programme

---

[28] Tax expenditures (tax sanctions) are defined as exceptions from the general rules in the tax system that are applied to certain groups or certain activities and imply lower (higher) government tax revenue. Norway uses revenue forgone method for calculating tax expenditures. There are different benchmarks for calculating tax expenditures related to excise duties and environmental taxes. Excise duties are treated individually which means that each excise tax expenditure calculation relies on a different benchmark.

[29] From the FY2010/11, this table can be found in the budget document labelled as Prop. 1LS (2010-2011).

[30] In Norway both tax expenditures and tax sanctions (negative tax expenditures) are reported in the national budget. A tax sanction is that part of tax revenue collected by the government that corresponds to taxing a specific sector or type of consumption at a tax rate above the general (*i.e.* benchmark) tax rate. The vast majority of the tax sanctions related to energy that were reported for the FY2010/11 stem from a higher-than-the-benchmark CO_2 tax rate. This higher CO_2 tax rate is levied on petrol, fuel used in domestic aviation and fuel used on the continental shelf.

committing them to achieving NO_x-reduction targets. Sectors benefitting from this exemption are petroleum, shipping, fishing, industry and aviation.

This item comprises annual amounts reported for the petroleum sector; we have allocated them to diesel and natural gas, on the basis of the IEA's Energy Balances for the oil and gas extraction sector.

Sources: Ministry of Finance (various years), NO_x Tax (2011).

Tag: NOR_te_02

NO_x Tax Exemption for Shipping (data for 2008-)

Fuels used in domestic shipping are all exempted from the NO_x tax.

The annual amounts reported are allocated to diesel, gasoline and fuel oils, on the basis of the IEA's Energy Balances for the domestic navigation sector.

Sources: Ministry of Finance (various years), NO_x Tax (2011).

Tag: NOR_te_03

NO_x Tax Exemption for Fisheries (data for 2008-)

Fuels used in the fisheries sector are all exempted from the NO_x tax.

Since the fisheries sector relies predominantly on diesel, we have allocated this support measure entirely to this particular fuel.

Sources: Ministry of Finance (various years), NO_x Tax (2011).

Tag: NOR_te_04

NO_x Tax Exemption for Industry (data for 2008-)

Fuels used in industry are all exempted from the NO_x tax.

The annual amounts reported are allocated, among other fuels, to bituminous coal, diesel, fuel oil, natural gas and LPG, on the basis of the IEA's Energy Balances for the industry sector.

Sources: Ministry of Finance (various years), NO_x Tax (2011).

Tag: NOR_te_05

NO_x Tax Exemption for Aviation (data for 2008-)

Fuels used in domestic shipping are all exempted from the NO_x tax.

We have allocated the annual amounts reported to kerosene type jet fuel only, on the basis of the IEA's Energy Balances for the domestic aviation sector.

Sources: Ministry of Finance (various years), NO_x Tax (2011).

Tag: NOR_te_06

Lower Tax Rate on Diesel Compared to Petrol (data for 1999-)

When it comes to the tax levied on road users, Norway levies a lower tax rate on diesel in comparison to petrol. According to the national budget, that constitutes a tax expenditure.

Tractors, construction machinery, chainsaws, boats and snowmobiles used off-the-road are also exempted from the abovementioned tax, but they are not included under this item.

From 2010, this tax expenditure has started covering the lower tax rate on biodiesel as well. Since the budget states that the amount of tax expenditure related to biodiesel is about 10%, this amount is subtracted from the figure for 2010.

Source: Ministry of Finance (various years).

Tag: NOR_te_07

Concessions on Basic Tax on Mineral Oil (data for 2001-)

A basic tax on mineral oil was introduced in 2000 in order to prevent overconsumption of heating oil in light of the newly introduced higher tax rates on consumption of electricity. The general tax rate on mineral oil has been increasing over time and it now corresponds to the general tax rate on consumption of electricity (including a levy on the electricity distribution tariffs).

The wood processing and pigment industries are granted a lower tax rate on mineral oil while the herring meal and fishmeal industries are exempted from this tax.

Sources: Ministry of Finance (various years).

Tag: NOR_te_08

Concessions on SO$_2$ Tax on Mineral Oil (data for 1999-2005)

An SO$_2$ tax on mineral oil was introduced in 1971 and was gradually increased over time. Norway provides domestic aviation and the supply fleet with a reduction on the SO$_2$ general tax rate. This tax expenditure terminated in 2005.

Exemptions from this tax are currently granted to international shipping, international aviation and fishing in foreign waters.

Sources: Ministry of Finance (various years).

Tag: NOR_te_09

General Services Support Estimate

Petroleum R&D Funding (data for 2005-)

The Research Council of Norway offers financial support for petroleum research and development activities through funding provided by the Ministry of Petroleum and Energy. In 2011, about 10% of the Council's budget of over NOK 7 billion was devoted to research related to petroleum and energy.

The following programmes are focused on research and development for the sector: PETROMAKS, introduced in 2004, assists the government in the implementation of its research strategy initiative, *Oil and Gas in 21st Century*. The main objective of the programme is to secure gas production in the future through the development of new technologies related to exploration, cost-effective petroleum extraction and transportation, health and safety, and the environment. PETROSAM assists the government in investing into projects related to petroleum activities in the field of social sciences. DEMO 2000 is a programme that provides funding for the demonstration and pilot-testing of technologies developed under PETROMAKS.

Payments are allocated to the GSSE since they do not increase current production or consumption of petroleum products.

Data are available for the 2005-10 period. They comprise funding devoted to PETROMAKS, DEMO 2000, PETROSAM and other strategic research projects related to oil and gas. We use production data from the IEA to allocate the annual amounts reported in budget documents to oil and natural gas extraction.

Sources: Ministry of Petroleum and Energy, Research Council of Norway (2011), PETROMAKS (2010).

Tag: NOR_dt_01

NPD Seismic Investigations (data for 2007-09)

The government of Norway provides funding for the research activities of the Norwegian Petroleum Directorate (NPD). The NPD concentrates on acquiring knowledge connected to the Norwegian continental shelf, which is then effectively used by the oil and gas industry (access to the NPD resources is granted after a small lump-sum payment).

Payments are allocated to the GSSE since they do not increase current production or consumption of petroleum products.

Data are available for the 2005-10 period. The upsurge in expenditure for the years 2008 and 2009 is due to the fact that the NPD received significant additional state-funding for exploration research efforts in the Nordland VI, VII and Troms II areas. We use production data from the IEA to allocate the annual amounts reported in budget documents to oil and natural gas extraction.

Sources: Ministry of Petroleum and Energy (various years), Norwegian Petroleum Directorate (2011).

Tag: NOR_dt_02

References

Policies or transfers

Barentsobserver.com, *Norwegian state grants extra funding to Spitsbergen coal company, Article from 28 November 2005,* Available at: http://www.barentsobserver.com/index.php?id=288059&xxforceredir=1&noredir=1.

CO_2 Tax (2011) *Tax Policy Department,* Available at: http://www.regjeringen.no/en/dep/fin/tema/skatter_og_avgifter/saravgifter/co2-avg ift.html?id=558367.

Ministry of Finance (1999) *St. meld. nr.1 (Nasjonalbudsjettet),* Available at: http://www.regjeringen.no/mobil/nb/dep/fin/dok/regpubl/stmeld/19992000/stmeld-nr-1-1999-2000-/4.html?id=133761.

Ministry of Finance (2000) *St. meld. nr.1 (Nasjonalbudsjettet),* Available at: http://www.regjeringen.no/mobil/nb/dep/fin/dok/regpubl/stmeld/20002001/stmeld-nr-1-2000-2001-/4.html?id=133902.

Ministry of Finance (2001) *St. meld. nr.1 (Nasjonalbudsjettet)*, Available at: http://www.regjeringen.no/mobil/nb/dep/fin/dok/regpubl/stmeld/20012002/stmeld-nr-1-2001-2002-/4.html?id=134297.

Ministry of Finance (2002) *St. meld. nr.1 (Nasjonalbudsjettet)*, Available at: http://www.regjeringen.no/mobil/nb/dep/fin/dok/regpubl/stmeld/20022003/stmeld-nr-1-2002-2003-/4.html?id=134641.

Ministry of Finance (2003) *St. meld. nr.1 (Nasjonalbudsjettet)*, Available at: http://www.regjeringen.no/mobil/nb/dep/fin/dok/regpubl/stmeld/20032004/stmeld-nr-1-2003-2004-/4.html?id=403211.

Ministry of Finance (2004) *St. meld. nr.1 (Nasjonalbudsjettet)*, Available at: http://www.regjeringen.no/mobil/nb/dep/fin/dok/regpubl/stmeld/20042005/stmeld-nr-1-2004-2005-/4.html?id=136126.

Ministry of Finance (2005) *St. meld. nr.1 (Nasjonalbudsjettet)*, Available at: http://www.regjeringen.no/mobil/nb/dep/fin/dok/regpubl/stmeld/20052006/stmeld-nr-1-2005-2006-/4.html?id=136323.

Ministry of Finance (2006) *St. meld. nr.1 (Nasjonalbudsjettet)*, Available at: http://www.regjeringen.no/mobil/nb/dep/fin/dok/regpubl/stmeld/20062007/stmeld-nr-1-2006-2007-/4.html?id=136645.

Ministry of Finance (2007) *St. meld. nr.1 (Nasjonalbudsjettet)*, Available at: http://www.regjeringen.no/mobil/nb/dep/fin/dok/regpubl/stmeld/2007-2008/stmeld-nr-1-2007-2008-/4.html?id=482983.

Ministry of Finance (2008) *St. meld. nr.1 (Nasjonalbudsjettet)*, Available at: http://www.regjeringen.no/mobil/nb/dep/fin/dok/regpubl/stmeld/2008-2009/stmeld-nr-1-2008-2009-/4.html?id=529324.

Ministry of Finance (2009) *St. meld. nr.1 (Nasjonalbudsjettet)*, Available at: http://www.regjeringen.no/mobil/nb/dep/fin/dok/regpubl/stmeld/2009-2010/meld-st-1-2009-2010/4/4.html?id=579819.

Ministry of Finance (2010) *St. meld. nr.1 (Nasjonalbudsjettet)*, Available at: http://www.regjeringen.no/mobil/nb/dep/fin/dok/regpubl/prop/2010-2011/prop-1-ls-20102011/49.html?id=618749.

Norwegian Petroleum Directorate (2011) *The Norwegian Petroleum Directorate: About us*, Available at: http://www.npd.no/en/About-us/.

NO$_x$ Tax (2011) *Tax Policy Department*, Available at: http://www.regjeringen.no/nb/dep/fin/pressesenter/pressemeldinger/2006/utslippsavgift-pa-nox.html?id=271754.

Petroleum Taxation Act (1975) *Act of 13 June 1975 No. 35 relating to the Taxation of Subsea Petroleum Deposits, etc. Last amended by Act of 29 June 2007 No. 51*, Available at: http://www.regjeringen.no/en/dep/fin/Selected-topics/taxes-and-duties/Act-of-13-June-1975-No-35-relating-to-th.html?id=497635.

PETROMAKS (2010) *Work Programme for the PETROMAKS, Optimal Management of Norwegian Petroleum Resources*, Available at: http://www.forskningsradet.no/servlet/Satellite?c=Page&cid=1226993690917&pagename=petromaks%2FHovedsidemal.

Research Council of Norway (2011) *The Research Council*, Available at:
http://www.forskningsradet.no/en/The_Research_Council/1138785832539.

Store Norske Spitsbergen Grubekompani AS (various years) *Annual Report and
Accounts, Longyearbyen, Norway,* Available at:
http://www.snsk.no/annual-report-and-accounts.148181.en.html.

Energy statistics

IEA, *Energy Balances of OECD Countries*, 2010 Edition, International Energy Agency,
Paris.

Figure 19.1. Shares of fossil-fuel support by fuel, average for 2008-10 – Norway

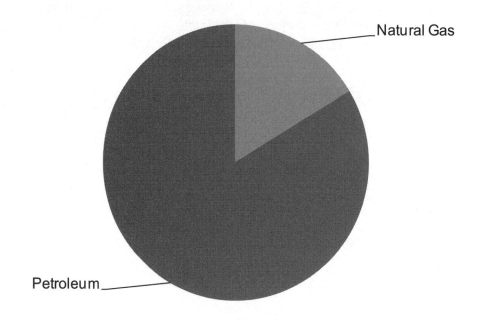

Source: OECD.

Figure 19.2. Shares of fossil-fuel support by indicator, average for 2008-10 – Norway

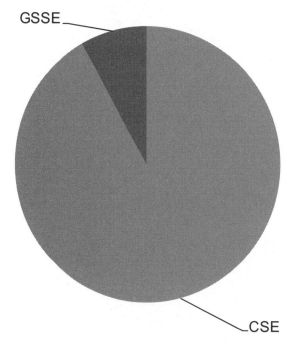

Source: OECD.

INVENTORY OF ESTIMATED BUDGETARY SUPPORT AND TAX EXPENDITURES FOR FOSSIL FUELS © OECD 2011

Table 19.1. Summary of fossil-fuel support to coal – Norway

(Millions of Norwegian kroner, nominal)

Support element	Jurisdiction	Avg 2000-02	Avg 2008-10	2008	2009	2010p
Producer Support Estimate						
Income support						
Operating Subsidy for Store Norske	–	n.a.	n.a.	n.a.	n.a.	n.a.
Consumer Support Estimate						
Consumption						
NOₓ Tax Exemption for Industry	–	n.a.	7.45	8.59	6.87	6.87
General Services Support Estimate (n.a.)						

Note: Tax expenditures for any given country are measured with reference to a benchmark tax treatment that is generally specific to that country. Consequently, the estimates contained in the table above are not necessarily comparable with estimates for other countries. In addition, because of the potential interaction between them, the summation of individual measures across fuel types was done by the OECD Secretariat based on the IEA's Energy Balances.

Source: OECD.

Table 19.2. Summary of fossil-fuel support to petroleum – Norway

(Millions of Norwegian kroner, nominal)

Support element	Jurisdiction	Avg 2000-02	Avg 2008-10	2008	2009	2010p
Producer Support Estimate						
Support for intermediate inputs						
NO$_x$ Tax Exemption for the Petroleum Sector	–	n.a.	27.36	29.58	25.51	26.99
Consumer Support Estimate						
Consumption						
CO$_2$ Tax Exemption for Fisheries	–	2 178.33	166.67	130.00	135.00	235.00
NO$_x$ Tax Exemption for Shipping	–	n.a.	585.00	625.00	590.00	540.00
NO$_x$ Tax Exemption for Fisheries	–	n.a.	131.67	125.00	140.00	130.00
NO$_x$ Tax Exemption for Industry	–	n.a.	11.74	13.55	10.84	10.84
NO$_x$ Tax Exemption for Aviation	–	n.a.	45.00	20.00	60.00	55.00
Lower Tax Rate on Diesel Compared to Petrol	–	1 200.00	3 270.00	3 100.00	3 200.00	3 510.00
Concessions on Basic Tax on Mineral Oil	–	92.50	100.00	100.00	105.00	95.00
Concessions on SO$_2$ Tax	–	433.33	n.a.	n.a.	n.a.	n.a.
General Services Support Estimate						
Petroleum R&D Funding	–	n.c.	137.15	148.42	120.63	142.40
NPD Seismic Investigations	–	n.c.	81.27	103.34	140.46	0.01

Note: Tax expenditures for any given country are measured with reference to a benchmark tax treatment that is generally specific to that country. Consequently, the estimates contained in the table above are not necessarily comparable with estimates for other countries. In addition, because of the potential interaction between them, the summation of individual measures for a specific country may be problematic. The allocation of particular measures across fuel types was done by the OECD Secretariat based on the IEA's Energy Balances.

Source: OECD.

Table 19.3. Summary of fossil-fuel support to natural gas – Norway

(Millions of Norwegian kroner, nominal)

Support element	Jurisdiction	Avg 2000-02	Avg 2008-10	2008	2009	2010p
Producer Support Estimate						
Support for intermediate inputs						
NO$_x$ Tax Exemption for the Petroleum Sector	–	n.a.	712.64	770.42	664.49	703.01
Consumer Support Estimate						
Consumption						
NO$_x$ Tax Exemption for Industry	–	n.a.	2.48	2.86	2.28	2.28
General Services Support Estimate						
Petroleum R&D Funding	–	n.c.	102.18	110.58	89.87	106.10
NPD Seismic Investigations	–	n.c.	60.55	76.99	104.64	0.01

Note: Tax expenditures for any given country are measured with reference to a benchmark tax treatment that is generally specific to that country. Consequently, the estimates contained in the table above are not necessarily comparable with estimates for other countries. In addition, because of the potential interaction between them, the summation of individual measures for a specific country may be problematic. The allocation of particular measures across fuel types was done by the OECD Secretariat based on the IEA's Energy Balances.

Source: OECD.

Chapter 20

Poland

This chapter identifies, documents, and provides estimates of the various budgetary transfers and tax expenditures that relate to the production or use of fossil fuels in *Poland*. An overview of *Poland's* energy economy is first given to place the measures listed into context. A data-documentation section then describes those measures in a systematic way. Whenever possible, the description details a measure's formal beneficiary, its eligibility criteria and functioning, and the fuels whose production or use stand to benefit from the measure. The chapter ends with a set of charts and tables that provide, subject to availability, quantitative information and estimates for the various measures listed.

20. POLAND

Energy resources and market structure

Fossil fuels provide the bulk of Poland's energy. It relies heavily on indigenous bituminous coal, which accounts for 55% of its total primary energy supply and more than 90% of electricity generation. Oil provides a quarter, all but 5% of which is imported, and natural gas for a further 13%, about two-thirds of which is imported. Russia supplies over 94% of its oil imports and over 80% of its imports of natural gas. Although its gas reserves are in decline, Poland is thought to have significant unconventional resources, notably shale gas. Exploratory drilling started only recently. Domestically produced biomass, the only significant renewable energy source, accounts for the remaining 6% of primary supply. The government's medium-term objective is to diversify its energy mix away from coal by introducing nuclear power and expanding the role of renewable energy.

The structure of Poland's energy sector has changed dramatically since the early 1990s, following the collapse of the communist bloc. Some assets were privatised, but the state has retained large stakes in most of the main companies. The state holds 100% of shares of two out of three biggest coal producers, Katowicki Holding Węglowy S.A. and Kompania Węglowa S.A. and it holds a majority share of the remaining one, Jastrzębska Spółka Węglowa S.A. The extraction of hard coal is also carried out by other, smaller companies, like Południowy Koncern Węglowy S.A., LW Bogdanka S.A., ZG Siltech Sp. z o.o., PG Silesia Sp. z o.o. Two vertically integrated power utilities, PGE S.A. and PAK S.A., mine lignite for their own use from four open-pit mines(Konin, Adamów, Bełchatów, Turów). Together with a small lignite mine, Sieniawa, these four open-pit mines account for the total lignite extraction in Poland.

There are half a dozen oil-producing companies in Poland, of which the Polish Oil and Gas Company (PGNiG), which is majority government owned, is by far the largest, accounting for 98% of production, most of which comes from on-shore wells. Another state-controlled company, PetroBaltic, produces small volumes offshore. Oil refining is undertaken by PKN Orlen, established in 1999 through the merger of two former state-owned enterprises, and by the LOTOS Group. Both companies are majority state-owned. A wholly state-owned company, PERN (Przedsiębiorstwo Eksploatacji Rurociągów Naftowych S.A., or "Przyjaźń"), operates oil storage and pipeline facilities. Distribution and retailing is carried out by PKN Orlen S.A. and the LOTOS Group, as well as a number of foreign companies.

PGNiG S.A., through subsidiaries, continues to dominate the downstream gas sector following the implementation of market reforms in recent years to comply with EU directives. The company controls virtually all gas imports and owns all the transmission pipelines and underground storage facilities, though the system is operated by an independent transmission system operator, OGP GAZ-SYSTEM S.A. – a wholly state-owned enterprise set up in 2004. Small quantities of liquefied natural gas (LNG) are transported by road in tanks by independent companies. PGNiG S.A. also owns six regional distribution companies covering most of the country, though they have been legally unbundled from the rest of the company. PGNiG S.A. dominates the retail market too. Several other companies (including G.EN Gaz Energia, CP Energia S.A., EWE Polska Sp. z o.o., Enesta Sp. z o.o. and KRI S.A.) have entered the market, but their total market share was only about 2% in 2009. As they have no access to gas resources, they purchase gas from PGNiG and resell it to final customers, often via their own local distribution networks. Customer switching is negligible.

There are more than 100 companies licensed to generate electric power in Poland, but four companies that were formed in 2007 out of the old state monopoly, Polskie Sieci Energetyczne S.A. (PSE), control most of the market: Polska Grupa Energetyczna (PGE), Tauron Polska Energia, Energa and Enea. They are vertically integrated, with activities in generation, distribution and direct supply. Poland's transmission grid is operated and owned by PSE Operator S.A., which remains in state ownership. There are 14 distribution system operators (DSOs) that were legally unbundled in 2007 from the former distribution companies, owned by the four main Polish power companies and two foreign companies (Vattenfall and RWE), as well as six so-called local distribution operators that were not subject to unbundling. The supply branch of each group sells most of its electricity to the customers connected to their distribution networks; the rate of customer switching to independent suppliers remains very low.

Prices, taxes and support mechanisms

Prices for coal, oil and oil products are set by the market and are neither regulated nor subsidised. The Energy Regulatory Authority, ERO, still regulates natural gas prices for all consumer groups. It also approves tariffs for electricity and gas transmission and distribution. End-user electricity prices are not regulated except for household tariffs, which are subject to approval by the ERO.

Sales of all fuels in Poland include a 23% value-added tax (VAT).[31] All oil products and electricity sales (both commercial and non-commercial) are subject to excise taxes; a road tax is levied on motor fuels. Excise taxes on gasoline are considerably higher than on diesel and automotive LPG, which has boosted demand for the latter fuels. Some off-road uses of petroleum fuels (fisheries, aviation) are exempt from excise taxes.

The heavy costs of restructuring the Polish hard-coal industry have been borne mainly by the state. Since Poland joined the European Union in 2004, the European Commission has taken a number of decisions on the compatibility of restructuring plans with the EU competition rules and on conditions for approving state aid for the hard-coal-mining industry. In recent years, the selling prices of locally produced steam coal, coking coal and lignite sold in Poland have been freely negotiated. Coal sales are not subsidised and state aid is no longer given to support operating costs or to maintaining access to already exploited coal reserves.

Most of the costs currently associated with aiding the restructuring of the hard-coal industry are associated with historic liabilities, namely: the entitlement by retired mineworkers to free coal; the costs of mine closures; benefits paid to redundant miners;

---

[31] In 2011, the basic VAT was increased from 22 to 23% until the end of 2013. However, the government announced it may further increase it, depending on the public-debt-to-gross-domestic-product ratio.

the costs of managing water, gas and fire risks at closed mines; and the restoration and clean-up of damage caused by past mining activity. The total cost to the national budget of these liabilities over the period 1999 to 2009 is estimated to be above PLN 20 billion. Almost 90% of these government expenses covered exemption or deferral of social-contribution, tax and fine payments. Since 2007, the costs of mine closures have been met by a dedicated fund, established for this purpose by the remaining mining enterprises.

Data documentation

General notes

The fiscal year in Poland normally coincides with the calendar year. Corporations, however, may choose a different starting point of the fiscal year.

Producer Support Estimate

Most of Polish state aid to the energy sector is apportioned to the coal industry. Poland's heavy reliance on coal stems from both a large domestic endowment of this fuel and the fact that in the communist period Poland had limited foreign-exchange earnings with which it could import other fuels. Because coal-mining was considered a strategic sector, the state subsidised production of coal, providing various social benefits to coal miners and regulating coal prices to keep them low.

With the economic transition of the early 1990s, the state envisioned to transform coal mines into self-reliant commercial companies that would adapt to the conditions of a free-market economy. The continued policy of price controls, however, meant that the industry had a very limited potential for economic growth and, hence, needed further state assistance.

All subsequent plans for restructuring the coal sector throughout the 1990s supported capacity adjustment, shutting down unprofitable mines and reducing employment to levels that would improve productivity. The overarching objective of those programmes was thus to make the coal-mining sector profitable.

These programmes proved ineffective due to the lack of consensus between the government and the trade unions. This changed in 1998 as the new government, supported by *Solidarność* (the biggest Polish trade union), devised a coal-mining restructuring plan, the *Reforma górnictwa węgla kamiennego w Polsce w latach 1998-2002*. The plan provided additional funding for social schemes and expressed a commitment to write-off of the debt which the mines had accumulated over the years. Another plan adopted in 2003 – the *Program restrukturyzacji górnictwa węgla kamiennego w Polsce w latach 2003-2006* – pursued similar objectives.

When Poland joined the European Union in 2004, state aid became subject to the Community rules. In practice, this development meant that coal-mining restructuring plans would have to be compatible with the common market, and that the European Commission would need to approve any state-aid scheme before it reaches recipients.

The Council of Ministers has so far adopted two documents regarding restructuring of the sector: the *Restrukturyzacja górnictwa węgla kamiennego w latach 2004-2006 oraz strategia na lata 2007-10*, which was then replaced by *Strategia działalności górnictwa węgla kamiennego w Polsce w latach* 2007-15. Poland does not provide subsidies to coal-mining under article 5-3 (current production aid). All current subsidies therefore result from article 7 (aid to cover exceptional costs) and are associated either with mine decommissioning or investment aid to operating mines (for up to 30% of the total investments made). The former measures are mainly allocated to the GSSE as most of them do not increase current production or consumption of coal. The latter are allocated to the PSE since they directly support coal producers.

The coal-mining sector underwent major restructuring through a series of management mergers and mine closures. At the beginning of the transition, the industry comprised 71 independent mines. In 1993, the management of hard-coal production was taken over by seven joint-stock holding companies that held the assets of 60 mines. Four mines remained stand-alone enterprises, while the rest was shut down on unprofitability grounds.

The Polish coal-mining sector now comprises 31 mines grouped into seven joint-stock holding companies and is dominated by three state-owned companies: Europe's largest hard-coal company, Kompania Węglowa S.A. (KW), Katowicki Holding Węglowy S.A. (KHW) and Jastrzębska Spółka Węglowa S.A. In 2000, two state-owned liquidation companies, Spółka Restrukturyzacji Kopalń S.A. (SRK) and Bytomska Spółka Restrukturyzacji Kopalń Sp. z o.o. (BSRK), were given responsibility to manage mine decommissioning. Since 2006, only two companies in Poland have been benefitting from state aid: KW and KHW. Aid is also being envisaged for the SRK (BSRK was consolidated into SRK in 2009).

Rehabilitation of Regions Damaged by Coal-Mining Activity (data for 1996-)

This item forms part of the broader restructuring programme. It provides funding for the rehabilitation of regions damaged by both past coal-mining activity and the reactivation of abandoned mining sites. Funding provided for the rehabilitation of regions damaged by the latter is a producer subsidy but it is impossible to isolate this single item from the reports (see the GSSE part of the cookbook).

Data for the 2001-03 period are not reported since they cannot be isolated from total state-aid for restructuring. The data reported for 2006 are an underestimate since no report is available for that particular year. The report for January–November 2006 is used instead.

Sources: Ministry of Economy (various years), Office of Competition and Consumer Protection (various years).

Tag: POL_dt_02

Exemption or Deferral of Social Contributions (data for 1996-2003)

This item comprises annual payments made by the state to the Social Insurance Office (ZUS) on behalf of coal mines. State aid took the form of both social-contribution exemptions and deferrals.

Both types of aid were granted on the basis of two government acts: *Rozporządzenie Rady Ministrów z dnia 15 września 1982 r. w sprawie zasad umarzania i udzielania ulg w spłacaniu należności państwowych (Dz. U. Nr 30, poz. 211 z 1982 r. z późn. zm.)* and *Ustawa z dnia 27 sierpnia 1997 r. o restrukturyzacji finansowej jednostek górnictwa węgla kamiennego oraz wprowadzeniu opłaty węglowej (Dz.U. Nr 113, poz.735 art 7)*. Aid was available for both operating coal mines and the liquidation companies dealing with shutting down the unprofitable mines.

State support provided through social-contribution exemptions and deferrals seems to date back to 1982 but data are only available for the 1996-2003 period. According to the document adopted by the Council of Ministers (*Strategia działalności górnictwa węgla kamiennego w Polsce w latach 2007-15*), the scheme terminated in 2006.

Amounts reported under this item were estimated as the product of the value of deferred contribution payments and the interest rate on these payments.

Payments are allocated to the PSE since they subsidise one of the production factors, labour.

Sources: Office of Competition and Consumer Protection (various years).

Tag: POL_dt_03

Exemption or Deferral of Taxes and Fines (data for 2001-03)

This item comprises annual payments made by the state to exempt or defer tax and fine payments on behalf of the coal-mining sector. State aid covered unpaid income taxes and fines, including environmental charges paid to the Environmental and Water Management Fund (NFOŚiGW) and fines paid to the Disability Fund (PFRON). Aid was available for both operating coal mines and liquidation companies dealing with shutting down the unprofitable mines.

The state is committed to continue the programme until at least 2015, as outlined in a document adopted by the European Council, *Strategia działalności górnictwa węgla kamiennego w Polsce w latach 2007–2015*.

The annual amounts for tax and fine deferrals were estimated as the product of the value of deferred payments and the interest rate on these payments.

Payments are allocated to the PSE since they constitute a production tax credit.

Sources: Office of Competition and Consumer Protection (various years).

Tag: POL_dt_04

NFOŚiGW Aid for Environmental Protection (data for 1996-2000)

The Environmental and Water Management Fund (NFOŚiGW) provides funding for the coal-mining industry to support environmental protection programmes. It can also write-off fines whenever the industry proves unable to pay them. These fines are imposed by the NFOŚiGW to partially internalise the social costs associated with coal-mining.

Data are available for the 1996-2000 period only since the amounts for later years cannot be distinguished from total aid for restructuring.

Sources: Office of Competition and Consumer Protection (various years).

Tag: POL_dt_05

R&D Funding from the Research Committee (data for 1996-2000)

This item comprises annual grants obtained from the Research Committee by the coal-mining industry for financing their R&D programmes.

The Research Committee provides funding for financing research and development to companies which apply for R&D grants.

Data are available for the 1996-2000 period. From 2001, data are unavailable since they cannot be isolated from total state-aid for restructuring.

Sources: Office of Competition and Consumer Protection (various years).

Tag: POL_dt_06

Stranded-Costs Compensation (data for 2008-)

This item comprises subsidies provided to power plants to compensate them for the termination of long-term Power Purchase Agreements (PPAs).

In the mid-1990s, the Polish government decided to launch a programme designed to modernise the domestic electricity sector and bring it into line with the technical and environmental standards of Western Europe. The programme initially launched a tender procedure with a view to selecting projects for new or modernised electricity generation plants. The selected projects would be awarded long-term PPAs for their generation capacity. The PPAs were signed between 1994 and 1998 and most of them had been concluded for a period of more than 15 years. The last PPA was to expire in 2027.

Under these agreements, the state network operator had a purchase obligation for a guaranteed volume of electricity at a guaranteed price. Power plants charged the electricity network operator an amount equivalent to all their fixed and variable costs plus a profit margin. The PPAs thus provided price-support to the power plants that had signed such agreements with the network operator (the PPAs covered around 40% of Polish electricity generation).

In November 2005, the Commission opened an in-depth investigation on the PPAs in Poland. During 2006 and 2007, the Polish authorities worked out a draft law that foresees the end of the PPAs and a compensation system to the power plants in line with the Commission's methodology for analysing state aid linked to stranded costs. That methodology allows stranded-cost compensations to alleviate the effect of liberalisation without threatening the continuation of electricity supply. Such compensations should be proportionate, and not discourage the entrance of new companies into the generation market.

The programme started in 2008 and funding is planned until the end of 2025. The biggest Polish power plants, *PGE Elektrownia Opole S.A.* and *PGE Elektrownia Turów S.A.*, received most of the payments. Payments are financed from a parafiscal levy imposed on all consumers to make up a fund which is then disbursed among the power plants. This fund is run by a special purpose company that is fully-owned and controlled by the state.

The formula for calculating these payments provides for the state to cover the losses associated with certain types of cost, plus depreciation and fuel costs, if the revenue collected on the market is not sufficient for that purpose. This implies that state payments cover the costs and risks normally borne by the power plants under normal market conditions. Since Polish power plants rely mainly on coal (more than 90% of Polish electricity is produced out of coal), this scheme is an implicit subsidy to the coal sector. These payments are therefore allocated to the PSE.

Sources: European Commission, Office of Competition and Consumer Protection (various years).

Tag: POL_dt_13

Initial Investment Aid for Hard-Coal-Mining Sector (data for 2010-)

This item comprises investment aid for hard-coal-mining sector. Aid was granted to investment projects related to ensuring access to coal reserves and was not granted for covering costs related to the production-process itself.

Grant was provided by the Ministry of Economy in form of a grant that covered initial investment costs and it covered fixed capital costs directly related to infrastructure work or to the equipment necessary for the mining of coal resources in existing mines (such as pits and main dip headings, roadways and other infrastructure work, mechanical installations, modern managements equipment, washrooms and surface installations).

The scheme operated only in 2010, with a planned budget of 400 million PLN. It followed the EU regulation stating that the state can reimburse up to 30% of the qualifying investment costs incurred by coal producers.

Sources: Ministry of Economy (2010).

Tag: POL_dt_14

Consumer Support Estimate

Coal Allowances in Coal-Mining Sector (data for 2004-)

Traditional in-kind benefits for miners include free provision of coal which used to serve heating and water-warming purposes. With time, however, most miners have obtained access to distributed heating systems and the benefit in-kind lost its rationale. The in-kind coal support is now being phased out with the introduction of cash equivalents.

Data for the period 2001-03 are not reported since they cannot be isolated from total state-aid for restructuring. The data reported for 2006 are an underestimate since no report is available for that particular year. The report for January – November 2006 is used instead.

Sources: Ministry of Economy (various years), Office of Competition and Consumer Protection (various years).

Tag: POL_dt_11

Rebates on Diesel-Fuel Tax in Farming (data for 2006-)

In 2006, Poland adopted the EU Council Directive 2003/96/EC – *Restructuring the Community Framework for the Taxation of Energy Products and Electricity*, which requires each member state to apply a minimum tax rate of 21 euros per 1000 litres to diesel fuel when used for farming purposes.

Rebates are financed out of the state budget and their value cannot exceed 86 litres per hectare of utilised agricultural area. The Minister of Agriculture and Rural Development determines the exemption rate on a yearly basis. Polish farmers can obtain rebates by submitting the relevant invoices to the local authority twice a year.

Data for this scheme were provided by the Ministry of Agriculture and Rural Development and are available at the Polish Business in Agriculture website.

Sources: Ministry of Agriculture and Rural Development (various years).

Tag: POL_te_01

General Services Support Estimate

Aid for Coal-Mine Decommissioning (data for 1996-)

The coal-mine decommissioning programme started in 1991. It became an official government policy in 1993 as part of the plan to make the coal-mining sector profitable. The state is committed to continue the programme until at least 2015, as outlined in a document adopted by the European Council, *Strategia działalności górnictwa węgla kamiennego w Polsce w latach 2007–2015.*

Throughout the existence of the programme, numerous mines have been either partially or completely shut down. The state has been covering the costs of dismantling the equipment, protecting the land above from subsistence, and ensuring that neighbouring coal mines are secured from water, gas and fire hazards.

Data for the 2001-03 period are not reported since they cannot be isolated from total state-aid for restructuring. The data reported for 2006 are an underestimate since no report is available for that particular year. The report for January – November 2006 is used instead.

Payments are allocated to the GSSE as they do not increase current production or consumption of hard coal.

Sources: Ministry of Economy (various years), Office of Competition and Consumer Protection (various years).

Tag: POL_dt_01

Rehabilitation of Regions Damaged by Coal-Mining Activity (data for 1996-)

This item forms part of the broader restructuring programme. It provides funding for the rehabilitation of regions damaged by both past coal-mining activity and the reactivation of abandoned mining sites.

State support for the scheme was regulated by a document adopted in 1994: *Prawo geologiczne i górnicze (Dz. U. Nr 27, poz. 96, z późn. zm.).* The state is committed to continue the programme until at least 2015, as outlined in a document adopted by the European Council, *Strategia działalności górnictwa węgla kamiennego w Polsce w latach 2007–2015.*

Payments are allocated to the GSSE as most of them do not increase current production or consumption of coal. Funding provided for the rehabilitation of regions damaged by the reactivation of abandoned mining sites is a producer subsidy but it is impossible to isolate this single item from the reports.

Data for the 2001-03 period are not reported since they cannot be isolated from total state-aid for restructuring. The data reported for 2006 are an underestimate since no report is available for that particular year. The report for January – November 2006 is used instead.

Sources: Ministry of Economy (various years), Office of Competition and Consumer Protection (various years).

Tag: POL_dt_02

Aid for Employment Restructuring (data for 1998-)

The employment restructuring programme was established in 1993. The item comprises various social schemes over the last two decades but its aim has always been to bring about a reduction in unemployment in the mining sector without a significant loss of the dismissed workers' welfare.

The aid devoted to employment restructuring was substantially increased with the introduction of the 1998 coal-mining restructuring programme, *Reforma górnictwa węgla kamiennego w Polsce w latach 1998–2002*. The programme introduced two different sets of measures.

The first set aimed at reemployment of younger miners in other sectors of the economy and provision of welfare benefits to dismissed workers while looking for a new job. Miners were to choose from a soft loan for the establishment of a business, social-assistance benefits and two different kinds of severance-payment schedules. Also, workers from closed mines were offered alternative forms of employment and access to active-labour-market policies.

The other set of measures was to provide social protection for older employees. Miners who had five or fewer years of work left before becoming eligible for a pension were entitled to receive a "mining leave" (equal to 75% of the wage paid when on a holiday leave). Miners two or fewer years away from qualifying for a pension obtained a prospect of a secure job in the coal-mining sector.

Data for the 2001-03 period are not reported since they cannot be isolated from total state-aid for restructuring. The data reported for 2006 are an underestimate since no report is available for that particular year. The report for January – November 2006 is used instead.

Payments are allocated to the GSSE as they do not increase current production or consumption of coal.

Sources: Ministry of Economy (various years), Office of Competition and Consumer Protection (various years).

Tag: POL_dt_07

Investment Aid from the Ministry of Economy (data for 1998-2000)

This item comprised aid to investment in environmental protection and research and development. Aid was provided by the Minister of the Economy in the form of direct transfers.

Data are available for the 1998-2000 period.

Payments are allocated to the GSSE as a more detailed description of the programme was not available.

Sources: Office of Competition and Consumer Protection (various years).

Tag: POL_dt_08

Severance Payments for the Coal-Mining Industry (data for 1999-2000)

Severance payments were granted to those miners who agreed to leave the coal-mining industry.

Data are available for the 1998-2000 period.

Payments are allocated to the GSSE as they do not increase current production or consumption of coal.

Sources: Office of Competition and Consumer Protection (various years).

Tag: POL_dt_09

Aid for Restructuring of the Coal-Mining Sector (data for 2001-03)

The reports do not specify the purpose of this item so payments are allocated to the GSSE. Aid was mainly provided by the Ministry of the Economy in form of direct transfers.

Sources: Office of Competition and Consumer Protection (various years).

Tag: POL_dt_10

Early-Retirement Benefits for Laid-Off Miners (data for 2004-)

The state provided aid to all miners from liquidated hard-coal mines in the form of early-retirement benefits, provided they were five or fewer years away from retirement.

Payments are allocated to the GSSE as they do not increase current production or consumption of coal.

Sources: Ministry of Economy (various years), Office of Competition and Consumer Protection (various years).

Tag: POL_dt_12

References

Policies or transfers

European Commission, *Stranded Costs Compensation in Poland,* Available at: http://ec.europa.eu/competition/sectors/energy/electricity/electricity_en.html.

Ministry of Agriculture and Rural Development (various years), Available at: http://www.portalspozywczy.pl/agrobiznes/wiadomosci/720-mln-zl-na-doplaty-do-paliwa-rolniczego-w-2011-r,37534.html.

Ministry of Economy (various years), *Informacja dla Rady Ministrów o przebiegu restrukturyzacji górnictwa węgla kamiennego,* Available at: http://www.mg.gov.pl/Gospodarka/Gornictwo.

Office of Competition and Consumer Protection (various years), *Raport o pomocy publicznej w Polsce udzielonej przedsiębiorcom,* Available at: http://www.uokik.gov.pl/raporty_i_analizy2.php#.

Figure 20.1. Shares of fossil-fuel support by fuel, average for 2008-10 – Poland

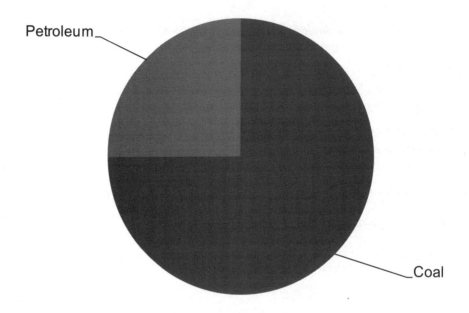

Source: OECD.

Figure 20.2. Shares of fossil-fuel support by indicator, average for 2008-10 – Poland

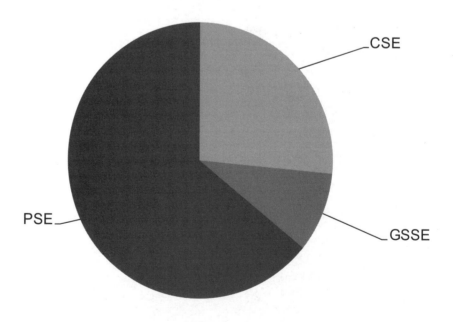

Source: OECD.

INVENTORY OF ESTIMATED BUDGETARY SUPPORT AND TAX EXPENDITURES FOR FOSSIL FUELS © OECD 2011

Table 20.1.   Summary of fossil-fuel support to coal – Poland

(Millions of Polish zloty, nominal)

Support element	Jurisdiction	Avg 2000-02	Avg 2008-10	2008	2009	2010p
Producer Support Estimate						
Support to unit returns						
Exemption or Deferral of Taxes and Fines	–	418.75	n.c.	..	..	..
Stranded Costs Compensations	–	n.a.	1 419.18	1.75	2 127.90	2 127.90
Support for land (*e.g.* royalty concessions)						
NFOSiGW Aid for Environmental Protection	–	n.c.	n.c.	..	..	..
Support for capital formation						
Initial Investment Aid for Hard Coal Mining	–	n.a.	n.a.	n.a.	n.a.	400.00
Support for labour						
Exemption or Deferral of Social Contributions	–	342.49	n.a.	n.a.	n.a.	n.a.
Support for knowledge creation						
R&D Funding from the Research Committee	–	n.c.	n.c.	..	..	..
Consumer Support Estimate						
Consumption						
Coal Allowances in Coal Mining Sector	–	n.c.	30.19	30.65	37.34	22.56
General Services Support Estimate						
Aid for Coal Mine Decommissioning	–	n.c.	191.52	186.71	193.14	194.70
Rehabilitation of Regions Damaged by Coal Mining	–	n.c.	14.13	22.23	7.46	12.70
Investment Aid from the Ministry of Economy	–	n.c.	n.a.	n.a.	n.a.	n.a.
Aid for Restructuring of the Coal Mining Sector	–	948.77[1]	n.a.	n.a.	n.a.	n.a.
Aid for Employment Restructuring	–	n.c.	n.a.	n.a.	n.a.	n.a.
Early Retirement Benefits for Laid Off Miners	–	n.a.	21.21	23.82	24.20	15.62

Note: Tax expenditures for any given country are measured with reference to a benchmark tax treatment that is generally specific to that country. Consequently, the estimates contained in the table above are not necessarily comparable with estimates for other countries. In addition, because of the potential interaction between them, the summation of individual measures for a specific country may be problematic. The allocation of particular measures across fuel types was done by the OECD Secretariat based on the IEA's Energy Balances. ([1]) Aid for Restructuring in the Coal Mining Sector is a broad category which for three years (2001-03) replaced a more detailed breakdown of support measures to coal in the government document. This category comprises, among others, NFOSiGW Aid for Environmental Protection, R&D Funding from the Research Committee, Aid for Coal Mine Decommissioning, Investment Aid from the Ministry of Economy, and Aid for Employment Restructuring.

Source: OECD.

Table 20.2. Summary of fossil-fuel support to petroleum – Poland

(Millions of Polish zloty, nominal)

Support element	Jurisdiction	Avg 2000-02	Avg 2008-10	2008	2009	2010p
Producer Support Estimate (n.a.)						
Consumer Support Estimate						
Consumption						
Rebates on Diesel Fuel Tax in Farming	–	n.a.	609.00	498.00	609.00	720.00
General Services Support Estimate (n.a.)						

Note: Tax expenditures for any given country are measured with reference to a benchmark tax treatment that is generally specific to that country. Consequently, the estimates contained in the table above are not necessarily comparable with estimates for other countries. In addition, because of the potential interaction between them, the summation of individual measures for a specific country may be problematic. The allocation of particular measures across fuel types was done by the OECD Secretariat based on the IEA's Energy Balances.

Source: OECD.

Chapter 21

Spain

This chapter identifies, documents, and provides estimates of the various budgetary transfers and tax expenditures that relate to the production or use of fossil fuels in *Spain*. An overview of *Spain's* energy economy is first given to place the measures listed into context. A data-documentation section then describes those measures in a systematic way. Whenever possible, the description details a measure's formal beneficiary, its eligibility criteria and functioning, and the fuels whose production or use stand to benefit from the measure. The chapter ends with a set of charts and tables that provide, subject to availability, quantitative information and estimates for the various measures listed.

21. SPAIN

Energy resources and market structure

The only fossil-fuel domestic resource of any consequence in Spain is coal, but most production is uneconomic. Almost all of the oil and gas used in Spain is imported, with less than 1% being domestically produced. Oil is by far the most important fuel, meeting 47% of the country's primary energy needs, followed by natural gas (24%), nuclear power (12%) and coal (6%). Renewable energy, mainly in the form of biomass, makes up the rest (11%). Production of wind and solar power contributes 17% to electricity generation and has been growing rapidly in recent years, thanks to large subsidies. Counting nuclear power as an indigenous resource, national production covers about a quarter of total energy use.

Spain's coal-mining industry is consolidating and production is declining. The National Plan for Strategic Coal Reserves 2006-12 sets out targeted reductions in production, staffing and subsidies, supply guarantees and economic restructuring policies for the coal-mining regions. Most companies have an annual production capacity below 500 000 tonnes, with some employing fewer than 25 miners. The largest is UMINSA, a privately owned company that resulted from a merger of 15 independent companies. The other major operator in terms of staff is the state-owned HUNOSA. Use of Spanish coal at power plants, the principal market, is based on volume quotas set by the government. Power producers contract directly with mining companies for the volume and price of coal under their quota.

Spain's oil sector is entirely deregulated and privately owned. Of the country's ten refineries, four are fully-owned and one is partly owned by Repsol YPF, amounting to about 56% of total refining capacity; three others are owned by Cepsa (about 33%) and one by BP (11%). There are a large number of companies active in the wholesale and retail markets. The gas sector is also privately owned, with a number of players active in one or more parts of the supply chain. Gas Natural, the former monopoly gas company, still accounts for half of all gas imported into Spain and almost half of retail sales. Ibredrola is the next largest importer and retailer. Enagás is the sole operator of the transmission system operator and also holds half of the country's LNG regasification capacity. The retail market for industrial customers is fairly competitive; competition in the residential market is much more limited.

Spain was among the first EU countries to embark on power-sector liberalisation in the 1990s, resulting in a major restructuring of the sector and changes in ownership. Today, three-quarters of electricity is generated by just three companies: Iberdrola, Endesa (almost 100% owned by the Italian utility, ENEL) and Unión Fenosa (owned by Gas Natural). Iberdrola and Endesa alone account for the bulk of retail sales, though the market is fully contestable. Because of subsidised retail prices for low-voltage consumers, supplier switching has hardly developed. REE, in which the state holds a 20% stake, operates the high-voltage transmission grid as the exclusive transmission system operator in co-ordination with the market operator; it owns almost the entire 400 kV grid and two-thirds of the 220 kV grid. Iberdrola, Endesa and Unión Fenosa are the largest distributors, although there are more than 300 small local distributors.

Prices, taxes and support mechanisms

All energy prices in Spain are determined by free-market competition, with the exception of LPG, the prices of which are set according to a formula based on international prices and a distribution margin, and electricity and gas tariffs for the smallest customers, who are eligible for a cost-covering last-resort tariff. The government has nominated five suppliers of gas (Gas Natural, Endesa, Iberdrola, Naturgas and Unión Fenosa) and five for electricity (Endesa, Iberdrola, Unión Fenosa, Hidrocantábrico and E.ON) under this tariff. Together with tariffs for third-party access to all basic gas infrastructures (pipelines, LNG facilities, and underground storage), last-resort tariffs are proposed by National Energy Commission (CNE) and approved by the Minister of Industry, Tourism and Trade.

Spain levies excise taxes on oil products and electricity. All energy products are subject to an 18% rate of VAT. Biofuels are exempted from tax, as are fuels used in aviation, navigation and rail transport. The tax on diesel fuel used in farming is refunded. Excise taxes on gasoline and diesel were previously relatively low, but have risen in recent years as Spain's derogation of the EU timetable to raise minimum taxes on automotive diesel expired.

The main source of support to energy production in Spain is the financial assistance to hard-coal mining. This assistance is subject to EU rules on state aid and approval by the European Commission. The principal form of aid is transfer payments by the government to private coal companies to compensate them for the difference between their operating costs and the prices at which they sell their output to local power plants (which are negotiated directly). Under the National Plan, operating aid is to be reduced by 1.25% per year for underground mines and 3.25% per year for opencast mines. Production is due to fall from 12.1 million tonnes in 2005 to 9.2 Mt in 2012, and employment from 8 310 to 5 302. Inherited liabilities aid can be used to pay benefits to former miners and cover the costs of mine closures. Aid is also available to finance mine closures, for industrialisation projects and for developing infrastructure in the affected mining regions. Another government measure provides funding to power plants for purchases of domestic coal for stockpiling. The government is also spending on R&D to develop clean-coal technology, including carbon capture and storage.

Data documentation

General notes

The fiscal year in Spain coincides with the calendar year. Following OECD convention, amounts prior to 1999 are expressed as 'euro-fixed series', meaning that we applied the fixed EMU conversion rate (1 EUR = 166.386 ESP) to data initially expressed in the Spanish Peseta (ESP).

Producer Support Estimate

Operating Aid to HUNOSA (data for 2002-)

The Spanish government has been providing financial assistance to the coal industry for several decades. Support is usually granted as part of a series of overarching, pluri-annual plans that aim at progressively rationalising and downsizing the Spanish coal industry. A dedicated agency – the Instituto para la Reestructuración de la Minería del Carbón y Desarrollo Alternativo de las Comarcas Mineras (Institute for the Restructuring of Coal Mining and the Alternative Development of Mining Areas) – was created in 1998 alongside the 1998-2005 Coal Mining Plan to manage state aid and promote the development of mining regions. More recently, the Ministry of Industry, Tourism, and Trade negotiated a new National Coal Plan covering the 2006-12 period with CARBUNIÓN (the Spanish coal producer association) and trade unions.

The estimates included in the database under this heading pertain to the amount of support granted to Hulleras del Norte S.A. (HUNOSA) to cover its operating costs. HUNOSA is a major state-owned producer of hard coal in the central Asturian basin. Accordingly, we allocate the entire programme to hard coal. Data prior to 2002 are not available at the present level of detail.

Sources: Ministerio de Economía y Hacienda (various years).

Tag: ESP_dt_01

Operating Aid to Coal Producers (data for 1998-)

This item corresponds to the amounts of price support granted by the Spanish government to domestic coal producers (see also "Operating Aid to HUNOSA" above). Transfer payments are being made to private coal companies to compensate them for the difference between their operating costs and the prices at which they sell their output to local power plants. Those prices are negotiated directly between coal producers and energy utilities.

We use production data from the IEA to allocate the annual amounts reported in budget documents to the various types of coal concerned (bituminous and sub-bituminous coal, lignite, and coking coal). Data are not available for the years 2000 and 2001, and prior to 1998.

Sources: Ministerio de Economía y Hacienda (various years), IEA.

Tag: ESP_dt_02

Subsidy for the Inter-basin Transport of Coal (data for 1998-)

This programme benefits private coal producers through budgetary transfers that support the transport of coal across basins whenever local supply conditions meet certain criteria. Additional information about this item could not be found.

We use production data from the IEA to allocate the annual amounts reported in budget documents to the various types of coal concerned (bituminous and sub-bituminous coal, lignite, and coking coal). Data are not available for the years 2000 and 2001, and prior to 1998.

Sources: Ministerio de Economía y Hacienda (various years), IEA.

Tag: ESP_dt_04

Adjustment Aid to Coal Producers (data for 1998-)

This item comprises transfers made by the Spanish government to private coal producers to ease the decline of the coal-mining sector.

We use production data from the IEA to allocate the annual amounts reported in budget documents to the various types of coal concerned (bituminous and sub-bituminous coal, lignite, and coking coal). Data are not available for the years 2000 and 2001, and prior to 1998.

Sources: Ministerio de Economía y Hacienda (various years), IEA.

Tag: ESP_dt_05

Consumer Support Estimate

Funding for Coal Stockpiles (data for 1998-)

This measure provides funding to power plants to support their constitution of coal stockpiles. Those stockpiles are meant to guarantee over 720 hours of power generation. Plants are, however, specifically required to accumulate domestic coal.

We use production data from the IEA to allocate the annual amounts reported in budget documents to the various types of coal concerned (bituminous and sub-bituminous coal, lignite, and coking coal). Data are not available for the years 2000 and 2001, and prior to 1998.

Sources: Ministerio de Economía y Hacienda (various years), IEA.

Tag: ESP_dt_03

Fuel-Tax Exemptions (data for 1996-)

The Spanish Tax Code exempts certain users from the fuel tax that is normally levied on sales of petroleum products. Major eligible activities include aviation, navigation, and railway transport.

We use data from the IEA on consumption volumes in the domestic aviation sector to estimate the share of the total amount of revenue foregone that can be ascribed to kerosene-type jet fuel. A benchmark rate of EUR 0.08 per litre is used for that purpose. Deducting this estimated share from the total tax expenditure leaves us with an amount that is mainly attributable (and that we attribute) to diesel fuel. Although this approach yields plausible estimates of the revenue foregone due to the exemption for aviation, it may overlook the small amounts of heavy fuel used in navigation and LPG used in certain activities (*e.g.* chemical reductions for the steel industry).

Sources: Ministerio de Economía y Hacienda (various years), IEA.

Tag: ESP_te_01

Fuel-Tax Reductions (data for 1996-)

This tax provision provides both the farming and mining sectors with a reduced rate of excise tax on petroleum products.

We allocate the annual amounts reported in official budget documents to diesel fuel, heavy fuel, and LPG on the basis of the IEA's Energy Balances for the agriculture and mining sectors.

Sources: Ministerio de Economía y Hacienda (various years), IEA.

Tag: ESP_te_02

General Services Support Estimate

Inherited Liabilities Due to Coal Mining (data for 2002-)

This programme provides certain non-profit organisations – along with coal miners and their families – with budgetary transfers to help address the social and technical costs that stem from the decline of the coal-mining sector.

The measure is allocated to the GSSE as it does not increase current production or consumption of coal. We use production data from the IEA to allocate the annual amounts reported in budget documents to the various types of coal concerned (bituminous and sub-bituminous coal, lignite, and coking coal). Data are not available prior to 2002 at the present level of detail.

Sources: Ministerio de Economía y Hacienda (various years), IEA.

Tag: ESP_dt_06

References

Policies or transfers

Ministerio de Economía y Hacienda (various years) Presupuestos Generales del Estado, Secretaría de Estado de Hacienda y Presupuestos, Available at: http://www.sgpg.pap.meh.es/sitios/sgpg/en-GB/Presupuestos/PresupuestosEjercici osAnteriores/Paginas/PresupuestosEjerciciosAnteriores.aspx.

Energy statistics

IEA, *Energy Balances of OECD Countries*, 2010 Edition, International Energy Agency, Paris.

Figure 21.1.   Shares of fossil-fuel support by fuel, average for 2008-10 – Spain

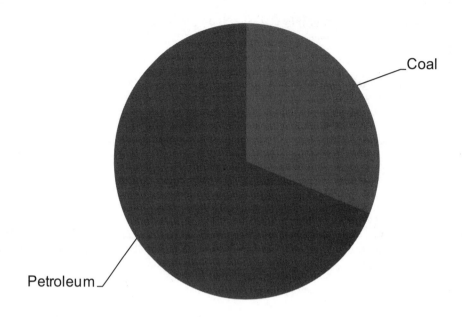

Source: OECD.

Figure 21.2.   Shares of fossil-fuel support by indicator, average for 2008-10 – Spain

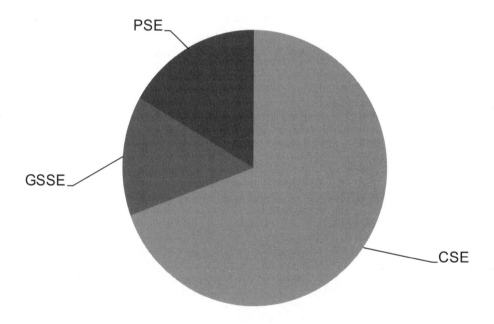

Source: OECD.

Table 21.1. Summary of fossil-fuel support to coal – Spain

(Millions of euros, nominal)

Support element	Jurisdiction	Avg 2000-02	Avg 2008-10	2008	2009	2010p
Producer Support Estimate						
Support to unit returns						
Operating Aid to HUNOSA	–	100.43	80.56	85.30	80.38	76.00
Operating Aid to Coal Producers	–	334.75	256.34	266.50	252.53	250.00
Subsidy for the Interbasin Transport of Coal	–	3.13	12.73	11.35	14.04	12.80
Income support						
Adjustment Aid to Coal Producers	–	54.05	30.07	40.00	40.00	10.20
Consumer Support Estimate						
Consumption						
Funding for Coal Stockpiles	–	12.02	7.25	2.92	6.34	12.50
General Services Support Estimate						
Inherited Liabilities Due to Coal Mining	–	155.06	322.05	302.55	328.00	335.60

Note: Tax expenditures for any given country are measured with reference to a benchmark tax treatment that is generally specific to that country. Consequently, the estimates contained in the table above are not necessarily comparable with estimates for other countries. In addition, because of the potential interaction between them, the summation of individual measures for a specific country may be problematic. The allocation of particular measures across fuel types was done by the OECD Secretariat based on the IEA's Energy Balances.

Source: OECD.

Table 21.2. Summary of fossil-fuel support to petroleum – Spain

(Millions of euros, nominal)

Support element	Jurisdiction	Avg 2000-02	Avg 2008-10	2008	2009	2010p
Producer Support Estimate (n.a.)						
Consumer Support Estimate						
Consumption						
Fuel Tax Exemptions		–	621.93	634.30	641.90	589.58
Fuel Tax Reductions		–	952.04	660.79	827.33	1 368.00
		733.27				
		670.10				
General Services Support Estimate (n.a.)						

Note: Tax expenditures for any given country are measured with reference to a benchmark tax treatment that is generally specific to that country. Consequently, the estimates contained in the table above are not necessarily comparable with estimates for other countries. In addition, because of the potential interaction between them, the summation of individual measures for a specific country may be problematic. The allocation of particular measures across fuel types was done by the OECD Secretariat based on the IEA's Energy Balances.

Source: OECD.

Chapter 22

Sweden

This chapter identifies, documents, and provides estimates of the various budgetary transfers and tax expenditures that relate to the production or use of fossil fuels in *Sweden*. An overview of *Sweden's* energy economy is first given to place the measures listed into context. A data-documentation section then describes those measures in a systematic way. Whenever possible, the description details a measure's formal beneficiary, its eligibility criteria and functioning, and the fuels whose production or use stand to benefit from the measure. The chapter ends with a set of charts and tables that provide, subject to availability, quantitative information and estimates for the various measures listed.

22. SWEDEN

Energy resources and market structure

Sweden has minimal fossil-energy resources, but important supplies of renewable energy, mainly in the form of biomass and hydropower. All of the country's oil, gas and coal needs are imported. Nuclear energy also plays a large role, accounting for 30% of the country's total primary energy supply (TPES), followed by biomass from the forest industry (22%). Small amounts of fuel peat are harvested in Sweden, augmented by a roughly equal amount of imported fuel peat, mainly from Belarus. Most of this peat, equal to about 1% of TPES, is used to generate hot water in district-heating plants. Non-fossil energy source together contribute two-thirds of supply – the highest share of any OECD country after Iceland. Electricity generation is almost CO_2-free: depending on hydrological conditions, hydro and nuclear power typically account for at least 90% of total annual generation in roughly equal amounts. On the other hand, energy intensity – measured as the amount of energy consumed per unit of GDP – is very high, because of the large energy requirements of heavy industry, mostly pulp and paper and iron and steel, as well as the cold climate and sparse population.

Sweden takes a free-market approach to energy policy, which puts the emphasis on competition in ensuring efficient energy supply within a policy framework that aims to encourage renewables. The only major energy company owned by the Swedish state is Vattenfall, which is one of several major players in the Swedish electricity market. It also has overseas operations, some of which are owned by foreign governments. Most of the small local electricity distribution companies and four gas distributors are owned by municipalities.

The Swedish oil market is privately owned and fully open to competition. A Saudi-owned company, Preem, owns two of the country's five refineries and is the fourth-largest marketer of oil products after QK-Q8, Statoil and Hydro. The other three refineries are also foreign-owned, one by St1 and two jointly by Neste Oil and Petroleos de Venezuela. The natural gas market is dominated by a small number of vertically integrated companies, and most gas is supplied under long-term contracts. The Swedish gas transmission network gas is owned by Swedegas, owned by a group of private-equity funds, and E.ON Gas Sverige (a subsidiary of Germany's E.ON). Two companies import gas into Sweden: E.ON Gas Sverige, which purchases its supplies from E.ON Ruhrgas in Germany, and DONG Energy, which procures gas from Denmark. These two companies also dominate the retail gas market. The four other suppliers are municipal companies that own local networks. Except for Swedegas and DONG Energy, all gas companies are part of energy companies with operations in the electricity or district heating market in Sweden.

The Swedish electricity market is fully liberalised and all customers are free to choose their own supplier. Svenska Kraftnät, the TSO, owns the transmission grid and is unbundled from the other parts of the industry; grid access for third parties is guaranteed and a regulator, EMI, oversees market operations. Three companies – Vattenfall, Fortum (majority-owned by the Finnish government), and E.ON Sverige – generate the overwhelming bulk of power in Sweden, own most of the distribution assets and account for around half of retail sales. More than half of electricity consumers have switched suppliers, a rate well above the average for rest of the European Union.

Prices, taxes and support mechanisms

All energy prices are freely determined by the market in Sweden, except for electricity and gas network tariffs. EMI regulates electricity and gas network access charges through price controls set every four years (three years for natural gas). Those controls set the maximum amount of revenue energy-network owners can collect through the charges they levy on users of their networks. Prices are meant to cover the costs to owners of the network for the period in question.

Energy is subject to an energy tax, a CO_2 tax and a sulphur tax. There is also a levy on NO_X emissions. Rates of tax vary by fuel and according to whether the fuel is being used for heating or in transport, whether by manufacturing industry, energy industry or households, and, in the case of electricity, what it is being used for and whether it is being used in the north or in the rest of the country. There are also several exemptions. The energy tax is levied on all fuels except peat, natural gas and LPG used as motor fuels and biofuels. The CO_2 tax is paid on all fuels except bioenergy and peat. However, almost all users of energy peat are obliged to buy emission rights (EU-ETS) for CO_2. In addition, several user groups are wholly or partly exempt (it is charged fully in transport, space heating and heat generation except co-generation). The sulphur tax is paid on bunker fuel, coal, petroleum coke and peat. Most tax revenues come from oil. There is also a tax on nuclear power, the rate of tax being set on the basis of the maximum permissible thermal power rating of each reactor.

Data documentation

General notes

The fiscal year in Sweden coincides with the calendar year.

Producer Support Estimates

No producer support estimates were identified.

Consumer Support Estimates

The Ministry of Finance (MoF) publishes official tax-expenditure estimates as part of its budget documentation every fiscal year (Ministry of Finance, various years). Numerous energy- and CO_2-tax exemptions and reductions are listed in its tax-expenditure report.

Calculations of tax-expenditure estimates related to the energy tax are based on the assumption that all the fuels should be subject to the same tax rate per unit of energy content, with two caveats: First, a higher benchmark rate is applied to electricity, to reflect the fact that one energy unit of electricity is equivalent to more than one energy unit of fuel (due to energy loss in the energy-generation process). Second, the benchmark rate Sweden applies to transport fuels is higher than that applied to heating and processing fuels since the tax revenue collected from the former covers costs associated with road transport, such as wear and tear of roads, noise and traffic accidents, among other societal costs. As for tax expenditures related to the CO_2 tax, no differentiation is made in terms of a benchmark - *i.e.* the same benchmark rate is applied to every usage of the fuel.

Reduced Energy-Tax Rate on Diesel Used in Transport (data for 2004-)

The energy-tax rate on diesel (SEK 0.133 per kWh in 2010) is lower than the official benchmark for transport fuels, which is the energy-tax rate on gasoline in environmental class 1 (SEK 0.338 per kWh). This tax expenditure will be reduced over time since the energy-tax rate on diesel will be increased to SEK 0.153 per kWh in 2011 and to SEK 0.173 per kWh in 2013.

Source: Ministry of Finance (various years).

Tag: SWE_te_01

Energy-Tax Exemption for Natural Gas and LPG Used in Transport (data for 2007-)

This tax expenditure reflects the fact that both natural gas and LPG used as fuel in transport are exempted from energy-tax payments. The benchmark against which this tax expenditure is calculated is the energy-tax rate on gasoline in environmental class 1.

The annual amounts reported in the tax-expenditure reports are allocated to natural gas only, since the IEA's Energy Balances show that LPG consumption by the road-transport sector in Sweden is negligible.

Source: Ministry of Finance (various years).

Tag: SWE_te_02

Energy-Tax Exemption for Diesel-Powered Trains (data for 2004-)

Diesel used as fuel in diesel-powered trains is exempted from the energy tax. The benchmark against which this tax expenditure is calculated is the energy-tax rate on gasoline in environmental class 1.

Source: Ministry of Finance (various years).

Tag: SWE_te_03

Energy-Tax Exemption for Domestic Shipping (data for 2004-)

Fuel used in commercial domestic shipping is exempted from the energy tax. The benchmark against which this tax expenditure is calculated is the energy-tax rate on gasoline in environmental class 1.

The annual amounts reported in the tax-expenditure reports are allocated to diesel and fuel oils, on the basis of the IEA's Energy Balances for the domestic navigation sector.

Source: IEA, Ministry of Finance (various years).

Tag: SWE_te_04

Energy-Tax Exemption for Domestic Aviation (data for 2007-)

Fuel used for commercial domestic aviation is exempted from the energy tax. Until 1 July 2008, fuel used for private domestic aviation was also exempted from the energy tax; this is no longer the case. The benchmark against which this tax expenditure is calculated by the MoF is the energy-tax rate on gasoline in environmental class 1.

We have allocated the annual amounts reported in the tax-expenditure reports to kerosene type jet fuel only, on the basis of the IEA's Energy Balances for the domestic aviation sector. No amounts were allocated to aviation gasoline since its share in fuel consumption by the domestic aviation sector is negligible (below 2%).

Source: Ministry of Finance (various years).

Tag: SWE_te_05

Reduced Energy-Tax Rate for Fossil Fuels Used for Heating (data for 2004-10)

The benchmark against which this tax expenditure is calculated is the energy-tax rate on heating oil. Energy-tax rates on LPG, natural gas and coal were equalised with the value of the benchmark at the beginning of 2011, which implies that this tax expenditure will effectively disappear from Sweden's tax-expenditure reports.

The annual amounts reported in the tax-expenditure reports are allocated to LPG and natural gas, on the basis of the IEA's Energy Balances for the manufacturing sector.

Source: IEA, Ministry of Finance (various years).

Tag: SWE_te_06

Energy-Tax Exemption for Industrial Consumers (data for 2004-10)

Until 2011, the industrial sector was granted a full energy-tax rebate for fossil fuels used in manufacturing processes. The benchmark against which this tax expenditure is calculated is the energy-tax rate on heating oil. In 2011, the energy-tax exemption was replaced by a 30% reduction in the standard tax rate on heating fuels.

The annual amounts reported in the tax-expenditure reports are allocated to LPG, natural gas and coal, on the basis of the IEA's Energy Balances for the manufacturing sector.

Source: IEA, Ministry of Finance (various years).

Tag: SWE_te_09

Energy-Tax Exemption for Heating in Greenhouses and Agriculture (data for 2004-10)

Until 2011, greenhouses and the agricultural sector were granted a full energy-tax rebate for fossil fuels used for heating. The benchmark against which this tax expenditure is calculated is the energy-tax rate on heating oil. In 2011, the energy-tax exemption was replaced by a 30% reduction in the standard tax rate on heating fuels.

The annual amounts reported in the tax-expenditure reports are allocated to LPG and natural gas, on the basis of the IEA's Energy Balances for the agricultural sector.

Source: IEA, Ministry of Finance (various years).

Tag: SWE_te_10

Reduced CO₂-Tax Rate for Industrial Consumers outside EU ETS (data for 2004-)

> Industries outside the EU ETS are granted a 79% reduction of the CO_2-tax rate on all fossil fuels used for heating purposes. The benchmark against which this tax expenditure is calculated is the standard CO_2-tax rate of SEK 1.05 per kg of CO_2. This reduction is planned to be diminished to 70% in 2011 and to 40% in 2015.

> The annual amounts reported in the tax-expenditure reports are allocated to LPG, natural gas and coal, on the basis of the IEA's Energy Balances for the manufacturing sector.

> Source: IEA, Ministry of Finance (various years).

> Tag: SWE_te_11

Reduced CO₂-Tax Rate for Natural Gas and LPG Used in Transport (data for 2007-)

> Natural gas and LPG used in transport are subject to lower CO_2-tax rates. In 2010, these fuels were granted a 41% and 48% CO_2-tax rate reduction respectively. The benchmark against which this tax expenditure is calculated is the standard CO_2-tax rate of SEK 1.05 per kg of CO_2. This reduction has been declining over time and further reductions are planned: from a 30% reduction on both fuels in 2011, through a 20% reduction in 2013, to a complete phase out of this tax expenditure in 2015.

> The annual amounts reported in the tax-expenditure reports are allocated to natural gas only, since the IEA's Energy Balances show that LPG consumption by the road-transport sector in Sweden is negligible.

> Source: Ministry of Finance (various years).

> Tag: SWE_te_12

Reduced CO₂-Tax Rate for Energy-Intensive Companies (data for 2004-)

> Fuels used for heating purposes by energy-intensive companies are granted a 24% CO_2-tax reduction for that value of the CO_2-tax that exceeds 0.8% of their sales value. This reduction can never imply lower CO_2-tax payments than the EU-stipulated minimum. The benchmark against which this tax expenditure is calculated is the standard CO_2-tax rate of SEK 1.05 per kg of CO_2.

> This tax expenditure is planned to be phased out in two steps. In 2011, the reduction will only apply to CO_2 tax exceeding 1.2% of a company's sales value. The plan is to completely phase out the reduction from 2015 onwards.

> The annual amounts reported in the tax-expenditure reports are allocated to coal, gas and diesel products, on the basis of the IEA's Energy Balances for combined chemicals and iron and steel sectors.

> Source: IEA, Ministry of Finance (various years).

> Tag: SWE_te_13

Specific CO₂-Tax Reduction for Greenhouses and Agriculture (data for 2008-)

> Fuels used for heating in greenhouses and the agricultural sector are granted a 24% CO_2-tax reduction for that value of the CO_2-tax that exceeds 0.8% of their sales value. This reduction can never imply lower CO_2-tax payments than the EU-stipulated minimum. The benchmark against which this tax expenditure is calculated is the standard CO_2-tax rate of SEK 1.05 per kg of CO_2.

This tax expenditure is planned to be phased out in two steps. In 2011, the reduction will only apply to CO_2 tax exceeding 1.2% of a company's sales value. The plan is to completely phase out the reduction from 2015 onwards.

The annual amounts reported in the tax-expenditure reports are allocated to diesel, LPG, natural gas and fuel oil, on the basis of the IEA's Energy Balances for the agricultural sector.

Source: IEA, Ministry of Finance (various years).

Tag: SWE_te_14

General CO_2-Tax Reduction for Greenhouses and Agriculture (data for 2004-)

Fossil fuels used for heating in greenhouses and the agricultural sector are subject to a lower CO_2-tax rate. In 2010 these sectors were granted a 79% reduction for the CO_2-tax rate on all fossil fuels used for heating. The benchmark against which this tax expenditure is calculated is the standard CO_2-tax rate of SEK 1.05 per kg of CO_2. This reduction has been declining over time and further reductions are planned: industrial consumers will be granted a 70% reduction in 2011 and a 40% reduction in 2015.

The annual amounts reported in the tax-expenditure reports are allocated to diesel, LPG, natural gas and fuel oil, on the basis of the IEA's Energy Balances for the agricultural sector.

Source: IEA, Ministry of Finance (various years).

Tag: SWE_te_15

CO_2-Tax Reduction for Diesel Used in Agriculture and Forestry (data for 2005-)

Diesel used as fuel for machinery in agriculture and forestry is subject to a lower CO_2-tax rate. In 2010, these sectors were granted a 79% reduction of the CO_2-tax rate. The benchmark against which this tax expenditure is calculated is the standard CO_2-tax rate of SEK 1.05 per kg of CO_2. This reduction, corresponding to SEK 2.38 per litre, has been decreasing over time and further reductions are planned – SEK 2.10 per litre in 2011, SEK 1.70 per litre in 2013, SEK 0.90 per litre in 2015.

Source: Ministry of Finance (various years).

Tag: SWE_te_16

CO_2-Tax Exemption for Diesel-Powered Trains (data for 2004-)

Diesel used as fuel in diesel-powered trains is fully exempted from the CO_2-tax. The benchmark against which this tax expenditure is calculated is the standard CO_2-tax rate of SEK 1.05 per kg of CO_2.

Source: Ministry of Finance (various years).

Tag: SWE_te_18

CO_2-Tax Exemption for Domestic Aviation (data for 2007-)

Fuel used for commercial domestic aviation is fully exempted from the CO_2 tax. Until 1 July 2008, fuel used for private domestic aviation was also exempted from the CO_2 tax; this is no longer the case. The benchmark against which this tax expenditure is calculated is the standard CO_2-tax rate of SEK 1.05 per kg of CO_2.

The annual amounts reported in the tax-expenditure reports are allocated to kerosene type jet fuel only, on the basis of the IEA's Energy Balances for the domestic aviation sector. No amounts were allocated to aviation gasoline since its share in fuel consumption by the domestic aviation sector is negligible (below 2%).

Source: Ministry of Finance (various years).

Tag: SWE_te_19

CO_2-Tax Exemption for Domestic Shipping (data for 2004-)

Fuel used in commercial domestic shipping is exempted from the CO_2 tax. The benchmark against which this tax expenditure is calculated is the standard CO_2-tax rate of SEK 1.05 per kg of CO_2.

The annual amounts reported in the tax-expenditure reports are allocated to diesel and fuel oils, on the basis of the IEA's Energy Balances for the domestic navigation sector.

Source: IEA, Ministry of Finance (various years).

Tag: SWE_te_20

CO_2-Tax Exemption for Peat (data for 2004-09)

Peat is fully exempted from the CO_2 tax. Since the beginning of 2011, Sweden has not treated this exemption as a tax expenditure since almost all peat used in Sweden is now included in the EU ETS.

Source: Ministry of Finance (various years).

Tag: SWE_te_22

References

Policies or transfers

Ministry of Finance (various years), *Redovisning av skatteutgifter* (Report on Tax Expenditures), Available at: http://www.regeringen.se.

Energy statistics

IEA, *Energy Balances of OECD Countries,* 2010 Edition, International Energy Agency, Paris.

Figure 22.1. Shares of fossil-fuel support by fuel, average for 2008-10 – Sweden

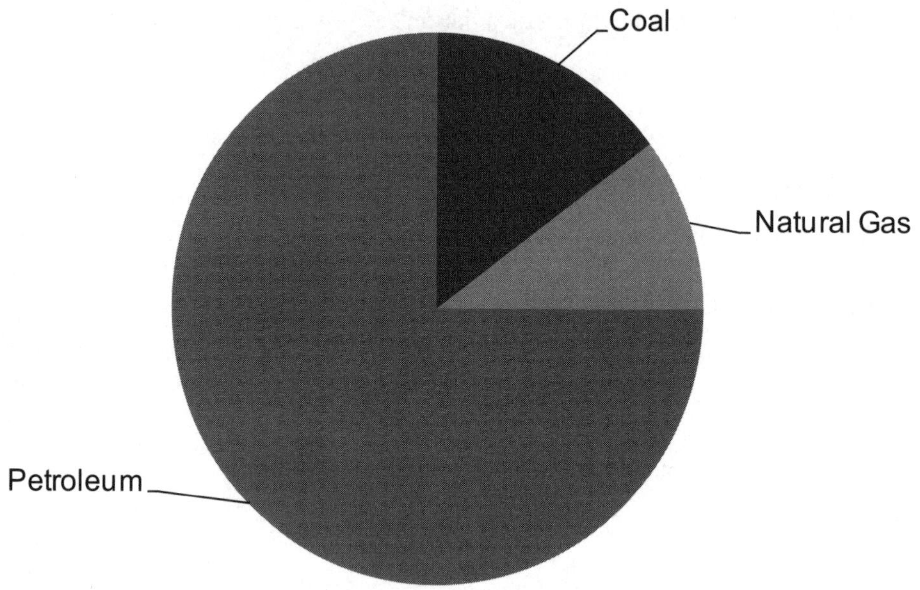

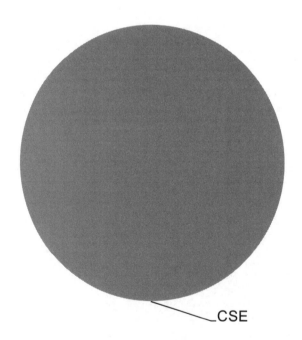

Source: OECD.

Figure 22.2. Shares of fossil-fuel support by indicator, average for 2008-10 – Sweden

Source: OECD.

INVENTORY OF ESTIMATED BUDGETARY SUPPORT AND TAX EXPENDITURES FOR FOSSIL FUELS © OECD 2011

Table 22.1.   Summary of fossil-fuel support to coal – Sweden

(Millions of Swedish kronor, nominal)

Support element	Jurisdiction	Avg 2000-02	Avg 2008-10	2008	2009	2010p
Producer Support Estimate (n.a.)						
Consumer Support Estimate						
Consumption						
Energy Tax Exemption for Industrial Consumers		n.c.	366.14	428.09	361.72	308.62
Reduced CO$_2$ Tax Rate for Industrial Consumers outside EU ETS		n.c.	1 316.34	1 898.19	1 602.84	448.00
CO$_2$ Tax Reduction for Energy Intensive Companies		n.c.	5.28	9.51	3.17	3.17
CO$_2$ Tax Exemption for Peat		n.c.	1 860.00	1 900.00	1 840.00	1 840.00
General Services Support Estimate (n.a.)						

Note: Tax expenditures for any given country are measured with reference to a benchmark tax treatment that is generally specific to that country. Consequently, the estimates contained in the table above are not necessarily comparable with estimates for other countries. In addition, because of the potential interaction between them, the summation of individual measures for a specific country may be problematic. The allocation of particular measures across fuel types was done by the OECD Secretariat based on the IEA's Energy Balances.

Source: OECD.

Table 22.2.   Summary of fossil-fuel support to petroleum – Sweden

(Millions of Swedish kronor, nominal)

Support element	Jurisdiction	Avg 2000-02	Avg 2008-10	2008	2009	2010p
Producer Support Estimate (n.a.)						
Consumer Support Estimate						
Consumption						
Reduced Energy Tax Rate for Diesel used in Transport	–	n.c.	11 386.67	11 300.00	10 830.00	12 030.00
Energy Tax Exemption for Diesel Powered Trains	–	n.c.	30.00	30.00	30.00	30.00
Energy Tax Exemption for Domestic Shipping	–	n.c.	550.00	610.00	350.00	690.00
Energy Tax Exemption for Domestic Aviation	–	n.c.	1 043.33	1 070.00	1 010.00	1 050.00
Reduced Energy Tax Rate for Fossil Fuels Used for Heating	–	n.c.	181.86	149.42	163.32	232.82
Energy Tax Exemption for Industrial Consumers	–	n.c.	357.35	417.81	353.03	301.21
Energy Tax Exemption for Heating in Greenhouses and Agriculture	–	n.c.	17.68	18.08	18.08	16.88
Reduced CO_2 Tax Rate for Industrial Consumers outside EU ETS	–	n.c.	1 284.74	1 852.62	1 564.36	437.24
CO_2 Tax Reduction for Energy Intensive Companies	–	n.c.	11.39	20.49	6.83	6.83
Specific CO_2 Tax Reduction for Greenhouses and Agriculture	–	n.c.	23.73	17.80	26.70	26.70
General CO_2 Tax Reduction for Greenhouses and Agriculture	–	n.c.	415.29	427.16	436.06	382.66
CO_2 Tax Reduction for Diesel used in Agriculture and Forestry	–	n.c.	1 346.67	1 330.00	1 350.00	1 360.00
CO_2 Tax Exemption for Diesel-Powered Trains	–	n.c.	20.00	20.00	20.00	20.00
CO_2 Tax Exemption for Domestic Commercial Aviation	–	n.c.	963.33	990.00	930.00	970.00
CO_2 Tax Exemption for Domestic Shipping	–	n.c.	490.00	540.00	310.00	620.00
General Services Support Estimate (n.a.)						

Note: Tax expenditures for any given country are measured with reference to a benchmark tax treatment that is generally specific to that country. Consequently, the estimates contained in the table above are not necessarily comparable with estimates for other countries. In addition, because of the potential interaction between them, the summation of individual measures for a specific country may be problematic. The allocation of particular measures across fuel types was done by the OECD Secretariat based on the IEA's Energy Balances.

Source: OECD.

INVENTORY OF ESTIMATED BUDGETARY SUPPORT AND TAX EXPENDITURES FOR FOSSIL FUELS © OECD 2011

Table 22.3. Summary of fossil-fuel support to natural gas – Sweden

(Millions of Swedish kronor, nominal)

Support element	Jurisdiction	Avg 2000-02	Avg 2008-10	2008	2009	2010p
Producer Support Estimate (n.a.)						
Consumer Support Estimate						
Consumption						
Energy Tax Exemption for Natural Gas and LPG used in Transport	–	n.c.	163.33	120.00	200.00	170.00
Reduced Energy Tax Rate for Fossil Fuels Used for Heating	–	n.c.	341.48	280.58	306.68	437.18
Energy Tax Exemption for Industrial Consumers	–	n.c.	379.84	444.10	375.25	320.17
Energy Tax Exemption for Heating in Greenhouses and Agriculture	–	n.c.	128.99	131.92	131.92	123.12
Reduced CO_2 Tax Rate for Industrial Consumers outside EU ETS	–	n.c.	1 365.58	1 969.19	1 662.80	464.76
Reduced CO_2 Tax Rate for Natural Gas and LPG Used in Transport	–	n.c.	40.00	30.00	50.00	40.00
Specific CO_2 Tax Reduction for Greenhouses and Agriculture	–	n.c.	2.94	2.20	3.30	3.30
General CO_2 Tax Reduction for Greenhouses and Agriculture	–	n.c.	51.37	52.84	53.94	47.34
General Services Support Estimate (n.a.)						

Note: Tax expenditures for any given country are measured with reference to a benchmark tax treatment that is generally specific to that country. Consequently, the estimates contained in the table above are not necessarily comparable with estimates for other countries. In addition, because of the potential interaction between them, the summation of individual measures for a specific country may be problematic. The allocation of particular measures across fuel types was done by the OECD Secretariat based on the IEA's Energy Balances.

Source: OECD.

Chapter 23

Turkey

This chapter identifies, documents, and provides estimates of the various budgetary transfers and tax expenditures that relate to the production or use of fossil fuels in *Turkey*. An overview of *Turkey's* energy economy is first given to place the measures listed into context. A data-documentation section then describes those measures in a systematic way. Whenever possible, the description details a measure's formal beneficiary, its eligibility criteria and functioning, and the fuels whose production or use stand to benefit from the measure. The chapter ends with a set of charts and tables that provide, subject to availability, quantitative information and estimates for the various measures listed.

23. TURKEY

Energy resources and market structure

Turkey has negligible fossil-fuel resources, and imports practically all of the oil and natural gas it uses from countries to the east. It is, however, a major energy transit route owing to its proximity to major oil and gas reserves. Turkey depends on imports for about 72% of its total primary energy supply (TPES). In 2008, fossil fuels accounted for nearly 90% of TPES while renewable energy sources provided the remaining 10%. Natural gas is the leading fossil fuel in TPES, accounting for 31% and followed by oil (30%) and coal (29%). Since 2000, Turkey's electricity supply has increased by around 50%. In 2009, natural gas fuelled half of power generation, while coal provided 28%, hydropower 19%, and oil 3%. Only a half percent of Turkey's electricity is exported. In order to meet the growing demand for electricity, Turkey has already started the construction of its first nuclear plant, and is planning to build a second one.

Turkey produces both hard coal and lignite. However, domestic production only covered around 57% of total domestic consumption in 2008. Although its hard-coal resources are meagre, the country is richly endowed when it comes to lignite, with several production facilities scattered all over the country. Turkey consumes all the lignite it produces but imports around 90% of its total coal needs.

Following the enactment of the 2001 Electricity Law, Turkey unbundled its state-owned vertically-integrated enterprises into different business activities, notably generation, transmission, distribution, wholesale trading and retail supply. Since 2003, private-sector investment in generation capacity has increased significantly while the government has already started to privatise a significant share of its state-owned generation assets. In 2005, the government-owned distribution company was divided into 20 different companies, and privatisation of these has already begun. The electricity law also mandated an independent regulatory authority, namely the Energy Market Regulatory Authority (EMRA), to issue licenses; determine and approve tariffs; sett the eligibility limits for market opening; draft secondary legislation; and solve disputes and apply penalties in electricity, natural gas, petroleum and LPG markets.

In 2001, Turkey passed the Natural Gas Market Law with the objective of establishing a competitive natural-gas market. Although the law requires the government-owned Petroleum Pipeline Corporation (BOTAŞ) to unbundle its import, transmission, storage and trade activities, BOTAS remains a major player in the natural-gas market. The natural-gas market reform prioritises contract transfer in order to limit the share of any importer or wholesaler in the domestic market to 20%. In 2006, BOTAS gave four companies the right to import around 12% of total natural-gas imports for a period of 15 years. Third-party access (TPA) to the transmission and distribution network is regulated by EMRA, and is non-discriminatory. As part of its market reform, Turkey has also started to privatise gas-distribution activities with a view to extending the network. EMRA granted licenses for a total of 60 cities, 53 of which are new distribution areas and include an obligation to build a gas network.

Turkey's domestic oil and natural-gas transmission network is owned and operated by BOTAS. Owing to its location between Europe, the Middle-East and the Caspian region, Turkey has become a major hub for international pipeline connections. Gas from Russia is transported to Bulgaria through the Russia-Turkey Bluestream and the Russia-Turkey West gas pipelines, while gas from Azerbaijan is transported through the Baku-Tbilisi-Erzurum pipeline. There are also a number of projects that are being contemplated and which would increase Turkey's international pipeline connections. The Nabucco pipeline is one such project that would enable new suppliers from the Middle-East and the Caspian region to access the European gas market.

Prices, taxes and support mechanisms

As part of the gas and electricity markets reform, Turkey is moving towards a fully cost-reflective tariff structure. Although wholesale prices for the gas and electricity markets are already cost-based, the retail prices remain regulated by means of a uniform national retail tariff, which is approved by EMRA. Hence, the retail tariff does not reflect the differences in costs across the distribution regions.

Retail prices for electricity remained constant between 2002 and 2007 in spite of a significant increase in generation costs, which itself resulted from high input prices. Since 2008, tariffs have been adjusted quarterly to take into account input prices, inflation and exchange rates. The transition to this system involved by three large tariff increases, in January, July and October 2008) which raised the average retail tariff by about 50%.

The Automatic Pricing Mechanism (APM), which operated between July 1998 and the end of 2004, set a ceiling on the prices of almost all oil products. In the beginning of 2005, the government decided to remove the price caps, which led to an increase in pre-tax prices. Since then, oil prices have been set by the market.

Turkey levies an 18% value-added tax (VAT) on all energy products. Turkish gasoline and diesel prices are among the highest in the OECD, owing to the relatively high excise taxes that are reflected at the level of retail prices. As of July 2011, the excise tax for regular gasoline (TRL 1.8915 per litre) was higher than that for diesel (TRL 1.3045 per litre). Excise taxes in Turkey are identical for both commercial and non-commercial users. Jet kerosene and aviation gasoline are, however, exempted from excise taxes.

The most important measure supporting energy production in Turkey is the financial assistance benefitting the hard-coal industry. Support is mostly provided through transfer payments from the Turkish Treasury to Turkish Hard-Coal Enterprises. The Ministry of Energy & Natural Resources distributes coal for heating purposes to assist poor families. Turkey is also supporting R&D connected to clean-coal technologies, including coal gasification, CO_2 storage and transport, and fuel production from biomass and coal blends. Meanwhile, there are a number of tax exemptions and rebates targeting specific fuels and specific sectors. These include: fuels used in domestic maritime shipping and in vehicles for national security; diesel used in agriculture for specific crops; oil and gas exploration, transportation and distribution; and public transportation.

Data documentation

Producer Support Estimate

Aid to the Hard-Coal Industry (data for 1991-)

Turkey's reserves of hard-coal are relatively small compared with those of lignite, and producers receive significant amounts of support to compensate them for costs that exceed revenues. Production costs for hard coal from Turkish Hard Coal Enterprises (TTK) stood at an average of USD 289 per tonne in 2008. Meanwhile, steel producers and power generators could purchase coal at prices ranging between USD 50 and USD 180 per tonne. State aid per tonne of coal has increased significantly over the years while production has declined.

Sources: IEA (2009; 2005).

Aid to the Lignite Industry (no data available)

Lignite makes a significant contribution to Turkey's domestic total coal supply. Turkish Coal Enterprise (TKI) is responsible for the exploration, production and marketing of both domestic lignite and asphaltite. Since 1995, the company has been able to cover its costs and make a profit.

Sources: IEA (2009; 2005).

Tax Exemption for Oil and Gas Exploration and Transportation (no data available)

This tax exemption was introduced in 1984 to encourage the exploration of oil and precious metals. According to the Turkish VAT Law (No. 3065), the Corporate Tax Law (No. 5520), and the Special Consumption Tax Law (No. 4760), activities connected to the exploration, processing, enrichment and refining of gold, silver and platinum, and those falling under the scope of the Oil Law (No. 6326), are entitled to tax-free provisions of services and delivery of goods. Eligible companies must be involved in certified oil-exploration activities. In addition, the delivery of machines and equipment to the owner of an investment-incentive certificate is exempted from value-added tax.

Sources: VAT Law No. 3065, Special Consumption Tax Law No. 4760, Tax Expenditure Report (2007).

Tax Exemption for the Transportation and Distribution of Oil and Gas (no data available)

This tax exemption was also introduced in 1984. It allows the transportation of foreign crude oil, natural gas and their products (including the construction and the services involved such as stations, pumps, measurement and communication tools) through pipelines to be exempted from both VAT and property tax.

Sources: Property Tax Law No. 1319, Tax Expenditure Report (2007).

Consumer Support Estimate

Tax Exemption for LPG Consumption (no data available)

Between 1999 and 2001, the government supported the use of LPG by households for cooking purposes by foregoing both VAT and the special consumption tax. Those tax exemptions resulted in the price of LPG being below that of both gasoline and diesel. As regular motor engines cannot use LPG, the government expected its use in cars to remain limited. However, an underground industry soon developed to make gasoline and diesel engines compatible with LPG. With a payback period of less than two years, the operation proved sufficiently simple and cheap for drivers to convert massively their vehicles to LPG use. Alerted by the resulting loss of tax revenue, the government began to phase out this tax expenditure at the end of 2000. This provision resulted in significant increases in LPG consumption.

Sources: IEA (2001).

Tax Exemption for Public Transportation (data for 2007)

According to the New Turkish Corporate Tax Law passed in 2006, public transport companies owned and managed by municipalities, villages or special provincial administrations are exempt from tax.

Sources: Corporate Tax Law No. 5520, Tax Expenditure Report (2007).

Rebate for Diesel Used in Agriculture (data for 2008-)

In Turkey, the tax rate on diesel fuel is very high, thereby creating a burden for farmers whose profit margins are significantly low. This programme was introduced by the Ministry of Agriculture in 2007 to help farmers grow specific crops. There are three different types of crops defined by the ministry which correspond to different aid levels. The amounts of aid are calculated according to the area of the land (in decares) used in growing specified crops, and paid according to a schedule defined by the cabinet. There are no restrictions on how grant money is spent. The measure is to be phased out.

Sources: Ministry of Agriculture and Rural Affairs (2007), Turkish Grand National Assembly.

Tax Exemption for Domestic Commercial Aviation (no data available)

In addition to the VAT, the Turkish government levies a "Special Consumption Tax" for every litre of fuel consumed. While gasoline, LPG and diesel are all subject to this tax, the domestic consumption of aviation and jet fuel has been exempted since the introduction of the excise tax law in 2002

Sources: Government of Turkey, Revenue Administration http://www.gib.gov.tr/fileadmin/mevzuatek/otv_oranlari_tum/31_12_2009.htm.

Aid for Coal to Poor Families (data for 2009-)

This programme was initiated in 2003 by the Ministry of Energy and Natural Resources to assist poor families. In Turkey, a significant number of families still burn lignite for heating purposes. The supply of coal is ensured by TKI and distributed by local governments. According to the Minister of Energy, an average of 1.7 million families received coal aid between 2003 and 2009. However, quantifying the total amount spent by the ministry is hampered due to lack of data.

Sources: Ministry of Energy and Natural Resources (2010), Turkish Court of Accounts (2009).

Fuel-Tax Exemption for Ships in Cabotage Lines (data for 2007)

This fuel-tax exemption was introduced by the government in 2003 to support the domestic maritime transport sector. The high special consumption tax on fuel was at the time considered to be a major barrier to the development of the sector in Turkey. Thus, the government decided to abolish the special consumption tax applying to sales of fuel for qualified ships. Qualified ships are those carrying cargo and passengers within the cabotage lines registered with the Turkish International Ship Registry and National Ship Registry, commercial yachts, and service and fishing ships.

Sources: Tax Expenditure Report (2007), Ministry of Finance.

Fuel-Tax Exemption for Vehicles used for National Security (no data available)

Fuel purchased by the Ministry of Defence, the General Command of Gandermarie, the General Command of Coast Guard, and the National Intelligence Agency is fully exempt from both VAT and the special consumption tax. This exemption was granted to these institutions for projects included in Turkish Armed Forces Strategic Aim Plan, Ministry of National Defense or Ministry of Interior, according to the relevance, is authorised to undertake commitments carried over to following years within the framework of Law No 3833 dated 1992.

Sources: Tax Expenditure Report (2007), Ministry of Finance.

References

Policies or transfers

Ministry of Agriculture and Rural Affairs (2007), *Annual Report,* Available at: http://sgb.tarim.gov.tr/anasayfa/faaliyet_raporlari/2007_YILI_BAKANLIK_FALI YET_RAPORU.pdf.

Ministry of Energy and Natural Resources (2010) *Budget Proposal,* Available at: http://www.enerji.gov.tr/yayinlar_raporlar/2010_Plan_ve_Butce_Komisyonu_Kon usmasi.pdf.

Ministry of Finance, General Directorate of Budget and Fiscal Control, *Budget for 2011,* Available at: http://www.bumko.gov.tr/EN/Genel/Default.aspx?17A16AE30572D313AAF6AA8 49816B2EF2858DA18F4388CDD.

Property Tax Law No. 1319, Available at: http://www.mevzuat.adalet.gov.tr/html/457.html.

Special Consumption Tax Law No. 4760, Available at: http://www.gib.gov.tr/fileadmin/mevzuatek/otv_oranlari_tum/31_12_2009.htm.

Turkish Court of Accounts (2009) *Treasury Accounting Report*, Available at:
http://www.sayistay.gov.tr/rapor/hazine/islemler/2009/2009_Hazine_Islemleri_Rap
oru.pdf.

Turkish Government Tax Expenditure Report (2007), Available at:
http://www.gep.gov.tr/fileAdmin/Statistics/Reports/VergiHarcamalari.pdf.

VAT Law No. 3065, Available at: http://www.gib.gov.tr/index.php?id=1028.

Energy Statistics

IEA (2009) *Energy Policies of IEA Countries: Turkey 2009 Review*, OECD Publications,
Paris.

IEA (2005) *Energy Policies of IEA Countries: Turkey 2005 Review*, OECD Publications,
Paris.

IEA (2001) *Energy Policies of IEA Countries: Turkey 2005 Review*, OECD Publications,
Paris.

Figure 23.1. Shares of fossil-fuel support by fuel, average for 2008-10 – Turkey

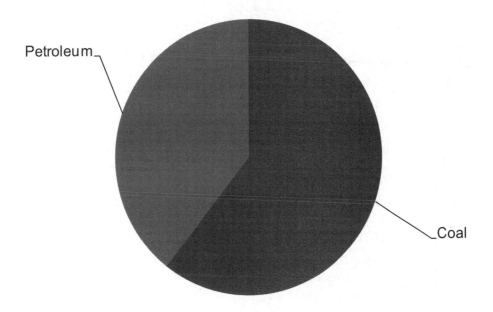

Source: OECD.

Figure 23.2. Shares of fossil-fuel support by indicator, average for 2008-10 – Turkey

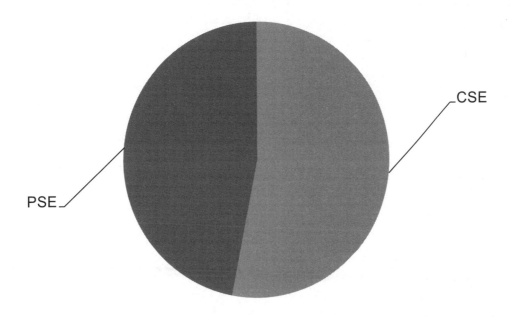

Source: OECD.

Table 23.1.   Summary of fossil-fuel support to coal – Turkey

(Millions of Turkish lira, nominal)

Support element	Jurisdiction	Avg 2000-02	Avg 2008-10	2008	2009	2010p
Producer Support Estimate						
Support to unit returns						
Aid to the Hard Coal Industry[1]	–	266.90	398.00	398.00	398.00	398.00
Consumer Support Estimate						
Consumption						
Aid for Coal to Poor Families	–	n.a.	252.00	..	252.00	252.00
General Services Support Estimate (n.a.)						

Note: Tax expenditures for any given country are measured with reference to a benchmark tax treatment that is generally specific to that country. Consequently, the estimates contained in the table above are not necessarily comparable with estimates for other countries. In addition, because of the potential interaction between them, the summation of individual measures for a specific country may be problematic. The allocation of particular measures across fuel types was done by the OECD Secretariat based on the IEA's Energy Balances.

(1) The amounts reported for this measure are in current USD.

Source: OECD.

Table 23.2. Summary of fossil-fuel support to petroleum – Turkey

(Millions of Turkish lira, nominal)

Support element	Jurisdiction	Avg 2000-02	Avg 2008-10	2008	2009	2010p
Producer Support Estimate						
Support for intermediate inputs						
Tax Exemption for Oil and Gas Exploration and Transportation	–	n.c.	n.c.	..	..	..
Tax Exemption for the Transportation and Distribution of Oil and Gas	–	n.c.	n.c.	..	..	..
Consumer Support Estimate						
Consumption						
Tax Exemption for Public Transportation	–	n.a.	n.c.	..	..	..
Rebate for Diesel used in Agriculture	–	n.a.	484.33	473.00	468.00	512.00
Fuel-Tax Exemption for Ships in Cabotage Lines	–	n.a.	n.c.	..	..	..
Tax Exemption for Commercial Aviation and Jet Fuel	–	n.a.	n.c.	..	..	..
Fuel-Tax Exemption for vehicles used for National Security	–	n.c.	n.c.	..	..	..
General Services Support Estimate (n.a.)						

Note: Tax expenditures for any given country are measured with reference to a benchmark tax treatment that is generally specific to that country. Consequently, the estimates contained in the table above are not necessarily comparable with estimates for other countries. In addition, because of the potential interaction between them, the summation of individual measures for a specific country may be problematic. The allocation of particular measures across fuel types was done by the OECD Secretariat based on the IEA's Energy Balances.

Source: OECD.

Table 23.3. Summary of fossil-fuel support to natural gas – Turkey

(Millions of Turkish lira, nominal)

Support element	Jurisdiction	Avg 2000-02	Avg 2008-10	2008	2009	2010p
Producer Support Estimate						
Support for intermediate inputs						
Tax Exemption for Oil and Gas Exploration and Transportation	–	n.c.	n.c.	..	..	..
Tax Exemption for the Transportation and Distribution of Oil and Gas	–	n.c.	n.c.	..	..	..
Consumer Support Estimate (n.a.)						
General Services Support Estimate (n.a.)						

Note: Tax expenditures for any given country are measured with reference to a benchmark tax treatment that is generally specific to that country. Consequently, the estimates contained in the table above are not necessarily comparable with estimates for other countries. In addition, because of the potential interaction between them, the summation of individual measures across fuel types was done by the OECD Secretariat based on the IEA's Energy Balances.

Source: OECD.

Chapter 24

United Kingdom

This chapter identifies, documents, and provides estimates of the various budgetary transfers and tax expenditures that relate to the production or use of fossil fuels in the *United Kingdom*. An overview of the *United Kingdom's* energy economy is first given to place the measures listed into context. A data-documentation section then describes those measures in a systematic way. Whenever possible, the description details a measure's formal beneficiary, its eligibility criteria and functioning, and the fuels whose production or use stand to benefit from the measure. The chapter ends with a set of charts and tables that provide, subject to availability, quantitative information and estimates for the various measures listed.

24. UNITED KINGDOM

Energy resources and market structure

The United Kingdom has been a major producer of oil and natural gas from the continental shelf in the North Sea since the 1980s, though output has been declining steadily for several years with the depletion of reserves. Historically, the country was a big coal producer too, but high costs have rendered most production uneconomic and output is now modest. Today, about a quarter of oil supplies are imported, about 30% of gas and almost two-thirds of coal. Natural gas is the dominant fuel in the primary energy mix, accounting in 2004 for 39% of total supply, followed by oil (33%) and coal (13%). Nuclear power contributes a further 9% and biomass for most of the remaining 3%. Since the 1980s, gas has displaced coal and oil, especially in power generation. Although UK import dependence has risen in recent years, the country still obtains all but a fifth of its energy supplies from indigenous sources (counting nuclear power as domestic production).

The United Kingdom has been a pioneer in deregulating and liberalising energy markets through price decontrol, the closure of inefficient coal mines, the removal of subsidies, privatisation and the introduction of competition and open access to electricity and natural gas networks, regulated by an independent regulatory body. Today, there is virtually no state ownership of energy assets and all markets are competitive.

The state-owned British Coal Corporation was sold in 1994, since which time all coal mining in Great Britain has been carried out by the private sector. The state, in the form of the Coal Authority (a non-departmental public body), remains the freehold owner of unworked coal reserves. With the phasing out of state aid to the coal industry, production has fallen sharply since the 1980s. Oil and gas exploration and production are carried out by a large number of private companies, including major international ones. Similarly, there is no state ownership within the downstream sector. The country's eleven refineries are owned mainly by international oil companies.

The gas sector was transformed in the 1980s and 1990s with the privatisation of the monopoly gas utility, British Gas, and the introduction of competition. Today, there are a large number of licensed wholesale and retail suppliers. The high-pressure transmission grid throughout Great Britain is operated by the National Grid. Five low-pressure gas distribution networks are owned by four gas distribution companies. Since the introduction of consumer choice in the 1990s, well over half of all retail customers have switched from the incumbent suppliers (British Gas, now Centrica in most parts of the country).

The UK electricity sector began a fundamental transformation in 1990 through a process of unbundling and privatisation. Today, the entire industry is privately-owned, apart from the 1.9 GW of old Magnox nuclear power stations that the government was not able to sell. The break-up of the former monopoly generating company, the entry of a wide range of new independent producers and divestitures by the largest initial generation companies throughout the 1990s has resulted in a high degree of fragmentation of ownership of generation assets, creating a competitive market structure. The National Grid owns and operates the England and Wales transmission system; the Scottish transmission system is owned by Scottish Power and Scottish and Southern Energy, and the Northern Ireland network by Northern Ireland Electricity. Licences for 14 distribution areas in Great Britain are currently held by seven different companies. Retail supply, which is unbundled from distribution, is dominated by six large companies which supply virtually all consumers. The majority of consumers have switched away from their incumbent supplier.

Prices, taxes and support mechanisms

There are no energy-price controls in the United Kingdom and all prices are set freely by the market. The Office of Gas and Electricity Markets (Ofgem) regulates electricity and gas network access charges through five-year price control periods that set the maximum amount of revenue which energy network owners can take through charges they levy on users of their networks. These prices are meant to cover their costs and earn them a return, while providing incentives to be efficient and to innovate technically.

Oil and gas production is subject to three taxes: the Petroleum revenue tax (PRT), which is levied at a rate of 50% on gross profits made on fields that were approved for development before 16 March 1993; the ring-fence corporation tax (30%); and a supplementary charge (which was raised from 20% to 32% in March 2011). PRT is a deductible expense for corporation tax and the supplementary charge. Various allowances are available in computing tax liabilities, including a new-field allowance that was introduced in 2009 for small, ultra-high-pressure and high-temperature oil fields, ultra-heavy oil fields, and (from 2010) remote deep-water gas fields to the west of Shetland. Other measures to support certain types of production include Promote licences, which allow small and start-up companies to obtain a production license first and secure the necessary operating capacity and financial resources later through reduced rent for the first two years.

Energy sales are subject to VAT (at a rate of 20%), excise taxes, and a Climate Change Levy (CCL). A reduced rate of VAT of 5% is applied to domestic fuel and power, as well as to the installation of certain energy-saving materials into domestic properties. Excise taxes are levied on oil products used for both commercial and non-commercial purposes. Businesses users pay the CCL on purchases of oil products (excluding transport fuels), natural gas, coal and electricity, though there are discounts and exemptions, depending on the source and use of the fuel (power generators are exempt, for example).

There are very few measures other than tax exemptions or reductions that support energy consumption in the United Kingdom. Schemes such as winter fuel payments for the elderly or cold-weather payments do not depend on the price of fuels and are provided in-cash to eligible households. Most of the remaining measures target consumption technologies such as low-carbon vehicles and hydrogen refuelling equipment rather than energy use *per se*.

Data documentation

General notes

The fiscal year in the United Kingdom runs from 1 April to 31 March. Following OECD convention, data are allocated to the starting calendar year so that data covering the period April 2005 to March 2006 are allocated to 2005.

Producer Support Estimate

Taxation of the oil and gas sector in the United Kingdom occurs through a variety of taxes. Fields approved for development prior to 16 March 1993 remain subject to the old Petroleum Revenue Tax (PRT), which was instituted in 1975. The PRT is a project-based tax that is levied at a rate of 50% of the profits from a given field. It allows for the full deduction of both operating and capital expenditures. The PRT does not, however, allow the deduction of interest costs and other financing charges from taxable profits.

Meanwhile, oil and gas corporations are also subject to a modified version of the regular corporation tax, namely the Ring-Fence Corporation Tax (RFCT). The imposition of a "ring fence" around upstream oil and gas activities means that these particular activities are to be treated separately for tax purposes from any other trade in which oil and gas companies may be engaged. This therefore allows upstream oil and gas activities to be taxed differently at the company-level. Differences in taxation include, for instance, the impossibility for companies to use losses in other activities as deductions against the income arising from oil and gas extraction.

While all fields are subject to the RFCT, those that were approved for development prior to 16 March 1993 can deduct the amount of PRT taxes paid from their RFCT tax base. This ensures that the fields that are still subject to the old PRT regime are not taxed twice on the same profits. In addition, all types of fields are liable to the so-called Supplementary Charge (SC), which was introduced in the Finance Act of 2002. The SC is a 20% tax on profits from oil and gas production that is levied on top of the RFCT.

The immediate write-off of both capital and exploration-and-development expenditures is normally considered under the systems in many countries to amount to a preferential tax treatment. The reason is that in calculating taxable profits in most income-tax systems, capital expenses are allocated over the period to which they contribute to earnings. Allowing the immediate writing-off these types of expenditure therefore provides companies with something akin to a zero-interest loan from the government since it delays the collection of taxes. A present-value calculation would indeed show a positive transfer from the government to the companies benefiting from such provisions.

However, when combined with an impossibility for companies to deduct interest costs and other financing charges, the immediate write-off of both capital and exploration-and-development expenditures may not be considered a preferential tax treatment. This is due to the fact that this particular combination of tax provisions may approximate what is known as a "cash-flow" tax system. Cash-flow tax systems can be theoretically equivalent to the more common imputed-income tax systems where the objective is to levy a neutral business tax (Boadway and Bruce, 1984). For that reason, provisions such as the expensing of exploration and development costs may not be preferential tax provisions in the particular case of the United Kingdom.

PRT Exemption for Sales to British Gas (data for 1997-)

Proceeds from the sale of natural gas to what was formerly the British Gas Corporation are exempted from the PRT if contracts were signed prior to 30 June 1975. This provision still applies to those contracts that have not been subject to any kind of "fundamental alteration".

Sources: HM Revenue & Customs (various years), HM Revenue & Customs (2008).

Tag: GBR_te_01

PRT Tariff Receipts Allowance (data for 1997-)

This provision was introduced in 1983 and excludes some tariff receipts from taxable profits under the PRT regime. Tariffs are here understood as payments to a company for the use of its assets by other oil and gas companies.

We use production data from the IEA to allocate the annual amounts reported in budget documents to oil and natural gas extraction.

Sources: HM Revenue & Customs (various years), HM Revenue & Customs (2008), IEA.

Tag: GBR_te_02

PRT Uplift for Certain Capital Expenditures (data for 1997-2007)

The 1975 Oil Taxation Act allows oil and gas companies subject to the PRT regime to obtain an additional 35% deduction for certain qualifying capital expenditures. Eligible types of expenditure would include the costs incurred in "substantially improving the rate of production or transportation". HM Revenue & Customs (2008) also mentions that the PRT uplift is meant to compensate companies for the non-deductibility of interest costs and other financing charges (cf. introductory remark).

This relief is available only while the field in question is in its initial phase and has yet to recover its start-up costs. Since PRT only applies to fields that were given development consent prior to 16 March 1993, availability of the uplift is restricted to a limited number of cases.

We use production data from the IEA to allocate the annual amounts reported in budget documents to oil and natural gas extraction. Data are not available for the years following FY2007/08.

Sources: HM Revenue & Customs (various years), HM Revenue & Customs (2008), IEA.

Tag: GBR_te_03

PRT Oil Allowance (data for 1997-)

The Oil Allowance was introduced in 1975 to encourage the development of small and marginal fields. It is a relief against PRT applicable to profits after all losses and expenditures have been relieved. The value of the allowance itself is determined using a statutory formula that depends in part on the date at which the field was developed and its location. The Oil Allowance is normally available for a period of ten years but relief can be claimed for a much longer period if there are sufficient profits to absorb all of the deductions available.

We use production data from the IEA to allocate the annual amounts reported in budget documents to oil and natural gas extraction.

Sources: HM Revenue & Customs (various years), HM Revenue & Customs (2008), IEA.

Tag: GBR_te_04

PRT Safeguard (data for 1997-2007)

The PRT Safeguard is a provision contained in the Oil Taxation Act of 1975. Safeguard, like the Oil Allowance, forms part of a package of measures designed to reduce the incidence of PRT on small, marginal fields. The PRT Safeguard is a relief against the amount of tax payable, and so applies only if there remains a tax liability once all expenditure and other reliefs have been taken into account. As for the PRT Uplift for Certain Capital Expenditures, Safeguard is only applicable to a limited number of fields.

We use production data from the IEA to allocate the annual amounts reported in budget documents to oil and natural gas extraction. Data are not available for the years following FY2007/08.

Sources: HM Revenue & Customs (various years), HM Revenue & Customs (2008), IEA.

Tag: GBR_te_05

Ring-Fence Expenditure Supplement (no data available)

The Ring-Fence Expenditure Supplement (RFES) was introduced in January 2006 to replace the former Exploration Expenditure Supplement (EES). Both schemes provide oil and gas companies with a yearly 6% increase in the value of unclaimed deductions for expenses related to exploration and appraisal. This annual supplement will be increased to 10% as of 1 January 2012.

No estimates are available for this provision.

Sources: HM Revenue & Customs (2008).

Field Allowance (no data available)

This new allowance was introduced in 2009 and extended in 2010 to encourage the development of small or technically-challenging fields. Qualifying fields must be small in size, feature ultra-high pressure or temperature, possess ultra-heavy-oil reserves, or be remote deep-water gas fields. The allowance provides companies with a partial exemption from the Supplementary Charge (cf. introductory remark). Relief is calculated at the level of the field but is provided at the company-level. Unclaimed allowances can be carried forward.

No estimates are available for this provision.

Sources: HM Revenue & Customs (2011[a]).

UK Coal Operating Aid Scheme (data for 2000-02)

The UK Coal Operating Aid Scheme (UKCOAS) was a temporary programme designed to provide short-term financial support to otherwise viable coal producers. It was introduced in 2000 for a period of three years over which a total amount of GBP 162 million was to be spent in four tranches. The programme was approved by the European Commission under the rules of the former European Coal and Steel Community. Applications were closed after 31 December 2002.

We use production data from the IEA to allocate the annual amounts reported in official documents to the various types of coal concerned.

Sources: DECC (2006[a]), IEA.

Tag: GBR_dt_01

Coal Investment Aid (data for 2004-08)

The Coal Investment Aid (CIA) was introduced in 2003 to reimburse up to 30% of the qualifying investment costs incurred by coal producers. Transfers were meant to secure access to reserves at twelve deep mines. Applications are now no longer accepted.

We use production data from the IEA to allocate the annual amounts reported in official documents to the various types of coal concerned.

Sources: DECC (2006[b]), IEA.

Tag: GBR_dt_02

Mineral Extraction Allowance (no data available)

The Mineral Extraction Allowance (MEA) was introduced in 1986 to provide mining companies (including coal, oil, and natural gas producers) with faster rates of depreciation for qualifying expenditures. The latter include the acquisition of mineral rights or deposits and expenditures connected to access to the reserves. Prescribed rates vary with the type of expenditure to which the provision applies. Analysis of this provision is, however, complicated by the interaction of the MEA with the general tax regime that applies to oil and gas extraction (*cf.* introductory remark). These caveats do not apply to coal though.

Although this provision applies to the mining sector as a whole, data from the OECD's STAN database indicate that mining of fossil fuels accounts for nearly 90% of total gross output for the mining and quarrying sector (as defined in the standard ISIC Rev.3 sector classification).

No estimates of the revenue foregone due to the MEA are available.

Sources: HM Revenue & Customs (2008), Office of Tax Simplification (2011).

Abandonment Costs (no data available)

This provision allows capital expenditures connected to the abandonment of fields and mines to be deducted in full in the year in which they are incurred. Deductions are coupled with a carry-back provision which makes it possible for companies to use losses arising from decommissioning costs against profits earned in earlier years. This may therefore result in tax refunds.

Although this provision applies to the mining sector as a whole, data from the OECD's STAN database indicate that mining of fossil fuels accounts for nearly 90% of total gross output for the mining and quarrying sector (as defined in the standard ISIC Rev.3 sector classification).

No estimates of the revenue foregone due to the expensing of abandonment costs are available.

Sources: HM Revenue & Customs (2008).

Consumer Support Estimate

Reduced Rate of VAT for Fuel and Power (data for 1997-)

The domestic consumption of both heating fuel and power in the United Kingdom is subject to a much lower rate of VAT than that applied to regular products (20% as of January 2011). Domestic fuel and power were initially zero-rated when VAT was first introduced in 1973 but subsequently became liable to a 8% rate with the VAT Act of 1994. The latter rate was eventually lowered to 5% (the EU minimum) in 1997.

We use the IEA's Energy Balances for the residential sector to allocate the amounts reported in official budget documents to fossil fuels, biomass, waste and electricity. Only those amounts that pertain to fossil fuels are here being considered.

Sources: HM Revenue & Customs (various years), IEA.

Tag: GBR_te_06

Reduced Rate of Excise for Red Diesel (no data available)

The use of "red diesel" (*i.e.* dyed diesel) and other such petroleum products in the United Kingdom is subject to a reduced rate of excise duty. Eligible uses include off-road vehicles such as those used for agriculture, road construction or clearing snow.

No estimates of the revenue foregone due this provision are available.

Sources: HM Revenue & Customs (2011[b]).

General Services Support Estimate

Inherited Liabilities Related to Coal-Mining (data for 1997-2009)

The Coal Authority was created by the Coal Industry Act of 1994 to address those inherited liabilities for which no licensed coal-mine operator can be held responsible. The abandoned mining sites handled by the Coal Authority include all former British Coal Corporation pits. Mine subsidence and historic liabilities such as the treatment of mine-water discharges are the Authority's two programmes that figure prominently here.

Data come from the Coal Authority's annual reports where yearly operating income and expenses are reported for each class of business. We thus report for each year the sum of the net expenses associated with each of these classes (excluding those classes that do not constitute general support like "licensing" or "mining assets").

We use production data from the IEA to allocate the annual amounts reported in official documents to the various types of coal concerned.

Sources: Coal Authority (various years), IEA.

Tag: GBR_dt_03

References

Policies or transfers

Boadway, Robin and Neil Bruce (1984) 'A General Proposition on the Design of a Neutral Business Tax', *Journal of Public Economics*, Vol. 24, No. 2, pp. 231-239.

Coal Authority (various years) *Annual Report and Accounts*, Available at: http://www.coal.gov.uk/publications/financial/index.cfm.

DECC (2006[a]) *Awards made under UK Coal Operating Aid Scheme (UKCOAS)*, Department of Energy & Climate Change, Government of the United Kingdom, Available at: http://www.decc.gov.uk/en/content/cms/what_we_do/uk_supply/energy_mix/coal/industry/industry.aspx.

DECC (2006[b]) *Awards made under Coal Investment Aid (CIA) scheme*, Department of Energy & Climate Change, Government of the United Kingdom, Available at: http://www.decc.gov.uk/en/content/cms/what_we_do/uk_supply/energy_mix/coal/industry/industry.aspx.

HM Revenue & Customs (2008) *A Guide to UK and UK Continental Shelf – Oil and Gas Taxation*, Government of the United Kingdom, Available at: http://www.hmrc.gov.uk/international/ns-fiscal3.htm.

HM Revenue & Customs (2011[a]) *Field Allowance: What is the field allowance?*, Government of the United Kingdom, Available at: http://www.hmrc.gov.uk/manuals/otmanual/ot21405.htm.

HM Revenue & Customs (2011[b]) *Excise Duty on Oils (Duty Liability): Rebated oils (for off- road and other qualifying uses)*, Government of the United Kingdom, Available at: http://www.hmrc.gov.uk/manuals/otemanual/HCOTEG12780.htm.

HM Revenue & Customs (various years) *Tax Expenditures and Ready Reckoners*, Government of the United Kingdom, Available at: http://www.hmrc.gov.uk/stats/tax_expenditures/menu.htm.

Office of Tax Simplification (2011) *Review of Tax Reliefs*, HM Treasury, Government of the United Kingdom, Available at: http://www.hm-treasury.gov.uk/ots_taxreliefsreview.htm.

Energy statistics

IEA, *Energy Balances of OECD Countries*, 2010 Edition, International Energy Agency, Paris.

Figure 24.1. Shares of fossil-fuel support by fuel, average for 2008-10 – United Kingdom

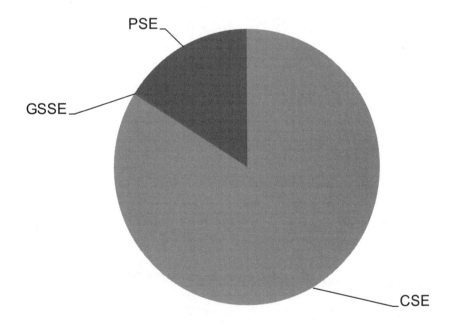

Coal

Petroleum

Natural Gas

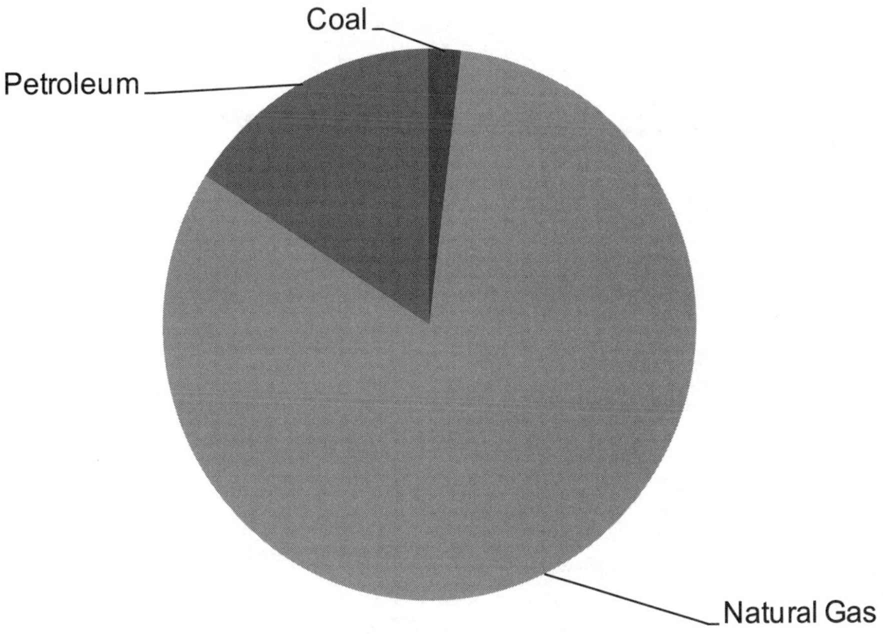

Source: OECD.

Figure 24.2. Shares of fossil-fuel support by indicator, average for 2008-10 – United Kingdom

PSE

GSSE

CSE

Source: OECD.

Table 24.1.   Summary of fossil-fuel support to coal – United Kingdom

(Millions of British pounds sterling, nominal)

Support element	Jurisdiction	Avg 2000-02	Avg 2008-10	2008	2009	2010p
Producer Support Estimate						
Income support						
UK Coal Operating Aid Scheme	–	54.06	n.a.	n.a.	n.a.	n.a.
Support for capital formation						
Coal Investment Aid	–	n.a.	n.a.	1.45	n.a.	n.a.
Consumer Support Estimate						
Consumption						
Reduced Rate of VAT for Fuel and Power	–	51.60	56.28	58.50	47.39	62.94
General Services Support Estimate						
Inherited Liabilities Related to Coal Mining	–	24.79	9.64	12.40	8.26	8.26

Note: Tax expenditures for any given country are measured with reference to a benchmark tax treatment that is generally specific to that country. Consequently, the estimates contained in the table above are not necessarily comparable with estimates for other countries. In addition, because of the potential interaction between them, the summation of individual measures for a specific country may be problematic. The allocation of particular measures across fuel types was done by the OECD Secretariat based on the IEA's Energy Balances.

Source: OECD.

Table 24.2. Summary of fossil-fuel support to petroleum – United Kingdom

(Millions of British pounds sterling, nominal)

Support element	Jurisdiction	Avg 2000-02	Avg 2008-10	2008	2009	2010p
Producer Support Estimate						
Support to unit returns						
PRT Tariff Receipts Allowance	–	33.11	32.61	32.61	32.61	32.61
PRT Oil Allowance	–	295.68	248.17	364.10	179.33	201.07
PRT Safeguard	–	138.81	n.c.	..	..	..
Support for capital formation						
PRT Uplift for Certain Capital Expenditures	–	117.42	n.c.	..	..	..
Consumer Support Estimate						
Consumption						
Reduced Rate of VAT for Fuel and Power	–	121.06	255.34	265.42	215.03	285.58
General Services Support Estimate (n.a.)						

Note: Tax expenditures for any given country are measured with reference to a benchmark tax treatment that is generally specific to that country. Consequently, the estimates contained in the table above are not necessarily comparable with estimates for other countries. In addition, because of the potential interaction between them, the summation of individual measures for a specific country may be problematic. The allocation of particular measures across fuel types was done by the OECD Secretariat based on the IEA's Energy Balances.

Source: OECD.

Table 24.3.   Summary of fossil-fuel support to natural gas – United Kingdom

(Millions of British pounds sterling, nominal)

Support element	Jurisdiction	Avg 2000-02	Avg 2008-10	2008	2009	2010p
Producer Support Estimate						
Support to unit returns						
PRT Exemption for Sales to British Gas	–	190.00	16.67	20.00	20.00	10.00
PRT Tariff Receipts Allowance	–	25.22	27.39	27.39	27.39	27.39
PRT Oil Allowance	–	225.99	208.50	305.90	150.67	168.93
PRT Safeguard	–	106.19	n.c.	..	..	..
Support for capital formation						
PRT Uplift for Certain Capital Expenditures	–	89.24	n.c.	..	..	..
Consumer Support Estimate						
Consumption						
Reduced Rate of VAT for Fuel and Power	–	1 147.96	2 539.75	2 640.00	2 138.74	2 840.51
General Services Support Estimate (n.a.)						

Note: Tax expenditures for any given country are measured with reference to a benchmark tax treatment that is generally specific to that country. Consequently, the estimates contained in the table above are not necessarily comparable with estimates for other countries. In addition, because of the potential interaction between them, the summation of individual measures for a specific country may be problematic. The allocation of particular measures across fuel types was done by the OECD Secretariat based on the IEA's Energy Balances.

Source: OECD.

Chapter 25

United States

This chapter identifies, documents, and provides estimates of the various budgetary transfers and tax expenditures that relate to the production or use of fossil fuels in the *United States*. An overview of the *United States's* energy economy is first given to place the measures listed into context. A data-documentation section then describes those measures in a systematic way. Whenever possible, the description details a measure's formal beneficiary, its eligibility criteria and functioning, and the fuels whose production or use stand to benefit from the measure. The chapter ends with a set of charts and tables that provide, subject to availability, quantitative information and estimates for the various measures listed.

25. UNITED STATES

Energy resources and market structure

The United States is the leading producer and consumer of energy in the world, with large and diverse energy resources. Reserves and production of oil and gas were in decline until recently, but have been boosted by new hydrocarbon discoveries in the Gulf of Mexico and by the deployment of new technologies that have made possible the economic development of vast new resources of unconventional gas, notably shale gas. The United States is fully self-sufficient in coal, exporting small volumes, and is largely self-sufficient in natural gas, importing a small share of its gas needs as LNG and by pipeline from Canada. By contrast, it is heavily dependent on imports of oil, which contribute 58% of its total oil supply. Overall, the United States produces 70% of its energy needs domestically, down from almost 85% in 1990.

Fossil fuels make up about 85% of US primary energy supply, a relatively high share by OECD standards. Oil is the leading fuel, accounting for 37% of supply, followed by natural gas (25%) and coal (22%). Nuclear power contributes a further 1%, with renewables – mainly biomass – making up the remaining 5%. The fuel mix has barely changed over the last decade. Energy use rose steadily between 1981 and 2007, but fell sharply as a result of the economic crisis; by 2009, it was 7% below its peak, though it is thought to have rebounded since.

The United States has a strong tradition of private ownership in energy and takes a market-based approach to energy policy. It was among the first countries to deregulate the upstream oil and gas sector (in the 1980s) and to pursue structural reforms in wholesale natural gas and electricity markets to boost the role of competition as a means of achieving more efficient supply and lower prices.

The coal industry is entirely privately owned. Significant deposits lie on federal lands in the west, which are leased out to mining companies. The three largest coal producers account for 40% of total coal production, with the top producer, Peabody Energy, alone accounting for 18%. Most of the coal produced is used for power generation, for which coal is the leading fuel input nationally.

The US oil market is fully deregulated and open to competition. Oil and gas production is fully in the hands of private enterprises, even though about four-fifths of the country's recoverable resources are on federal land or in federally controlled offshore waters. There are more than 15 000 operating companies active in oil and gas exploration and production, including many foreign companies. The US downstream oil sector is also fully privately-owned. There are 148 refineries, the largest number anywhere in the world, most of which are relatively sophisticated with a large capacity to upgrade low-quality crude oil into light products. The distribution network comprises common-carrier and proprietary pipelines, barge and tanker fleets, and storage installations. Companies active in the sector can be fully integrated or operate as independent traders in specific market segments. The retail sector is characterised by a large number of suppliers, ranging from vertically integrated major companies to independent operators.

The natural gas market is dynamic and highly competitive, with a very active spot and futures market. Regional US markets are highly integrated, thanks to an extensive national network of high-pressure transmission pipelines, market centres and hubs, and are also well-integrated with the markets of Canada and Mexico. The industry has a high degree of private ownership with little vertical integration. Production, transmission and distribution are for the most part carried out by separate companies. Only a few large gas distributors own transmission pipelines. There are roughly 1 400 local gas distribution companies, most of which are small companies with a few thousand customers, though there are several with over a million customers. The only public ownership in the United States gas industry is in gas distribution; around 950 municipality-owned gas utilities account for about 7% of all domestic gas sales. Retailing is carried out by a mixture of unbundled independent marketers and incumbent distributors, according to the degree to which retail markets have been opened to competition (which varies widely across states).

The structure of the electricity-supply industry is complex and fragmented. Less than half of the investor-owned utilities (IOUs) are vertically integrated, owning transmission and distribution assets, while three-quarters of the publicly-owned or co-operative utilities are involved solely in local distribution. Retail sales are dominated by IOUs, accounting for more than two-thirds of total sales, while wholesale power purchases are primarily undertaken by power marketers and energy service providers. Independent power producers (IPPs) mostly sell their output on the wholesale market only; few of them supply power on the retail market. Generation is dominated by the IOUs, which account for around 60% of generation by volume, while IPPs account for about 30%. The remainder is produced by subsidiaries of three federal agencies (of which only the Tennessee Valley Authority generates any electricity from fossil fuels) and by the small number of municipally owned and co-operatively owned electric utilities that generate electric power.

The US electricity industry and the downstream gas industry are subject to regulation at the local, state and federal levels. Intra-state activities are subject to regulation by state regulatory commissions, which approve plant and transmission line construction, and retail prices for the incumbent utilities. Where a utility activity crosses state boundaries, it is subject to federal regulation by the Federal Energy Regulatory Commission (FERC). Wholesale prices, plus other matters such as hydro-electric and nuclear plant permitting issues, are under federal regulation. States have responsibility for making decisions about liberalisation of intra-state markets, but have been encouraged to do so by FERC and the federal government in recent years. Electricity market liberalisation has progressed less rapidly than in the gas sector and in some other OECD countries, primarily as a consequence of the electric-power crisis in California a decade ago, which resulted in part from poorly designed reforms, and of broader concerns about system reliability in a competitive environment. Moves to introduce or expand competition in wholesale and retail electricity markets have been suspended or halted completely in a number of states.

Prices, taxes and support mechanisms

In general, non-network forms of energy are not subject to any price controls in the United States. However, some states have the power to implement price ceilings for oil products. Electricity and gas prices are generally regulated by the FERC at the wholesale level and by state regulatory commissions at the retail level. Prices and network charges are set on a cost-of-service basis.

Compared with other IEA member countries, energy is taxed at a relatively low rate in the United States. Taxes are levied by the states and by the federal government. In nearly all states, a sales tax is levied on all sales of goods and services to non-commercial users. The rates vary between the states, but generally automotive fuels are exempt from sales tax, as special taxes on these fuels are always levied at the state and, in some cases, local level. At the federal level, excise taxes are levied on automotive fuels only. Special federal taxes apply to aviation gasoline and jet fuel sold used for domestic flights.

Mineral rights for the production of coal, oil or natural gas on federal lands and in federal offshore waters are subject to federal taxation and royalties. Royalties, bonuses and rents paid by minerals companies for mining on federal land are collected by the Minerals Management Service and are shared on a 50/50 basis with the state in which the land lies. The state revenues are distributed in part to the counties in which production occurs. In non-federal onshore areas and offshore state waters, each state determines what royalties and rents are to be paid.

Federal tax breaks are available for some types of offshore oil and gas production. For example, oil and gas producers are allowed to expense a share of intangible exploration and production drilling costs rather than amortise them over time; non-integrated oil and gas producers can amortise geological and geophysical expenditure over a two-year period and integrated producers over seven years; and oil producers are granted a tax credit amounting to 15% of the investment costs related to the use of enhanced oil recovery methods (when the real price of crude is below a set level). Some states also give favourable tax treatment to some types of oil and gas production. Federal tax breaks are available for refiners also, notably a provision in the 2005 Energy Policy Act (EPAct) allowing them to expense 50% of the cost of capital equipment. EPAct also shortened the depreciation period for natural gas distribution pipelines from 20 years to 15 years – well below their normal working life. Support to coal mining includes favourable tax treatment of royalty income, partial expensing of advanced mine safety equipment and reduced severance tax rates for thin-seamed coal in West Virginia.

In the electric power sector, municipally owned utilities, as well as other publicly owned utilities, are able to issue low cost, tax-exempt debt to finance construction of power plants and other long-lived capital facilities. EPAct provides for tax credits on investment in clean-coal technologies, such as integrated gas combined cycle, with a view to encourage the development of advanced coal-fired power plants; another measure allows power generators to amortise certain pollution-control facilities over a period of seven years.

There are a number of programmes and measures relating to fossil-energy consumption. At the federal level, the Low Income Home Energy Assistance Program, set up in 1981, provides grants to poor households to help them pay their energy bills. Off-road users of gasoline and diesel fuels, including the farming, fishing, forestry and mining sectors, are exempted from both federal and excise taxes on fuel; most states also grant exemptions or levy reduced rates of excise tax on fuels used by these sectors.

The Strategic Petroleum Reserve (SPR), created in 1975 to provide a secure reserve of petroleum that could be accessed quickly in the event of a major disruption in supply, is also a source of support to the oil industry, as the cost is covered entirely by the federal government. The SPR accounts for about half of the US emergency stocks in terms of days of net imports, with the rest being held by the private sector. Another important source of support is the federal fossil-energy research and development programme, which provides funding for developing technologies related to fossil energy such as fuels conversion or coal liquefaction. The programme has a long history, but funding was increased substantially under the 2009 American Recovery and Reinvestment Act. A number of states also provide support to the production and consumption of coal, oil or natural gas, mainly through the tax system.

Data documentation

General notes

The fiscal year in the United States runs from 1 October to 30 September. Following OECD convention, data are allocated to the ending calendar year so that data covering the period October 2005 to September 2006 are allocated to 2006. States may, however, have a different fiscal year.

Since the United States is a federal country, the data collection exercise was also conducted for a sample of three states. Those three states are: West Virginia (WV), Texas (TX), and Alaska (AK).

Producer Support Estimate

Alternative Fuels Production Credit (data for 1987-)

Early versions of this measure predate the Internal Revenue Code of 1986. Since then, the Alternative Fuels Production Credit has changed markedly in terms of fuel coverage. The Energy Policy Act of 2005 provided a temporary income-tax credit equal to USD 3 (generally adjusted for inflation) per Btu oil-barrel equivalent for coke and coke gas produced in the United States. This credit applies to coke or coke gas produced during a four-year period beginning on the later of 1 January 2006 or the date at which the qualified facility[32] was placed in service. The amount of credit-eligible coke produced at any one facility may not exceed an average of 4 000 barrels of oil-equivalent a day.

An income-tax credit was also available through 2002 for oil produced from shale and tar sands, as well as natural gas produced from geo-pressured brine, Devonian shale, coal seams, and tight formations, provided that the wells were drilled before 1993. For natural gas produced from biomass, and synthetic fuels produced from coal or lignite, the credit was available through 2007, provided that the facility was placed in service before July 1998. Credits can be carried forward 20 years since the Alternative Fuels Production Credit is part of the general business credit.

Prior to 2007, this measure primarily benefited synthetic coal obtained through the use of bituminous coal as feedstock (EIA, 2008). Starting in 2007, the credit now only applies to coke and coke gas, which are both produced from coking coal. We therefore allocate the measure entirely to hard coal.

---

[32]   For purposes of the credit as it applies to coke, the qualified facilities are those that were placed in service before 1 January 1993 or after 30 June 1998, and before 1 January 2010. Qualified facilities do not include facilities that produce petroleum-based coke or coke gas.

Sources: EIA (2008), OMB (various years).

Tag: USA_te_01

Refined Coal Credit (no data available)

This measure is meant to encourage the production of refined coal in the United States. As such, it comprises two separate tax credits: one for the production of refined coal used to generate steam, and one for the production of fuel for the steel industry. Both credits are described below.

A first temporary income-tax credit is available for producing certain types of refined coal used to generate steam. Eligible companies may generally claim the credit during a ten-year period commencing with the date at which the qualified facility was placed in service. Qualified facilities must have been placed in service after 22 October 2004 and before 1 January 2010.

Meanwhile, each barrel-of-oil equivalent of steel-industry fuel produced at a qualified facility generally receives an income-tax credit. A qualified facility is any facility capable of producing steel-industry fuel and that was placed in service before 1 January 2010. Steel-industry fuel is defined as a fuel produced through a process of liquefying coal-waste sludge, distributing the liquefied product on coal, and using the resulting mixture as feedstock for the manufacture of coke. The credit is generally available for one year starting at the date at which the facility was placed in service or 31 December 2009.

This tax credit is part of the broader Energy Production Credit as reported in OMB (various years). The OMB does not, however, produce a separate annual estimate of the associated tax expenditure. Meanwhile, the Joint Committee on Taxation estimates this tax expenditure to be less than USD 50 million per year (see JCT, various years).

Sources: OMB (various years), JCT (various years).

Indian Coal Credit (no data available)

Producers of coal from lands owned by Native Americans are eligible to receive a temporary income-tax credit. The measure is available for a seven-year period beginning 1 January 2006 and ending 31 December 2012. A qualified coal facility is a facility that was placed in service before 1 January 2009, and that produces coal from reserves.

This tax credit is part of the broader Energy Production Credit as reported in OMB (various years). The OMB does not, however, produce a separate annual estimate of the associated tax expenditure. Meanwhile, the Joint Committee on Taxation estimates this tax expenditure to be less than USD 50 million per year (see JCT, various years).

Sources: OMB (various years), JCT (various years).

Capital Gains Treatment of Royalties on Coal (data for 1987-)

This tax provision allows individual owners of coal-mining rights to benefit from the more favourable capital gains tax rate rather than the regular income-tax regime when receiving royalties. The measure was introduced in 1951 with the intention of boosting coal production.

We use production data from the IEA to allocate the annual amounts reported in budget documents to the various types of coal concerned (bituminous and sub-bituminous coal, lignite, and coking coal).

Sources: EIA (2008), OMB (various years), IEA.

Tag: USA_te_03

Partial Expensing for Advanced Mine Safety Equipment (data for 2006-)

This measure was introduced in 2006 to encourage the adoption of advanced mine safety equipment in coal extraction. For tax purposes, the Internal Revenue Code allows a 50% expensing of qualifying equipment as opposed to a regular amortisation.

We use production data from the IEA to allocate the annual amounts reported in budget documents to the various types of coal concerned (bituminous and sub-bituminous coal, lignite, and coking coal).

Sources: EIA (2008), OMB (various years), IEA.

Tag: USA_te_05

Expensing of Exploration and Development Costs (data for 1987-)

This measure dates back to 1986 in its present form although older versions go as far back as 1916. It allows independent oil and natural-gas producers to deduct immediately (*i.e.* expense) intangible drilling costs (IDCs) associated with investments in domestic oil and gas wells, and exploration and development costs for other fuels. IDCs consist of wages, machinery used for grading and drilling, and unsalvageable materials used in developing a well. Integrated oil and natural-gas companies may deduct up to 70% of such costs and recover the remaining 30% over a five-year period. Because these expenses occur prior to production and are properly attributable to future output, normal income-tax rules would treat them as capital costs and allow deductions for depletion only as the resources from the well are extracted. Similar rules apply in the case of mining exploration and development costs for minerals other than oil and natural gas.

We use production data from the IEA to allocate the annual amounts reported in budget documents to oil and natural gas extraction. As is the case for most accelerated capital-depreciation provisions (of which expensing is a particular type), annual budgetary estimates can sometimes be negative. This is for instance the case when the industry to which the provision applies declines, thereby slowing (or even reversing) capital accumulation. Accelerated depreciation causes tax revenues in the later years of a given asset's useful life to exceed what they would have been had the asset been depreciated in a conventional way. Thus, a decline in capital investment may result in tax deductions on new equipment proving not sufficient to outweigh the higher revenue flow arising from the older equipment being already depreciated for tax purposes.

Sources: EIA (2008), OMB (various years), IEA.

Tag: USA_te_06

Excess of Percentage over Cost Depletion (data for 1987-)

Under normal income-tax treatment, expenses that are capitalised into the basis of mineral properties would be recovered over time as output is extracted from the wells or mines. Under percentage depletion, producers can, however, recover these costs by claiming as a depletion allowance a fixed percentage of gross income from the property. Over time, the sum of these deductions can be several times the original cost of the investment. For oil and natural-gas properties, the percentage ranges from 15% to 25% and, except in the case of marginal wells, the deduction may not exceed 100% of the net income from the property. In addition, the percentage depletion deduction for oil and gas properties may not exceed 65% of the taxpayer's overall taxable income.

Only independent producers and royalty owners (in contrast to integrated oil companies) qualify for the percentage depletion deduction. In addition, oil and gas producers may claim percentage depletion only on up to 1 000 barrels of average daily production of domestic crude oil or an equivalent amount of domestic natural gas.

A taxpayer may also qualify for percentage depletion with respect to coal and other hard-mineral fossil-fuel properties. The amount of the deduction is a statutory percentage of the gross income from the property. The percentage is 10% for coal and lignite, and 15% for shale oil.[33] The deduction may not exceed 50% of the taxable income from the property (determined before the deductions for depletion and domestic manufacturing).

Official budget documents provide estimates of the excess deductions stemming from the use of percentage depletion by oil & gas and coal-mining companies (the baseline being the use of cost depletion). We use production data from the IEA to allocate the annual amounts reported in budget documents to oil, natural-gas and coal extraction.

Sources: EIA (2008), OMB (various years), IEA.

Tag: USA_te_07

Amortisation of Geological Expenditure (data for 2006-)

This measure allows non-integrated oil and gas producers to amortise geological and geophysical expenditure over a two-year period. The amortisation period is lengthened to seven years for integrated producers. This tax provision was introduced as part of the Energy Policy Act of 2005.

We use production data from the IEA to allocate the annual amounts reported in budget documents to oil and natural gas extraction.

Sources: EIA (2008), OMB (various years), IEA.

Tag: USA_te_08

---

[33]   Other than shale oil to which a 7.5% depletion rate applies because it is used for certain non-fuel purposes.

Accelerated Depreciation of Natural-Gas Distribution Pipelines (data for 2006-)

The Energy Policy Act of 2005 established a statutory 15-year recovery period for natural-gas distribution pipelines placed in service after 11 April 2005 and before 1 January 2011. Prior to this, natural-gas distribution pipelines were assigned a 20-year recovery period under the Modified Accelerated Cost Recovery System. According to the IRS, the actual working life of most natural gas pipelines is typically on the order of 20 to 25 years.

Sources: EIA (2008), OMB (various years).

Tag: USA_te_09

Exception from Passive Loss Limitation (data for 1988-)

This measure dates back to 1986 and allows partnerships and individuals having interests in oil and gas properties to offset passive losses against active income. The IRS defines "passive losses" as losses on activities in which the taxpayer does not materially participate (*e.g.* rents, royalties or dividends). Normally, these losses cannot be deducted from active income (*e.g.* wages) but can be carried forward for later use against future passive-income flows. The present tax provision is an exception to this rule.

We use production data from the IEA to allocate the annual amounts reported in budget documents to oil and natural gas extraction.

Sources: EIA (2008), OMB (various years), IEA.

Tag: USA_te_10

Temporary Expensing of Equipment for Refining (data for 2006-)

This temporary tax provision was introduced as part of the Energy Policy Act of 2005. It allows eligible producers to expense 50% of the cost of any qualified property used for processing liquid fuel from crude oil or other qualified fuels. The remaining 50% are then recovered under the otherwise applicable rules.

The annual amounts reported in budget documents have been allocated to the different fuels on the basis of the IEA's Energy Balances for the refining sector. Because the EIA mentions that it is a 'transportation fuel subsidy', we exclude such non-liquid refinery products such as paraffin wax and bitumen.

Sources: EIA (2008), OMB (various years), IEA.

Tag: USA_te_11

Aid to Small Refiners for EPA Capital Costs (data for 2005-)

Small-business refiners were allowed to immediately deduct as an expense 75% of the costs paid or incurred for purposes of complying with the Highway Diesel Fuel Sulfur Control requirement of the Environmental Protection Agency (EPA). Costs qualifying for the deduction were those costs paid or incurred during the period beginning on 1 January 2003 and ending on 31 December 2009 at the latest. Small-business refiners were defined as crude-oil refiners that had no more than 1 500 individuals engaged in refinery operations on any given day, and that had an average daily refinery run (or average retained production) of not more than 205 000 barrels for the one-year period ending on 31 December 2002.

Small-business refiners were also allowed to claim a credit of USD 0.05 per gallon for each gallon of low-sulphur diesel fuel produced during a taxable year. The total production credit claimed by a given taxpayer could not exceed 25% of the qualified costs incurred in complying with the EPA diesel fuel requirements. Costs qualifying for the credit were those costs paid or incurred with respect to any facility of a small-business refiner during the period beginning on 1 January 2003 and ending on 31 December 2009 at the latest.

Sources: EIA (2008), OMB (various years).

Tag: USA_te_12

Enhanced Oil Recovery Credit (data for 1993-)

This provision gives oil producers a tax credit amounting to 15% of the investment costs related to the use of enhanced oil recovery methods. Such "tertiary recovery methods" make it possible to extract more oil from a given reservoir than is the case with conventional primary or secondary methods. Starting in 2004, the measure also applies to capital investment connected to transportation of the Alaskan natural gas. A phase-out provision ensures, however, that the credit becomes unavailable when the real price of crude exceeds a certain level. This has proved to be the case since FY2006.

We use production data from the IEA to allocate the annual amounts reported in budget documents to oil and natural gas extraction.

Sources: EIA (2008), OMB (various years), IEA.

Tag: USA_te_13

Qualified Capital Expenditure Credit (data for 2007-)

The State of Alaska introduced this provision alongside the Petroleum Profits Tax (PPT) in 2006. It was then retained in the Clear and Equitable Share (ACES) tax which was enacted in 2007. The Qualified Capital Expenditure Credit allows oil and gas companies to obtain a tax credit for as much as 20% of the qualified capital expenditures incurred in a given fiscal year. Those credits can be carried forward or transferred to other companies, and are to be set against the company's PPT liability. Qualifying capital expenditure includes drilling equipment, infrastructure, and some exploration costs. New legislation adopted in 2010 expanded the original credit and now also provides for a 40% tax credit on qualified well lease expenditure incurred south of 68 degrees North latitude.

Some tax credits related to oil and gas production may not constitute tax expenditures under an alternative baseline where severance taxes (or production taxes) vary with market conditions and production costs. We include here the annual amounts of credit claimed as reported by the Alaska Department of Revenue (2010).

We use production data from the IEA to allocate the annual amounts reported in budget documents to oil and natural gas extraction. The Alaska Department of Revenue confirmed, however, that data were only available for the years 2007 to 2009.

Sources: Alaska Department of Revenue (2010), IEA.

Tag: USA_te_19

Development Credit for Certain Producers (data for 2007-)

The State of Alaska provides certain producers with a full tax credit on the amounts of oil and gas produced in the state. This measure was adopted in 2006 alongside the new Petroleum Profits Tax. Two categories of producers are eligible for the credit. The first includes those companies that operate outside the North Slope and Cook Inlet areas and that produce less than 100 000 barrels of oil equivalent a day. The second category is broader and comprises all companies producing less than 100 000 barrels of oil equivalent a day. Credits available to the first category are capped at USD 6 million per company per year while those for the second category are capped at USD 12 million. In both cases, producers are required to have a positive tax liability before other tax credits are applied, and cannot transfer nor carry the credits forward.

Some tax credits related to oil and gas production may not constitute tax expenditures under an alternative baseline where severance taxes (or production taxes) vary with market conditions and production costs. We include here the annual amounts of credit claimed as reported by the Alaska Department of Revenue (2010).

We use production data from the IEA to allocate the annual amounts reported in budget documents to oil and natural gas extraction. The Alaska Department of Revenue confirmed, however, that data were only available for the years 2007 to 2009.

Sources: Alaska Department of Revenue (2010), IEA.

Tag: USA_te_20

Alternative Credit for Exploration (data for 2007-)

This tax provision was introduced by the State of Alaska in 2003. It allows oil and gas companies operating in the state to get a tax credit for certain qualifying exploration expenditures. The credit was initially worth 20-30% of eligible expenditures but was subsequently increased to 30-40% with the 2007 tax reform.

Some tax credits related to oil and gas production may not constitute tax expenditures under an alternative baseline where severance taxes (or production taxes) vary with market conditions and production costs. We include here the annual amounts of credit claimed as reported by the Alaska Department of Revenue (2010).

We use production data from the IEA to allocate the annual amounts reported in budget documents to oil and natural gas extraction. The Alaska Department of Revenue confirmed, however, that data were only available for the years 2007 to 2009.

Sources: Alaska Department of Revenue (2010), IEA.

Tag: USA_te_21

Alaska Gasline Inducement Act (data for 2009-)

This item comprises a stream of matching funds that were granted by the State of Alaska to TransCanada (a natural gas transmission company) to subsidise construction of a gas pipeline through Alaska and Canada. The Alaska Gasline Inducement Act (AGIA) was enacted in 2007 to provide incentives to a licensee for completion of a pipeline that would bring North Slope gas to the market. The licensee was to be selected among a pool of applicants from which TransCanada was eventually chosen in 2008.

The incentives are to be mostly provided in the form of reimbursements worth a total of USD 500 million, spread over several years. Expenditures that qualify for such reimbursements are certain transportation commitments, financing charges, the costs stemming from compliance with certain administrative and regulatory requirements, etc. TransCanada submitted its first request for reimbursements in late 2009. In addition, the State of Alaska has made a commitment not to provide financial and fiscal assistance to other projects that could compete with the AGIA pipeline.

Data on annual transfers can be found in a 2011 follow-up report on AGIA prepared by the State of Alaska. Sums are entirely allocated to natural gas.

Sources: State of Alaska (2011).

Tag: USA_dt_08

Sales Tax Exemption for Oil & Gas Equipment (data for 2001-)

The Texas Tax Code exempts certain sales of equipment destined to oil and natural-gas exploration or production from the sales tax that normally applies in such cases. Qualifying equipment consists of certain tangible assets used offshore (*e.g.* drill pipes). This exemption dates back to 1967.

We use production data from the IEA to allocate the annual amounts reported in budget documents to oil and natural gas extraction.

Sources: Texas Comptroller of Public Accounts (various years), IEA.

Tag: USA_te_15

Severance Tax Exemptions for Crude Oil (data for 2001-)

Production of crude oil in the State of Texas is subject to two different taxes. The production tax applies a rate of 4.6% to the market value of oil produced in the state while the regulation tax amounts to 3/16 of a U.S. cent per barrel. Several exemptions are, however, granted depending on whether wells are high-cost or have been inactive for a few years, or whether producers use specific recovery methods like enhanced oil recovery. Marginal and orphaned wells are also eligible for a tax relief.

Since data on individual exemptions are not available, and given that the Texas Comptroller of Public Accounts only provides estimates for a single year (see Texas Comptroller of Public Accounts, 2008), we estimate the revenue foregone by comparing actual revenues and revenues as calculated using official data on production and prices in the State of Texas. All exemptions are therefore being bundled together, a method that does not allow making distinctions among them. Data on production come from the Railroad Commission of Texas – which is also the source used in official estimates – and data on taxable prices and tax revenues come from the Texas Comptroller of Public Accounts. This method yields estimates that are close to and consistent with those appearing in Texas Comptroller of Public Accounts (2008).

Some exemptions may not constitute tax expenditures under an alternative baseline where severance taxes vary with market conditions and production costs. We assume here that the baseline corresponds to the standard rates of severance tax that apply to oil and natural gas production in Texas.

Sources: Texas Comptroller of Public Accounts (2008), Texas Comptroller of Public Accounts (2011), Railroad Commission of Texas (2010).

Tag: USA_te_17

Severance Tax Exemptions for Natural Gas (data for 2001-)

Production of natural gas in the State of Texas is taxed at the rate of 7.5% of the market value of gas produced and kept within the state. Several exemptions are, however, granted depending on whether wells are high-cost or have been inactive for a few years. Marginal and orphaned wells are also eligible for tax relief.

Since data on individual exemptions are not available, and given that the Texas Comptroller of Public Accounts only provides estimates for a single year (see Texas Comptroller of Public Accounts, 2008), we estimate the revenue foregone by comparing actual revenues and revenues as calculated using official data on production and prices in the State of Texas. All exemptions are therefore being bundled together, a method that does not allow making distinctions among them. Data on production come from the Railroad Commission of Texas – which is also the source used in official estimates – and data on taxable prices and tax revenues come from the Texas Comptroller of Public Accounts. This method yields estimates that are close to and consistent with those appearing in Texas Comptroller of Public Accounts (2008).

Some exemptions may not constitute tax expenditures under an alternative baseline where severance taxes vary with market conditions and production costs. We assume here that the baseline corresponds to the standard rates of severance tax that apply to oil and natural gas production in Texas.

Sources: Texas Comptroller of Public Accounts (2008), Texas Comptroller of Public Accounts (2011), Railroad Commission of Texas (2010).

Tag: USA_te_18

Exclusion of Low-Volume Oil & Gas Wells (data for 2008-)

Oil and gas wells in West Virginia that produce less than one-half barrel per day or less than 5 000 cubic feet per day are exempted from the severance tax usually levied on resource extraction.

Estimates from official tax-expenditure reports are only available for a single year (FY2008). We use production data from the IEA to allocate the amounts reported to oil and natural gas extraction.

Sources: West Virginia State Tax Department (2009), IEA.

Tag: USA_te_25

Coalbed Methane Exemption (data for 2008-)

The West Virginia Tax Code exempts coalbed-methane wells placed in service after 1 January 2000 from the regular severance tax. This exemption can be used for five consecutive years and is meant to encourage the capture and use of coalbed methane. Subsequent legislation added a provision making the exemption only applicable to coalbed-methane wells placed in service before 1 January 2009. Qualifying wells can, however, continue to use their five-year exemption provided they were placed in service before 1 January 2009.

Estimates from official tax-expenditure reports are only available for a single year (FY2008).

Sources: West Virginia State Tax Department (2009).

Tag: USA_te_26

Reduced Tax for Thin-Seamed Coal (data for 2008-)

Those coal mines in West Virginia that feature thin seams – defined as seams having "less than forty-five inches [114 cm] in average thickness" – are eligible for a reduced rate of severance tax. The severance tax is usually levied at a rate of 5% of the gross value of coal extracted, but the present measure entitles eligible producers to a rate of 1% or 2% (depending on the thickness of the seams). Only new underground mines may qualify for this reduction.

Estimates from official tax-expenditure reports are only available for a single year (FY2008). We allocate the measure entirely to bituminous coal.

Sources: West Virginia State Tax Department (2009).

Tag: USA_te_27

Consumer Support Estimate

Low-Income Home Energy Assistance Program (data for 1981-)

This federal programme was created in 1981 to help low-income households pay their energy bills. It covers the costs associated not only with heating, but also cooling in order to ensure that those states that are located in warmer areas gain access to federal funding too. Being a block grant programme, the federal government uses a complex formula to allocate total funding for LIHEAP between the different states. The latter then have some discretion in administrating the grants. Home energy assistance is often provided in-kind to households as payments can be made directly to energy providers or landlords.

Only those components of the scheme that are directly related to fossil fuels are being reported here. This includes both heating benefits and crisis benefits, but excludes items such as cooling benefits or weatherisation aid. We allocated the annual amounts reported in official documents to fuel oil, natural gas, and LPG on the basis of the IEA's Energy Balances for the residential sector.

Sources: U.S. Dep. of Health and Human Services (2009), LIHEAP Clearinghouse, Kaiser and Pulsipher (2003), IEA.

Tag: USA_dt_01

Credit for Investment in Clean Coal (data for 2006-)

An investment tax credit is available for power-generation projects that use integrated gasification combined cycle (IGCC) or other advanced coal-based electricity generation technologies. As originally enacted in the Energy Policy Act of 2005, the credit amounts to 20% for investments in qualifying IGCC projects, and 15% for investments in qualifying projects that use other advanced coal-based electricity generation technologies. The Treasury may allocate up to USD 800 million of credits to IGCC projects, and USD 500 million to the other eligible ones. Under the 2008 amendments to this provision, the credit rate was increased to 30% for new IGCC and other advanced coal projects, and the Treasury is now permitted to allocate an additional USD 1.250 billion of credits to qualifying projects. The 2008 amendments also provide that qualifying projects must include equipment that separates and sequesters 65% percent of the project's total CO_2 emissions.

A tax credit of 20% is also available for investments in certain qualifying gasification projects, with a ceiling set at USD 350 million in credits. Under the 2008 amendments to the provision, the credit rate for gasification projects was increased to 30% and the Treasury was granted permission to allocate an additional USD 250 million in credits to qualified projects that separate and sequester at least 75% of total CO_2 emissions.

Fuel allocation by type of coal relies on the EIA description of the programme. This results in bituminous coal, sub-bituminous coal, and lignite getting most of the tax expenditure (62%). A significant share of the programme's estimated cost (38%) remains, however, unallocated since it is directed towards 'other advanced coal technologies' in general. For that reason, we used production data from the IEA to allocate the remaining amounts to the various types of coal concerned.

Sources: EIA (2008), OMB (various years), IEA.

Tag: USA_te_02

Amortisation of Certain Pollution Control Facilities (data for 2008-)

Taxpayers can generally recover the cost of any certified pollution control facility over a period of 60 months. A certified air-pollution control facility is defined as a new, identifiable treatment facility which is used in connection with a plant in operation before 1 January 1976 to abate or control water or atmospheric pollution or contamination.

A certified air-pollution control facility (but not a water-pollution control facility) used in connection with an electric-generation plant which is primarily coal-fired is eligible for 84-month amortisation if the associated plant or other property was not in operation prior to 1 January 1976. This provision was added by the Energy Policy Act of 2005, and is generally applicable to property that was constructed or acquired after 11 April 2005.

Because a report by the Joint Committee on Taxation mentions that this measure applies primarily to coal-fired power plants, we allocate it entirely to that fuel using the IEA's Energy Balances to distinguish between the various types of coal used in power generation.

Sources: JCT (various years), IEA.

Tag: USA_te_04

Small Municipality Energy Assistance Program (data for 2005-08)

This programme was created in October 2004 and provides grants to certain small municipalities of Alaska to help them pay for their fuel purchases. Qualifying municipalities are those cities that had a population of less than 2 500 residents in 2003. Grants must first be used to repay any remaining debt that municipalities have with the Bulk Fuel Revolving Loan Fund. The latter is a loan programme that is managed by the Alaska Energy Authority. If repayments do not exhaust the grants, funds from the Small Municipality Energy Assistance Program can then be used to directly finance purchases of fuels.

The numbers reported in the database for this programme are based on appropriations. We allocated the measure entirely to heating oil.

Sources: Alaska OMB (various years).

Tag: USA_dt_05

Power Cost Equalization (data for 1988-)

This programme grants indirect financial assistance to power consumers located in remote areas of Alaska where provision of electricity can be very costly. The Alaska Energy Authority (AEA) administers the scheme but the level of support for each utility participating in it is set by the Regulatory Commission of Alaska. This level is in turn determined by a specific formula which compares the actual generation costs of a given utility to a floor (a ceiling) under (above) which PCE assistance becomes unavailable (capped). Participating utilities must also meet certain efficiency standards.

Although the Power Cost Equalization scheme is an electricity subsidy, virtually all of the participating utilities generate power using diesel fuel only. The programme is thus indirectly supporting consumption of diesel and we allocate it entirely to the corresponding fuel category. The data reported in the database are actual disbursements that can be found in annual reports of the AEA.

Sources: Alaska Energy Authority (various years).

Tag: USA_dt_06

Alaska Heating Assistance Program (data for 2009-)

This programme was created in 2008 by the state of Alaska to supplement the federally-funded LIHEAP (see above). While LIHEAP targets households with incomes below 150% of the poverty line, the Alaska Heating Assistance Program (AKHAP) does so for households with incomes between 150% and 225% of the same threshold. AKHAP thus extends LIHEAP eligibility criteria. Both programmes are implemented in the same way with most of the payments being given directly to energy suppliers. These payments are then passed onto final consumers through credits on their heating bills.

Data from the U.S. Census Bureau (2008) suggest that heating in the state as a whole mainly comes from natural gas (about 55%) and heating oil or diesel fuel (roughly 45%). The latter share is higher here than it is at the federal level given that rural communities in Alaska rely heavily on diesel fuel. The use of coal and wood being very marginal, we omit them from the breakdown.

The numbers reported in the database for this programme are based on appropriations.

Sources: Alaska OMB (various years), U.S. Census Bureau (2008).

Tag: USA_dt_07

Sales-Tax Exemption for Natural Gas (data for 2001-)

The Texas Tax Code exempts certain uses of natural gas and electricity from the sales tax that normally applies to sales of such products. Qualifying uses include processing a product for sale; exploring for or producing and transporting a material extracted from the earth; agricultural operations; gas and electricity used by an electric utility; gas and electricity used in residences; and gas and electricity used in timber operations.

Exempting intermediate inputs from sales tax is generally not considered a tax expenditure. In this case, the exemption serves to prevent the cascading of taxes on the final sale of the product considered. For that reason, we only consider the part of the exemption that relates to the use of natural gas and electricity in the residential sector. However, the Texas Tax Code also provides that cities retain the right to tax the use of natural gas and electricity. This latter provision calls for additional caution in interpreting the value of this tax expenditure.

The Texas State report on tax expenditures contains a breakdown by industry but not by fuel (electricity or gas). For that reason, we use EIA data to estimate the share of natural gas in total consumption (of electricity and natural gas) by the residential sector in Texas (about 31%).

Sources: Texas Comptroller of Public Accounts (various years), EIA.

Tag: USA_te_14

Gasoline Tax Exemptions (data for 2001-)

The off-road use of gasoline in the state of Texas is exempt from the motor-fuels tax that applies to on-road users. Eligible users include the following sectors: federal government, public schools, maritime navigation, agriculture, construction, industry, and some commercial services.

Under a baseline that considers the motor-fuels tax to be a substitute for a road-user fee, exempting motor fuel used on farms and off-highway from excise taxes does not constitute a tax expenditure. Under an alternative baseline where all uses of motor fuels are taxed in the same way, an exemption from the motor-fuel tax would be considered a tax expenditure. This baseline implicitly assumes that the motor-fuel excise tax is specifically intended to raise general revenue by raising the price of the taxed item, or to reduce externalities associated with the consumption of the fuel, but not the externalities associated with the use of vehicles on highways, or the direct cost of funding the highway system. We choose to adopt the latter approach here.

Sources: Texas Comptroller of Public Accounts (various years).

Tag: USA_te_16

Non-Utility Sales of Natural Gas (data for 2008-)

This provision was introduced in 1987 by the state of West Virginia and exempts non-utility sales of natural gas from the local Business and Occupation Tax that normally applies in such cases.

Estimates from official tax-expenditure reports are only available for a single year (FY2008).

Sources: West Virginia State Tax Department (2009).

Tag: USA_te_22

Industrial Expansion and Revitalization Credit (data for 2008-)

This measure provides eligible companies of West Virginia with a tax credit worth 10% of certain qualifying investment expenditures in both real and tangible property. The overall amount of tax credits that can be claimed cannot, however, exceed 50% of the total Business and Occupation Tax liability in a given year. Although the credit was initially broadly destined to industry, it has been narrowed down to electricity producers only for those investments made starting in January 2003.

Since almost all of West Virginia's electricity comes from coal-fired power plants, this tax provision indirectly supports consumption of coal. Official budgetary documents mention that the scheme is being predominantly used to invest in both plant modernisation and pollution control facilities.

Estimates from official tax-expenditure reports are only available for a single year (FY2008). We allocate the measure entirely to bituminous coal.

Sources: West Virginia State Tax Department (2009).

Tag: USA_te_23

Credit for Reducing Utility Charges (data for 2008-)

This tax provision applies in West Virginia and is meant to compensate electricity and gas utilities for the lower rates they are required to charge low-income households. Credits can be used against the full amount of the utilities' Business and Occupation Tax liabilities.

Estimates from official tax-expenditure reports are only available for a single year (FY2008). Data from the U.S. Census Bureau (2008) suggest that use of natural gas in the state tends to be 1.5 times bigger than electricity for residential heating purposes. We therefore use this ratio to allocate the measure to natural gas and bituminous coal (from which nearly all of West Virginia's electricity comes).

Sources: West Virginia State Tax Department (2009), U.S. Census Bureau (2008).

Tag: USA_te_24

Fuel-Tax Exemption for Aviation (data for 2008-)

The West Virginia Tax Code exempts sales of aviation fuel from the state excise tax usually levied on sales of motor fuels. Under a baseline that considers the motor-fuels tax to be a substitute for a road-user fee, exempting motor fuel used on farms and off-highway from excise taxes does not constitute a tax expenditure. The

State of West Virginia thus justifies the exemption for aviation fuels on the grounds that it benefits off-highway users (see also "Fuel Tax Exemptions for Farmers"). It does not consider this provision to be a tax expenditure.

Under an alternative baseline where all uses of motor fuels are taxed in the same way, an exemption from the motor-fuel tax would be considered a tax expenditure. This baseline implicitly assumes that the motor-fuel excise tax is specifically intended to raise general revenue by raising the price of the taxed item, or to reduce externalities associated with the consumption of the fuel, but not the externalities associated with the use of vehicles on highways, or the direct cost of funding the highway system. We adopt this approach in measuring provisions that support consumption of fossil fuels in the aviation sector in West Virginia.

We allocate the measure entirely to kerosene-type jet fuel since the sales volumes of aviation gasoline in West Virginia are fairly small. Estimates from official tax expenditure reports are only available for a single year (FY2008).

Sources: West Virginia State Tax Department (2009).

Tag: USA_te_29

Fuel-Tax Exemption for Dyed Diesel (data for 2008-)

As is generally the case in the United States, the West Virginia Tax Code exempts sales of dyed diesel from the state excise tax levied on sales of motor fuels. This exemption may not be considered a tax expenditure depending on the baseline used to measure it (see "Fuel-Tax Exemption for Aviation" and "Fuel-Tax Exemptions for Farmers" for a discussion of the baseline and its consequences).

To avoid double-counting, we deduct from the reported amounts the value of the exemption we estimated for the farming sector of West Virginia (see "Fuel Tax Exemptions for Farmers" below). The resulting number thus excludes the amounts of dyed diesel used in agriculture.

Estimates from official tax expenditure reports are only available for a single year (FY2008).

Sources: West Virginia State Tax Department (2009), EIA (various years), FHA (2011).

Tag: USA_te_30

Fuel-Tax Exemption for Propane (data for 2008-)

The West Virginia Tax Code exempts sales of propane from the state excise tax levied on sales of motor fuels. This exemption may not be considered a tax expenditure depending on the baseline used to measure it (see "Fuel-Tax Exemption for Aviation" and "Fuel-Tax Exemptions for Farmers" for a discussion of the baseline and its consequences).

We allocate the measure entirely to LPG. Estimates from official tax expenditure reports are only available for a single year (FY2008).

Sources: West Virginia State Tax Department (2009).

Tag: USA_te_31

Fuel-Tax Exemption for County Boards of Education (data for 2008-)

The West Virginia Tax Code exempts sales of motor fuels to county boards of education from the state excise tax levied on such fuels. This provision is meant to reduce the costs of operating school buses.

We allocate the measure entirely to diesel fuel. Estimates from official tax expenditure reports are only available for a single year (FY2008).

Sources: West Virginia State Tax Department (2009).

Tag: USA_te_32

Fuel-Tax Exemptions for Farmers (data for 1984-)

The off-road use of motor fuels in the United States is exempted from federal excise taxes on fuels. This exemption is not treated as a tax expenditure. The United States does not measure excise tax expenditures because of the difficulties in determining the appropriate baseline. Under a baseline that considers the motor-fuels tax to be a substitute for a road-user fee, exempting from tax the motor fuel used on farms and off-highway uses does not constitute a tax expenditure. However, there are several exceptions for fuel used by on-highway vehicles. Under this baseline, exemptions to the excise tax on fuel used by on-highway vehicles could constitute tax expenditures. Under current U.S. tax law these exemptions include: (i) an exemption for intracity buses; (ii) an exemption for school buses; (iii) a reduced rate for intercity buses; (iv) an exemption for state and local governments; and (v) an exemption for qualified blood collectors.

Under an alternative baseline where all uses of motor fuels are taxed in the same way, an exemption from the motor-fuel tax would be considered a tax expenditure. This baseline implicitly assumes that the motor-fuel excise tax is specifically intended to raise general revenue by raising the price of the taxed item, or to reduce externalities associated with the consumption of the fuel, but not the externalities associated with the use of vehicles on highways, or the direct cost of funding the highway system. We adopt this approach in measuring provisions that support consumption of fossil fuels in the farming sector.

Annual estimates of the value of the fuel-tax exemptions benefitting the U.S. farming sector were estimated using official sales data from the EIA combined with historical data on federal and state tax rates from the Federal Highway Administration (FHA). Since undertaking this for every single state would not be practical, we selected a few ones on the basis of their agricultural production. Although being very small primary producers of agricultural commodities, Alaska and West Virginia are also part of the sample (*cf.* introductory remark) which therefore comprises: Alaska, Arkansas, California, Illinois, Iowa, Kansas, Minnesota, Nebraska, Texas, and West Virginia.

Data are available for the years 1984 to 2009 for both diesel fuel and kerosene.

Sources: EIA (various years), FHA (2011).

Tag: USA_te_28

Fuel-Tax Exemption for Certain Public Administrations (data for 2008-)

The West Virginia Tax Code exempts certain public administrations from the state excise tax normally levied on sales of motor fuels. Eligible administrations include municipalities, urban mass transit authorities, county governments, and fire departments.

Documentation on fuel use by local administrations suggests that the use of gasoline may be twice that of diesel. Vehicles used by police forces, and smaller fire and rescue vehicles, tend to run on gasoline, whereas larger fire trucks, garbage trucks, heavy-duty road-working equipment and snow plows tend to have diesel-powered engines. Consequently, we use this ratio (2:1) to split the reported amounts between those two types of motor fuel. Estimates from official tax expenditure reports are only available for a single year (FY2008).

Sources: West Virginia State Tax Department (2009).

Tag: USA_te_33

Fuel-Tax Exemption for Certain Off-Highway Uses (data for 2008-)

The State of West Virginia exempts certain off-highway uses of motor fuel from the state excise tax levied on sales of both diesel and gasoline. Few details are available but eligible uses seem to include stationary engines, heating, commercial watercraft, railroad locomotives, and use as a solvent or lubricant. Double-counting is avoided since exemptions related to diesel used in farming have already been netted out (see "Fuel-Tax Exemption for Dyed Diesel" above).

This exemption may not be considered a tax expenditure depending on the baseline used to measure it (see "Fuel-Tax Exemption for Aviation" and "Fuel-Tax Exemptions for Farmers" for a discussion of the baseline and its consequences).

We allocate the measure entirely to diesel fuel. Estimates from official tax expenditure reports are only available for a single year (FY2008).

Sources: West Virginia State Tax Department (2009).

Tag: USA_te_34

General Services Support Estimate

Strategic Petroleum Reserve (data for 1980-)

The Strategic Petroleum Reserve (SPR) was created in 1975 to provide a secure reserve of petroleum that could be accessed quickly in the event of a major disruption in supply. The SPR consists of several storage facilities located mainly in Texas and Louisiana. It accounts for about half of the United States' emergency stocks in terms of days of net imports, with the rest being held by the private sector.

Most OECD countries use stockpiling in order to meet their IEA obligations relating to energy security. Public provision of stockpiling does not, however, necessarily entail a transfer from taxpayers to the oil industry. In some cases, governments may charge the industry a fee to cover the costs associated with running storage facilities (*e.g.* as in France). In others, regulatory requirements may mandate the private sector to build and maintain the necessary stockpiles (*e.g.* as in the United Kingdom). In the case of the SPR, support comes from the fact that the government actually pays for it. The U.S. Department of Energy is responsible for the programme while funding is provided through annual budgetary transfers.

The value of public provision of oil stockpiling is best measured not through the direct budgetary transfers involved, but rather as the government making an investment that indirectly benefits the industry. Estimating the support element associated with the SPR is therefore not straightforward. The method used here follows that of Koplow and Martin (1998), which estimates how much the SPR would cost had it been provided by the private sector. This cost includes various elements such as capital depreciation, operating and management costs, imputed interest charges on capital, or the gains (losses) on sales of SPR oil. While management costs appear as such in budget documents, we use Koplow and Martin's estimated breakdown of expenditures related to SPR facilities to separate operating costs (30%) from capital-related expenditures (70%). It is assumed that capital depreciates over a 35-year period using the straight-line method. Imputed interest charges on both capital and inventories are estimated using the interest rate on U.S. Treasury bonds with a constant 30-year maturity (data for which are available on the website of the Federal Reserve System).

The entire programme is allocated to crude oil. Because the SPR benefits the oil sector as a whole and – depending on the value of the relevant elasticities – may also benefit consumers, we allocated the measure to the GSSE.

Some of the numbers reported in the database for this programme are based on appropriations.

Sources: U.S. Dep. of Energy (2009), Koplow and Martin (1998).

Tag: USA_dt_02

Fossil Energy R&D (data for 1994-)

This programme provides funding for research and development expenses related to fossil energy such as fuels conversion or coal liquefaction. Its creation dates back to the late 1980s but it recently gained in importance with the 2009 American Recovery and Reinvestment Act (ARRA) which provided significant extra funding. A breakdown by objective is available in budget documents, thereby allowing allocation of funds to the various energy sources (*i.e.* coal, natural gas, and oil). Available information does not, however, make a distinction between basic and applied research. For that reason, we allocate the measure to the GSSE as it is not clear whether this programme increases current consumption or production of fossil fuels.

For those components of the programme that cannot be directly ascribed to any particular fuel (such as programme direction or plant and capital equipment), we allocate funds using the shares of each fuel in total (fuel-specific) expenses. Since these shares tend to vary substantially from one year to the next, we use moving averages with a five-year window in order to smooth the series over time. This accounts for the fact that energy R&D is a long-term investment for which large yearly changes in administrative and equipment charges cannot realistically be reported. Data for the years prior to 1994 are not available.

The numbers reported in the database for this programme are based on appropriations.

Sources: U.S. Dep. of Energy (various years), IEA.

Tag: USA_dt_03

Northeast Home Heating Oil Reserve (data for 2000-)

The Northeast Home Heating Oil Reserve (NEHHOR) was created in 2000 to act as a buffer stock in the event of a severe disruption in the supply of heating oil. Its name comes from the fact that most households relying on heating oil reside in the Northeast region. Contrary to the Strategic Petroleum Reserve (see above), the NEHHOR does not have its own dedicated storage facilities. The government therefore relies on the private sector for both leasing of the storage tanks and acquisition of the heating oil to be stored. Since funding was initially not available in the first year of the reserve's existence, an agreement was reached whereby the U.S. Department of Energy would swap SPR barrels of crude oil in exchange for leasing of the storage tanks and acquisition of the first two million barrels of heating oil.

The subsidy component of the NEHHOR is thus easier to estimate than in the case of the SPR since the federal government does not own the premises. For the year 2000, the average acquisition cost of crude oil by refiners is used to calculate the implicit leasing fee effectively paid by the government in the case of the swap agreement. For the other years, we use official data on actual NEHHOR expenditures that were provided by the U.S. Department of Energy. To remain consistent with our estimates for the SPR, heating oil inventories are treated as government-owned assets while we also account for gains and losses on sales of NEHHOR barrels. This means that imputed interest charges on inventories are also estimated using the interest rate on U.S. Treasury bonds with a constant 30-year maturity (data for which are available on the website of the Federal Reserve System).

The entire measure is allocated to heating oil. Because the NEHHOR benefits consumers and producers of heating oil as a whole, we allocated the measure to the GSSE.

Sources: U.S. Dep. of Energy (various years).

Tag: USA_dt_04

References

Policies or transfers

Alaska Department of Revenue (2010) *Fall 2010 Revenue Sources Book*, Tax Division, Available at: http://www.tax.alaska.gov/programs/sourcebook/index.aspx.

Alaska Energy Authority (various years) *Statistical Report of the Power Cost Equalization Program*, Available at: http://www.akenergyauthority.org/programspce.html.

Alaska OMB (various years) *Budget Reports*, Office of Management and Budget, Office of the Governor of the State of Alaska, Available at: http://omb.alaska.gov/html/budget-report/fy-2012-budget.html.

EIA (2008) *Federal Financial Interventions and Subsidies in Energy Markets 2007*, Energy Information Administration, Available at: http://www.eia.doe.gov/oiaf/servicerpt/subsidy2/index.html.

EIA (various years) *Fuel Oil and Kerosene Sales*, Energy Information Administration, Available at: http://www.eia.doe.gov/oil_gas/petroleum/data_publications/fuel_oil_and_kerosene_sales/foks.html.

FHA (2011) *Monthly Motor Fuel Reported by States*, Motor Fuel & Highway Trust Fund, Federal Highway Administration, U.S. Department of Transportation, Available at: http://www.fhwa.dot.gov/ohim/mmfr/index.cfm.

JCT (various years) *Estimates of Federal Tax Expenditures*, Joint Committee on Taxation, Congress of the United States, Available at: http://www.jct.gov/publications.html?func=select&id=5.

Kaiser, Mark J., and Allan G. Pulsipher (2003) 'LIHEAP reconsidered', *Energy Policy*, Vol. 31, No. 14, pp.1441-1458.

Koplow, Douglas and Aaron Martin (1998) *Fueling Global Warming: Federal Subsidies to Oil in the United States*, Washington DC: Greenpeace by Industrial Economics, Inc.

OMB (various years) *Analytical Perspectives – Budget of the United States Government*, Office of Management and Budget, Executive Office of the President of the United States, Available at: http://www.gpoaccess.gov/usbudget/browse.html.

Railroad Commission of Texas (2010) *Data & Statistics: Production*, Available at: http://www.rrc.state.tx.us/data/production/index.php.

State of Alaska (2011) *AGIA Fund Disbursement Report*, Report for the State legislature prepared jointly by the Department of Revenue and the Department of Natural Resources, Available at: http://gasline.alaska.gov/newsroom/newsroom.html.

Texas Comptroller of Public Accounts (2008) *The Energy Report*, Research and Analysis Division, May 2008, Available at: http://www.window.state.tx.us/specialrpt/energy/.

Texas Comptroller of Public Accounts (2011) *Biennial Revenue Estimate 2012-2013*, Window on State Government, Financial Reports, Available at: http://www.window.state.tx.us/taxbud/bre2012/.

Texas Comptroller of Public Accounts (various years) *Tax Exemptions and Tax Incidence*, Window on State Government, Financial Reports, Available at: http://www.window.state.tx.us/finances/morefinancial.html.

U.S. Census Bureau (2008) *Census of Housing*, Housing and Household Economic Statistics Division, Available at: http://www.census.gov/hhes/www/housing/census/historic/fuels.html.

U.S. Dep. of Energy (2009) *Strategic Petroleum Reserve Annual Report for Calendar Year 2009*, Assistant Secretary for Fossil Energy, Office of Petroleum Reserves, Available at: http://www.fe.doe.gov/programs/reserves/publications/Pubs-SPR/Annual_Report_2009_Final.pdf.

U.S. Dep. of Energy (various years) *DOE's Fossil Energy Budget*, Available at: http://www.fossil.energy.gov/aboutus/budget/index.html.

U.S. Dep. of Health and Human Services (2009) *LIHEAP Report to Congress for Fiscal Year 2006*, Available at: http://www.acf.hhs.gov/programs/ocs/liheap/publications/publications_reports.html.

West Virginia State Tax Department (2009) *West Virginia Tax Expenditure Study – Special Business Tax, Business License Tax, Excise Tax, and Property Tax Expenditures*, January 2009, Available at: http://www.wvtax.gov/websiteUpdates.2009.01.html.

Energy statistics

IEA, *Energy Balances of OECD Countries*, 2010 Edition, International Energy Agency, Paris.

EIA, *Residential Sector Energy Consumption Estimates*, 2008, Energy Information Administration, Washington D.C.

Figure 25.1. Shares of fossil-fuel support by fuel, average for 2008-10 – United States

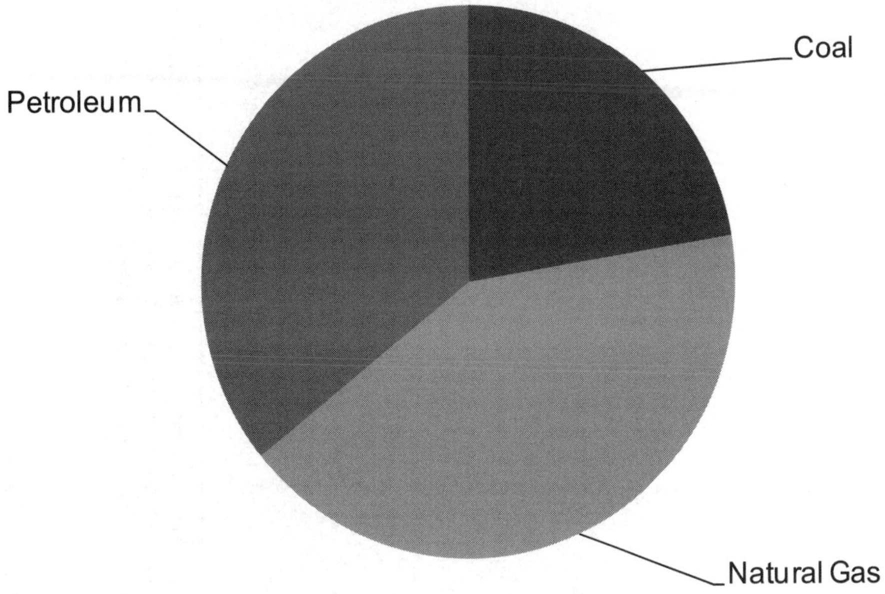

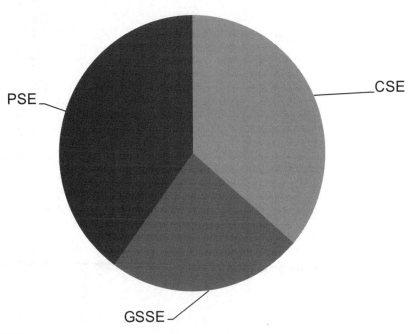

Source: OECD.

Figure 25.2. Shares of fossil-fuel support by indicator, average for 2008-10 – United States

Source: OECD.

Table 25.1. Summary of fossil-fuel support to coal – United States

(Millions of U.S. dollars, nominal)

Support element	Jurisdiction	Avg 2000-02	Avg 2008-10	2008	2009	2010p
Producer Support Estimate						
Support to unit returns						
Alternative Fuels Production Credit	Federal	1 143.33	273.33	590.00	60.00	170.00
Reduced Tax for Thin-Seamed Coal	WV	n.c.	37.00	37.00	37.00	37.00
Support for land (*e.g.* royalty concessions)						
Capital Gains Treatment of Royalties on Coal	Federal	90.00	76.67	110.00	70.00	50.00
Support for capital formation						
Partial Expensing for Advanced Mine Safety Equipment	Federal	n.a.	6.67	20.00	0.00	0.00
Excess of Percentage over Cost Depletion	Federal	162.17	317.07	390.68	144.38	416.16
Consumer Support Estimate						
Consumption						
Credit for Investment in Clean Coal	Federal	n.a.	150.00	30.00	180.00	240.00
Amortisation of Certain Pollution Control Facilities	Federal	n.a.	100.00	100.00	100.00	100.00
Industrial Expansion and Revitalization Credit	WV	n.c.	44.80	44.80	44.80	44.80
Credit for Reducing Utility Charges	WV	n.c.	1.72	1.72	1.72	1.72
General Services Support Estimate						
Fossil Energy R&D	Federal	373.31	1 866.92	686.40	1 008.75	3 905.60

Note: Tax expenditures for any given country are measured with reference to a benchmark tax treatment that is generally specific to that country. Consequently, the estimates contained in the table above are not necessarily comparable with estimates for other countries. In addition, because of the potential interaction between them, the summation of individual measures for a specific country may be problematic. The allocation of particular measures across fuel types was done by the OECD Secretariat based on the IEA's Energy Balances.

Source: OECD.

Table 25.2. Summary of fossil-fuel support to petroleum – United States

(Millions of U.S. dollars, nominal)

Support element	Jurisdiction	Avg 2000-02	Avg 2008-10	2008	2009	2010p
Producer Support Estimate						
Support to unit returns						
Severance Tax Exemptions for Crude Oil	TX	35.29	97.08	140.10	67.51	83.64
Development Credit for Certain Producers	AK	n.a.	11.80	8.35	13.53	13.53
Exclusion of Low-Volume Oil & Gas Wells	WV	n.c.	3.18	3.18	3.18	3.18
Income support						
Exception from Passive Loss Limitation	Federal	7.38	7.96	3.98	7.96	11.94
Support for capital formation						
Expensing of Exploration and Development Costs	Federal	32.55	489.35	656.44	652.47	159.14
Excess of Percentage over Cost Depletion	Federal	105.64	170.91	210.59	77.83	224.32
Temporary Expensing of Equipment for Refining	Federal	n.a.	626.67	350.00	770.00	760.00
Aid to Small Refiners for EPA Capital Costs	Federal	n.a.	13.33	30.00	10.00	0.00
Enhanced Oil Recovery Credit	Federal	140.40	0.00	0.00	0.00	0.00
Sales Tax Exemption for Oil & Gas Equipment	TX	n.c.	41.31	25.62	49.77	48.54
Qualified Capital Expenditure Credit	AK	n.a.	207.01	155.56	232.74	232.74
Alternative Credit for Exploration	AK	n.a.	13.26	7.16	16.31	16.31
Support for knowledge creation						
Amortisation of Geological Expenditure	Federal	n.a.	27.85	7.96	15.91	59.68
Consumer Support Estimate						
Consumption						
Low-Income Home Energy Assistance Program	Federal	265.73	463.60	250.35	570.23	570.23
Small Municipality Energy Assistance Program	AK	n.a.	n.a.	48.69	n.a.	n.a.
Power Cost Equalization	AK	15.65	34.07	28.14	37.03	37.03
Alaska Heating Assistance Program	AK	n.a.	n.a.	n.a.	4.50	2.25
Gasoline Tax Exemptions	TX	73.45	78.07	77.70	77.60	78.90
Fuel Tax Exemptions for Farmers	both	1 187.98	988.08	1 118.17	923.03	923.03

Table 25.2. continued over page

INVENTORY OF ESTIMATED BUDGETARY SUPPORT AND TAX EXPENDITURES FOR FOSSIL FUELS © OECD 2011

Table 25.2. Summary of fossil-fuel support to petroleum – United States

(continued)

Support element	Jurisdiction	Avg 2000-02	Avg 2008-10	2008	2009	2010p
Consumer Support Estimate						
Consumption						
Fuel Tax Exemption for Aviation	WV	n.c.	2.30	2.30	2.30	2.30
Fuel Tax Exemption for Dyed Diesel	WV	n.c.	68.60	68.60	68.60	68.60
Fuel Tax Exemption for Propane	WV	n.c.	13.40	13.40	13.40	13.40
Fuel Tax Exemption for County Boards of Education	WV	n.c.	13.60	13.60	13.60	13.60
Fuel Tax Exemption for Certain Public Administrations	WV	n.c.	1.80	1.80	1.80	1.80
Fuel Tax Exemption for Certain Off-Highway Uses	WV	n.c.	84.80	84.80	84.80	84.80
General Services Support Estimate						
Strategic Petroleum Reserve	Federal	1 262.57	1 090.89	1 101.47	1 093.85	1 077.35
Fossil Energy R&D	Federal	85.57	11.40	10.45	6.43	17.32
Northeast Home Heating Oil Reserve	Federal	6.88	10.54	15.55	12.84	3.22

Note: Tax expenditures for any given country are measured with reference to a benchmark tax treatment that is generally specific to that country. Consequently, the estimates contained in the table above are not necessarily comparable with estimates for other countries. In addition, because of the potential interaction between them, the summation of individual measures for a specific country may be problematic. The allocation of particular measures across fuel types was done by the OECD Secretariat based on the IEA's Energy Balances.

Source: OECD.

Table 25.3. Summary of fossil-fuel support to natural gas – United States

(Millions of U.S. dollars, nominal)

Support element	Jurisdiction	Avg 2000-02	Avg 2008-10	2008	2009	2010p
Producer Support Estimate						
Support to unit returns						
Severance Tax Exemptions for Natural Gas	TX	201.36	1 122.89	919.98	1 133.79	1 314.89
Development Credit for Certain Producers	AK	n.a.	17.86	12.65	20.47	20.47
Exclusion of Low-Volume Oil & Gas Wells	WV	n.c.	4.82	4.82	4.82	4.82
Coalbed Methane Exemption	WV	n.a.	4.00	4.00	4.00	4.00
Income support						
Exception from Passive Loss Limitation	Federal	9.28	12.04	6.02	12.04	18.06
Support for capital formation						
Alaska Gasline Inducement Act	AK	n.a.	18.37	..	4.36	32.38
Expensing of Exploration and Development Costs	Federal	40.78	740.65	993.56	987.53	240.86
Excess of Percentage over Cost Depletion	Federal	132.18	258.68	318.73	117.79	339.52
Accelerated Depreciation of Distribution Pipelines	Federal	n.a.	93.33	80.00	80.00	120.00
Enhanced Oil Recovery Credit	Federal	176.26	0.00	0.00	0.00	0.00
Sales Tax Exemption for Oil & Gas Equipment	TX	n.c.	62.52	38.78	75.33	73.46
Qualified Capital Expenditure Credit	AK	n.a.	313.32	235.44	352.26	352.26
Alternative Credit for Exploration	AK	n.a.	20.07	10.84	24.69	24.69
Support for knowledge creation						
Amortisation of Geological Expenditure	Federal	n.a.	42.15	12.04	24.09	90.32

Table 25.3. continued over page

Table 25.3.   Summary of fossil-fuel support to natural gas – United States

(continued)

Support element	Jurisdiction	Avg 2000-02	Avg 2008-10	2008	2009	2010p
Consumer Support Estimate						
Consumption						
Low-Income Home Energy Assistance Program	Federal	1 037.81	2 340.73	1 264.00	2 879.10	2 879.10
Alaska Heating Assistance Program	AK	n.a.	n.a.	n.a.	5.50	2.75
Sales Tax Exemption for Natural Gas	TX	162.83	247.81	242.42	245.40	255.63
Non-Utility Sales of Natural Gas	WV	n.c.	17.00	17.00	17.00	17.00
Credit for Reducing Utility Charges	WV	n.c.	2.58	2.58	2.58	2.58
General Services Support Estimate						
Fossil Energy R&D	Federal	64.56	61.88	30.33	29.24	126.08

Note: Tax expenditures for any given country are measured with reference to a benchmark tax treatment that is generally specific to that country. Consequently, the estimates contained in the table above are not necessarily comparable with estimates for other countries. In addition, because of the potential interaction between them, the summation of individual measures for a specific country may be problematic. The allocation of particular measures across fuel types was done by the OECD Secretariat based on the IEA's Energy Balances.

Source: OECD.

GLOSSARY

Accelerated depreciation – A provision in a country's tax code that allows businesses to allocate the costs of past expenditures on fixed assets over a shorter accounting period than using straight-line depreciation.

Anthracite – A shiny hard coal with a high carbon content and little volatile matter that produces little smoke when it burns.

Aviation gasoline – Gasoline (petrol) specially formulated for use in ignition-combustion engines used generally in small airplanes.

Biodiesel – A diesel-equivalent, processed fuel made from the esterification (a chemical process which removes the glycerine from the oil) of both vegetable oils and animal fats.

Biofuels – Generally liquid fuels derived from biomass or waste feedstocks and include ethanol and biodiesel.

Biogas – A mixture of methane and CO_2 produced by bacterial degradation of organic matter and used as a fuel.

Bituminous coal – A dense coal, usually black, sometimes dark brown, often with well-defined bands of bright and dull material, used primarily as fuel in steam-electric power generation, with substantial quantities also used for heat and power applications in manufacturing and to make coke. Its moisture content usually is less than 20%. The heat content of bituminous coal ranges from 21 to 30 million Btu per ton on a moist, mineral-matter-free basis.

Brown coal – A collective term for lignite and sub-bituminous coal (see respective category definitions).

Buildings – A sector that includes energy used in residential, commercial and institutional buildings. Building energy use includes space heating and cooling, water heating, lighting, appliances and cooking equipment.

Bunkers – Refers to both international marine bunkers and international aviation bunkers (see respective category definitions).

Clean coal technologies – Technologies designed to enhance the efficiency and the environmental acceptability of coal extraction, preparation and use.

Coal – A collective term that refers to both peat, primary coal (brown coal and hard coal) and derived fuels (including patent fuel, brown-coal briquettes, coke-oven coke, gas coke, coke-oven gas, blast-furnace gas and oxygen steel furnace gas).

Coalbed methane – Methane found in coal seams. Coalbed methane (CBM) is a source of unconventional natural gas.

Coke (coal) – A solid carbonaceous residue derived from low-ash, low-sulfur bituminous coal from which the volatile constituents are driven off by baking in an oven at temperatures as high as 2 000 degrees Fahrenheit so that the fixed carbon and residual ash are fused together. Coke is used as a fuel and as a reducing agent in smelting iron ore in a blast furnace. Coke from coal is grey, hard, and porous and has a heating value of 24.8 million Btu per ton.

Coke (petroleum) – A residue high in carbon content and low in hydrogen that is the final product of thermal decomposition in the condensation process in cracking. This product is reported as marketable coke or catalyst coke. The conversion is 5 barrels (of 42 U.S. gallons each) per short ton. Coke from petroleum has a heating value of 6.024 million Btu per barrel.

Coal-to-liquids – Coal-to-liquids (CTL) refers to the transformation of coal into liquid hydrocarbons. It can be achieved through either coal gasification into syngas (a mixture of hydrogen and carbon monoxide), combined with Fischer-Tropsch or methanol-to-gasoline synthesis to produce liquid fuels, or through the less developed direct-coal liquefaction technologies in which coal is directly reacted with hydrogen.

Condensates – Liquid hydrocarbon mixtures recovered from associated or non-associated gas reservoirs. They are composed of C5 and higher carbon number hydrocarbons and normally have an API between 50° and 85°.

Electricity generation – Defined as the total amount of electricity generated by power only or combined heat and power plants including generation required for own use. This is also referred to as gross generation.

Ethanol – Ethyl alcohol that is normally produced from fermenting any biomass high in carbohydrates (starches and sugars) or cellulose and hemicelluloses (the fibrous material that makes up the bulk of most plant matter) using advanced techniques.

Excise tax – A special tax levied on a specific kind of goods, typically alcoholic beverages, tobacco and fuels; it may be imposed at any stage of production or distribution and are usually assessed by reference to the weight or strength or quantity of the product.

Fossil fuel – A fuel derived from the remains of ancient plant and animal life. Fossil fuels include peat, lignite, bituminous and sub-bituminous coal, petroleum (derived from conventional geological formations, oil sands or oil shale), and natural gas (derived from conventional geological formations, coal seams, natural-gas shales, or methane clathrate).

G-20 – The Group of Twenty countries: Argentina, Australia, Brazil, Canada, China, France, Germany, India, Indonesia, Italy, Japan, Korea, Mexico, the Russian Federation, Saudi Arabia, South Africa, Turkey, the United Kingdom, and the United States. The European Union.

Gas – Gas includes natural gas (both associated and non-associated with petroleum deposits, but excluding natural gas liquids) and gas-works gas.

Gas-to-liquids – Gas-to-liquids refers to a process featuring reaction of methane with oxygen or steam to produce syngas followed by synthesis of liquid products (such as diesel and naphtha) from the syngas using Fischer-Tropsch catalytic synthesis. The process is similar to those used in coal-to-liquids or biomass-to-liquids.

Hard coal – Coal of gross calorific value greater than 5 700 kilocalories per kilogramme on an ash-free but moist basis. Hard coal can be further disaggregated into anthracite, coking coal and other bituminous coal.

Heat energy – Heat is obtained from fuel combustion, nuclear reactors, geothermal reservoirs, capture of sunlight, exothermic chemical processes and heat pumps which can extract it from ambient air and liquids. It may be used for heating or cooling or converted into mechanical energy for transport vehicles or electricity generation. Commercial heat sold is reported under total final consumption with the fuel inputs allocated under power generation.

Heavy petroleum products – A collective term referring to heavy fuel oil.

Hydro-electric power – Kinetic energy of water converted into electricity in hydroelectric plants. It excludes output from pumped storage and marine (tide and wave) plants.

Industry – A sector that includes fuel used within the manufacturing and construction industries. Key industry sectors include iron and steel, chemical and petrochemical, non-metallic minerals, and pulp and paper. Use by industries for the transformation of energy into another form or for the production of fuels is excluded and reported separately under other energy sector. Consumption of fuels for the transport of goods is reported as part of the transport sector.

Intangible drilling costs (IDCs) – The costs incurred by oil and gas producers when preparing and developing a well before production begins. These include wages, repairs, fuel, and hauling. The costs associated with development work or drilling done by a contractor are also sometimes considered IDCs.

International aviation bunkers – Deliveries of aviation fuels to aircraft for international aviation. Fuels used by airlines for their road vehicles are excluded. The domestic-international split is determined on the basis of departure and landing locations and not by the nationality of the airline. For many countries this incorrectly excludes fuels used by domestically owned carriers for their international departures.

International marine bunkers – This category covers those quantities delivered to ships of all flags that are engaged in international navigation. The international navigation may take place at sea, on inland lakes and waterways, and in coastal waters. Consumption by ships engaged in domestic navigation is excluded. The domestic/international split is determined on the basis of port of departure and port of arrival, and not by the flag or nationality of the ship. Consumption by fishing vessels and by military forces is also excluded and included in residential, services and agriculture.

Jet fuel, kerosene type – A medium-distillate used for aviation turbine power units that has the same distillation characteristics and flash point as kerosene (between 150 degrees C and 300 degrees C but not generally above 250 degrees C). In addition, it has particular specifications (such as freezing point) which are established by the International Air Traffic Association (IATA).

Kerosene – Generally refers t a medium-distillate used for heating and wick lamps, with a flash point between 150 degrees C and 300 degrees C but not generally above 250 degrees C.

Light petroleum products – A collective term referring to liquefied petroleum gas (LPG), naphtha and gasoline.

Lignite – A non-agglomerating coal with a gross calorific value less than 4 165 kilocalories per kilogramme (kcal/kg).

Low-carbon technologies – Refers to technologies that produce low- or zero-greenhouse-gas emissions while operating. In the power sector this includes fossil-fuel plants fitted with carbon capture and storage, nuclear plants and renewable-based generation technologies.

Lower heating value – The heat liberated by the complete combustion of a unit of fuel when the water produced is assumed to remain as a vapour and the heat is not recovered.

Middle distillates – A collective term referring to jet fuel, diesel and heating oil.

Natural decline rate – The base production decline rate of an oil or gas field without intervention to enhance production.

Natural gas liquids (NGLs) – The liquid or liquefied hydrocarbons produced in the manufacture, purification and stabilisation of natural gas. These are those portions of natural gas which are recovered as liquids in separators, field facilities, or gas processing plants. NGLs include but are not limited to ethane, propane, butane, pentane, natural gasoline and condensates.

Non-energy use – Fuels used for chemical feedstocks and non-energy products. Examples of non-energy products include lubricants, paraffin waxes, coal tars, and oils used as timber preservatives.

Nuclear energy – The primary heat equivalent of the electricity produced by a nuclear power plant with an average thermal efficiency of 33%.

Nuclear energy – The electricity produced by a nuclear power plant.

Observed decline rate – The production decline rate of an oil or gas field after all measures have been taken to maximise production. It is the aggregation of all the production increases and declines of new and mature oil or gas fields in a particular region.

Oil – A collective term that refers to crude oil, condensates, natural gas liquids, refinery feedstocks and additives, other hydrocarbons (including emulsified oils, synthetic crude oil, mineral oils extracted from bituminous minerals such as oil shale, bituminous sand and oils from CTL and GTL) and petroleum products (refinery gas, ethane, LPG, aviation gasoline, motor gasoline, jet fuels, kerosene, gas or diesel oil, heavy fuel oil, naphtha, white spirit, lubricants, bitumen, paraffin waxes and petroleum coke).

Petroleum – See Oil.

Petroleum coke – see Coke (petroleum.

Reticulated natural gas – Natural gas distributed to end-users by a system of pipelines.

Royalty – In energy, a term used to describe either the regular payments made by the lessees of subsoil assets to the owners of the assets.

Severance tax – A tax imposed by a state (or other sub-national unit) on the extraction of a nonrenewable resource (such as crude oil, natural gas or coalbed methane) that is sold outside the state or during a certain period.

Sub-bituminous coal – A non-agglomerating coal with a gross calorific value between 4 165 kcal/kg and 5 700 kcal/kg.

Tax sanction – A negative tax expenditure. It is that part of tax revenue collected by the government that corresponds to taxing a specific sector or type of consumption at a tax rate above the general (*i.e.* benchmark) tax rate. A tax sanction can also be referred to as "surtax" or "supertax".

Total final consumption (TFC) – The sum of consumption by the various end-use sectors. TFC is broken down into energy demand in the following sectors: industry, transport, buildings (including residential and services) and other (including agriculture and nonenergy use). It excludes international marine and aviation bunkers, except at world level where it is included in the transport sector.

Total primary energy demand (TPED) – Domestic energy demand. It is broken down into power generation, other energy sector and total final consumption.

Total primary energy supply (TPES) – The sum of energy production and imports, minus both exports and international aviation bunkers. To that are also added changes in stocks. TPES is thus equivalent to primary energy demand.

Sources

OECD on-line glossary (http://stats.oecd.org/glossary/index.htm)

U.S. Energy Information Administration on-line glossary
(http://www.eia.gov/tools/glossary/)

Internal Revenue Service
(http://www.irs.gov/publications/p535/ch07.html#en_US_2010_publink1000208883)

ORGANISATION FOR ECONOMIC CO-OPERATION AND DEVELOPMENT

The OECD is a unique forum where governments work together to address the economic, social and environmental challenges of globalisation. The OECD is also at the forefront of efforts to understand and to help governments respond to new developments and concerns, such as corporate governance, the information economy and the challenges of an ageing population. The Organisation provides a setting where governments can compare policy experiences, seek answers to common problems, identify good practice and work to co-ordinate domestic and international policies.

The OECD member countries are: Australia, Austria, Belgium, Canada, Chile, the Czech Republic, Denmark, Estonia, Finland, France, Germany, Greece, Hungary, Iceland, Ireland, Israel, Italy, Japan, Korea, Luxembourg, Mexico, the Netherlands, New Zealand, Norway, Poland, Portugal, the Slovak Republic, Slovenia, Spain, Sweden, Switzerland, Turkey, the United Kingdom and the United States. The European Union takes part in the work of the OECD.

OECD Publishing disseminates widely the results of the Organisation's statistics gathering and research on economic, social and environmental issues, as well as the conventions, guidelines and standards agreed by its members.

OECD PUBLISHING, 2, rue André-Pascal, 75775 PARIS CEDEX 16
(22 2011 05 1 P) ISBN 978-92-64-12872-9 – No. 59631 2011-02